Communications
in Computer and Information Science   186

James J. Park   Javier Lopez
Sang-Soo Yeo   Taeshik Shon
David Taniar (Eds.)

Secure and Trust Computing, Data Management, and Applications

8th FTRA International Conference, STA 2011
Loutraki, Greece, June 28-30, 2011
Proceedings

 Springer

Volume Editors

James J. Park
Seoul National University of Science and Technology, Seoul, South Korea
E-mail: parkjonghyuk1@hotmail.com

Javier Lopez
University of Malaga, Spain
E-mail: jlm@lcc.uma.es

Sang-Soo Yeo
Mokwon University, Daejeon, South Korea
E-mail: ssyeo@mokwon.ac.kr

Taeshik Shon
Ajou University, Suwon, South Korea
E-mail: taeshik.shon@gmail.com

David Taniar
Monash University, Clayton, VIC, Australia
E-mail: david.taniar@infotech.monash.edu.au

ISSN 1865-0929   e-ISSN 1865-0937
ISBN 978-3-642-22338-9   ISBN 978-3-642-22339-6 (eBook)
DOI 10.1007/978-3-642-22339-6
Springer Heidelberg Dordrecht London New York

Library of Congress Control Number: Applied for

CR Subject Classification (1998): D.2, C.2, E.3, H.4, K.4.4, K.5, K.6.5

Typesetting: Camera-ready by author, data conversion by Scientific Publishing Services, Chennai, India

Printed on acid-free paper

Springer is part of Springer Science+Business Media (www.springer.com)

Preface

On behalf of the Organizing Committees, it is our pleasure towelcome you to the proceedings of the 8th FTRA International Conference on Secure and Trust Computing, Data Management, and Application (STA 2011),which was held in Loutraki, Greece, June 28–30, 2011.

STA 2011 was the first conference after the merger of the successful SSDU, UbiSec, and TRUST symposium series previously held as SSDU 2010 (Xi'an, China, 2010), SSDU 2008 (Kunming, China, 2008), SSDU 2007 (Nanjing, China, 2007), UC-Sec 2009 (Las Vegas, USA, 2009) and TRUST 2008 (Shanghai, China, 2008), TRUST 2007 (Taipei, Taiwan, 2007), and TRUST 2006 (Seoul, Korea, 2006).

STA 2011 addressed the various theories and practical applications of secure and trust computing and data management in future environments. It presented important results for improving the application services and solving various problems within the scope of STA 2011. In addition, we believe it triggered further related research and technology developments which will improve our lives in the future.

We sincerely thank all our Chairs and Committees that are listed on the following pages. Without their hard work, the success of STA 2011 would not have been possible.We hope you find the proceedings of STA 2011 enjoyable and we would welcome any suggestions for improvement.

David Chadwick
Javier Lopez
Sang-Soo Yeo

Message from the Program Chairs

Welcome tothe 8th FTRA International Conference on Secure and Trust Computing, Data Management, and Application (STA 2011),will be held in Loutraki, Greece, June 28-30, 2011.

STA 2011will foster state-of-the-art research in the area of security and trust computing include most types of platform and network, data management and smart home, smart sensor issues as well as algorithms and performance evaluation and measurement in Secure and Trust Computing, Data Management, and Applications. The STA 2011 will also provide an opportunity for academic and industryprofessionals to discuss the latest issues and progress in the area of secure and trust computing, data management, and applications.

Due to many high quality paper submissions and the lack of space in proceedings, the review process was verytough and we had no choice but to reject several good papers. Each paper was accessed by at least three peer reviewers.

Finally, we would like to thank you all for your participation in our symposium, and thank all the authors, reviewersand organizing committee members.

Thank you and enjoy the conference!

TaeshikShon
Lambrinoudakis Costas
David Taniar
Andreas Wombacher

Conference Organization

Steering Chairs

James J. (Jong Hyuk) Park   Seoul National University of Science and
Technology, Korea

General Chairs

David Chadwick   University of Kent, UK
Javier Lopez   University of Malaga, Spain
Sang-Soo Yeo   Mokwon University, Korea

General Vice-Chair

Changhoon Lee   Hanshin University, Korea

Program Chairs

Security and Trust Computing Track

Taeshik Shon   Samsung Electronics, Korea
Lambrinoudakis Costas   University of the Aegean, Greece

Data Management Track

     Monash University, Australia
David Taniar
Andreas Wombacher   University of Twente, The Netherlands

Workshop Chairs

Security and Trust Computing Track

Jean-Marc Seigneur   University of Geneva, Switzerland
Panagiotis Rizomiliotis   University of the Aegean, Greece

Data Management Track

     University of Linz, Austria
Roland R. Wagner
Xiaofang Zhou   The University of Queensland, Australia

International Advisory Board

Bart Preneel   KatholiekeUniversiteit Leuven, Belgium
Gail-Joon Ahn   Arizona State University, USA
Wanlei Zhou   Deakin University, Australia
Stefanos Gritzalis   University of the Aegean, Greece
Hsiao-Hwa Chen   National Sun Yat-Sen University, Taiwan
Feng Bao   Institute for Infocomm Research (I2R),
                                  Singapore
Xiaobo Zhou   University of Colorado at Colorado Springs,
                                  USA
Tok Wang Ling   National University of Singapore, Singapore
Philip S. Yu   University of Illinois at Chicago, USA

Publicity Chairs

Sotiris Ioannidis   Foundation for Research and Technology,
                                  Greece
Jong-Hyouk Lee   INRIA, France
Andreas Wombacher   University of Twente, The Netherlands
Deqing Zou   Huazhong University of Science and
                                  Technology, China
Lei Shu   Osaka University, Japan
Sang Yep Nam   Kookje College, Korea

International Liaison Chairs

Guojun Wang   Central South University, P.R. China
Bernady O. Apduhan   Kyushu Sangyo University, Japan
Jongsung Kim   Kyungnam University, Korea
Muhammad Khurram Khan   King Saud University, Saudi Arabia

Program Committee

Security and Trust Computing Track

Song Bo-Yeon   Korea University, Korea
Marcel Winandy   Ruhr University Bochum, Germany
Roberto Caldelli   University of Florence, Italy
Vincent Rijmen   TU Graz, Austria and KU Leuven,
                                  Belgium
Gildas Avoine   UCL, Louvain-la-Neuve, Belgium
Jongsub Moon   Korea University, Korea
Walter Colin   University of London, UK
Ruth Breu   University of Innsbruck, Austria
Cliff Zou   University of Central Florida, USA

Chang-Tsun Li	University of Warwick, UK
Yong Lee	ChungJu University, Korea
Xiaofeng Chen	Ministry of Education, Xidian University, China
Thomas Risse	Fraunhofer IPSI, Germany
Hyohyun Choi	Inha Technical College, Korea
Schahram Dustdar	Technical University of Vienna, Austria
Gerald R. DeJean	Microsoft Research, USA
Christos Kaklamanis	Computer Technology Institute, Greece
Levente Buttyan	Budapest University of Technology and Economics, Hungary
Panos Vassiliadis	University of Ioannina, Greece
Won Joo Lee	Inha Technical College, Korea
Thaier Hayajneh	The Hashemite University, Jordan
Sandra Steinbrecher	TU Dresden, Germany
Karl M. Goeschka	Vienna University of Technology, Austria
Wei-ChuenYau	Multimedia University, Malaysia
Harald Kosch	University of Passau , Germany
Kyusuk Han	KAIST, Korea
Soon M. Chung	Wright State University, USA
Lingyu Wang	George Mason University, USA
Anna Squicciarini	UniversitatAutonoma de Barcelona, Spain
Hongmei Chi	Florida A&M University, USA
Hongbin Zhang	Beijing University of Technology, China
Dave Singelee	research group COSIC, Belgium
Vijay Varadharajan	Macquarie University, Australia
Ling Liu	Georgia Tech, USA
Jaeik Cho	Korea University, Korea
Wei Feng Chen	California University of Pennsylvania, USA
Jin Li	Guangzhou University, China
ByoungCheon Lee	Joongbu University, Korea
Masoom Alam	Institute of Management Sciences, Pakistan
Peng Wang	Limewire, USA
Thomas Wook Choi	Hankuk University of Foreign Studies, Korea
Chan Yeun Yeob	Khalifa University of Science Technology and Research, UAE
Han-You Jeong	Pusan University, Korea
Rodrigo Roman Castro	University of Malaga, Spain
Jeong Hyun Yi	Soongsil University, Korea
Jose A. Onieva	University of Malaga, Spain
Sunwoong Choi	Kookmin University, Korea
Edward Hua	QED Systems, USA
Vishal Kher	VMware, USA
Jae-il Lee	KISA, Korea
Ruben Rios del Pozo	University of Malaga, Spain

Data Management Track

Agustinus Borgy Waluyo	Monash University, Australia
Kefeng Xuan	Monash University, Australia
Geng Zhao	Monash University, Australia
Maria Indrawan	Monash University, Australia
Eric Pardede	La Trobe University, Australia
Jinli Cao	La Trobe University, Australia
Wenny Rahayu	La Trobe University, Australia
Torab Torabi	La Trobe University, Australia
Farookh Hussain	Curtin University of Technology, Australia
Vidyasagar Potdar	Curtin University of Technology, Australia
Yun Sing Koh	Auckland University of Technology, New Zealand
Nathan Rountree	Otago University, New Zealand
Hui Ma	Victoria University of Wellington, New Zealand
Mafruz Ashrafi	Institute for Infocomm Research, Singapore
Hamidah Ibrahim	Universiti Putra Malaysia, Malaysia
Ali Mamat	Universiti Putra Malaysia, Malaysia
Manhyun Chung	Korea University, Korea
Mustafa Mat Deris	KUSTEM, Malaysia
RuzanaIshak	Malaysia
Pradeep Kumar	India
Thanh C. Nguyen	HCMC University of Technology, Vietnam
Tran Khanh Dang	Vietnam National University of Ho Chi Minh City, Vietnam
Maytham Safar	Kuwait University, Kuwait
Mourad Ykhlef	King Saud University, Saudi Arabia
Simon So	Hong Kong Institute of Education, Hong Kong
Hui-Huang Hsu	Tamkang University, Taiwan
Ilsun You	Korean Bible University, Korea
Tomoya Enokido	Rissho University, Japan
Yusuke Gotoh	Okayama University, Japan
Ailixier Aikebaier	Seikei University, Japan
Shusuke Okamoto	Seikei University, Japan
Kai Cheng	Kyushu Sangyo University, Japan
Imam Machdi	Tsukuba University, Japan
Alfredo Cuzzocrea	University of Calabria, Italy
Luke Liming Chen	University of Ulster, UK
Muhammad Younas	Oxford Brookes University, UK

Table of Contents

STA2011 - Security Track

STA2011 - Data Management Track

Embedding High Capacity Covert Channels in Short Message Service (SMS)

M. Zubair Rafique[1], Muhammad Khurram Khan[1],
Khaled Alghatbar[1], and Muddassar Farooq[2]

[1] Center of Excellence in Information Assurance
King Saud University, Riyadh, Saudi Arabia
[2] Next Generation Intelligent Networks Research Center
nexGIN RC, NUCES, FAST-Islamabad, Pakistan
{zrafique.c,mkhurram,kalghtbar}@ksu.edu.sa,
muddassar.farooq@nexginrc.org

Abstract. Covert Channels constitute an important security threat because they are used to ex-filtrate sensitive information, to disseminate malicious code, and, more alarmingly, to transfer instructions to a criminal (or terrorist). This work presents zero day vulnerabilities and weak-nesses, that we discovered, in the Short Message Service (SMS) protocol, that allow the embedding of high capacity covert channels. We show that an intruder, by exploiting these SMS vulnerabilities, can bypass the existing security infrastructure (including firewalls, intrusion detection systems, content filters) of a sensitive organization and the primitive content filtering software at an SMS Center (SMSC). We found that the SMS itself, along with its value added services (like picture SMS, ring tone SMS), appears to be much more susceptible to security vulnerabilities than other services in IP-based networks. To demonstrate the effectiveness of covert channels in SMS, we have used our tool GeheimSMS[1] that practically embeds data bytes (not only secret, but also hidden) by composing the SMS in Protocol Description Unit (PDU) mode and transmitting it from a mobile device using a serial or Bluetooth link. The contents of the overt (benign) message are not corrupted; hence the secret communication remains unsuspicious during the transmission and reception of SMS. Our experiments on active cellular networks show that 1 KB of a secret message can be transmitted in less than 3 minutes by sending 26 SMS without raising an alarm over suspicious activity.

Keywords: Short Message Service (SMS), SMS Covert Channels, SMS PDU.

1 Introduction

Covert channels based attacks on modern distributed systems pose a serious security threat as they are widely used in leaking sensitive information, secret Botnets

---

[1] The demo of GeheimSMS has been presented in Black Hat USA Arsenal event.
http://www.blackhat.com/html/bh-us-10/
bh-us-10-specialevents arsenal.html#rafique

J.J. Park et al. (Eds.): STA 2011, CCIS 186, pp. 1–10, 2011.
© Springer-Verlag Berlin Heidelberg 2011

communication, the dissemination of malicious codes and the propagation of terrorists instructions. The major component that is exploited through such channel is the privacy assurance of the modern systems. A covert storage channel involves the embedding of secret and hidden messages by the sender and the interpretation of these secret and hidden messages by the receiver [1].

The current state-of-the-art research mainly concentrates on the embedding of a covert storage channel by exploiting the vulnerabilities in common Internet protocols such as TCP/IP [2] [3] [4] [5], UDP [6], HTTP [7], VoIP [8], SSH [9] and FTP [10]. The underlying idea of embedding a covert channel is based on the theory proposed by Lampson in [11]. The National Computer Security Center, a branch of the United States' National Security Agency (NSA), has established a standard called "Trusted Computer Security Evaluation Criteria (TCSEC)," which specifically refers to secret disseminating of information from a higher classification compartment to a lower classification in secure systems [1].

While previous research on covert storage channels was based on Internet based protocols, there has been no work done (to the best of our knowledge) to analyze the covert channel susceptibility of cellular services. We therefore undertook an empirical study to analyze the susceptibility of SMS to covert channel vulnerabilities. Note that SMS has become the most used cellular service, which is substantiated by a recent report that more than 5.5 trillion text messages were sent over carrier networks world-wide in 2009 [12]. The trend appears to be increasing as a survey projects that 6.6 trillion messages will be exchanged globally during 2010 [12].

This work presents zero day vulnerabilities and weaknesses, which we discovered, in the Short Message Service (SMS) protocol, which is the most used cellular networks service that allows the embedding of high capacity covert channels. The major contribution of our work is demonstration that intruders can exploit vulnerabilities in the SMS protocol: (1) to secretly communicate or transfer sensitive data (from inside or outside an organization) by embedding high capacity covert channels in legitimate (overt) SMS, (2) to bypass the existing IP based security infrastructures (including firewalls, Intrusion Detection Systems (IDSs), content filters) of an enterprise; which would allow, disgruntled employees to covertly leak sensitive and secret information of an organization, and (3) to embed high capacity covert channels using different SMS value-added-services; which would make it possible for a 1 KB of file to be transferred in less than 3 minutes. To demonstrate the effectiveness of covert channels in SMS, we practically embed data bytes (not only secret, but also hidden) by composing the SMS in Protocol Description Unit (PDU) mode and transmitting it from a mobile device using a serial or Bluetooth link. To conclude, our pilot studies showed that we need to quickly fix the vulnerabilities in the SMS protocol;-before this important service can be exploited by intruders. The security analysis of an SMS covert channel is not within the scope of this paper.

The rest of the paper is organized as follows. Section 2 provides a brief description of the SMS structure. We demonstrate the embedding of a covert channel by exploiting SMS vulnerabilities in Section 3. Our real world experiments on an active network, with more than 172 million subscribers, are discussed in Section 4. Finally, we conclude our paper in Section 5.

2   SMS Overview

Mobile Originated (MO) messages are sent and received through SMSC, which has store and forward functionality. Once SMSC receives a message, it tries to forward it to the user; if the user is not available, it queues SMS and tries to retransmit it later. Once a mobile phone receives SMS from SMSC, it is processed by the GSM modem – the interface between GSM network and the application processor – of a mobile phone. An SMS can be sent and received in two modes: (1) PDU, and (2) text. Most of the well known services – Wireless Application Protocol (WAP), voice mail notifications, information retrieval, Multimedia Messaging Service (MMS), secure transaction services (mobile banking), and Over-the-Air (OTA) – use the PDU mode of SMS protocol. In the next section, we briefly describe the PDU mode. An interested reader, however, is referred to [13] for details of SMS.

2.1   SMS Encoding Modes

As mentioned before, PDU and text are two well known modes for sending and receiving SMS. In the text mode, plain text is given to the GSM modem, which selects a suitable scheme to encode the given text and puts it in the user data (payload) of an SMS. Moreover, it also attaches a default SMS header to the payload and sends it. In comparison, in the PDU mode, it is possible to manipulate the fields of an SMS header and also modify the contents of the user data. (The complete SMS is encoded in hexadecimal octets or decimal semi-octets.) In the PDU mode, an SMS is transferred from a mobile phone to SMSC by composing it using the SMS-SUBMIT format. Similarly, an SMS is received at a mobile phone in the SMS-DELIVER format from SMSC. Figures 1(a) and 1(b) depict the formats of the SMS-SUBMIT and SMS-DELIVER PDU's. A user can send maximum of 140 bytes of user data in single SMS message. More information is transfer through CSMS.

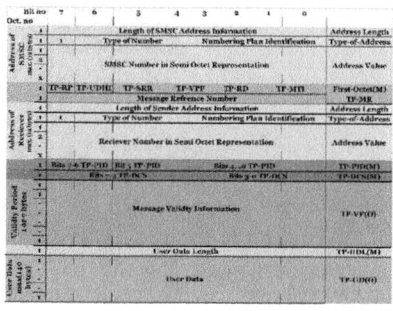

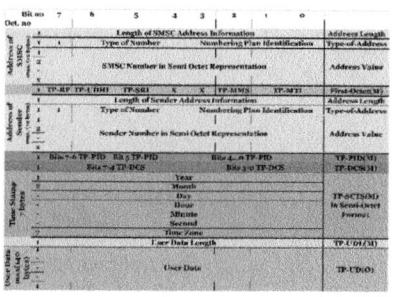

(a) SMS-SUBMIT PDU Format   (b) SMS-DELIVER PDU Format

Fig. 1. SMS PDU Formats

2.2   Concatenated SMS (CSMS)

CSMS makes it possible to fragment a long SMS into small messages and send them separately using different SMS-SUBMIT PDUs. The application at the receiver does the reassembly and they appear as a single SMS to the end user. In order to send a CSMS, the TP-UDHI (see Figure 1) bit is set in the headers of all of the fragmented SMSs. This bit indicates that an optional User Data Header (UDH) is present in the payload, which the receiving device uses to concatenate the different fragments. The fields of a typical UDH are shown in Table 1.

Table 1. Fields of CSMS UDH

Fields	Description
1	It indicates the length of UDH.
2	(Information Element Identifier (IEI)): It tells the receiving device about the objective of using UDH.
3	(Information Element Data Length (IEDL)): It indicates the number of fields in UDH.
4	(Information Element Data (IED)): It contains a CSMS reference number to identify different fragments of the same CSMS.
5	It indicates the total number of fragments of a CSMS.
6	It indicates the sequence number of the currently received fragmented SMS.

3   SMS Covert Channel (SMSCC)

This secret communication through SMS is a modified version of the prisoner problem introduced by Simmons [14]. We here demonstrate how sender (Alice) and receiver (Bob) can exploit vulnerabilities in the SMS header and user data to covertly transfer information in an otherwise benign SMS. The objective is to embed covert information in such a way that to an independent warden (Wendy), it is a benign SMS containing characters, pictures and ring tones. Once Bob receives the benign SMS, he extracts the covert information from it. Similarly, Bob can also send covert information to Alice using the same information hiding technique (this makes the covert channel bidirectional). Moreover, the SMS covert channel has a high capacity because it is possible to transfer multiple bytes in a single SMS. Figure 2 shows the covert channel communication through SMS.

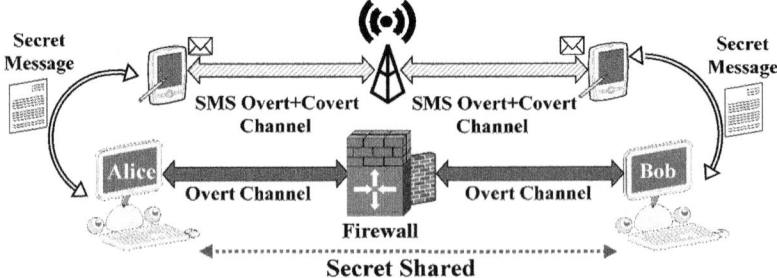

Fig. 2. SMS Covert Channel

In order to embed a convert channel, we make use of AT[2] commands. These commands are used to control – through serial or blue tooth connections – the GSM modem of a mobile phone using an external controller. The external controller allows the users to compose an SMS in PDU mode and modify different header fields in the SMS-SUBMIT and SMS-DELIVER formats. As a result, Alice can covertly transfer information in these fields. (The challenge, however, is that it should not affect the benign SMS.) Now, we will discuss six vulnerabilities that allow covert channel communication through SMS. (Our pilot studies show that, utilizing these techniques, Alice can secretly communicate with Bob on any active cellular network using a variety of mobile phones.)

3.1　Vulnerability 1: Single Text SMS

Recall from Table 2.2 that UDH is used to transmit a concatenated SMS. In this case, Field 5 and Field 6 indicate the total number of fragments and the sequence number of the current fragment, respectively. We exploit a vulnerability by setting both fields to 01, which tricks the receiving device into thinking that the concatenated SMS consists of just one fragment and the current SMS is that fragment. We have empirically found that a mobile phone uses UDH in a single text message. (Ideally, this option should not have been allowed because the purpose of CSMS is to transmit messages having user data of more than 140 bytes.) As a result, the reference number, i.e., Field 4, has become redundant and Alice can covertly send data in it.

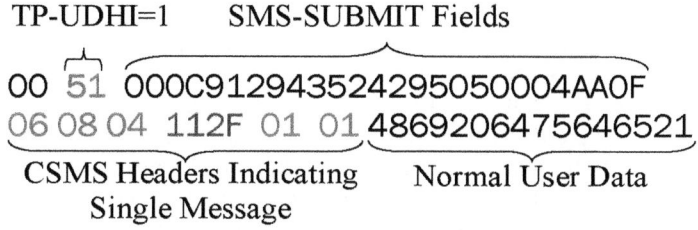

Fig. 3. (Vulnerability 1) Single Text SMS

Figure 3 shows the encoding of a single text message by exploiting the UDH of CSMS. In Figure 3, the "00" in the first octet tells the GSM modem to use the default SMSC information stored in the Subscriber Identity Module (SIM) of a mobile phone. Then, the TP-UDHI bit is set to "1" to indicate that particular SMS contains a UDH. Alice is sending the secret information "112F" in Field 4 of the UDH. With this technique, Alice has 16 Symbols S because of hexadecimal representation and 4 semi-octets (2 bytes) n available for covert communication. This leads to a channel capacity of $\log_2(S^n)$ (16 bits) per SMS.

---

[2] AT commands are the de' facto standard for controlling the modems.

3.2 Vulnerability 2: Misusing Reference Number

By logically extending the previous vulnerability, we can misuse the reference number for Field 4 of an actual CSMS to covertly communicate secret information. (Remember from Section 2.2, that the reference number field is mandatory for the reassembly of a fragmented SMS at the destination device.) Because a sending device can put any value in the reference number, this technique is hard to detect compared with the previous one. Again, Alice has 16 Symbols S because of hexadecimal representation and 4 semi-octets (2 bytes) n available for covert communication. This leads to a channel capacity of $\log_2(S^n)$ (16 bits) per CSMS. Figure 4 shows an example of a CSMS in which the "4F4B" reference number is chosen to secretly communicate "OK".

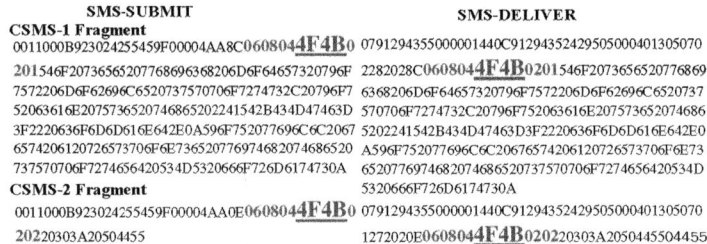

Fig. 4. CSMS Reference Number Misuse

3.3 Vulnerability 3: Misusing Originator Port in Picture SMS

With the advent of Value Added Services (VAS), which provide pictures, tones, and logos etc., the use of SMS has significantly increased. A destination port field of "158A" in the extended UDH (see Figure 5) is used to indicate to the receiving device that SMS contains a picture. (A picture SMS is sent using CSMS because of its large size.) The picture (to be sent) is first converted into the Over the Air (OTA) format (a standard size of 72x28 pixels). It is then encoded in an hexadecimal format and sent in the user data of CSMS [13]. The UDH of a picture (see Figure 5) also contains the picture display options (e.g., height, width, etc.). The originator port (we empirically determined that any value between "0000" and "FFFF" is legal in the case of a picture SMS) is not used by the receiving device. As a result, Alice can misuse it for covert communication with Bob.

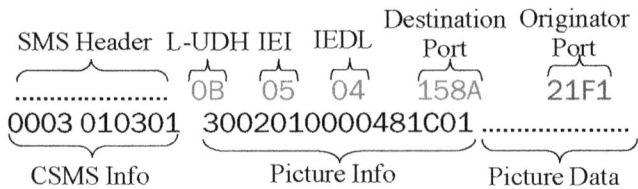

Fig. 5. Picture SMS Header

In this technique, the channel capacity is directly proportional to the number of fragments in the concatenated SMS used to transmit a picture. If Alice uses m fragments, then the channel capacity would be $m * \log_2(S^n)$ bits per picture SMS, where we have 16 Symbols S because of hexadecimal representation and 4 semi-octets (2 bytes) n (of originator port) available for covert communication. If we combine it with Vulnerability 2, our capacity increases to $(m * \log_2(S^n) + 16)$ bits per picture SMS. Alice can use 256 pictures (each having two fragment concatenated SMSs) and encode the covert data (2 bytes) in the originator port field of each fragment of a CSMS. If we assume that the average transfer rate of a GSM modem (send/receive) is 10 SMS per minute, a 1 KB file can be transmitted secretly in 512 fragmented SMSs, which is expected to take less than 52 minutes.

3.4 Vulnerability 4: Melodious Sound

iMelody is the standard format used for creating *user defined* monophonic sounds with the basic Enhanced Messaging Service (EMS) [15]. An iMelody sound consists of the iMelody sound header, sound body and sound footer. Figure 6 shows the basic iMelody format and its encoded PDU.

Once a mobile phone receives an EMS containing the sound, the mobile set uses the Sound Data Length (as indicated in Figure 6), headers and footers of iMelody to parse the enclosed sound data. After decoding the iMelody sound body, it finally plays the tone. This methodology is vulnerable to data injection because it allows for the padding of extra data – a secret message or a malicious code – after the iMelody footer in the PDU of the user data. Our investigations validate that the extra padding has no effect on the quality of the sound and also that the padded data is not visible to a mobile user. The channel capacity in this scenario depends on the size of the sound data and iMelody structure.

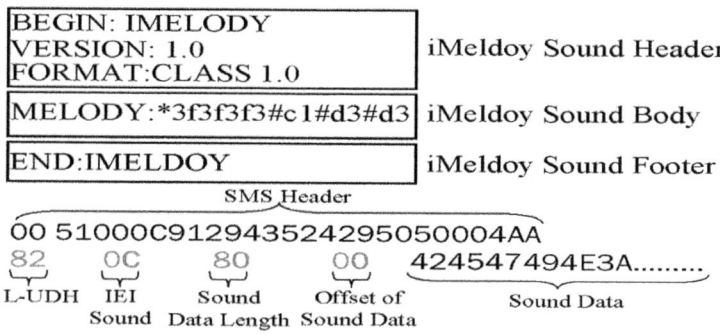

Fig. 6. iMelody Format for Sounds/Music

It is possible to use a CSMS in which all of the fragments have the same iMelody header and footer, but the melody data is portioned among these fragments [15]. (Note that SMS can carry a maximum of l = 280 semi-octets (140 bytes) of data.)Let z be the cumulative size of UDH including iMelody header, footer, and sound body of (in semi-octets). As a result, Alice has l-z semi-octets per SMS remaining at her disposal to secretly communicate with Bob. If the melody is encoded in m fragments of CSMS, then the capacity of the covert channel is m*$\log_2(S^{l\text{-}z})$ (S = 16) bits per melody (EMS) message. In Figure 6, the value of z with 32 bytes of melody data is 192 semi-octets. If we add 8 semi-octets for the sound EMS header, the total size would become 200 semi octets. As a result, Alice can now covertly send 80 semi-octets (or 40 bytes) in a single sound message. To conclude, Alice can secretly transfer 1 KB file in just 26 (1024/40) tone messages. If we assume a 10 SMS per minute send/receive rate for a GSM modem, then the time required to covertly transfer a 1 KB message should be less than 3 minutes.

3.5 Vulnerability 5: Encoding Option

Recall from Figure 1, that TP-DCS is used to indicate a 7 bit, 8 bit or 16 bit data encoding scheme for an SMS [13]. Our pilot studies show that Alice can secretly send 1 bit of data to Bob assuming that the covert data is "0" (when text is encoded in 7 bit or 16 bit) or "1" (when 8 bit text encoding is used). Figure 7 shows that Alice covertly sends 2 bits of covert data "01" in an overt text "hi" (7 bit encoding) and "Gud" (8 bit encoding). This technique has a low capacity but is very hard to detect.

```
                  7 bit Encoding   "hi"
0011000B923024255459F00000AA02E834    0791294355000001040C912943524295050000
                  8 bit Encoding  "Gud"  0130103005640202E834
0011000B923024255459F00004AA03477564    0791294355000001040C912943524295050004
                                         01301030258102034775 64
        SMS-SUBMIT                       SMS-RECEIVE
```

Fig. 7. TP-DCS used for Covert Channel

3.6 Vulnerability 6: Status Report

The TP-SRR Status Report Request bit in the first octet of SMS-SUBMIT demands an acknowledgment from the receiving device. The field appears in the TP-SRI of the first octet of SMS-DELIVER and asks the receiving device to acknowledge a received SMS (see Figure 1). This allows Alice to embed a 1 bit capacity covert channel (see Figure 8) in SMS. Our pilot studies show that some operators do not support the status report feature to reduce the SMS load on SMSC.

```
     TP-SRR=1                              TP-SRI=1
0031000B923024255459F00004AA026869 0791294355000001240C912943524295050004
                                    01301030258102026869
        SMS-SUBMIT                       SMS-RECEIVE
```

Fig. 8. TP-SRR used for Covert Channel

4 Experiments and Results

We now report the results of our experiments – on real world active cellular networks using a number of different types of mobile phones. We ran our experiments on the GSM network of one of the largest mobile operators, with more than 172 million active subscribers world-wide. Its network core consists of an NSN infrastructure with (GSM 900/1800) specifications.

We wanted to transfer a 1 KB file – by embedding covert channels through the above-mentioned six vulnerabilities – using our GeheimSMS tool. Our goal was to understand the end-to-end delay for transferring this file by utilizing different SMS send rates per minute. We have tabulated the results of a 10 SMS per minute send rate in Table 2. It took 51 minutes to transfer the file by exploiting vulnerability 1 (single text). In the case of reference number vulnerability, it took approximately twice the time (1 hour 48 minutes) to transfer the same file. We used 256 pictures and transmitted each of them in 256 concatenated SMS CSMSs having 2 fragments each. The transfer time in this case was 57 minutes as compared with an estimated time of 52 minutes (see vulnerability 4 in Section 3). We used 26 single SMS ring tones transferring 40 bytes of secret data on the average and the same file was transferred in less than 3 minutes. As expected, the transfer time using the last two vulnerabilities was about 16 hours.

Table 2. Timing Results for Transferring 1-KB Covert Message on Active GSM Network

Vul. No.	Transfer Time	No. of SMS
1	51 minutes	512 SMS
2	1 hour 48 minutes	512 CSMS
3	57 minutes	256 Pictures
4	2 minutes 50 sec	26 Ring Tones
5 and 6	16 hour 12 minutes	8192 SMS

5   Conclusion

In this paper, we prove that intruders (or terrorists) can exploit vulnerabilities in SMS to secretly organize and execute criminal (or terrorist) activities by embedding high capacity covert channels in SMS. We empirically proved that it is possible to send multiple covert bytes within a single SMS; as a result, 1 KB of data can be transferred in less than 3 minutes. We also proved that intruders (or terrorists) can exploit the vulnerabilities in SMS to secretly organize and execute criminal (or terrorist) activities. Our pilot studies showed that the appearance of an overt SMS (with an embedded covert channel) remains unaffected, and encoded messages can be easily sent/received on active cellular networks without raising an alarm about suspicious activity. The detection of SMS covert channels will be the subject of our future research.

References

1. National Computer Security Center, US DoD: Trusted computer system evaluation criteria. Technical Report, DOD 5200.28-STD (December 1985)
2. Ahsan, K., Kundur, D.: Practical data hiding in TCP/IP. In: Proc. of the 9th Workshop on Multimedia & Security, pp. 25–34. ACM, Texas (2002)

3. Rowland, C.: Covert channels in the TCP/IP protocol suite. First Monday 2(5-5) (1997)
4. Giffin, J., Greenstadt, R., Litwack, P., Tibbetts, R.: Covert messaging through TCP. In: Dingledine, R., Syverson, P.F. (eds.) PET 2002. LNCS, vol. 2482, pp. 194–208. Springer, Heidelberg (2003)
5. Murdoch, S., Lewis, S.: Embedding covert channels into TCP/IP. In: Barni, M., Herrera-Joancomartí, J., Katzenbeisser, S., Pérez-González, F. (eds.) IH 2005. LNCS, vol. 3727, pp. 247–261. Springer, Heidelberg (2005)
6. Fisk, G., et al.: Eliminating steganography in internet traffic with active wardens. In: Petitcolas, F.A.P. (ed.) IH 2002. LNCS, vol. 2578, pp. 18–35. Springer, Heidelberg (2003)
7. Bauer, M.: New covert channels in http: adding unwitting web browsers to anonymity sets. In: Proc. of the 2003 ACM Workshop on Privacy in the Electronic Society, pp. 72–78. ACM, NY (2003)
8. Mazurczyk, W., Kotulski, Z.: New VoIP traffic security scheme with digital watermarking. Computer Safety, Reliability, and Security, 170–181 (2006)
9. Lucena, N., Pease, J., Yadollahpour, P., Chapin, S.: Syntax and semantics-preserving application-layer protocol steganography. In: Fridrich, J. (ed.) IH 2004. LNCS, vol. 3200, pp. 164–179. Springer, Heidelberg (2005)
10. Zou, X., Li, Q., Sun, S., Niu, X.: The Research on Information Hiding Based on Command Sequence of FTP Protocol. In: Khosla, R., Howlett, R.J., Jain, L.C. (eds.) KES 2005. LNCS (LNAI), vol. 3683, pp. 1079–1085. Springer, Heidelberg (2005)
11. Lampson, B.: A note on the confinement problem. Communications of the ACM 16(10), 613–615 (1973)
12. Portio-Research: Mobile Messaging Future (2010-2014), http://www.portioresearch.com/
13. GSM-ETSI: 03.40. Technical realization of the Short Message Service (SMS) (1998), http://www.3gpp.org/ftp/Specs/html-info/0340.htm
14. Simmons, G.J.: The prisoners problem and the subliminal channel. In: Proc. of Advances in Cryptology (CRYPTO), pp. 51–67 (1984)
15. Le Bodic, G.: Mobile Messaging technologies and services: SMS, EMS and MMS. John Wiley Sons Inc., Chichester (2005)
16. The Trusted System Evaluation Criteria. Fred Cohen Associates, http://all.net/books/orange/chap8.html

A Framework for Detecting Malformed SMS Attack

M Zubair Rafique[1], Muhammad Khurram Khan[1],
Khaled Alghathbar[1], and Muddassar Farooq[2]

[1] Center of Excellence in Information Assurance
King Saud University, Riyadh, Saudi Arabia
[2] Next Generation Intelligent Networks Research Center, nexGIN RC
NUCES-FAST, Islamabad Pakistan
{zrafique.c,mkhurram,kalghtbar}@ksu.edu.sa,
muddassar.farooq@nexginrc.org

Abstract. Malformed messages in different protocols pose a serious threat because they are used to remotely launch malicious activity. Furthermore, they are capable of crashing servers and end points, sometimes with a single message. Recently, it was shown that a malformed SMS can crash a mobile phone or gain unfettered access to it. In spite of this, little research has been done to protect mobile phones against malformed SMS messages. In this paper, we propose an SMS malformed message detection framework that extracts novel syntactical features from SMS messages at the access layer of a smart phone. Our framework operates in four steps: (1) it analyzes the syntax of the SMS protocol, (2) extracts syntactical features from SMS messages and represents them in a suffix tree, (3) uses well-known feature selection schemes to remove the redundancy in the features' set, and (4) uses standard distance measures to raise the final alarm. The benefit of our framework is that it is lightweight-requiring less processing and memory resources-and provides a high detection rate and small false alarm rate. We evaluated our system on a real-world SMS dataset consisting of more than 5000 benign and malformed SMS messages. The results of our experiments demonstrated that our framework achieves a detection rate of more than 99% with a false alarm rate of less than 0.005%. Last, but not least, its processing and memory requirements are relatively small; as a result, it can be easily deployed on resource-constrained smart phones or mobile devices.

Keywords: Short Message Service (SMS), SMS Fuzzing, SMS PDU.

1 Introduction

Crafty attackers can launch sophisticated attacks on smart phones by exploiting vulnerabilities in the syntax or implementation (or both) of a protocol. Recently, it was shown that the extent of the damage can increase exponentially when a malformed message[1] attacks target smart phones and mobile devices [2] [3] . (We use

---

[1] Malformed network messages do not conform to the standard of a protocol and aim to exploit vulnerabilities in the implementation of protocols [1]. In the context of our paper we use term malformed message, fuzzed message and malicious message interchangeably.

J.J. Park et al. (Eds.): STA 2011, CCIS 186, pp. 11–20, 2011.
© Springer-Verlag Berlin Heidelberg 2011

the terms mobile phones, mobile devices, and smart phones interchangeably in this paper.) A recently published survey about emerging smart phone security lists fuzzed (SMS) attacks [4] as a serious emerging threat. A fuzzed SMS attack gives control of the instructions executed within a phone's processor to an imposter; as a result, he can get unfettered access to personal information. Moreover, he can also use a malformed SMS to identify vulnerabilities in a mobile device that could be exploited to launch self-propagating attacks (such as worms).

Despite the severity of the problem, malformed message detection in mobile phones has received little attention. Mostly researchers follow one of two approaches for malformed messages detection: (1) signature-based intrusion detection [5], and (2) anomaly detection [6]. It is now a well known fact that signature-based techniques cannot cope with an exponential increase in new malware because not only will the size of the signature database not scale but the time to match signatures also increases significantly [7]. In comparison, non-signature based systems mostly utilize attributes that are specific to a particular protocol [6] [8]; as a result, the tight coupling between the attributive distinctiveness and a particular service make them unsuitable for mobile services that run on resource constrained smart phones [9]. Therefore, we believe that the domain of malformed SMS detection is open to novel research.

The major contribution of this paper is a malformed message detection framework that automatically extracts novel syntactical features to detect a malformed SMS at the access layer of mobile phones. Our framework operates in four steps: (1) it analyzes the syntax of the SMS protocol, (2) extracts syntactical features from SMS messages and represents them in a suffix tree, (3) uses well-known feature selection schemes to remove redundancy in the features' set, and (4) uses standard distance measures to raise the final alarm. Consequently, our proposed framework consists of four modules: the message analyzer module, feature extraction module, feature selection module, and detection module.

We evaluated our proposed detection framework on a real world dataset of SMS. The malformed SMS dataset consisted of more than 5000 messages and was generated using the SMS injection framework presented in [3]. We also collected more than 5000 benign SMS messages using our customized *mobile terminal interface*. The benign SMS messages were obtained from the mobile phones of users with diverse socioeconomic backgrounds including engineers, students, housewives, professionals, and corporate employees. The results of our experiments show that our framework achieves a detection rate of more than 99% with a false alarm rate $\leq$ 0.005% for distinguishing between a benign and malformed SMS. Its processing and memory requirements are relatively small; therefore, it can easily be integrated into resource constrained smart phones.

The rest of this paper is organized as follow. We present our threat model in Section 2. We describe our performance evaluation strategy in Section 3, which includes the characteristics of our real-world datasets and a description of the attack injection process in the collected benign traffic. In Section 4, we propose the methodology of our detection framework for fuzzing attacks. We describe the results of our experiments in Section 5, followed by related work in Section 6. Finally, we conclude the paper with an overview of our future work in Section 7.

2 Threat Model

We now outline our threat model for SMS. As mentioned before, that intelligently crafted malformed SMS messages can be used to launch DoS attacks by exploiting vulnerabilities in the implementation of the SMS handling modules inside smart phones. The SMS received by the Short Message Service Center (SMSC) on a mobile phone is handled through a GSM modem. The GSM modem is controlled through standardized AT[2] commands. Moreover, the modem also provides an interface with the GSM network and the application processor of a smart phone. The SMS received from the modem is delivered to the operating system of the mobile phone through the telephony stack, which has a multiplexing layer that allows multiple applications to access the modem at the same time. Furthermore, the telephony stack decodes the API-calls (Application Program Interface calls) into corresponding AT commands and the AT result codes into different category messages/API-calls. An imposter provides a fuzzed SMS as the AT result codes to the application processor of a mobile phone in order to trick it into reaching an undefined state. This, might result in significant processing delays, unauthorized access, or denial of access to the legitimate user.

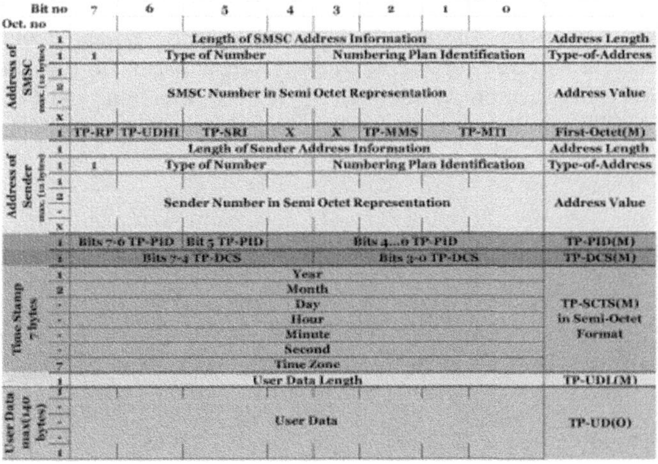

Fig. 1. SMS-DELIVER format of receiving SMS on modem of a mobile devices through SMSC. The fields are encoded in hexa-decimal octets representation.

3 Data Acquisition

We developed a *modem terminal interface* that can read an SMS from the memory of a mobile phone in the SMS-DELIVER [10] format. Our interface interacts serially with the modem of a mobile device through AT commands. It first configures the modem to operate in PDU mode by giving the AT+CMGF=0 command. Once the

---

[2] AT commands represent are the standard language for controlling the modems.

modem is configured in PDU mode, using AT+CMGL=ALL, all of the messages in the memory of the mobile phone are redirected to the terminal. We used our *modem terminal interface* to collect a real world dataset in the SMS-DELIVER format from people belonging to different socioeconomic backgrounds: engineers, students, housewives, professionals, and corporate employees. This gave us a real world benign SMS dataset (more than 5000) that covered a broad spectrum of the messages that can be received by a user on his/her mobile set.

For malformed dataset we deployed a testbed that launches fuzzing attacks targeting smart phones. Our testbed consists of an *I-Mate Windows Mobile* and the injection framework (*injector*) specially created by the authors of [4] for launching SMS attacks on a smart phone. This injection framework was used in conjunction with the Sulley fuzzing framework [11] to generate malformed SMS messages. Using this method, we generated more than 5000 malformed SMS messages. In our dataet the sixe of 50.89% of the benign messages and 51.83% of the malformed messages lies in range of 320 to 380 bytes. (This made it a challenge to detect a malformed SMS because its size was the same as that of a benign SMS.)

4   Malformed SMS Detection Framework

In this section, we discuss the architecture and working principle of our proposed malformed detection framework. Our architecture consists of four modules: (1) a message analyzer, (2) feature extraction, (3) feature selection, and (4) classification (see Figure 2). We now discuss each module separately.

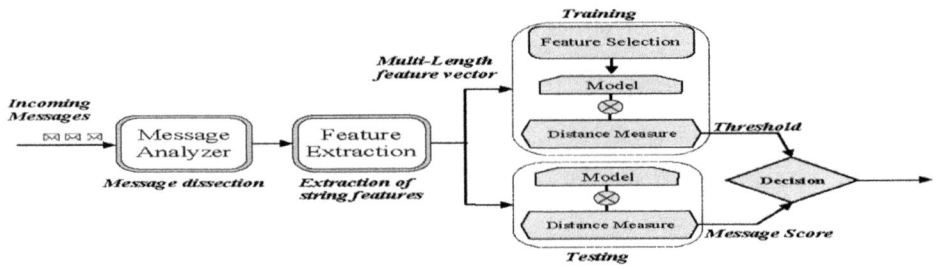

Fig. 2. Architecture of Malformed SMS Detection Framework

4.1   Message Analyzer

The core functionality of the message analyzer module involves transforming incoming SMS messages into a format from which we can extract intelligent features. As mentioned before, the SMS messages received by a modem through SMSC are in the SMS-DELIVER format. Similarly, the messages that are sent through a mobile phone to SMSC are in the SMS-SUBMIT format. Because our framework is designed to operate with local detection (operates on incoming messages), we focus our attention on the SMS-DELIVER format.

4.2 Feature Extraction

We exploited the properties of a *suffix tree* to operate as our feature entrenching function. Suffix tree is a data-structure used for efficient string processing. In its compact representation, it corresponds to the suffixes of a given string where all of the nodes with one child are merged with their parents [12].

We define a set of attribute strings "A" to model the content of an incoming SMS message "m" from the message analyzer module. We extract syntactical attributes A from the suffix tree, such that for every attribute $a \in A$ the length of a can vary from $a=1:|A|$. With each attribute string a such that $a \in A$, we calculate the number of occurrences of a in m. This gives us an (attribute, value) pair for each attribute $a \, \varepsilon \, m$ and the value of its frequency, $f(a,m)$. An entrenching function, ψ (suffix tree), translates each incoming message m to the $|M|$ dimensional vector $\hat{v}$ space by taking into account $f(a,m)$ and the a that belongs to a particular A. where $\psi: m \rightarrow \hat{v}^{|M|}$ with $\psi(m) \rightarrow (a, f(a,m))_{a \in A}$.

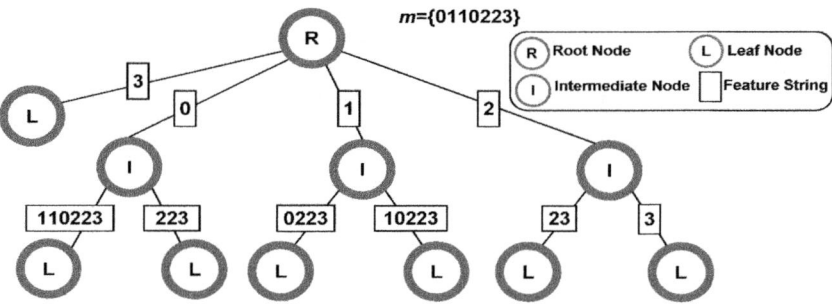

Fig. 3. Suffix Tree construction for a given message $m=\{0110223\}$

Figure 3 illustrates the extraction of feature strings and feature space using a suffix tree from an incoming SMS message m. A suffix tree is constructed for each m received from the message analyzer module. The entrenching function, ψ, extracts the (attribute, value) pair of features string a and its frequency from the nodes of the suffix tree. We define the set of messages used for training as $K = \{m_1, \cdots, m_k\}$. After each $m \in k$ passes through ψ, we have a set of M dimensional feature vectors as $\hat{V} = \{\hat{v}_1, \dots, \hat{v}_k\}$ with $\psi(m_i) \rightarrow \hat{v}_i^{|M|}$. In terms of (attribute, value) pairs, we have:

$$\hat{V} = \begin{bmatrix} (a_1, f(m_1, a_1)) & \cdots & (a_n, f(m_1, a_n)) \\ (a_1, f(m_2, a_1)) & \cdots & (a_n, f(m_2, a_n)) \\ \cdots & \cdots & \cdots \\ \cdots & \cdots & \cdots \\ (a_1 f(m_{k-1}, a_1)) & \cdots & (a_n, f(m_{k-1}, a_n)) \\ (a_n, f(m_k, a_1)) & \cdots & (a_n, f(m_k, a_n)) \end{bmatrix} \quad (1)$$

In order to create the ``normal model'' for our framework reflecting the vital characteristics of our training data we take the union of feature vectors to obtain raw features' set $\vec{\mathbf{X}}$ as:

$$\vec{X} = \{\hat{v}_1 \cup \hat{v}_2 \cup \hat{v}_3 \cdots \hat{v}_k\} \tag{2}$$

4.3 Feature Selection

We have now computed the raw feature set, $\vec{\mathbf{X}}$, that contains a number of extracted features (from the suffix tree) based on the syntactical formation of the messages in the training SMS dataset. It is possible that all of the features in $\vec{\mathbf{X}}$ might not be useful for detecting malformed messages. Furthermore, the high dimensionality of $\vec{\mathbf{X}}$ will result in large processing overheads, making the detection process infeasible for resource constrainted mobile devices. Therefore, it is logical to remove redundant features having low classification potential to reduce the dimensionality of the raw features' set, but not at the cost of a high false alarm rate. We, therefore, decide to reduce the dimensionality of the raw feature set by ranking the features based on statistics and information theory parameters. This helps us to determine the classification potential of each feature in $\vec{\mathbf{X}}$. We subsequently rank the features as a function of their classification potential and select the 500 top-ranked features for classification. We use Information Gain, Gain Ratio and Chi-squared for our selection module. The details on these feature selection canbe found in [13][14].

4.4 Classification

Once we have a distinct *model set* of attributes ($\hat{S}$) --obtained after reducing the dimensionality of the raw features' set--we can easily detect a malformed message by using well known distance/divergence measures. A large corpus of anomaly detection literature [15][6] or anomalous network payloads [16][17] share a common idea: anomalies are deviations from a learned ``normal model'' [8].

For our framework, we choose statistical distance measures to compute the deviations from the model set. Statistical distance measures are used in anomaly detection schemes because of their low processing overheads. However, the accuracy of these measures depends on the classification potential of the extracted features. In this study, we have empirically derived a short list of two well-known distance measures for our analysis: (1) Manhattan distance, and (2) Itakura-Saito Divergence. An interested reader can find details on these distance measures in [18].

Through our pilot studies on these measures, we found that the distance values of malformed SMS messages are normally greater than those of benign messages when compared with a model set ($\hat{S}$). We compute K distance scores as $D = \{d_1, d_2, \cdots\cdots d_k\}$ from incoming SMS message streams to model the deviation pattern of the benign messages. (Remember that the largest distance value in D still represents a normal message.) Hence, we only need to learn threshold value t with the help of the largest distance score of a message in the training data, K. If the distance of an SMS from the model is greater than threshold t, it is classified as a malformed SMS. Mathematically, the threshold value is:

$$t = \max(D_i), 1 \le i \le 100 \tag{3}$$

where t corresponds to the largest distance value from model set $\hat{S}$. Using Equation (11), we can raise an alarm just with a single `` $\geq$ " comparison using the threshold value. Furthermore, the calculation of this threshold value is linear in time with complexity $O(K)$.

5 Experimental Results and Analysis

In this section, we report the results of our malformed SMS detector on real world SMS traffic and malformed messages. We designed our experiments to select the best feature selection module and distance measure. We used standard definitions for the detection accuracy and false alarm rate with the help of four parameters: (1) detection of a malformed message, True Positive (TP), (2) detection of a benign message, False Positive (FP), (3) does not detect a malformed message, False Negative (FN), and (4) does not detect a benign message, True Negative (TN). We define the Detection Rate as $DR = \frac{TP}{TP+FN}$ and the False Alarm Rate as $FAR = \frac{FP}{FP+TN}$.

We trained our framework on 100 benign SMS messages to compute the threshold for each distance measure. We empirically determined that only 100 SMS messages are adequate to define the ``normal model". (Modern smart phones allow users to store more than 100 SMS in the inbox.) The framework was tested on 500 benign and 500 malformed messages. We repeated the procedure on a complete dataset and then reported the average results.

We plot the ROC curves for different experimental scenarios by varying the threshold for the output class probability [19]. The false alarm rate is on the x-axis and the detection rate is on the y-axis for different threshold values of distance measures. We show our detection rate results using the feature space of a suffix tree in Figure 4. We have also tabulated the training and testing overheads for the distance measures on different feature selection schemes in Table 1. The training overhead contains the time (in milliseconds) taken by our framework for the Feature Extraction (FE), computation of the Raw Feature set (RF), building the final model through Feature Selection (FS), and Threshold Calculation per 100 SMS messages.

It can be seen from our results that the classification of malformed SMS messages through distance measures using suffix tree feature space showed a higher classification accuracy when features were selected with the help of information gain. The detection accuracy was worse when features were selected through chi-squared. In particular for the SMS dataset, the detection accuracy of manhattan distance with IG was better than 99% (see Figure 4). Using isd, the detection accuracy of our framework was reduced to less than 98%. The accuracy of our framework with chi-squared feature selection is shown in Figure 4. It is obvious that both distance measures achieved relatively poor accuracy ($\leq 96\%$) with this selection scheme. The detection accuracy of our framework with gain ratio was less than the information gain using both distance measures.

A closer look at the training overheads (see Table 1) reveals no significant difference in the processing overheads of the different feature selection schemes. Our framework took an average of 3.5 seconds to train itself on 100 messages. (Note that training is only required in the beginning.) However, this training time is depended on the size of the incoming message. Similarly, during the testing phase, our framework took just 10 milliseconds to detect a malformed message. Our suffix tree features' set required just 2 KB of memory. To conclude, the manhattan distance in conjunction with the information gain provides the best detection accuracy, a low false alarm rate, and small training and testing overheads.

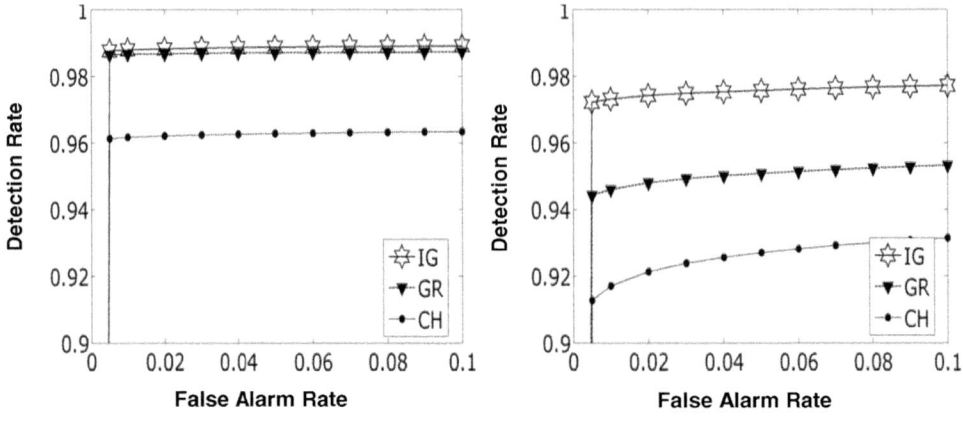

(a) ROC using Manhattan Distance   (b) ROC using Itakura-Saito Divergence

Fig. 4. Experimental Results on different feature selection schemes and distance measures

Table 1. Training and Threshold calculation overheads in (milliseconds/100 SMS) while Testing overheads in (milliseconds/1 SMS) using Information Gain, Gain Ratio and Chi-squared for Manhattan distance and Itakura-Saito Divergence

		IG		GR		CH	
		md	isd	md	isd	md	isd
Training Overhead	Feature Extraction	2485		2485		2485	
	Raw Feature	15		15		15	
	Feature Selection	47		26		48	
Threshold Calculation		1093	1101	1092	1101	1092	1101
Testing Time		10.73	10.851	10.782	10.81	10.722	10.871

To overcome this shortcoming, researchers have proposed anomaly-based detection schemes. Most of these systems utilize tokens or $n - grams$ to construct a features' set, and then use a similarity measure between the attributed $n - grams$/tokens derived from the protocol grammar. The works of D'ussel et al. [8] and Rieck et al. [6] are well known examples of anomaly-based systems.

In this context, our malformed detection framework uses a novel architecture, in which a suffix tree is used to construct a features' set. Subsequently, well known features selection schemes coupled with distance measures are used to detect a malformed message.

6   Conclusion and Future Work

The major contribution of our work is a real time malformed message detection framework. Currently, this framework has been tested on real datasets of SMS messages. The results of our experiments show that our framework using syntactical features successfully detects malformed messages with a detection accuracy of more than 99% and a false alarm rate of less than 0.005%. Once we successfully detect a malformed SMS, we can protect a mobile phone by taking effective flitering/blocking countermeasures; as a result, the threat of the instant unavailability of a service is mitigated. Our future research will focus on further optimizing the testing overhead of our scheme and deploying it on real world mobile devices and smart phones.

References

1. Bocan, V.: Developments in DOS research and mitigating technologies. Periodica Politehnica, Transactions on Automatic Control and Computer Science 49, 63 (2004)
2. Engel, T.: Remote Short Message Service (SMS) Denial of Service - Curse Of Silence (2008), http://berlin.ccc.de/tobias/cursesms.txt
3. Mulliner, C., et al.: Fuzzing the Phone in your Phone. In: Briefings of the Black Hat, Las Vegas, USA, Black Hat (2009)
4. Mulliner, C., et al.: Injecting SMS Messages into Smart Phones for Security Analysis. In: Proc. of the 3rd USENIX WOOT 2009, Montreal, Canada (2009)
5. Roesch, M.: Snort-lightweight intrusion detection for networks. In: Proc. of the 13th USENIX Conference on System Administration, Seattle, Washington, pp. 229–238 (1999)
6. Rieck, K., Wahl, S., Laskov, P., Domschitz, P., Müller, K.-R.: A self-learning system for detection of anomalous SIP messages. In: Schulzrinne, H., State, R., Niccolini, S. (eds.) IPTComm 2008. LNCS, vol. 5310, pp. 90–106. Springer, Heidelberg (2008)
7. Abdelnur, H.J., et al.: KiF: a stateful SIP fuzzer. In: Proc. IPTComm 2007, pp. 47–56. ACM, New York (2007)
8. Düssel, P., Gehl, C., Laskov, P., Rieck, K.: Incorporation of application layer protocol syntax into anomaly detection. In: Sekar, R., Pujari, A.K. (eds.) ICISS 2008. LNCS, vol. 5352, pp. 188–202. Springer, Heidelberg (2008)
9. Cheng, J., et al.: Smartsiren: virus detection and alert for smartphones. In: Proc. of the 5th International Conference on Mobile Systems, Applications and Services, pp. 258–271. ACM, New York (2007)
10. GSM-ETSI: 03.40. Technical realization of the Short Message Service (SMS) (1998)
11. Amini, P.: Sulley, Pure Python fully automated and unattended fuzzing framework
12. Ukkonen, E.: On-line construction of suffix trees. Algorithmica 14(3), 249–260 (1995)
13. Yang, Y., et al.: A comparative study on feature selection in text categorization. In: Proc. of International Conference on Machine Learning, pp. 412–420. Morgan Kaufmann Publishers Inc., Nashville (1997)
14. Moh'd, A., Mesleh, A.: Chi Square Feature Extraction Based Svms Arabic Language Text Categorization System. Journal of Computer Science 3(6), 430–435 (2007)
15. Gao, D., Reiter, M.K., Song, D.: Behavioral distance measurement using hidden markov models. In: Zamboni, D., Krügel, C. (eds.) RAID 2006. LNCS, vol. 4219, pp. 19–40. Springer, Heidelberg (2006)
16. Rieck, K., et al.: Language models for detection of unknown attacks in network traffic. Journal in Computer Virology 2(4), 243–256 (2007)

17. Wang, K., Parekh, J.J., Stolfo, S.J.: Anagram: A content anomaly detector resistant to mimicry attack. In: Zamboni, D., Krügel, C. (eds.) RAID 2006. LNCS, vol. 4219, pp. 226–248. Springer, Heidelberg (2006)
18. Cover, T., et al.: Elements of information theory. John Wiley & Sons Inc., Chichester (2006)
19. Fawcett, T.: ROC graphs: Notes and practical considerations for researchers. Machine Learning 31 (2004)
20. Paxson, V.: Bro: A system for detecting network intruders in real-time. Computer Networks: The International Journal of Computer and Telecommunications Networking 31, 2435–2463 (1999)

A Metadata Model for Data Centric Security

Benjmin Aziz[1], Shirley Crompton[2], and Michael Wilson[3]

[1] School of Computing, University of Portsmouth, Portsmouth, U.K.
benjamin.aziz@port.ac.uk
[2] e-Science Centre, STFC Daresbury Laboratory, Warringston, U.K.
shirley.crompton@stc.ac.uk
[3] e-Science Centre, STFC Rutherford Appleton Laboratory, Oxfordshire, U.K.
michael.wilson@stc.ac.uk

Abstract. Data-sharing agreements across organisations are often used to derive security policies to enforce the access, usage and routing or data across different trust and administrative domains. The data exchanged is usually annotated with metadata to describe its meaning in different applications and contexts, which may be used by the enforcement points of such data-sharing policies. In this paper, we present a metadata model for describing data-centric security, i.e. any security information that may be used to annotate data. Such metadata may be used to describe attributes of the data as well as their security requirements. We demonstrate an applicability scenario of our model in the context of organisations sharing scientific data.

Keywords: Metadata, Security, Semantic Web, Data Sharing, Legal Contracts.

1 Introduction

The process of data sharing on a large industrial and organisational scale often requires complex procedures starting from the setting up of data sharing agreements and dissemination contract among organisations and ending up with implementations of those agreements at the low level in the form of access, usage and routing control infrastructures. These infrastructures rely on formal statements of what constitutes acceptable sharing and usage of data in the form of security policies, which are consulted and enforced each time a request to access, use or route the data is received.

However, policy enforcement and decision points require information about the attributes of the requesting subject as well as the attributes of the data being requested in order to be able to match the request against the security policy controlling the data. These attributes, which are often pulled or pushed to the policy decision point at time of request, may express security information, such as the sensitivity level of the data and the clearance level of the subject. Security policies often require such meta-information about the data in order for the data to be *comprehensible* by the policy.

For example, in a multilevel security policy (e.g. one based on the security lattices of [1], there is a requirement that the data controlled by that policy be also classified with the same type of security levels as referenced in the policy, for that data to be comprehensible to the policy. Otherwise, the policy will simply not be enforceable or its enforcement will be meaningless at best.

J.J. Park et al. (Eds.): STA 2011, CCIS 186, pp. 21–28, 2011.
© Springer-Verlag Berlin Heidelberg 2011

The main contribution of this paper is to introduce a metadata model that can be used to describe some of the most common data security attributes used by policy decision points of various security models. The metadata model itself does not describe what the data *are*, but rather what the data *have*, in terms of their security metadata values. Hence, it is a metadata model of data-centric security.

2   Related Work

Despite the fact that there exist a few security ontologies in the literature, as far as we know, none has yet touched on the topic of data-centric security. In [2], the authors propose an extension of DAML-S [3] with ontologies that describe security properties and standards related to Web services. The ontologies presented include credentials such as smart and identity cards and X509 certificates as standardised by XML Signature [4] as well as security mechanisms such encryption functions, signatures and protocols. They also propose a reasoning engine based on the Java Theorem Prover (JTP) [5] for matching security requirements of the user and those proposed by the service it requests.

In [6] an OWL-S-based [7] ontology called the NRL Security Ontology is presented. NRL can be used at various levels of detail for annotating resources in general and not only Web services and furthermore, it is extensible, reusable and provides a higher-level mapping from security requirements to lower-level capabilities. NRL contains rich ontologies for describing credentials, security algorithms such as cryptographic functions, security assurances as well as service and agent security ontologies. Finally, [8] propose a computer security incident ontology, which is related to incidents of security breaches.

3   Motivating Scenario

Our main real world scenario motivating the work of this paper is based on a public-private research collaboration with limited lifetime, such as five years, co-funded by a key *public funding agency* in some scientific field, such as Biosciences, and a *small-to-medium enterprise* technology company, for example, with specialisation in bioinformatics. such collaborations typically involve academic researchers from *universities* or *industrial research departments* with relevant expertise, a *scientific facility provider*, whose facility provides the infrastructure for performing scientific experiments and finally, an *e-Science infrastructure owner* to provide the data management and dissemination technologies.

The award from the funding agency would cover capital and recurrent costs, a postgraduate studentship and industrial placements. The academic partners benefit from the financial support, gain experience of the private sector's applied research and development environment and insights on commercialising research. The industrial partner, in turn, gains access to cutting-edge research and technology to improve its products and the possibilities of recruiting appropriate trained staff at the end of the project. It licences a limited time-bounded access to its structure-based design algorithms and proprietary data to the partners. In line with the agency's funding criteria, the partners make agreements at the grant proposal stage on the licensing, ownership and exploitation of foreground and background intellectual property rights and the publication of research outputs. The agreement also includes a schedule on good data management practices, demanding the use of data portals and information cataloguing to manage research outputs and to share sensitive data.

In [9], we demonstrated that such a scenario entails at least the following use cases: data sharing agreement specification and policy administration, server based data accessing, peer-to-peer data sharing and offline data sharing. The use cases of this scenario lead to a natural technical problem; the *sharing of scientific data* resulting from cost-critical scientific experiments on large-scale facilities, for example the Large Hedron Collider (LHC) (http://lhc.web.cern.ch/lhc/). Such data are often considered to be sensitive due to the enormous cost of the experiments generating them thereby making it mandatory to protect the data from loss, corruption and in some cases, from leakage to unauthorised users. Nonetheless, the originating raw data will need to be disseminated to various scientific and commercial organizations for the purposes of analysis. This dissemination is usually controlled, at the highest levels, by well-defined *data sharing agreements* and *legal contracts* that make natural language statements about the manner in which data should be disseminated, accessed and used. These agreements are enforced, at the lower technical levels, by security policy enforcement infrastructures and mechanisms. The policies in these infrastructures represent the enforceable form of the data sharing agreements. Most of the current form of these policies (e.g. [10,11,12]) rely on some form of subject and object attributes (e.g. roles, identities, contexts and any other attributes).

4   A Security Metadata Model

We propose here a metadata model for describing data-centric security. Elements of this model are shown in Fig. 1 using OWL-like representation. The model consists of a top class called *DataSecurityInformation*, divided into the following subclasses:

- *Redundancy Information*: This subclass includes any redundancy information necessary for checking the integrity of the data. It consists further of the subclass: *Checksums*, which represent the classical error correcting codes, like the cyclic redundancy checks [13].
- *Freshness Information*: This subclass defines information necessary to detect whether the data is fresh or not, either with reference to some point in time or with reference to previous copies. It consists itself of the following two subclasses: *Timestamps*, which usually contain the time and date at which the data was created, based on for example, the ISO 8601 standard, and *Nonces*, which are random numbers, which must be fresh each time a new copy of the data is produced. A nonce, sometime also know as a *salt*, ensures that the new copy is distinguished from its previous ones, thus preventing replay attacks.
- *Contextual Information*: This subclass represents information about the permissible contexts in which the data may be accessed. A context in this sense is related to the time, date and location of the data or the subject accessing it. The following subclasses represent such information: *Permissible Time Range*, which indicates the time range in the day during which the data may be accessed/used

Fig. 1. The Data Security Metadata Model

(One could also use *Deniable Time Range* to indicate the times when the data should not be used or accessed), *Permissible Date Range*, which indicates the date range in the year during which the data may be used/accessed (similarly, a *Deniable Date Range* represents the days in which the data should not be used or accessed and *Permissible Location Set*, which represents the set of locations in which the data is allowed to be accessed or used (*Deniable Location Range*, on the contrary, represents the locations in which the data cannot be accessed).

- *Classification Information*: This subclass contains security information about the sensitivity of the data. This information could be for example, security levels [1], or conflict classes as used in the Chinese wall policies [14]. The following two subclasses can be used to capture such classifications: *Security Levels*, which represents the security classification of the data, taken possibly from a complete lattice structure (e.g. the Powerset lattice), and *Conflict Classes*, which represents the conflict group to which the data may belong, necessary to avoid accessing/using data belonging to the same group at the same time, which could lead to breach of security properties, such as confidentiality or anonymity.

- *Provenance Information*: This subclass represents the usual provenance information, which at a minimum includes the following information: *Place of Origin*, which represents the original place (e.g. IP-domain) where the data was first created, *Data Ownership*, which describes who the owner of the data is, e.g. the scientist who conducted the experiment or the funding body supporting the study, *Data Lineage* which represents the original time and date at which the data was created and *Original Identity*, which represents the original identity of the data (e.g. their unique identifier at the point of acquisition or creation).

- *Cryptography Information*: This subclass contains any cryptographic information associated with the data. This could include the following: *Encryption Algorithm*, indicating the algorithm used for encrypting the data (e.g. DES [15] and RSA [16]), *Digital Signatures*, including any digital signatures, such as DSS [17] and RSA [16], which may be used to sign the data, and *Hash Functions*: representing cryptographic hash functions, such as SHA and MD, which may be used for protecting the data integrity.

- *Environmental Information*: This subclass represents information on any environmental constraints on the access, usage and routing of the data. Currently, we envisage the following two subclasses under this class: *Permissible Network Route*, which represents the permissible network routes that the data may be communicated over (alternatively, one can also use *Non-Permissible Network Routes*) and *Permissible IP Domain*, which represents the permissible IP domains in which the data may be accessed and used (alternatively, one may also refer to *Non-Permissible IP Domain*).

- *Safety Information*: This subclass contains any safety information on accessing, using or routing the data. Currently, it contains a single subclass: *Permissible Operations*, which contains the list of operations that can be applied to the data. This could be either usage operations, such as read or write, or communication operations, such as send. It may also contain management operations such as updating any of its other metadata information.

- *History Information*: This subclass contains information about the history of the data. It consists of the following subclass: *Logs*, which represents the usual log files, which may record any of the access, usage and routing history of the data.

5   Applicability of the Model

Fig. 2 represents a possible sequence of actions that may be involved in the dissemination and routing of data from one organisation to others, and then finally, the access and usage of that data by a user.

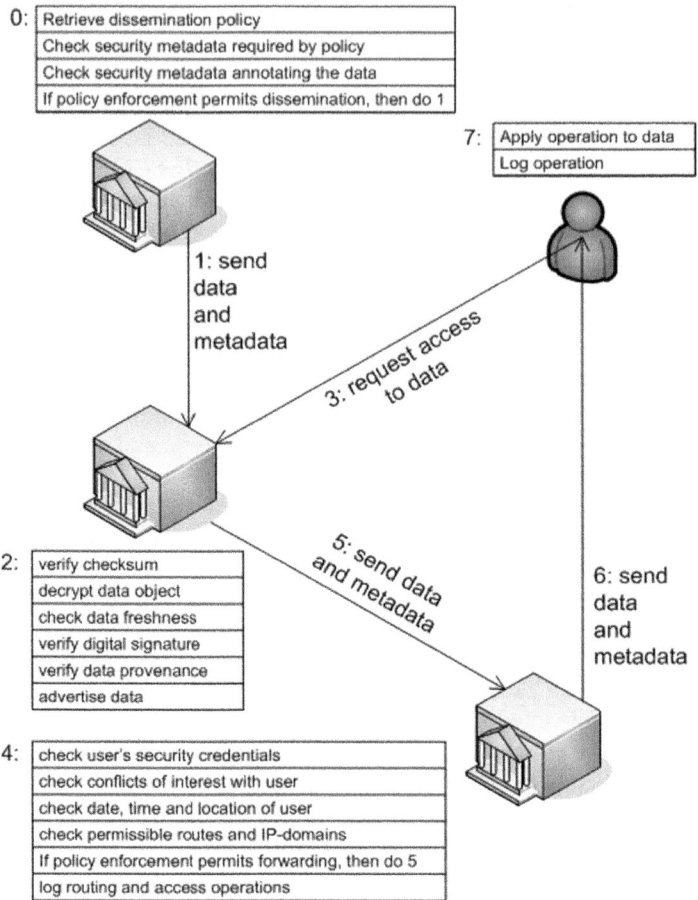

Fig. 2. Diagram representing a usage scenario of the security metadata

In this scenario, owner organisation, *Org1*, will either generate or acquire the data for example from conducting scientific experiments. It then annotates the data with some descriptive (e.g. scientific) metadata and the security metadata suggested in the previous section and stores the data either locally or on the Grid. Scientific metadata can describe the circumstances in which the data were generated, such as the experiment set-up, the investigation, the scientific study and so on. One common model for describing scientific data is the CSMD model [18].

Next, a collaborating organisation, *Org2*, will request to share the data with the source organisation. Upon receiving this request, the source organisation will check if the security metadata of the requested data is within the permissions of the dissemination policy of the source organisation. If this is the case, *Org1* will send the data and its metadata to *Org2*. *Org2* then conducts a set of possible security and cryptographic operations to make sure the data is acceptable to the local policy of storing data at *Org2*. These operations will be applied to the security metadata, for example, checking data freshness and provenance. Finally, a *User* requests to access the data.

The attributes and credentials of the *User* are compared against some of the security metadata, for example, whether the date and location of the *User* are within the permissible range allowed by the security metadata and whether it is possible to route the data to the *User* via certain IP-domains. If the latter is the case, *Org2* forwards the data to *Org3*, which may be running as a mirror for *Org2*. *Org3* then forwards the data with the metadata to the User for the latter to apply their operations. In this scenario, we assume the existence of an access, usage and routing control infrastructure to enforce the security requirements.

6 Conclusion

In this paper, we presented a metadata model for describing the security attributes usually associated to data during their dissemination, usage and routing across different organisations and by different users. We motivated the model by a use case from the domain of large-scale cost-critical scientific experiments, which often generate data that require protection from corruption, loss or leakage.

Our future plans are to build search and match tools that are based on this model and that can match security policies against the security metadata of the data being disseminated. We are also investigating the use of identity-based encryption as a secure means of propagating the security metadata in a manner not detachable from their data.

References

1. Denning, D.: A Lattice Model of Secure information Flow. ACM Transactions on Programming Languages and Systems 19(5), 236–243 (1976)
2. Denker, G., Kagal, L., Finin, T.W., Paolucci, M., Sycara, K.P.: Security for DAML Web Services: Annotation and Matchmaking. In: Fensel, D., Sycara, K., Mylopoulos, J. (eds.) ISWC 2003. LNCS, vol. 2870, pp. 335–350. Springer, Heidelberg (2003)
3. Ankolekar, A., Burstein, M.H., Hobbs, J.R., Lassila, O., Martin, D.L., McIlraith, S.A., Narayanan, S., Paolucci, M., Payne, T.R., Sycara, K.P., Zeng, H.: DAML-S: Semantic Markup for Web Services. In: SWWS, pp. 411–430 (2001)
4. Bartel, M., Boyer, J., Fox, B., LaMacchia, B., Simon, E.: XML Signature Syntax and Processing, 2nd edn. W3C Recommendation (June 2008)
5. Fikes, R., Jenkins, J., Frank, G.: JTP: A System Architecture and Component Library for Hybrid Reasoning. In: Proceedings of the Seventh World Multiconference on Systemics, Cybernetics, and Informatics, Orlando, Florida, USA (July 2003)
6. Kim, A., Luo, J., Kang, M.H.: Security Ontology for Annotating Resources. In: OTM Conferences, vol. (2), pp. 1483–1499 (2005)
7. Martin, D., Burstein, M., Hobbs, J., Lassila, O., McDermott, D., McIlraith, S., Narayanan, S., Paolucci, M., Parsia, B., Payne, T., Sirin, E., Srinivasan, N., Sycara, K.: OWL-S: Semantic Markup for Web Services. W3C Member Submission (November 2004)

8. Martimiano, L.A.F., dos Santos Moreira, E.: The evaluation process of a computer security incident ontology. In: de Freitas, F.L.G., Stuckenschmidt, H., Pinto, H.S., Malucelli, A. (eds.) Proceedings of the 2nd Workshop on Ontologies and their Applications (WONTO 2006). CEUR Workshop Proceedings, vol. 199. CEUR-WS.org (2006)

9. Crompton, S., Aziz, B., Wilson, M.: Sharing Scientific Data: Scenarios and Challenges. In: Proceedings of the W3C Workshop on Access Control Application Scenarios (2009)

10. Sandhu, R.S., Coyne, E.J., Feinstein, H.L., Youman, C.E.: Rolebased access control models. Computer 29(2), 38–47 (1996)

11. Wang, L., Wijesekera, D., Jajodia, S.: A logic-based framework for attribute based access control. In: FMSE 2004: Proceedings of the 2004 ACM Workshop on Formal Methods in Security Engineering, pp. 45–55. ACM, New York (2004)

12. Park, J., Sandhu, R.: The UCONabc Usage Control Model. ACM Transactions on Information and System Security 7(1), 128–174 (2004)

13. Peterson, W., Brown, D.: Cyclic Codes for Error Detection. Proceedings of the Institute of Radio Engineers 49, 228–235 (1961)

14. Brewer, D., Nash, M.: The chinese wall security policy. In: Proceedings of the 1989 IEEE Symposium on Security and Privacy, pp. 206–214. IEEE Computer Society Press, Oakland (1989)

15. N. B. of Standards, Data Encryption Standard, U.S. Department of Commerce. Tech. Rep. NBS FIPS PUB 46 (1997)

16. Rivest, R., Shamir, A., Adleman, L.: A Method for Obtaining Digital Signatures and Public-Key Cryptosystems. Communications of the ACM 21(2), 120–126 (1978)

17. N. I. of Standards and Technology, Digital Signature Standard, U.S. Department of Commerce. Tech. Rep. FIPS PUB 186 (1994)

18. Matthews, B., Sufi, S., Flannery, D., Lerusse, L., Griffin, T., Gleaves, M., Kleese, K.: Using a Core Scientific Metadata Model in Large-Scale Facilities. International Journal of Digital Curation 5(1), 106–118 (2010)

SecPAL4DSA: A Policy Language for Specifying Data Sharing Agreements

Benjamin Aziz[1], Alvaro Arenas[2], and Michael Wilson[3]

[1] School of Computing, University of Portsmouth, Portsmouth, U.K.
`benjamin.aziz@port.ac.uk`
[2] Department of Information Systems, Instituto de Empresa Business School, Madrid, Spain
`alvaro.arenas@ie.edu`
[3] e-Science Centre, STFC Rutherford Appleton Laboratory, Oxfordshire, U.K.
`michael.wilson@stfc.ac.uk`

Abstract. Data sharing agreements are a common mechanism by which enterprises can legalise and express acceptable circumstances for the sharing of information and digital assets across their administrative boundaries. Such agreements, often written in some natural language, are expected to form the basis for the low-level policies that control the access to and usage of such digital assets. This paper contributes to the problem of expressing data sharing requirements in security policy languages such that the resulting policies can enforce the terms of a data sharing agreement. We extend one such language, SecPAL, with constructs for expressing permissions, obligations, penalties and risk, which often occur as clauses in a data sharing agreement.

Keywords: Data Sharing Agreements, Deontic Logic, Security Policies.

1 Introduction

Data sharing is becoming increasingly important in modern enterprises. Every enterprise requires the regular exchange of data with other enterprises. Although the exchange of this data is vital for the successful inter-enterpriseal process, it is often confidential, requiring strict controls on its access and usage. In order to mitigate the risks inherent in sharing data between enterprises, Data Sharing Agreements (DSAs) are used to ensure that agreed data policies are enforced across enterprises [1].

A DSA is a legal agreement (contract) among two or more parties regulating who can access data, when and where, and what they can do with it. DSAs either include the data policies explicitly as clauses, or include existing enterpriseal data policies by reference. DSA clauses include deontic notions stating permissions for data access and usage, prohibitions on access and usage which constrain these permissions, and obligations that the principles to the agreement must fulfill. A DSA can be created between an enterprise and each of many collaborators. DSAs are represented in natural languages with their concomitant ambiguities and potential conflicts, which are exacerbated by DSA combinations. Therefore, analysing such natural language DSAs [2] is desirable before they can be enforced, which is usually done through a transformation into executable policy languages [3].

J.J. Park et al. (Eds.): STA 2011, CCIS 186, pp. 29–36, 2011.
© Springer-Verlag Berlin Heidelberg 2011

This paper is mainly concerned with defining an approach for the modelling and enforcement of DSAs based on the SecPAL policy language [4]; a simple and powerful language defined by Microsoft Research. The approach involves enriching SecPAL with deontic predicates expressing permissions and obligations. These predicates can then be used to model DSA clauses. Second we extend the definition of clauses to associate them with penalties, in case clauses are violated. Finally, we provide a risk-based approach for calculating SecPAL queries, which takes into consideration the level of assurance of the infrastructure or the reputation of the user and the penalty associated with clauses.

There has been a fresh interest in the concept of data sharing agreements, motivated mainly by models exploiting Internet as a technological platform for businesses, in which sharing data and information is central. An initial model of DSAs was proposed by Swarup et al in [5]. The model is based on dataflow graphs whose nodes are principals with local stores, and whose edges are channels along which data flows. Agreement clauses are modelled as obligation constraints expressed as distributed temporal logic predicates over data stores and data flows. In [6], an operational semantics expressing how a system evolves when executed under the restriction of DSA is defined, and in [9], the model is encoded in the Maude term-rewriting system and several DSA properties are automatically verified.

Our work has been influenced by the work of Arenas et al. [2] on using the Event-B specification language for modelling DSAs. There, a method is defined for representing deontic concepts into event-based models, and how those models can be exploited to verify DSA properties using model-checking techniques. However, our work goes further by using an implementable specification language, SecPAL, and by including quantitative factors such as penalties and their associated risk. Closer to our approach is the work on using SecPAL for modelling privacy preferences and data-handling policies [8]. The work focuses on defining a notion of satisfaction between a policy and a preference with the aims of developing a satisfaction-checking algorithm. By contrast, our work has concentrated on giving precise formal definitions to the notions of permissions and obligations as key concepts in DSAs.

2   Overview of Data Sharing Agreements

Data sharing requirements are usually captured by means of collaboration agreements among the partners. They usually contain clauses defining what data will be shared, the delivery/transmission mechanisms and the processing and security framework, among others. Following [5], a DSA consists of a definition part and a collection of agreement *Clauses*. The definition part includes the list of involved *Principals*; the start and end dates of the agreement; and the list of *Data* covered by the agreement.

Three types of clauses are relevant for DSAs: *Authorisation*, *Prohibition* and *Obligation* clauses. Authorisations indicate that specified roles of principals are authorised to perform actions on the data within constraints of time and location. Prohibitions act as further constraints on the authorisations, prohibiting actions by specific roles at stated times and locations. Obligations indicate that principals, or the underlying infrastructure, are required to perform specified actions following some event, usually within a time period. The DSA will usually contain processes to be followed, or systems to be used to enforce the assertions, and define penalties to be imposed when clauses are breached.

The set-up of DSAs requires technologies such as DSA authoring tools [6], which may include controlled natural language vocabularies to define unambiguously the DSAs conditions and obligations; and translators of DSAs clauses into enforceable policies. We represent DSA clauses as guarded actions, where the guard is a predicate characterising environmental conditions like time and location, or restrictions for the occurrence of the event, such as *"user is registered"* or *"data belongs to a project"*.

Definition 1: (**Action**). An action is a tuple consisting of three elements $\langle p,an,d\rangle$, where p is the principal, an is an action name, and d is the data.

Action $\langle p,an,d\rangle$ expresses that the principal p performs action name an on the data d. Action names represent atomic permissions, where actions are built from by adding the identity of the principal performing the action name and the data on which the action name is performed. We assume that actions are taken from a pre-defined list of actions, possibly derived from some ontology. An example of an action is *"Alice accesses product data"*. We shall consider in this paper two types of clauses only: permissions and obligations. Clauses are usually evaluated within a specific context represented by predicates for environmental conditions like location and time.

Definition 2: (**Agreement Clause**). Let G be a predicate and $a = \langle p,an,d\rangle$ be an action. The syntax of agreement clauses is defined as follows:

$$C ::= \text{IF } G \text{ THEN } P(a) \mid \text{IF } G \text{ THEN } O(a)$$

A permission clause is denoted as IF G THEN $O(a)$, which indicates that provided the condition G holds, the system may perform action a. An obligation clause, on the other hand, is denoted as IF G THEN $O(a)$, which indicates that provided the condition G holds, the system eventually must perform action a. A data sharing agreement can be defined as follows.

Definition 3: (**Data Sharing Agreement**). A DSA is a tuple $\langle Principals, Data, ActionNames, fromTime, endTime, \wp(C)\rangle$

Principals is the set of principals signing the agreement and abiding by its clauses. *Data* is the data elements to be shared. *ActionNames* is a set containing the name of the actions that a party can perform on a data. *fromTime* and *endTime* denotes the starting and finishing time of the agreement respectively; this is an abstraction representing the starting and finishing date of the agreement. Finally, $\wp(C)$ is the set of clauses of the data sharing agreement.

3   SecPAL4DSA: SecPAL for Data Sharing Agreements

SecPAL [4] is a declarative authorization language with a compact syntax and a succinct unambiguous semantics. It has been proposed for modelling various security policy idioms, such as discretionary and mandatory access control, role-based access control and delegation control, and within the scope of large-scale distributed systems like Grids [7]. It has also been recently suggested as a framework for modelling privacy preferences and data-handling policies [8].

A policy in SecPAL is represented as an *assertion context*, AC, which is simply a set of *assertions*, $A \in AC$, written according to the following syntax:

$AC ::= \{A_1,...,A_n\}$
$A ::= E$ says $fact_0$ if $fact_1 ... fact_n$ where c
$fact ::= e$ pred $e_1 ... e_m \mid e$ can say $fact$
$e ::= x \mid E$

Where c is a constraint in the form of a logical condition, E is some principal entity (such as a user or a system process), x is a variable, *fact* is a sentence stating a property on principals in the form of the predicate, e pred $e_1 ... e_m$ or allowing delegations in the form of e can say *fact*. A main feature of SecPAL is that it is extensible in the sense that any set of predicates e pred $e_1 ... e_m$ can be added to a specific instance of SecPAL. Such predicates will be defined based on the specific domain for which the policies are required, for example, in the domain of scientific experiments, predicates could include A *canVisualise(data)* or A *canAnalyse(data)*.

The main contribution of this paper is to propose a new instance of SecPAL for expressing assertions and queries on DSAs, called SecPAL4DSA. SecPAL4DSA extends the syntax of facts of the previous section with the following predicates:

$fact ::= permitted((an,d)) \mid obliged_{user}((an,d)) \mid obliged_{sys}((an,d))$

The *permitted((an,d))* predicate implies that the user is permitted to execute the action *an* on the data *d*. On the other hand, *obliged$_{user}$((an,d))* means that the user is obliged to execute *an* on *d* sometime in the future. Here, we do not deal with real-time temporal constraints on obligations, though these would be possible to incorporate. Finally, *obliged$_{sys}$((an,d))* means that the system infrastructure is obliged to execute *an* on *d* sometime in the future.

The extra predicates we define above represent the deontic operators of permissions and obligations for users and systems. Note that at present, SecPAL does not allow negative predicates in the language of assertions because of issues related to the complexity of assertion deductions. Therefore, we do not deal with prohibitions and assume that any action not permitted is prohibited by default.

Example 1. In the context of DSAs, a principal E may represent any of the *signatories* of the DSA. So, for example, assuming there are two signatories, A and B, then the following two assertions express a DSA that demands payments for data accesses:

(**Assert1**) A *says* B *permitted(access, data)* if A *hasFinished(authenticate, B)* where c

(**Assert2**) A *says* B *obliged$_{user}$(pay, amount)* if B *permitted(access, data)*, B *hasFinished(access, data)* where *currentTime* $\leq$ *PaymentDeadline*

The first assertion will allow A to grant B the permission to *access data* if A successfully authenticates B (modelled by the predicate *hasFinished*) and some condition c holds (which could be relevant to some of B's attributes). The second assertion states that whenever B has finished accessing the data, then it is obliged by A to pay an amount of money within some predefined deadline.

Next, we define precisely what we mean by the permitted and obliged deontic operators in the context of SecPAL4DSA.

3.1 Semantics of the Permission and Obligation Predicates

The semantics of permissions, user obligations and system obligations are given here in terms of Linear Temporal Logic (LTL). LTL formulae are defined based on a set of propositional variables, $p_1, p_2 \ldots$, which are in our case the predicates themselves, and logical operators ($\neg, \wedge, \vee, \rightarrow$) including future temporal operators such as $\Box$ (always), $\Diamond$ (eventually) and $\bigcirc$ (next). They may also include past versions of these. Here, we shall write $P \Rightarrow Q$ to denote the formula $\Box(P \Rightarrow Q)$, and we write the two-way conditional, $B \wr A \wr C$, to denote that if A is true, then C is true, otherwise if A is false, then B is true.

1. *Semantics of User Obligations*: We start with the semantics of user obligations. This semantics is defined in terms of two actions: bF and bS. bF represents a system action corresponding to the failure of executing an action by the user and bS is a system action corresponding to the success of the user in executing some action. bF would normally represent a penalty action that the system will execute in case of user failure. On the other hand, bS is a follow-up action that the system executes after the user successfully fulfils his obligation to carry some action. Either or both of bF and bS could be inactive actions, such as (*null, null*). However, more meaningful examples would be for bF to be the disabling of some system resources, bF=(*disable, resource*), and for bS to be the enabling of system resources, bS=(*enable, resource*). Now, assuming that $p(a)$ is the post condition of action a; this means that a has already occurred and its effect on the state of the system is modelled as the predicate $p(a)$, we can define the semantics of B *obliged$_{user}$*(a) (i.e. B is obliged to do a) in terms of the semantic function, [*fact*]=P defined as follows:

$$[B\ obliged_{user}(a)] = \exists bF,\ bS{:}\ G \Rightarrow \Diamond\ ([Sys\ obliged_{sys}(bF)]) \wr p(a) \wr [Sys\ obliged_{sys}(bS)]$$

where G is a general predicate on the current state of the system enabling and could include for example p(request), which is a predicate indicating that the action representing a request from the user to execute a has occurred. This meaning of user obligations is defined in terms of the meaning of system obligations, which we discuss next. The rationale behind this is that user obligation cannot be enforced; users by their nature can always violate an obligation. However, such violations can trigger corrective or compensatory system obligations.

2. *Semantics of System Obligations*: The semantics of system obligations, *Sys obliged$_{sys}$*(b), on the other hand, are defined in terms of [*fact*]=P, as:

$$[Sys\ obliged_{sys}(b)] = G \Rightarrow \Diamond p(b)$$

Where G is a general predicate (e.g. on the system state) that enables the obligation. This meaning implies that if the action b is obliged to be executed by the system, then it will *eventually* be executed as expressed by the LTL operator $\Diamond$. In general, $\Diamond$ has no time limit, but this can be constrained by the computational limits of the system or by the time limit of the DSA contract (i.e. its expiry date and time). The main aspect to note in the meaning of system obligations is that, unlike user obligations, system obligations can be enforced and their enforcement depends on the correct behaviour of the system components responsible for their fulfilment.

3. *Semantics of Permissions*: The semantics of permissions are also defined in terms of the special semantic function, [*fact*]=*P* as follows:

$$[User\ permitted(a)] = p(request) \Rightarrow \Diamond p(a)$$

This meaning simply says that to be permitted, as a user to execute an action, is the same as saying that when a request to execute that action occurs, this will eventually result in the execution of the action. Again, the $\Diamond$ operator leaves out any time constraints, which could be introduced using a real-time version of the operator or using next $\bigcirc$.

3.2 Mapping DSAs to SecPAL4DSA

Finally, we describe here an approach for mapping permission and obligation clauses in the language of [2] to assertions in SecPAL4DSA, such that DSAs can be enforced by a policy enforcement point.

As we mentioned earlier, one of the main features of SecPAL is that it expresses the root of authority in each individual assertion. This is equivalent to saying that each clause in a DSA must have a root of trust, which is more expressive than the normal DSA clauses. Therefore, we assume that for each clause in a DSA, a signatory, *A*, assumes the role of the root of trust for that clause. Based on this assumption, we define the transformation function, *F: C → A*, as follows:

$$F(\text{IF } G \text{ THEN } P((p,an,d))) = A \text{ says } p \text{ } permitted((an,d)) \text{ if } G$$
$$F(\text{IF } G \text{ THEN } O((p,an,d))) = A \text{ says } p \text{ } obliged((an,d)) \text{ if } G$$

where *obliged* is either $obliged_{sys}$ or $obliged_{user}$ depending on whether *p* is a system or a user, respectively. The transformation function uses the structure of actions in the language of DSAs to construct the corresponding parts of SecPAL4DSA permission and obligation assertions.

4 Penalties in SecPAL4DSA

Another construct, which we use to extend the language of SecPAL4DSA is that of *penalties*, which are added to the definition of assertions to form what we call *penalty clauses,* defined by the following syntax:

Penalty Clause ::= (*A, Penalty*)

Where *Penalty: Principal* → N is a utility function mapping principals to some values (e.g. natural numbers representing a monetary concept such as money). Going back to *Example 1*, we can define a couple of penalty clauses as follows.

Example 2. Define the new penalty clauses based on the permission and obligation clauses as follows.

(**Clause1**) (*A* says *B permitted*(*access, data*) if *A hasFinished*(*authenticate, B*) where *c*, (*A* → 10))

(**Clause2**) (*A* says *B obliged$_{user}$*(*pay, amount*) if *B permitted*(*access,data*) and *B hasFinished*(*access, data*) where *currentTime* ≤ *PaymentDeadline*, (B → 50))

In Clause1, the failure of permitting the assertion to happen will incur a penalty on *A* of 10 units. This means that even though *A* was meant to authorise *B* to access the data, it failed to do so, which corresponds to a denial of service. Instead, in Clause2, the failure is related to *B* failing to make a payment by the specified deadline, which corresponds to a violation of an obligation. Therefore, it incurs a penalty of 50 units.

4.1 Semantics of Penalty Clauses

We define the semantics of penalty clauses more formally in terms of the semantic function, *E*[(*A, Penalty*)], defined as follows:

$$E[(A, Penalty)] = Penalty \in Penalty_{Log} \{p(a)\} Penalty \notin Penalty_{Log}$$
where *A=A* says *B dsa$_{operator}$*(*a*) if *fact* where *c*
and *dsa$_{operator}$* ∈ {*obliged$_{user}$, obliged$_{sys}$, permitted*}

The meaning of a penalty clause depends essentially on whether or not the action of the deontic operator in an assertion has taken place or not. If this is the case, then the penalty specified in the clause does not belong to the state called *Penalty$_{Log}$*, which registers all the due penalties. Otherwise, if the action did not take place, then the penalty is logged in the state.

4.2 Policy Queries

The additional extensions of the deontic predicates and penalties that SecPAL4DSA incorporated into the policy language allow for richer semantics for the reference monitor interpreting queries generated as a result of user requests. One such interesting high-level semantics would be to include a risk-sensitive reference monitor that compares the probability of the failure of an assertion (i.e. failure of granting access, failure of fulfilling obligations) with the penalty incurred by that failure. For example, we could define a risk-calculation function, *R: Penalty Clause* → N, which returns the risk of the failure of an assertion part of a penalty clause compared to the penalty associated with that failure.

For example, taking the penalty clauses of *Example 2* and assuming that the probability of failure of the first assertion is 0.7 and for the second is 0.05, then *R*(Clause1) = ((0.7 × 10)/100) = 0.07 and *R*(Clause2) = ((0.05 × 50)/100) = 0.025. This demonstrates that the probability of failure combined with the penalty can give indicate how delicate an assertion (i.e. DSA clause) is.

5 Conclusion and Future Work

This paper presented an extension to a popular policy language called SecPAL, for modelling and expressing data sharing agreements among enterprises with different administrative domains. The new language, SecPAL4DSA, is capable of encoding permission and obligation clauses of a DSA, and can also express penalty clauses and provide a quantitative means based on risk levels for evaluating policy rules against requests submitted by external users for accessing and using local resources.

In its current form, SecPAL does not allow prohibitive clauses to be modelled due to issues related to decidability of queries. For future work, we plan to investigate other methods by which prohibitions can be modelled in terms of the current language constructs. Also, we are planning to consider other quantitative factors related to DSAs, such as modelling of bounded obligations. Finally, we plan to develop a query evaluation engine for the new language, SecPAL4DSA and evaluate its performance with regards to case studies taken from the domain of scientific data sharing.

References

1. Sieber, J.E.: Data Sharing: Defining Problems and Seeking Solutions. Law and Human Behaviour 12(2), 199–206 (1988)
2. Arenas, A.E., Aziz, B., Bicarregui, J., Wilson, M.: An Event-B Approach to Data Sharing Agreements. In: Méry, D., Merz, S. (eds.) IFM 2010. LNCS, vol. 6396, pp. 28–42. Springer, Heidelberg (2010)
3. Damianou, N., Dulay, N., Lupu, E., Sloman, M.: The Ponder Policy Specification Language. In: Sloman, M., Lobo, J., Lupu, E.C. (eds.) POLICY 2001. LNCS, vol. 1995, pp. 18–38. Springer, Heidelberg (2001)
4. Becker, M.Y., Fournet, C., Gordon, A.D.: SecPAL: Design and Semantics of a Decentralized Authorization Language. Journal of Computer Security 18(4), 597–643 (2010)
5. Swarup, V., Seligman, L., Rosenthal, A.: A Data Sharing Agreement Framework. In: Bagchi, A., Atluri, V. (eds.) ICISS 2006. LNCS, vol. 4332, pp. 22–36. Springer, Heidelberg (2006)
6. Matteucci, I., Petrocchi, M., Sbodio, M.L.: CNL4DSA a Controlled Natural Language for Data Sharing Agreements. In: 25th Symposium on Applied Computing, Privacy on the Web Track. ACM, New York (2010)
7. Dillaway, B.: A unified approach to trust, delegation, and authorization in large-scale grids. Microsoft Corporation, Tech. Rep. (2006)
8. Becker, M.Y., Malkis, A., Bussard, L.: A Framework for Privacy Preferences and Data-Handling Policies. Microsoft Research, Tech. Rep. MSR-TR-2009-128 (September 2009)
9. Colombo, M., Martinelli, F., Matteucci, I., Petrocchi, M.: Context- Aware Analysis of Data Sharing Agreements. In: 4th European Workshop on Combining Context with Trust, Security, and Privacy, CAT 2010, pp. 99–104 (2010)

Self-keying Identification Mechanism for Small Devices[*]

Krzysztof Barczyński, Przemysław Błaśkiewicz,
Marek Klonowski, and Mirosław Kutyłowski

Institute of Mathematics and Computer Science,
Wrocław University of Technology, Wrocław, Poland
{Przemyslaw.Blaskiewicz,Marek.Klonowski,
Miroslaw.Kutylowski}@pwr.wroc.pl

Abstract. We present a strong authentication mechanism intended for embedded systems based on standard but weak processors, without support for cryptographic operations. So far the main effort was to provide methods based on relatively short keys and complex computations, we make advantage of availability of non-volatile memory of larger size and confine ourselves to basic bit operations available on each processor.

Keywords: authentication, random walk, standard processor, self-keying.

1 Introduction

Process of introducing small and tiny electronic devices into everyday life continues. Tracking goods, fare collection in public transport, inventory keeping are some examples. A typical architecture of such a system would consist of a number of high-end terminals capable of querying a database and multitude of small devices, such as RFID tags, low-end microcontrollers, swipe- or wave- cards etc. By their nature, widespread systems like these are prone to many threats, such as cloning.

In contrast, hardware constraints in these devices call for special attention when designing security mechanisms. Each protocol must be tailored to the small available memory and be simple enough to save energy and time. As a consequence, the protocol should involve calculations that do not go beyond integer multiplication or squaring (common asymmetric practice of exponentiation to a large prime is strictly out of scope). Additionally, communication should be short, and therefore quick. The preferred type of interaction here is challenge-response.

Needless to say the protocol should be safe. However, it does not need to offer security comparable to that of RSA or other full-flavored cryptosystems: simply if such high security was needed, then more powerful (hence expensive, complex) devices would be deployed. In many cases a "deterrant-protocol" will be suitable: time to break it will be greater than possible gain to the attacker. We also do not assume that tiny device is in any way tamper-resistant; the economic model for here is that the vast number of devices is acceptable only if their price is low.

[*] Partially supported by Polish Ministry of Science and Higher Education, grants N N206 2701 33, NN 206 2573 35 and Foundation for Polish Science – Mistrz Programme.

J.J. Park et al. (Eds.): STA 2011, CCIS 186, pp. 37–44, 2011.

Recent implementations of RFID systems, sensor networks and even embedded systems all face similar problems of limited hardware capabilities. With exception of data storage that has become a cheap and abundant resource. It is tempting to utilize it to balance the drawbacks of hardware.

For a solution, we turn to a slightly modified concept of security: based not on hardness of an algebraic problem (as is the case in standard cryptography), but leveraging certain properties of simple processes and some level of randomness. General idea is presented in Sect. 3. and further extended in Sect. 4. Analysis of our approach in Sect. 5 is concluded with some remarks and intuitions in Sect. 6.

2 Previous and Related Work

Literature devoted to authentication methods is abundant, but designing such mechanisms for limited devices remains challenging. Many solutions for the so-called *light-weight cryptography* are still prohibitively demanding (e.g., require hash computation). There are notable exceptions, mainly motivated by applications in RFID-systems. Such methods usually do not provide security comparable to typical cryptographic methods, but rather offer *some* level of security for devices, having, say, at most dozen of hundreds logical gates and very limited memory. Such an approach is presented for example in [2,6,9]. The last of them presents probably the most known family of that type of protocols, namely HB/HB+ based on the protocol described in [4]. Despite its merits, the protocol was a subject of various attacks (see [3]). Other schemes that can be used for authenticating constrained devices can be found in the surveys [5,8].

3 Basic Mechanism

3.1 The Algorithm

The basic algorithm ([1]) performs a sequence of *jumps* between positions on a secret bit string S of length t that is stored securely on a device. We assume that t is a power of two, hence $l=\log(t)$ bits are required to address every position in S. Denote l bits of S starting at A_i by $S(A_i)$, then $S(A_i)$ can be treated as destination (address) of the next jump. The secret S is stored in a database which can be accessed by high-end authorization units (readers, access control terminals, etc.). Alternatively, it can be recovered with a pseudorandom number generator with the private key of the system provider (if the secret keys are created in this way). The following procedure is executed. Reader sends a challenge pair: (A_0, N) : A_0 is the starting address, N is the number of jumps to be made. The device performs:

```
ptr ← A₀
for i→0 to N-1 do
    ptr ← A_{i+1}=S(A_i +1).
```

Finally, the device responds with one bit from S at position *ptr*. Then the reader performs the same operations as above on all identifiers it stores in memory and selects possible candidates. Procedure is repeated with different challenges until a single candidate remains.

3.2 Properties

An analysis of the basic scheme is given in [1]. We report the main observations. First of all, the distribution of last jump addresses is uneven. There is an inherent property of the process that some positions in S are more probable to occur than others and hence the bits corresponding to these positions will be returned more often. Direct reason for that is the existence of *cycles*: there exist sets of indices C such that for all $i \in C$ there exists $S(A_i) \in C$. It has been shown that, in expectation, short cycles are indeed highly probable.

Secondly, a graph model of the process was developed and shown by simulation to be very similar to a random mapping with t vertices. Specifically, let $G_{alg}=(V,E)$ be the graph of the process and all vertices are labeled by integers $[0,t]$. Then $(v_1,v_2) \in E$ iff $S(v_1)=v_2$. Let $G_{rand}=(V',E')$ be a random graph, where $\Pr[(v_1,v_2) \in E=1/t$. Then, taking into consideration the strongest component size, average number of cycles with a given length and average number of elements in a cycle for analytic values for G_{rand} and experimental values for G_{alg} it was concluded that random mapping G_{rand} is a good approximation of the discussed scheme.

4 Extensions

The main algorithm suffers from the existence of cycles: whenever the address in such cycle is reached, the consecutive addresses are determined. To alleviate this we extend (following the idea put forward in [1]) the scheme so as to modify each next address by combining it with current jump counter (*cnt* in the following). This does not increase the demand for hardware as the jump counter must be implemented any-way. The following modifiers were considered:

flip: Flipping bits 0-3 with 4-7. This option was checked with for $t=8$ only.
shift: Cyclic shifting bits of the address by the value *cnt* mod l.
ADD: Adding (*cnt·M*) to the current address value (mod l). In this case M is a parameter defaulting to 1; by changing its value to the one with more 1's in binary representation, more bits in original address can be modified.
XOR: Bit-wise XOR of the current address value with (*cnt·M*) taken (mod l). Again, the parameter M defaulting to 1 is introduced to allow more bits to be flipped when binary representation of M has many 1's.
d-ADD, d-XOR: Take the **ADD** modification from above and run it on secret S. In parallel, run the non-modified algorithm as described in Sect. 3, with the following addition. When next-hop address is determined by the basic scheme, after calculating $A_{i+1}=S(A_i+1)$, ADD or XOR, respectively, it with the address in S used during i-th hop of the **ADD** modification.

5 Analysis

5.1 Experiments Methodology

To evaluate practical impact of the modifications on the basic scheme the following characteristics were considered. First, the number of different *address*es that were visited during one run of the algorithm. The more unique values of A_i a given modification produces, the less certain is the estimated location of the return bit. Likewise, if the number of these addresses is similar to N, it suggests that no cycle was hit. Secondly, randomness tests were run to check to what extent do the return bits behave like a random bit sequence. Obviously, multiple runs of the protocol for the same key but different challenges should yield independently both 0 and 1 with a probability close to 0.5, so that attacker's advantage in guessing is minimized.

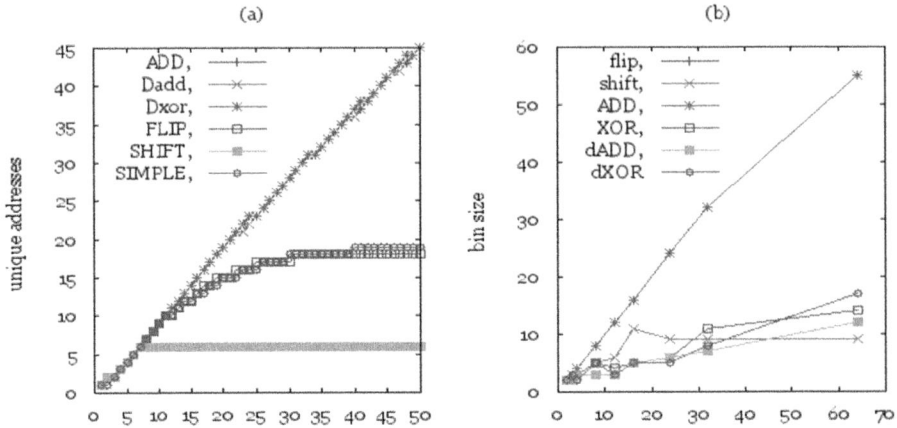

Fig. 1a. Average number of generated unique addresses as function of the number of jumps. Almost linear growth for ADD, XOR, d-ADD, d-XOR suggest immunity to cycles phenomenon.
Fig. 1b. Distribution of the number of unique addresses. Number of bins grows with the number of jumps. For *flip* and ADD this is a linear growth (lines overlay).

The scheme can be viewed as transforming one quasi-random bit string S into a sequence of also quasi-random bits. This transformation, in order to be useful for authentication, should yield results that can distinguish two devices. Therefore the third characteristic we studied was if the difference between two secrets is maintained in response bit strings corresponding to these secrets. To do this, the Hamming distance between two secrets S_1, S_2 was measured and the scheme was run for both of them for t rounds with random value of A_0 for each round. The Hamming distance was measured for the resulting streams of return bits.

5.2 Experimental Results

Number of unique addresses. To observe this property one can compare the number of hops executed on S and the number of unique addresses generated during the procedure. Fig. 1a shows this for all seven examined extensions. It is also important if the number of unique addresses is more or less constant for different strings S. The simulation involved generation of 7168 unique S's and running the six modifications on each of them. For each S, the number of unique addresses that were generated was calculated. Table 1 presents the distribution of these values for different numbers of jumps. The correlation of the number of different addresses and the number of jumps is presented in Fig. 1b. First of all, introducing modifications to the basic scheme

Table 1. Distribution of the number of unique addresses for each extension process. The first number in column is the size of the largest bin; the percentage value is the fraction of addresses that fall into this and two adjacent bins, over all addresses that have are generated in the process.

jumps:	3		4		8		12		16		24		32		64	
flip	3	98.5%	4	99.1%	8	87.7%	12	74.5%	16	66.9%	24	31.9%	32	20.3%	55	13.5%
shift	3	99.9%	4	99.6%	7	91.7%	10	84.3%	12	60.3%	11	68.1%	11	70.3%	11	75.4%
ADD	3	99%	4	96.8%	8	89.0%	12	76.5%	16	55.3%	24	43.1%	32	13.6%	20	13.8%
XOR	3	100%	4	99.8%	8	84.9%	12	96.0%	16	94.8%	23	78.0%	31	56.7%	57	41.1%
d-ADD	3	100%	4	99.9%	8	99.7%	12	98.6%	16	93.7%	23	92.4%	30	80.9%	56	46.6%
d-XOR	3	99.5%	4	100%	8	99.2%	12	98.4%	16	91.0%	23	91.5%	30	73.8%	58	43.8%

solves the problem of cycles. Indeed, the more jumps are performed, the more unique addresses are generated – loops are avoided.

On the other hand, first conclusions on the effectiveness of the modifications can be drawn. Both *flip* and ADD are shown to behave unevenly: for some strings S they manage to generate very few unique addresses, even with relatively large number of jumps. This fact is clearly seen in Fig. 1b, where number of bins grows almost linearly for them. That suggests that both ADD and *flip* can get stuck in a loop generating very few unique addresses.

Data presented in Table 1 add to this description. For example, for 12 hops only approximately 3/4 of all addresses generated during the simulation by *flip* and ADD belong to the three largest bins. Other extensions perform much better, obtaining score of more than 90%. This suggests that these algorithms are stable: they generate almost constant amount of unique addresses, regardless of S. Furthermore, it can be inferred that XOR, d-ADD and d-XOR are especially resistant to the effect of cycles: the size of the largest bin grows almost linearly with the number of jumps.

Randomness of output bits. To assess randomness of the output from the algorithms two standard tests were performed. First, a sliding window test with sizes 1, …, 6. Then, matrix rank tests for matrices of size 3, …, 6. Table 4 summarizes results of the sliding window test and Fig. 2 presents their part for window size 5. Results of the matrix rank test are given in Table 2.

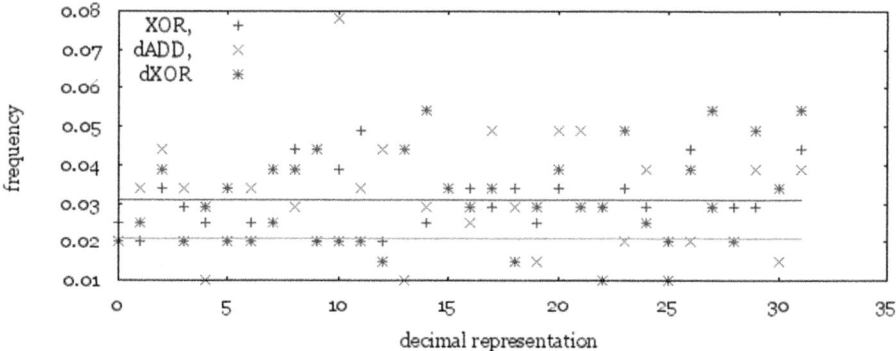

Fig. 2. Frequency of occurrence of binary strings of length $k=5$ in the output of XOR (average 0.031), d-ADD (0.021) and d-XOR (0.031) modifications

It may be concluded that all three algorithms present similar behavior, with slight advantage of XOR. This is reflected in the matrix test, since sliding window results are almost the same. The remaining three protocols have also been tested, due to scarcity of space they are not presented. Note that, as shown in previous section, rest of schemes displays worse properties in terms of unique address generation, hence their further analysis is not the subject of this paper.

Diversity of output. This feature is probably least important, since previous tests have shown relatively good random behavior of the three schemes. However, as the last step it was checked if the difference between two secrets S_1, S_2, given by Hamming distance, is reflected in the output of the schemes. If so, this would mean that it is in fact possible to use the output instead of the original S as sequence identifying the device. An excerpt from the simulation results is given in Table 3.

Table 2. Average (first) and standard deviation (second) for occurrences of given rank of rectangular matrix of size N

Rnk	XOR	d-ADD	d-XOR
3	.345; .046	.372; .088	.346; .051
2	.555; .053	.547; .076	.550; .056
<2	.100; .026	.081; .024	.104; .023
4	.299; .170	.315; .066	.378; .116
3	.547; .147	.558; .084	.524; .157
<3	.154; .089	.127; .063	.097; .071
5	.439; .098	.382; .081	.418; .086
4	.475; .089	.554; .092	.496; .047
<4	.086; .101	.064; .040	.086; .048
6	.423; .153	.449; .116	.439; .077
5	.500; .117	.474; .098	.480; .071
<5	.077; .075	.077; .081	.082; .064

Table 3. Hamming distances between two secrets (column -1-) and strings of output bits for given schemes (column -2-) run with these secrets to yield the same number of bits as have the secrets (here 256)

XOR		d-ADD		d-XOR	
-1-	-2-	-1-	-2-	-1-	-2-
119	132	123	125	126	128
124	124	119	133	125	123
115	121	150	124	147	113
134	121	120	126	124	120
128	130	131	123	113	115
132	118	128	122	117	123

5.3 Discussion of Results

The number of unique addresses visited by the processes in simulations suggests that they cover quite large part of secret S. Best performing modifications visit new address practically at each iteration and they spread uniformly in the range $\{0,...,t\}$. So, it does not seem vital that large number of jumps should be executed: the process is quickly likely to return a bit from a pseudo-random address. The modifications of the basic scheme were introduced to alleviate the problem of cycles. For some set C of integers from $0,...,t$ suppose addresses A_i: $i \in C$ form a cycle in the basic scheme. Then, modifying some A_j, $j \in C$ will have chances to escape the cycle defined by C. These chances are greater when $|C|$ is small, the case which is more frequent [1]. On the other hand, if $|C|$ is large, then such modification might not escape the cycle, but large cycles are less probable. Moreover, note that even if the process stays in the same cycle, it has exactly the same chances of leaving the cycle in the next iteration.

We note that, as simulations show, the protocols return pseudo-random bit generated by an also random sequence of bits in the secret S. Therefore it seems plausible to generate quasi-random numbers to be used in other protocols.

Table 4. Average (first) and standard deviation (second) for occurrences of k-bit long stings in outputs of the three algorithms

K	XOR	d-ADD	d-XOR	ideal
1	0.5000; 0.0113	0.5000; 0.0608	0.5000; 0.0778	1/2;
2	0.2500; 0.0199	0.2500; 0.0579	0.2503; 0.0459	1/4;
3	0.1281; 0.0120	0.1341; 0.0118	0.1279; 0.0353	1/8;
4	0.0623; 0.0242	0.0625; 0.0322	0.0623; 0.0300	1/16;
5	0.0312; 0.0078	0.0312; 0.0139	0.0313; 0.0130	1/32;
6	0.0178; 0.0087	0.0158; 0.0121	0.0160; 0.0122	1/64;

5.4 Security Considerations

Model of the attacker. Suppose the attacker wants to clone the tag so it can authenticate itself to any reader. She needs to learn the secret S. Assume that the only information available is from eavesdropping the legitimate communication. Hence, after listening to r runs of the protocol the adversary obtains the list of tuples: $\{(A_1, b_1), ..., (A_r, b_r)\}$, where A_i are the starting addresses and b_i bits returned by the tag.

Feasibility. The adversary must collect some amount of data to launch an attack. The devices in our scheme will not be authorized too often, nor will they protect highly valuable goods. Consequently, time needed to break one single secret S can be too big an expense to balance the possible gains. Also, breaking one S does not facilitate breaking other secrets, therefore a simple trick of timely updating S in the device forces the adversary to undergo the same procedure from scratch.

Intuition. Mathematical models are not provided, there are intuitions that argument for scheme's solidity against ordinary attacker. First of all, suppose the attacker overheard an authentication transmission, which provided him with r pairs (A_i, b_i). Our simulations show that if all A_i's are different then approximately 0.5 of b_i's will be zeroes. Moreover, in many cases the attacker may not know where exactly the b_i's come from in the secret S.

Conversely, assume that the attacker knows as much as a half of bits randomly chosen out in S. In the case of protocol with K jumps one can easily compute that all encountered addresses (understood as l-bit strings) in r jumps are disjoint is at least $\prod_{i=0}^{K-1}(1 - \frac{i(2l-1)}{t})$. Then, probability that all bits in all jumps are known to the adversary is $\frac{1}{2^{Kl}}$. More precise calculations show that in the case of two jumps, probability that all bits are known is smaller than $(\frac{3}{t})^2$. Thus for reasonable size of l advantage of the adversary, even having significant number of bits, is moderate.

Let us note also that at the heart of the scheme there is no particular algebraic problem, such as DLP or factorization. Indeed, the whole operation is performed on bit representations of numbers. Although inter-dependencies between binary representations of consecutive numbers occur (see [1] for analysis) there is no obvious "algebraic hack" that could potentially be used by the attacker, as is the case with some cryptographic schemes.

Replay attack. One simple strategy for an attacker is to collect all possible starting addresses A_i. To countermeasure this the reader can send additional number in its challenge, which must be combined with the *second* address produced in the process of jumping. Since all but first (starting) address remain unknown to the eavesdropper, this value will change the sequence of addresses in the process.

6 Conclusions

In this paper we presented a novel security solution tailored especially for simple devices with high hardware constraints. The scheme requires little memory and performs only basic bit operations on a preloaded random string. We present arguments for soundness of the scheme, yet no mathematical proof. This remains a task for future work.

References

1. Barczyński, K.: Coordinating communication in chosen RFID based systems. Master dissertation, Wrocław University of Technology, Wrocław, Poland (2008)
2. Cichoń, J., Klonowski, M., Kutyłowski, M.: Privacy protection for rfid with hidden subset identifiers. In: Indulska, J., Patterson, D.J., Rodden, T., Ott, M. (eds.) PERVASIVE 2008. LNCS, vol. 5013, pp. 298–314. Springer, Heidelberg (2008)
3. Gilbert, H., Sibert, H., Robshaw, M.: An active attack against a provably secure lightweight authentication protocol. IEEE Electronic Letters 41, 1169–1170 (2005)
4. Hopper, N.J., Blum, M.: Secure human identification protocols. In: Boyd, C. (ed.) ASIACRYPT 2001. LNCS, vol. 2248, pp. 52–66. Springer, Heidelberg (2001)
5. Juels, A.: Rfid security and privacy: a research survey. IEEE Journal on Selected Areas in Communications 24(2), 381–394 (2006)
6. Juels, A., Weis, S.A.: Authenticating Pervasive Devices with Human Protocols. In: Shoup, V. (ed.) CRYPTO 2005. LNCS, vol. 3621, pp. 293–308. Springer, Heidelberg (2005)
7. Peris-Lopez, P., Hernandez-Castro, J.C., Estevez-Tapiador, J.M., Ribagorda, A.: RFID systems: A survey on security threats and proposed solutions. In: Cuenca, P., Orozco-Barbosa, L. (eds.) PWC 2006. LNCS, vol. 4217, pp. 159–170. Springer, Heidelberg (2006)
8. Vajda, I., Buttyan, L.: Lightweight authentication protocols for low-cost rfid tags. In: Dey, A.K., Schmidt, A., McCarthy, J.F. (eds.) UbiComp 2003. LNCS, vol. 2864. Springer, Heidelberg (2003)

A Software Architecture for Introducing Trust in Java-Based Clouds

Siegfried Podesser and Ronald Toegl

Institute for Applied Information Processing and Communications (IAIK),
Graz University of Technology, Inffeldgasse 16a, A-8010 Graz, Austria
{siegfried.podesser,ronald.toegl}@iaik.tugraz.at

Abstract. The distributed software paradigms of grid and cloud computing offer massive computational power at commodity prices. Unfortunately, a number of security risks exist. In this paper we propose a software architecture which leverages the Trusted Computing principle of Remote Attestation to assess the trustworthiness of nodes in computing clouds. We combine hardware-security based on the Trusted Platform Module and Intel Trusted Execution Technology with an integrity-guaranteeing virtualization platform. Cloud services are offered by an easy-to-use Java middleware that performs role based access control and trust decisions hidden from the developer.

Keywords: Trusted Computing, Cloud Computing.

1 Introduction

Grid and its popular descendant Cloud computing promise to provide massive computational power by distributing the workload over a large pool of systems. "The Grid" provides flexible, secure and coordinated access to shared resources among dynamically changing virtual organizations [4]. Much like the power grid, it aims to make computational power at the level of supercomputing an ubiquitous commodity resource which is available at low costs. Not only large organizations provide resources, but also individual users may donate unused CPU cycles, bandwidth or memory. Especially commercially offered, easy-to-use Cloud computing resources have seen wide deployments in the last years. Such heterogeneous environments are ideally served by virtual machine based software [5] such as Java. Still, unsolved security issues exist. Many of those can be mitigated with Trusted Computing (TC).

In this paper we study a virtualized software architecture that allows Java applications access to public and private clouds to execute their grid applications, without giving up control over their code. Within the scope of a Public Key Infrastructure, we integrate role-based access control and TPM-based attestation mechanisms to enforce this in a practical implementation.

2 Challenges in Grid and Cloud Security

A number of security challenges occur in grid and cloud systems. A recent report of ENISA [3] lists several security risks, many of those are still not solved. A very

J.J. Park et al. (Eds.): STA 2011, CCIS 186, pp. 45–53, 2011.
© Springer-Verlag Berlin Heidelberg 2011

promising line of research [2,7,8] to overcome the security limitations of distributed computation networks is to incorporate Trusted Computing based on the widely available TPM. Specifically, we study the risk that code may not be executed correctly. Here, a remote node might report wrong answers back, either deliberately or by computing inaccurately. The code distributed could also be compromised or, if it contains precious intellectual property, stolen. Finally, also the data need to be secured and protected according to data protection requirements. Here it is especially important to proof that security facilities are actually used and not circumvented by malicious software. Current systems use only basic mechanisms to ensure trust. For instance, BOINC[1] is sending the same work-package to three different clients and validate if all clients report back the same answer. It will then ignore nodes that report dissenting answers. However, this only provides for correct computation but does not cover other risks.

3   Trusted Platforms

Trusted Computing as it is available today is based on specifications of the Trusted Computing Group (TCG). The core hardware component is the Trusted Platform Module (TPM) [13]. Similarly to a smart card the TPM features tamper-resilient cryptographic primitives, but is physically bound to its host device. The TPM helps to guarantee the integrity of measurements of software components by offering a set of Platform Configuration Registers (PCRs), which can only be written to via the one-way extend operation. PCRs are reset to defined values at platform boot. A PCR with index i, $i \geq 0$ in state t may then be extended with input x by setting $PCR^i_{t+1} = SHA-1(PCR^i_t//x)$. PCRs can be used to exactly document the software executed on a machine by implementing the transitive trust model, where each software component is responsible to measure the following component before invoking it. Ultimately, a chain of trust is established where the full Trusted Computing Base (TCB) and configuration of the platform is mapped to PCR values. If such a PCR configuration fulfills the given security or policy requirements, we refer to the system state as a trusted state.

The TPM is capable of signing the current values of the PCRs together with a supplied nonce. This is called a Quote operation. To protect the platform owner's privacy, the unique Endorsement Key, typically injected by the TPM manufacturer, is not used for this signature. Rather, a pseudonym is used: an Attestation Identity Key (AIK). The authenticity of an AIK can be certified by an online trusted third party, called PrivacyCA [10], or with the group-signature-based DAA scheme. The certificate vouches that the private signature key is securely held by a standard conforming TPM. With it, a remote Verifier can analyze the Quote result and decide whether to trust the given configuration or not. Modern platforms, featuring Intel Trusted Execution Technology (TXT) [6] or AMD SVM offer addtional CPU instructions and chipset modifications that allow to switch a system to a well-known system state. If this state is used as starting point for a chain of trust, it is referred to as

---

[1] http://boinc.berkeley.edu

Dynamic Root of Trust for Measurement (DRTM). In combination with hardware-based virtualization this helps to reduce the number of components involved and thus simplifies the description of system states.

4 Proposed Architecture

We now present an approach of how to apply TC in grids and clouds to solve security issues. Our goal is to include Remote Attestation seamlessly and transparently into the development of distributed applications. We also desire to create a trusted distributed system which is developer friendly. To this end we choose to extend a well-established cloud computing framework.

However, in general a large amount of complexity is introduced by applying TC mechanisms, especially in using the TPM and collecting a meaningful chain-of-trust. These issues can only be solved by changes to the system beneath the middleware-layer. Our approach to curb this complexity is to use a high-level Trusted Computing API to access the TPM, apply platform virtualization to isolate the grid services and Intel TXT as DRTM. The proposed architecture is realized in the Java programming environment, which offers comprehensive support for security mechanisms. We outline the architecture in figure 1 and describe the components and their integration in the remainder of this section.

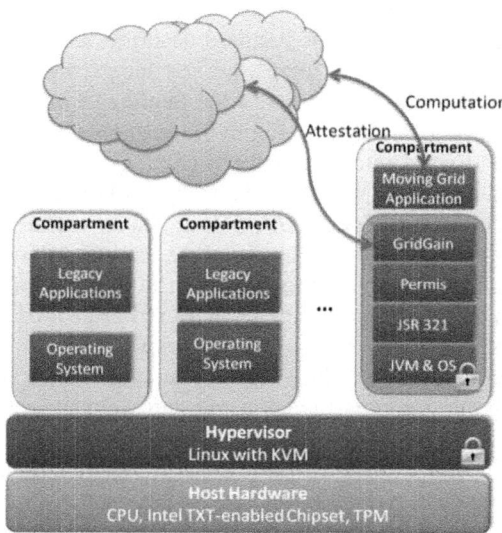

Fig. 1. Our proposed architecture

GridGain [9] is a feature-rich Java-based grid-and cloud computing frame-work. It completely abstracts the underlying hard- and software and provides all nodes with the same environment, be they local or remote. In consequence, the cloud becomes a natural extension of a local grid. The so-called "Zero Deployment model" allows to develop, deploy and run new code in (almost) real-time, as configurations such as grid size, code deployment, load balancing and execution parameters are done automatically. Java annotations provide developers a non-invasive way to take full control on distribution. For example it is possible to distribute a task by just adding the @Gridify tag to a method's signature. Currently, GridGain does not implement any access control mechanisms; it distributes tasks over all systems that make themselves available to the local grid or as cloud service.

Permis [1] is a Role Based Access Control (RBAC) policy-based decision-making engine. It is a comprehensive, Java-based system that offers a complete authorization-infrastructure with privilege-, and policy-management. The key domain of Permis is of course the protection of distributed resources. Access control decisions are made based on the access control policies and user roles. It ensures that the currently used policies have not been tampered or that individuals do not exceed their authorizations. In Permis users, roles and policies are defined and the roles assigned to the users; this task may also be delegated. Upon access to a resource, Permis validates that the operation is authorized and grants or denies it. Permis is a modular design, and can be adapted as needed. Currently, the Permis framework consists out of eight different packages, which provide for a wide variety of application such as the protection of web-services, hardware-resources or grid-computing. Unfortunately, Permis currently does not consider platform based trust evidence, for instance quotes from TPM-based Remote Attestation, in its decisions.

Java Specification Request # 321 [12] is the proposed standard Java API for Trusted Computing. Such a uniform API is a key requisite to allow code to migrate between different platforms. The draft standard describes a high-level object-oriented Java API for Trusted Computing. It maps the key hierarchies to an intuitive object-oriented inheritance hierarchy, offers tools for Sealing, Binding and Attestation. It integrates with the existing Java Cryptography Extensions (JCE) architecture. Overall, it provides a straightforward interface to high-level TC functionalities and supports developers by easing the task of writing code using the Trusted Platform Module.

Virtualization Platform: Toegl and Pirker have created acTvSM [11], an attestation-friendly platform to host the agent execution environment based on an Intel TXT Platform. In the architecture, a system boot leads to a late launch of the platform into a fresh, secure mode. Then, a Measured Launched Environment (MLE) is started in the form of a Linux base system from a measured and sealed file image on the platform's hard disk. This base system in turn runs a hypervisor, which is capable of protecting guest compartments using hardware support for the isolation of memory.

Integration: Java Annotations will be used to tag functions with trusted state descriptors for deployment. When GridGain assigns a new task to a node, it will verify at first if the node has correctly joined into the network and if it is still authorized to receive work units. Added GridGain functionality monitors every work unit deployment and reception and ensures that only the receiving node can send back the result as long as the connection to the server is continuous.

For every trustworthy grid/cloud configuration there is a Permis security certificate. Permis checks this certificate for authenticity before it compares for every new node the node state with the known-good configuration and also if the request to join the network is allowed according to the policy. Only if this succeeds, Permis forwards the request with the trusted state of the verified node to the local grid/cloud server, which may then deploy tasks to nodes, where their trusted state tag matches the required tag.

5 Public Key Infrastructure Design

To support our software architecture, a Public Key Infrastructure (PKI) is needed. A PKI represents a system for binding a public key to a specific and distinct user or device identity by means of digital certificates. Certificates are signed by a Certification Authority after a Registration Authority established the identity and revocation mechanisms blacklist compromised keys.

5.1 Attestation Identities

In our scheme a PrivacyCA acts as trusted third party for all cloud participants. The AIK certificates it issues are created during the registration process of the client's unique hardware platform. It ensures that a real hardware TPM is present on the registered hardware, and that the private part of each AIK will never be exposed by the TPM. Besides verification of the Quote operation, another use of AIK certificates is during every new connection or boot of the client platform by the GridGain client software for the authentication process to identify the hardware trying to connect.

This is done in two verifications steps. The first verification step ensures that the transmitted AIK certificate from the client is the same as the one presented during the registration process and that the certificate is still valid and has not been revoked. This is done by consulting the PrivacyCA's public revocation service. In a second later step, the client will be challenged to perform a Quote operation for the attestation protocol, thus proofing its possession of the AIK private part.

5.2 Enrollment

For every new user (operator) who wants to join the network it is necessary that he gets a TPM-based and TXT-capable platform assigned. The TPM must have been activated and the ownership taken. In the following we describe the registration process.

At first, the identity of the hardware platform is established. After the creation of the TPM-based AIK RSA pair, the public part is sent to the PrivacyCA server together with the Endorsement Key certificate. The PrivacyCA server validates and analyses the EK certificate and decides whether to trust the TPM or not. If the server believes the TPM to be authentic, the server then certifies the AIK and encrypts the fresh certificate with the public Endorsement Key of the TPM. This is returned to the platform and can only be decrypted there. Our PrivacyCA only supports the verification of Infineon TPMs, as currently no other hardware manufacturer is shipping EK certificates. The AIK certificate is permanently stored at the PrivacyCA to allow a later revocation of this certificate.

Step Two of the registration process requires the personal registration of the user or operator responsible for the hardware platform. The user registers himself together with his AIK certificate and his public AIK key at the registration authority of the server. The registration authority validates at first the given AIK certificate against the

PrivacyCA to check if the certificate is valid and if it has been successfully registered there. If the AIK certificate is valid then Permis mechanisms are used to verify if the appropriate role for this user is already existing or not. If not it is created. The next step involves the usage of a registration software utility. This utility is responsible for creating, storing, modifying and deleting of new or already registered users in an existing database. User profiles include the user name, a password, the AIK certificate, the AIK key and the credentials for the correct Permis authorization. The user name and the password are used for the authentication process. The AIK certificate is stored to allow a direct revocation, if needed. Further a domain-wide security level for this client is determined and assigned.

For instance, the security levels may be defined as the letters A, B and C and represent the public, internal use only and confidential security classifications. This classification later decides which classes of work units may be distributed to the client enrolled.

5.3 Seamless Attestation

We now describe how creation of a chain-of-trust, attestation, authentication and job distribution integrate to provide a trusted cloud environment. Figure 2 illustrates the process of joining a client platform to the cloud. When a user starts his client-computer (step 0), it boots at first the acTvSM platform via the DRTM mechanism that measures the hypervisor and configuration loaded. The hypervisor then continues to measures the complete Trusted Computing Base of the middleware client by extending its disk image into the PCRs. Only after the chain-of-trust is established, the client software is started automatically. After the successful start of the client-software, it tries to connect to the GridGain server to join into the network. The AIK certificate together with authentication credentials is then sent to the server (step 1). The server validates at first the AIK certificate with help of the PrivacyCA to immediately verify if the AIK certificate is valid and already successfully registered to the server (step 2).

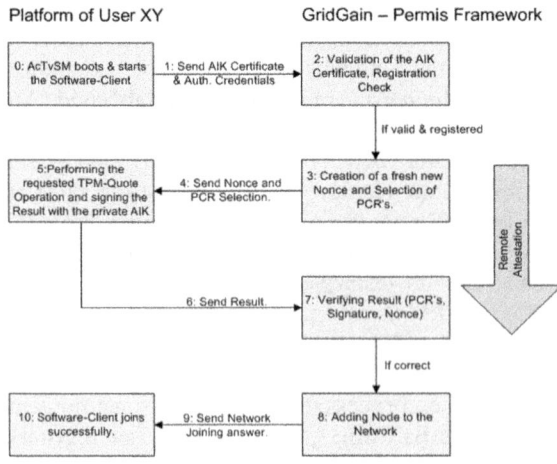

Fig. 2. Client Join Process

If the certificate is valid and registered then a new fresh nonce is created and the desired PCRs are chosen that will hold the desired client-system states (step 3). The nonce together with the PCR selection list is then sent to the client-platform (step 4). The client-platform performs a TPM Quote operation (step 5), via the JSR321 programming interface. The TPM signs the result of this operation with the private AIK. The quote information is sent back to the server (step 6). The Server is now responsible to verify the result which means it validates the PCR values based on the given nonce, the signature and the nonce itself (step 7). If everything is correct then the node is trusted and will be added into the network (step 8). The node then receives a positive response (step 9) and is automatically added into the network (step 10). If attestation fails, then the node gets marked as bad and the request is denied. If a node unsuccessfully attempts to connect several times, it will be permanently blocked and the administrator will be notified.

6 Implementation and Performance

We measure and enforce node integrity with the acTvSM virtualization platform [11]. Right at system boot a late launch is performed using the Intel Trusted Boot open source implementation tboot[2]. We use IAIK jTpmTools and IAIK jTSS[3] tools for configuration. Next, a low-footprint Linux operating system is started from a measured file system image using the MLE. The operating system runs the KVM/Qemu hypervisor which is capable of protecting guest compartments using hardware isolation.

The currently used application image for the GridClients is based on a minimal Gentoo system including a version 1.6.22 Java runtime environment.The controlling element of our GridGain/Permis/JSR321 integration is a modified GridGain framework. The control logic is added in three classes to GridGain for handling Permis access, JSR321 access and master control. Therefore, developers only need to write a simple Java annotation for a task to guarantee that a piece of code and its arguments are only deployed on remote nodes which follow the specified policy. See the code in Figure 3 for an example.

```
public final class compute_secLevelC {

  @Gridify(taskClass = GridifyTask_secLevelC.class)
  public static Long compute(long x)
    {
      //compute...
    }
}
```

Fig. 3. Example of annotation with security class descriptor

The so assembled grid execution environment is, together with its operating system, contained in an encrypted and sealed image file, which is also measured before execution by the virtualization platform. From within the virtual machine, we can access the TPM using our jTSS-based implementation of JSR321 to retrieve the Quote that reflects the system state. During the remote attestation protocol run PCRs 16, 18, and 19 are used to verify the system state of the client platform. Note that the chain of trust that covers the virtualization platform and the virtual application containing the computing framework is composed of only a few hashes from well-known (read-only) software images. This can easily be compared with (trusted) reference values.

When comparing the performance of our implementation with that of the original GridGain framework, only in the Client-Joining process on the server significant differences are found due to the security checks performed, with up to *8*[s] for attestation. This process is only done once for every client that joins and therefore it will not influence the actual work unit processing performance.

7 Conclusions and Outlook

In this paper, we propose a software architecture for distributed applications. It combines several powerful technologies to demonstrate a novel class of trusted services. Our prototype implementation suggests that it will be relatively easy to program and deploy distributed applications which can rely on trustworthy nodes that execute a known-good middleware service in hardware-guaranteed isolation. Our approach allows overcoming a number of security issues commonly found today. The next step will be to do a comprehensive security analysis. Overall, our framework is hardly slower than the original unprotected middleware but offers significantly more security features.

References

1. Chadwick, D.W., Zhao, G., Otenko, S., Laborde, R., Su, L., Nguyen, T.A.: Permis a modular authorization infrastructure. Concurrency and Computation: Practice and Experience 20(11), 1341–1357 (2008)
2. Cooper, A., Martin, A.: Towards a secure, tamper-proof grid platform. In: Cluster Computing and the Grid, CCGRID 2006 (2006)
3. Daniele Catteddu, G.H.: Cloud Computing benefits, risks and recommendations for information security. Tech. rep., ENISA (2009)
4. Foster, I., Kesselman, C., Tuecke, S.: The anatomy of the grid: Enabling scalable virtual organizations. Int. J. High Perform. Comput. Appl. 15(3), 200–222 (2001)
5. Getov, V., von Laszewski, G., Philippsen, M., Foster, I.T.: Multiparadigm communications in java for grid computing. Commun. ACM 44(10), 118–125 (2001)
6. Grawrock, D.: Dynamics of a Trusted Platform: A Building Block Approach, Richard Bowles. Intel Press, Hillsboro (2009) ISBN 978-1934053171
7. Löhr, H., Ramasamy, H.V., Sadeghi, A.-R., Schulz, S., Schunter, M., Stüble, C.: Enhancing grid security using trusted virtualization. In: Xiao, B., Yang, L.T., Ma, J., Muller-Schloer, C., Hua, Y. (eds.) ATC 2007. LNCS, vol. 4610, pp. 372–384. Springer, Heidelberg (2007)

8. Mao, W., Martin, A., Jin, H., Zhang, H.: Innovations for grid security from trusted computing. In: Security Protocols, pp. 132–149 (2009)
9. Ivanov, N., Setrakyan, D.: GridGain (2010), http://www.gridgain.com
10. Pirker, M., Toegl, R., Hein, D., Danner, P.: A PrivacyCA for anonymity and trust. In: Chen, L., Mitchell, C.J., Martin, A. (eds.) Trust 2009. LNCS, vol. 5471, pp. 101–119. Springer, Heidelberg (2009)
11. Toegl, R., Pirker, M., Gissing, M.: acTvSM: A dynamic virtualization platform for enforcement of application integrity. In: INTRUST 2011. LNCS. Springer, Heidelberg (in print, 2011)
12. Toegl, R., Winkler, T., Nauman, M., Hong, T.: Towards platform-independent trusted computing. In: Xu, S., Asokan, N., Nita-Rotaru, C., Seifert, J.P. (eds.) STC, ACM, New York (2009)
13. Trusted Computing Group: TCG TPM specification version 1.2 revision 103 (2007)

A Network Data Abstraction Method for Data Set Verification[*]

Jaeik Cho[1], Kyuwon Choi[2], Taeshik Shon[3], and Jongsub Moon[1]

[1] Graduate School of Information Security, Korea University, Seoul, Korea
[2] ECE, Illinois Institute of Technology, Chicago, USA
[3] College of Information Technology, Ajou University, Korea
{chojaeik,jsmoon}@korea.ac.kr, kchoi@ece.iit.edu,
taeshik.shon@gmail.com

Abstract. Network data sets are often used for evaluating the performance of intrusion detection systems and intrusion prevention systems[1]. The KDD CUP 99' data set, which was modeled after MIT Lincoln laboratory network data has been a popular network data set used for evaluation network intrusion detection algorithm and system. However, many points at issues have been discovered concerning the modeling method of the KDD CUP 99' data. This paper proposed both a measure to compare the similarities between two data groups and an optimization method to efficiently modeled data sets with the proposed measure. Then, both similarities between KDD CUP 99' and MIT Lincoln laboratory data that between our composed data set from the MIT Lincoln laboratory data and MIT Lincoln laboratory are compared quantitatively.

Keywords: Data set modeling; Intrusion detection system.

1 Introduction

In order to evaluate performance of security systems, specifically the Intrusion Detection System (IDS), it should be acknowledged that the data group is a standard data [2][3]. The data group should mimic the characteristics of the real network [4][5][6][7]. Many research groups tried to make such a test bed [8] that mimics the real network and the research is ongoing. MIT Lincoln Lab (MIT/LL), which is supported by DARPA since 1988 [9][10] has worked to gather a data group from the real network. A special interest group, called Knowledge Discovery and Data mining (KDD), also announced a data group for IDS performance test in 1999 (KDD CUP 99' Data) [11]. After KDD CUP 99' announced the data, many vendors and researchers have used the KDD CUP 99' data to test the performance of theirs IDS [12] [13][14][15][16].

This paper analyzes the MIT/LL data and KDD CUP 99' data set and proposes and statistical efficient method to compose data set. For the comparison of the composed data and the KDD CUP 99' data set, the MIT/LL network data will be used as the population data both data. Furthermore, for evaluation, a statistical method as a

[*] This research was supported by Korea University Grant.

measure will be used to relatively compare the composed data and the KDD CUP 99' data to the population data in a quantitative manner. The previous method used in composing network data set of KDD CUP 99' and MIT/LL did not have any statistical homogeneity test. However, this paper suggests a more effective optimized method for network data set based on homogeneity test.

2   Related Works

The MIT/LL research, concerning the network data is well-known throughout the nations. It has been ongoing since 1998 [18]. It is the most usable data that has been publicized and it is crucial for two reasons. First reason is that is used for intrusion detection algorithm or method development research, and it is also used after evaluation of detection efficiency [19][20][21].The experiment concerning the network data collection is necessary for the network data set. However, this is impossible in reality, because of violation of personal privacy and risk of classified information leakage [22]. Therefore, MIT/LL researchers publicized their network packet data after experimenting, collecting, and reconstructing without datagram part of a network packet data based on the Air Force under the supporting of DARPA [23][24]. The MIT/LL, they experimented with many network services and the incoming/outgoing network behavior of several kinds of virtual machines. Although, network packet data was effective in 1998, it is no longer effective with the current network environment such as network service type and network capacity. The network environment of today has surpassed the one in 1998. Also, network services have become more complicated and widely used than 1998, such as cloud network and mobile device connections.The data set of KDD CUP 99' was modeled after the packet data that had been collected by MIT/LL from the Air Force. The KDD CUP 99' expressed the data set with 41 features. All data sets of MIT/LLwas divided into two second segments and expressed each segment as one data set with 41 features [17].

3   A Proposed Method

We propose two methods. One is a measure to evaluate the similarities between groups and the other is a novel method to generate a data set from an original population data.We propose a Weighted Euclidean Distance method as a measure for similarity between groups. The Weighted Euclidean Distance method follows a Chi-square statistics in Correspondence Analysis theory. To use this measure we explain the Correspondence Analysis first.

- A Simple Correspondence Analysis

Let's assume a two way contingency Table 1 in which the number of row is p and the number of column is q each. The characteristics of a row and column are a categorical data or nominal data. Each element in the Table1 is of occurred frequency. We represent it as a Table 1 which is a Correspondence Matrix.

Table 1. A Correspondence Matrix

		Group 1	...	Group j	...	Group q	Total
	Category 1	f_{11}	...	f_{1j}	...	f_{1q}	f_{1+}
Features	...	...	...	...	...	...	...
	Category p	f_{p1}	...	f_{pj}	...	f_{pq}	f_{p+}
	Total	f_{+1}	...	f_{+j}	...	f_{+q}	N

A Correspondence Matrix is considered as,

$$F = (f_{ij}), f_{ij} = \frac{o_{ij}}{o_{++}}, i = 1, ..., p \text{ and } j = 1, ..., q \tag{1}$$

Such as Table 1, the profile vector, r_i, of row i in the matrix is defined as,

$$r_i = \frac{f_{i1}, f_{i2}, ..., f_{i(q-1)}, f_{iq}}{f_{i+}}, i = 1, ..., p \tag{2}$$

Therefore, a profile vector within each category is the ratio of the category. The distance between r_i and r_k in the Weighted Euclidean space is defined as Chi-square Distance as following Equation (3).

$$d(r_i, r_k) = \sum_i \left(\frac{f_{ij}}{f_{i+}} - \frac{f_{kj}}{f_{k+}} \right)^2 / f_{+j} \tag{3}$$

This Chi-square Distance is a criterion in measuring the similarity r_i and r_k which is differences between the two categories, i and k. If the value is small, then we can verify that the population of the two data group is similar. Also, a profile vector, c_j, of column j is defined as,

$$c_j = \frac{f_{1j}, f_{2j}, ..., f_{pj}}{f_{+j}}, j = 1, ..., q \tag{4}$$

Thus, the profile vector within each group is the ratio in the group. The distance between c_j and c_i in the Weighted Euclidean space is defining as Chi-square Distance as follows.

$$d(c_j, c_i) = \sum_i \frac{\left(\frac{f_{ij}}{f_{+j}} - \frac{f_{il}}{f_{+j}} \right)^2}{f_{i+}} \tag{5}$$

This Weighted Euclidean distance is a criterion in measuring the similarity and differences between two data groups, j and i. If the value of the Equation (6) is small, then we can verify the characteristics of the two data groups are similar.

If a distance value between two groups, c_j and c_l, is smaller than a distance value between other groups, c_j and c_k like Equation (6), then the group c_l is more similar with c_j, then c_k is with c_j.

$$d(c_j, c_l) < d(c_j, c_k) \tag{6}$$

3.1 An Effective Method for Composing Data Sets

This section describes a composition method of data sets which reflects the application's behavior using network by two different methods. We make the following assumptions in order to earn the statistical best-qualified samples from the original populations. There are only two classes. One is an original population and the other is a created class those elements are reconstructed from the original population. Moreover, both classes contain common features in order to evaluate how similar the two classes are. We consider a reduced Table 2, optimized from the Table 1 for two classes.

Table 2. Modified table from the Correspondence Table

	Class 1	Class 2	Total
Feature 1	f_{11}	f_{12}	f_{1+}
	...	...	...
Feature p	f_{p1}	f_{p2}	f_{p+}
Total	f_{+1}	f_{+2}	N

- **Distance between groups as measure**

The distance between two selected groups, Equation (5) isshortest when each ratio in a class is equal to the ratio of the corresponding feature between two classes. That is, the value of Equation (5) is "0" in this case. Since there are only two classes where 'class 1' is an original population and the 'class 2' is a derived class. The Equation (5) for the Table 1 is modified to Equation (5') for two classes. An ideal class from the population should be satisfying Equation (5') with the value of "0". In other words, the smaller the value of Equation (5') after extracting data from the population, the more similar the two classes are.

$$d(class_1, class_2) = \sum_{i=1}^{p} \frac{f_{+i}}{\left(\frac{f_{i1}}{f_{+1}} - \frac{f_{i2}}{f_{+2}}\right)^2} \tag{5'}$$

Where, $\forall i\, f_{i1}$ are all constants, because the number of data in the population is fixed. Therefore, the object is to maintain a sample group (class 2), those characteristics are to minimize Equation (5').

- **The number of composed data**

If the compose data is exactly the same as the population, the Equation (5') result should be "0". Even though, this is ideal case, this is meaningless, also. Because one important goal of sampling is to reduce the number of data from the original population as well as to reflect similar characteristics of the population at least network protocols. Thus, in order to reflect the number of sample, we suggest a cost function related with the number of samples - Equation (7).

$$N_{sample} = \sum_{i=1}^{p} o_{i2} \tag{7}$$

Where, O_{ij} is the occurred frequency defined in section 3.1. The purpose of Equation (7) is to reduce the number of samples.

- **Minimum number of composed data**

However, if the composed data size is too small or too small amount of specific feature's data, we cannot have any statistical confidence. Thus, the number of each feature should be over a certain minimum threshold. If some features of the original population do not exist, then the frequency of a corresponding feature of the sample class should be "0". This is expressed as Equation (8).

$$o_{i2} \geq n_i > 0, for \ \forall i \ such \ that \ o_{i1} > n_i \qquad (8)$$

Otherwise, $o_{i2} = 0$, where n_i is a minimum threshold.

3.1.1   The Object Function

The best efficiency generated data group from the original population class is the data which minimize Equation (9), that is a combination of Equation (5') and Equation (8). In this case, k should be large enough that balanced with Correspondence Analysis value and minimum threshold.

$$Criteria \left(f_{12}, f_{22}, \dots, f_{p2} \right) = d(c_1, c_2) + C \cdot N_{sample} + k \sum_{i=1}^{p} g(n_i - o_{i2})$$

$$where \ g(x) = \left. \begin{matrix} x, if \ x > 0 \\ 0, otherwise \end{matrix} \right\} \ and \ k \gg C$$

3.1.2   An Algorithm Extracting a Sample Group from the Original Population

There are two cases in consideration. First case is to generate an artificial data instead of extracting it from an original data group. The second case is generating the sample group by extracting real data from an original data group.

- **Artificial generation of a sample group that is similar to an original population**
  If this is the case, the method is trivial. A method is suggested as following.

  1. Predetermine each frequency of the feature in the sample group as a minimum value in order to satisfy Equation (8). This condition omits the third term of the Equation (9). Thus, the Equation (9) is transformed to the Equation (10).
  2. Find a feature which maximally decreases Equation (1) result or minimally increases Equation (10) result when a frequency of the feature is increased by one among all features. Since the purpose of the objective function is to maintain a minimum value, selecting a feature that has a maximum decrease is rational if the object is decreased the next time. The next time, if there is no feature to decrease, the best is to select the feature which increases minimally.

$$Let \ h \left(o_{12}, \dots, o_{i2}, \dots, o_{p2} \right) = \sum_{i=1}^{p} \frac{\left(\frac{f_{i1}}{f_{+1}} - \frac{f_{i2}}{f_{+2}} \right)^2}{f_{i+}} + C \cdot \sum_{i=1}^{p} o_{i1} \qquad (10)$$

  3. For the selected feature at step 1, if the number of a feature is already exceeding the predetermined threshold at step 1, discard this feature and go to step 2.
  4. Make a sample data which reflects the feature selected at step 2.
  5. Repeat step 2 to 4, if all frequency of features exceeds the predetermined frequency at step 1. Otherwise, stop repeat generation a sample data set.

4   Experiments and Result

In this section, we generated one sample data set from theMIT/LL network data. Then, we compare the object value(Equation (9)), distance value (Equation (5) and Equation(5')) between the generated sample data set and the MIT/LLdata. To show the enhanced degree of our composing algorithm,we compared the above two values between oursample group and the KDD CUP 99'. In order to an achievethe object value of Equation (9) and Equation (5) betweenKDD CUP 99' and MIT/LL. When we make a sample fromthe MIT/LL, we used both version of the algorithm.We need parameters to calculate Equation (9). Weused several parameters. Among them, following parametersshown in the Table 4 are selected.

- **Activation function R**

The function R generates data from a set of population datawhich consists of a network packet. In this experiment, R makes a packet with the protocol which is the most frequentlyappeared protocols in the set of population data.

Table 3. Predetermined frequency for MIT/LL and KDD CUP 99' (10% Sampled data)

Feature	MIT/LL(Group 1)	KDD CUP 99'
802.1D	0	0
ARP	0.724136512	1.561053
CDPv2	0.078185779	0
Fragment	0.471551254	0
ICMP	0.064329896	0.130639
Others	1.204608011	21.752216
TCP	87.59588830	47.810557
UDP	9.861300247	28.745535
Total	100	100

Table 4. Parameters for Equation (9)

C	$0.0001, 0.001, \cdots, 2.5, 5, 10$
K	$0.001, 0.002, \cdots, 0.009, 0.01$

	TCP	1261
	UDP	142
n_i	ARP	40
	ICMP	40
	Others	40

Table 5. The CA table of MIT/LL and sample group generated by each ending point and each version

Feature	MIT/LL Data	Sample group by version 1			Sample group by version 2		
		P1	P2	P3	P1	P2	P3
TCP	126185635	4151	91435	559005	15581	86020	3112048
UDP	14205622	467	10294	62931	1754	9684	350345
ARP	104321	40	76	462	40	71	2573
ICMP	92679	40	67	411	40	63	2285
Others	173593	40	126	769	40	118	4281
Total Number	140761850	4738	101998	623578	17455	95956	3471532
% ofMIT/LL	(100%)	(0.003%)	(0.072%)	(0.443%)	(0.012%)	(0.068%)	(2.466%)

$P_i = i^{th}$ ending point

The scale of composing a data set varies by the objective.A network data set is usually used for the evaluation of intrusiondetection system or an algorithm. At the generatinglarge number of data set, how many numbers of the sampleddata set is depending on the security policy of the system ornetwork. A data set may contain the

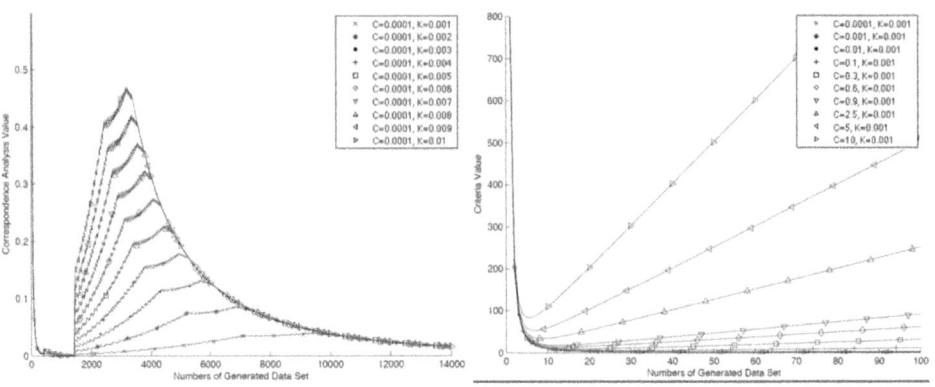

Fig. 1. Result by Equation 5'   **Fig. 2.** Criteria result by Equation 9

majority of informationcontained in the original population or generate a minimaldata set while having statistical homogeneity. In our experiments, criteria value showed a monotonicincrease after a considerable decrease. The first end pointis where a monotonic increase starts. With the parameter specified by the Table 4, we composedtwo sample data groups. One is composed by algorithm version1 and the other is version 2. The resultant CorrespondingAnalysis tables for both cases are shown in the Table 5.Also, the Table 5 shows the number of samples. The concludingconditions were considered. The optimized method by modified the CorrespondenceAnalysis that is proposed method generated effective dataset is much smaller than MIT/LL's original population data set. At the first ending point of the data set compositionusing by method version 1 size is 0.003% of the MIT/LLdata set that is enough short Euclidean Distance. Secondending point of the data set composition, at the point ofthe Euclidean Distance is first shorter point than first endingpoint's Euclidean Distance. At the third ending point of thecomposition is minimum limit of the homogeneity by Chi-squaretest which data set size is 0.443% of the MIT/LL'soriginal population.

As a result, the effectiveness of the experiments by the proposed method is from the protocol selecting which has a maximum decreasing or minimum increasing Criteria value. This graph result shows monotonic decrease of the Criteria value, it means every time composition method selecting most effective protocol for whole data set modeling efficiency. So, each time protocol selections are making more effective protocol selection on next steps protocol selection by Criteria value, also whole sampled data set is very similar to original population.

5   Conclusion

Since our method is more efficient than MIT's KDD CUP99', it is not appropriate to use KDD CUP 99' for evaluatingintrusion detection systems and other security methods,or systems. The data set obtained for this paper can be usedas a basis for network-related researches for a number ofreasons. First, it is crucial for network simulation research.For a more realistic network simulation, a more efficient networkdata set should be generated. To obtain data flowof many nodes, the datasetwhich is minimized and containsa sufficient amount of information is required. For instance,if the data set does not contain adequate amount of informationabout the original population, it will not be an accuratesimulation. Also, the size of the data set should be minimizedto guarantee an effective processing speed neededfor network simulation. Second, it can be utilized to researchof malicious software. Many researchers have beenusing reverse engineering or network packet data analysisfor malicious software's behaviors, which consumes an immenseamount of time and space. However, by using theproposed data set, we can analyze malicious behaviors moreefficiently. For future work, we plan to include the sequential data analysisto this method. This will be used for network data modelingfor distributed nodes activities and its associates. Inaddition, if we are able to find the distribution of each service,network behavior types, and associates, we will definethe general network data distribution.

References

[1] Bishop, M., Cheung, S.: The Threat from the Net. IEEE Spectrum (1997)
[2] Amoroso, E.: Intrusion Detection, Intrusion.Net Books (1999)
[3] Northcutt, S.: Network Intrusion Detection: An Analysis Handbook. Net Riders Publishing, Indianapolis (1999)
[4] Mariani, J., Cole, R.A., Mariani, J., Uskoriet, H., Zaenen, A., Zue, V.: Survey of the Evaluation. In: State of the Art in Human Language Technology. Cambridge University Press, Cambridge (1997)
[5] Puketza, N., Zhang, K., Chung, M., Mukherjee, B., Olsson, R.A.: A Methodology for Testing Intrusion Detection System. IEEE Transactions on Software Engineering 22, 719–729 (1996)
[6] Ko, C., Fink, G., Levitt, K.: Execution Monitoring of Security critgical Programs in Fistribution Systems: A Specification-based Approach. In: IEEE Symposium on Security and Privacy, pp. 134–144 (1997)
[7] Shipley, G.: ISS RealSecure Pushed Past Newer IDS Players. In: Network Computing. CMP Publication, Inc. (1999)
[8] Allen, J., Christie, A., Fithen, W., McHugh, J., Pickel, J., Stoner, E.: State of the Practice of Intrusion Detection Technologies, Technical Report, Carnegie Mellon University
[9] Lippmann, R.P., Fried, D.J., Graf, I., Haines, J.W., Kendall, K.R., McClurg, D., Weber, D., Webster, S.E., Wyschogrod, D., Conningham, R.K., Zissman, M.A.: Evaluating Intrusion Detection Systems: the 1998 DARPA Oine Intrusion Detection Evaluation. In: DARPA Information Survivabillity Conference and Exposition, vol. 2 (2000)
[10] Lippmann, R.P., Cunningham, R.K.: Improving Intrusion Detection Performance Using Keyword Selection and Neural Networks. Computer Networks 34(4), 597–603 (2000)
[11] Lippmann, R., Haines, J.W., Fried, D.J., Korba, J., Das, K.: The 1999 DARPA O-line Intrusion Detection Evaluation. Computer Networks 34(4), 579–595 (2000)
[12] MIT Lincoln Laboratory, LNKnet software (2002),
    http://www.ll.mit.edu/IST/lnknet/index.html
[13] Agarwal, R., Joshi, M.V.: PNrule: A NewFramework for Learning Classifier Models in Data Mining, Technical Report TR00-015, Department of Computer Science, University of Minnesota (2000)

[14] Levin, I.: KDD-99 Classifier Learning Contest LLSoft's Results Overview. SIGKDD Explorations, ACM SIGKDD 1(2), 6775 (2000)
[15] Yeung, D.Y., Chow, C.: Parzenwindow Network Intrusion Detectors. In: The Sixteenth International Conference on Pattern Recognition, pp. 11–15 (2002)
[16] Kendall, K.: A Database of Computer Attacks for the Evaluation of Intrusion Detection Systems, Master's Thesis, MIT, Boston, MA (1998)
[17] Knowledge Discovery and Data Mining (KDD), KDD CUP 99' Network Data Set (1999), http://kdd.ics.uci.edu/databases/kddcup99/kddcup99.html
[18] Durst, R., Champion, T., Witten, B., Miller, E., Spagnuolo Testing, L.: Evaluating Computer Intrusion Detection Systems. Communications of the ACM 42(7), 53–61 (1999)
[19] Cristianini, N., Shawe, J.: An Introduction to Support Vector Machines and other kernel-based learning methods. Cambridge Press, New York (2004)
[20] Lee, W., Stolfo, S.J., Mok, K.W.: A Data Mining Framework for Building Intrusion Detection Models. In: IEEE Symposium on Security and Privacy, p. 120132 (1999)
[21] Lee, W., Stolfo, S.J., Mok, K.W.: Mining in a Data Flow Environment: Experience in Network Intrusion Detection. In: The 5th ACM SIGKDD, pp. 114–124 (1999)
[22] Elkan, C.: Results of the KDD 99' Classifier Learning. ACM SIGKDD Explorations Newsletter (2000)
[23] Haines, J.W.: 1999 DARPA Intrusion Detection Evaluation, Technical Report 1062, MIT Lincoln Laboratory (2001)
[24] Haines, J.W., Lippmann, R.P.: 1999 DARPA Intrusion Detection Evaluation: Design and Procedure. MIT Licoln Laboratory (2001)

Efficient De-Fragmented Writeback
for Journaling File System[*]

Seung-Ho Lim[1], Hyun Jin Choi[2], and Jong Hyuk Park[3]

[1] Department of Digital Information Engineering
Hankuk University of Foreign Studies
slim@hufs.ac.kr
[2] Memory Division, Samsung Electronics Co. Ltd.
hyunjin.choi@gmail.com
[3] Seoul National University of Science and Technology
jhpark@seoultech.ac.kr

Abstract. Journaling file systems are widely used file systems to guarantee data integrity. However, the system performance is degraded due to data request fragmentations. We propose a technique that efficiently handles fragmented data workloads in journaling file system, which we call De-Fragmented Writeback(DFW). The first method of the DFW sorts write orders of the atomic data set in accordance with their disk block numbers before issuing into write requests. The second method of the DFW searches for data fragments in the sorted data set and tries to fill up holes between adjacent data fragments using dirty blocks in main memory. The filling of holes between data fragments converts fragmented data blocks into sequential ones so that this method lowers the number of write requests and reduces unnecessary disk-head movements to write the blocks.

Keywords: Journaling File System, Transaction, Atomic Data Set, De-Fragmented Writeback.

1   Introduction

When computer system crashes with such a reason of power failure, file system has to be recovered to a consistent state again. Recently, several solutions have been proposed to reduce file system recovery time, in which they keep some kind of log of the file system's metadata. If the system crashes, the log is replayed to recover the file system consistency. Among them, the journaling file system keeps a record of the changes made to the file system in a special part of the disk called a journal or log before actually reflecting those changes to itself [1][2][3][4][8]. Unlike a traditional file system, the journaling file system can be made consistent by re-executing the pending changes that were recorded in a few log records, rather than having to examine the whole file system.

---

[*] This work was supported by Hankuk University of Foreign Studies Research Fund of 2011.

J.J. Park et al. (Eds.): STA 2011, CCIS 186, pp. 63–70, 2011.
© Springer-Verlag Berlin Heidelberg 2011

The journaling file system generally takes a few seconds to recover. However, it always performs additional I/O operations to maintain recovery information, and these are mainly random fragmented I/O requests. Writes of fragmented data to a disk provides poor bandwidth compared to writes of sequential data, even if the amount of data is the same. Among many factors that affect the positioning time, we focus on the writeback policies of an operating system. This writeback policy primarily considers dirty blocks to reduce the possibility of files having time-disordered data in a disk layout. However, if the data blocks were fragmented, randomly dirty, and spread across a disk, this policy causes a penalty of uncontrolled seek overhead in writing the fragmented data. In accordance with the writeback policy, we consider the metadata write mechanism in journaling file system. In general, metadata are more frequently updated than data because metadata are considered as a more important part than data. The metadata logging reduces possibility of a file system losing its recent updates. However, this priority-based update policy causes different writeback timings of data and metadata. If metadata blocks were assigned in data regions of a file system, the frequent flushing of metadata blocks prevents a sequential writeback of physically adjacent data and metadata blocks.

In this paper, we present efficient writeback method to enhance the above-mentioned writeback policies of journaling file system, which is called a de-fragmented writeback (DFW). It is based on Ext3 journaling file system [1], and relies on the atomic writeback of data and metadata blocks grouped for a pre-defined time interval. The DFW consists of two novel methods; the first method, sorting the atomic data set, solves the problem of time-ordered data writebacks by considering where data will be written in a disk layout. This method prevents random movements of the disk heads and reduces the positioning time of a disk in writing the data blocks. The second method, filling holes between data fragments, converts fragmented data blocks into sequential ones, reducing the number of write requests. Furthermore, it enables a sequential writeback of physically adjacent data and metadata blocks. With these two methods, the DFW efficiently handles fragmented data workloads as well as does not harm the data consistency of the file system.

2   Background

At first, we briefly describe a journaling file system. These descriptions are made with the representative journaling file system in Linux, Ext3 file system [1][12]. The journaling file system offers three different journaling modes: writeback, ordered, and journaled mode. Each mode provides a different level of data consistency and run-time performance. In the writeback mode, only metadata blocks are logged to the journal, while data blocks are written directly to their home locations. It does not enforce any writing order between data and metadata blocks, so it does not guarantee data consistency, but affords the highest runtime performance. In ordered mode, only metadata blocks are logged, however, data blocks are ensured to be written to their home locations before their related metadata blocks are written to the journal. The write ordering guarantees that incompletely written data blocks at system crash do not become part of any file because they are not referenced by any metadata block. In journaled mode, all the data and metadata are logged together to the journal region, and later they are written to their home locations. The journaled mode provides the best guarantee of data consistency. However, it generally has a much slower run-time performance than the other modes. Journaling file systems such as Ext3 and ReiserFS use ordered mode as a default.

Transaction is a fundamental concept used for the consistency of the file system. The transaction in Ext3 contains two major lists in order to group data and metadata blocks; the *t_sync_datalist* list is a doubly linked circular list of data blocks to be directly written to their home locations. The *t_buffers* list is a doubly linked circular list of dirty blocks to be journaled. The transaction exists in several states over its lifetime; running, commit and checkpoint states. In running state, the dirty data and metadata blocks are grouped into the two lists. In some bounded conditions, such as transaction interval timeout or synchronization request, the running transaction is closed and goes to the commit state. At that time, a new transaction is created to group the next file system updates. In commit state, the closed transaction performs the task of writing its data and metadata blocks. All the data blocks of the *t_sync_datalist* are committed to their home locations, and then the metadata blocks of the *t_buffers* are committed to the journal region. In checkpoint state, the blocks of the journal region are copied to their home locations. When it is completed, the transaction is completed and the journal region for that transaction is reclaimed. If a system crash occurs before completion of the checkpoint, the transaction will be checked again during the journal recovery phase of mounting the file system.

The proposed algorithm is based on the journaling file system operating with the ordered mode. In this ordered journaling file system, data blocks and relative metadata blocks which were modified for a pre-defined time interval are grouped into a single unit of transaction and written to storage in an atomic way, so we call it atomic data set. This atomic writeback operation guarantees that either all grouped blocks are applied or none of them is applied during the system recovery. Thus, blocks of the atomic data set are handled as a whole, rearranging the write orders of the blocks can be performed with no restriction, i.e., with no harm to the system in terms of data consistency.

3   De-Fragmented Writeback

The DFW technique relies on the atomic set grouped in a transaction. The overview of the DFW is depicted in Fig. 1. We designed the DFW algorithm by adding conventional transaction processing of journaling file system. In the first added step, the DFW logs clean versions of metadata to the journal to guarantee the same data consistency with the ordered mode. In the second added step, the DFW does sorting data blocks of the *t_sync_datalist* with block number order. It globally minimizes the positioning time of a disk, i.e., the rotation and seek latency in writing data blocks of the data list. In the third added step, the DFW collects the pointers of buffer heads of cached data blocks, whose block numbers reside between the lowest and highest block numbers of the *t_sync_datalist*, that is, the first and last element of the data list. After that, the DFW looks up the fragments within the *t_sync_datalist*. If DFW finds fragmented holes, it tries to fill up the holes with the cached data blocks or modified

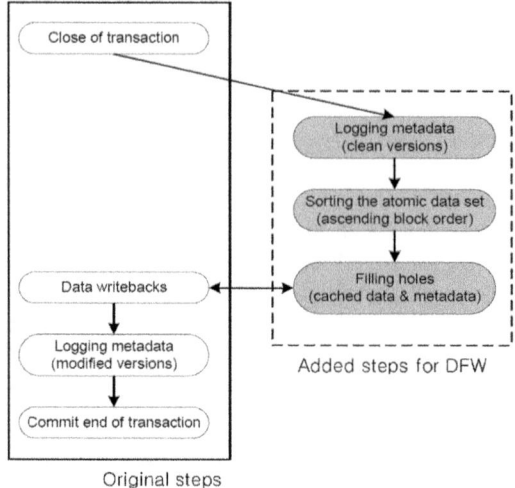

Fig. 1. The Overview of DFW

versions of metadata between adjacent data fragments. It repeats this operation until the end element of the *t_sync_datalist*, which converts fragmented data blocks into sequential ones. We explain the detailed algorithm in the following subsections.

3.1   Sorting the Atomic Data Set

In the original of ordered journaling, corresponding data blocks of the files are linked listed to the *t_sync_datalist* in the order they became dirty, and written back to a disk in that order. This time-ordered data writeback can lead to bad positioning of the disk heads to write the data blocks. Even though disk scheduler rearranges data blocks subsequently submitted from the data list, both the time and capacity limits restrict the optimization. Sorting the data blocks of the *t_sync_datalist* in terms of block numbers provides great performance benefit to the system. Fig. 2 describes the sorting of *t_sync_datalist*. This sorted data writeback of *t_sync_datalist* needs only half of time-ordered data writeback in the disk-head rotations and seek operations. Especially for highly random workloads, the sorted data writeback provides considerable performance benefits. In doing sorting data blocks, we adopt a radix sort algorithm [13]. In general, the radix sorting is the optimal algorithm for sorting integer numbers, i.e. disk block numbers. The overhead for sorting data blocks is negligible if the sorting is compared with the writeback of the data blocks.

3.2   Filling Holes with Data and Metadata

After sorting all the data blocks of the *t_sync_datalist* in commit transaction, the DFW searches for data blocks cached in the memory that are not members of the *t_sync_datalist*, which will be used for filling holes between data fragments. For this purpose, the DFW looks up the LRU list of a page cache and collects pointers of buffer heads of data blocks which were cached and mapped to a disk. Given a block number, the DFW performs the binary searching for the cached data. The filling hole with data is illustrated in Fig. 2. After sorting the data blocks of the *t_sync_datalist* and collecting the buffer heads of the cached blocks, the DFW starts searching for data fragments from the first element of the sorted list. If the block number of the next element is the same as the block number of the current element plus one, i.e., the next element is the contiguous block of the current element, DFW progresses forward to the next element and keeps searching for the data fragment. If the next element is not the contiguous block of the current element, DFW checks the distance between current and next elements, we call it stride distance. If the stride distance exceeds the pre-defined maximum distance, the DFW progresses to the next element. The maximum distance can be determined by running the stride benchmark, which analyzes the statistical and relative costs of discontinuous I/O over the contiguous I/O. For instance, the maximum distance can be set to 10 from the result of the stride benchmark. If the stride distance between current and next elements is within the distance, the DFW checks whether the holes between the two elements can be filled with cached data blocks. If the holes can be filled with some blocks, the DFW forces the found cached blocks to participate in the transaction. If the holes cannot be filled, the DFW progresses to the next element. This operation is repeated to the end element of the *t_sync_datalist*. This filling holes with data reduces the number of write requests by converting fragmented data blocks into sequential ones, and thus, enhancing the write throughput.

In the ordered mode, data must be written back to their home locations before writebacks of related metadata. This write ordering implies the different writeback timings of data and metedata. Thus, a sequential writeback of data and metadata blocks is not possible even if they are physically contiguous, and, as the result, additional disk rotations can occur. A simple experiment of the evaluation section for creating files larger than 48 KB generating indirect blocks shows this phenomenon. In Unix-like file systems, indirect blocks and directory entry blocks, which are kinds of metadata, are dynamically assigned within the data regions of the file systems. These kinds of metadata and data are generally contiguously assigned in data regions. Thus, without any special treatment of their writes, the sequential writeback of them cannot be achieved. The above mentioned problem is effectively solved by the filling holes with metadata. Since metadata blocks are in the *t_buffers* list of the transaction, metadata blocks of the *t_buffers* are checked to find out whether holes between adjacent data fragments can be filled with metadata blocks. If the holes can be filled with some metadata blocks, the metadata blocks are chosen for participation in data writebacks of the commit transaction. This method eliminates unnecessary additional disk rotations resulting from metadata blocks residing in the data regions of file systems.

By the filling holes with metadata, metadata can be written before related data are written, which is opposite of the write ordering of the ordered mode. Without addressing this break in the write ordering, the same data consistency as the ordered mode could not be guaranteed. For solving this problem, clean versions of metadata are written to the journal before the writing of the data blocks of the commit transaction is begun. Only after the safe logging of the clean metadata, the sequential writeback of physically adjacent data and modified versions of metadata is performed. With the help of this operation, the file system can recover from a failure by restoring the logged clean versions of metadata to their home locations of the file system.

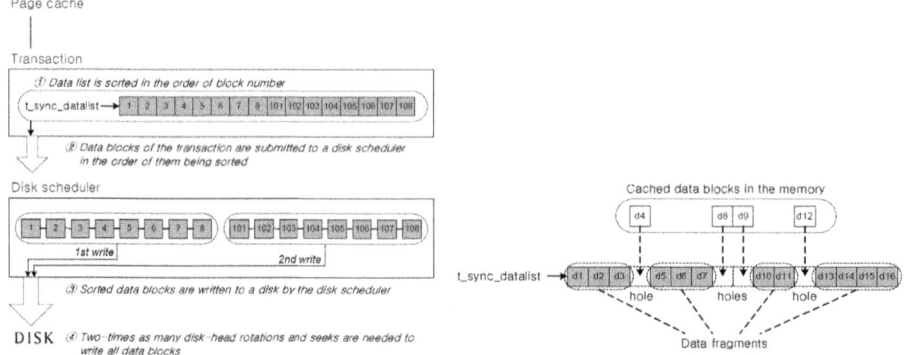

Fig. 2. A sorted data writeback and Filling holes with cached blocks method

4   Performance Evaluation

The proposed technique was implemented in the linux kernel 2.6.15. It was compared with the ordered mode (ORD) and journaled mode (JNL) of EXT3, and the EXT2. In the results, DFW1 represents the results of only applying of sorting effect, and DFW2 represents the results for both of sorting and filling holes. The block size and journal region were set to 4 KB and 100 MB, respectively, and the commit interval of a transaction was set to 5s, which was typically set as usual. They were executed on the same hardware environment with Intel 2.67GHz CPU with 2GB DRAM. The Seagate 10,000 RPM disk was used in the experiment. Postmark [14] is used to test our algorithm. It has been run with a cold file system cache for which test file systems are remounted whenever each benchmark is performed. For comparison between figures, in some graphs, the results of all tested file systems are normalized with respect to the result of EXT3(ORD) where the absolute result was written over each EXT3(ORD) bar of the benchmark results.

The Postmark benchmark performs four kinds of file operations, create, delete, append, and read operation. Two sets of workloads were prepared for the experiments. The first configuration consists of small files which do not generate indirect blocks, and the second configuration includes large files generating indirect blocks. At first, we measured creation times for small files. The benchmark randomly creates files across subdirectories while allocating subdirectories in different cylinders. As the number of subdirectories increases, the distribution of the created files also widely spreads across disk cylinders. As shown in Fig 8(a), this wide spreading of randomly created files severely lowered the performances of ORD and EXT2 because these file systems conduct time-ordered data writebacks make results that disk heads move randomly back and forth to write the files. On the contrary, the increase of randomness of the created files has little effect on the performance of both DFW1 and DFW2, because these file systems sort the created files in the ascending block order before their writebacks, from which the disk-head movements are optimized. DFW1 and DFW2 perform similarly in the first configuration, where indirect blocks (a kind of metadata) were not generated. Next, we measured creation times for large files. As shown in Fig 8(b), the generation of indirect blocks for large files greatly lowers the performance of DFW1, however, the performance of DFW2 is not affected by the indirect blocks because the method of filling holes enables DFW2 to perform the sequential writeback of data and metadata in the data regions. Fig 8(c) shows the results of the Postmark benchmark read and write running. For the small files, DFW performs about 20% better than ORD. DFW1 and DFW2 shows little performance difference because the read and write for small files do not generate indirect blocks IO. EXT2 provided similar performance to DFW. The JNL suffered from the overhead of full data logging. For the large files, DFW1 gets about 5% more performance gain than ORD due to the sorted data writebacks of files. The performance gain is less compared to that of the small file's running because the average file size is larger and data randomness is lowered than that of the small files' running. DFW2 gets about a 20% performance benefit against DFW1 with the benefit of filling holes where adjacent data and metadata are written together sequentially.

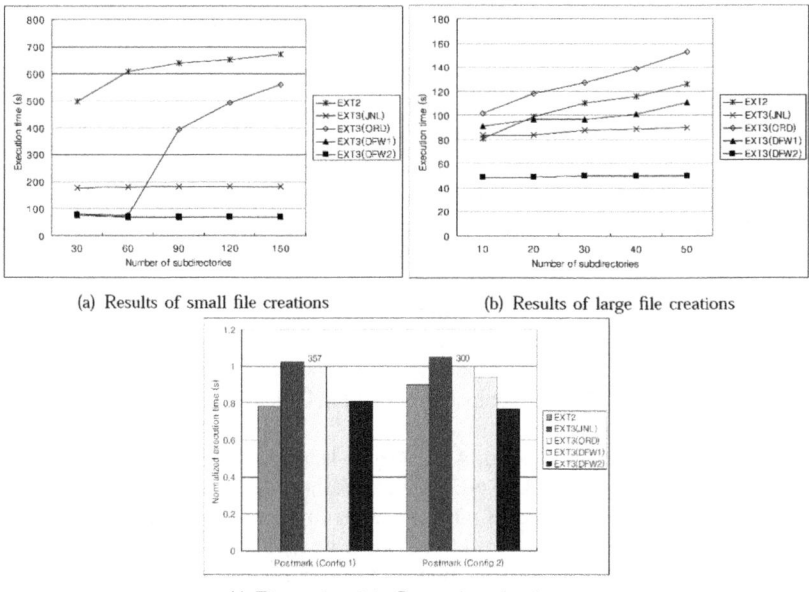

(a) Results of small file creations   (b) Results of large file creations

(c) The results of the Postmark read and write

Fig. 3. The results of file creations and random read/write of the Postmark benchmark

5   Conclusion

Based on the journaling file system operating with the ordered journaling, we have introduced an efficient technique, called de-fragmented writeback (DFW), which efficiently handles fragmented data workloads, and enables their rapid writeback. The DFW technique relies on the atomic writeback which guarantees that either all grouped blocks of the atomic data set are applied to the file system or none of them is applied during the file system recovery. At first, DFW considers where data blocks will be written in a disk layout rather than keeping their writeback orders based on their modification times, which minimizes the overall positioning time of a disk. Then, DFW reduces the number of write requests by making fragmented data blocks into sequential ones. It enables the sequential writeback of physically adjacent data and metadata blocks with no sacrifice of data consistency, which is fulfilled by logging the clean versions of metadata in advance of the data writeback. Overheads of the DFW are first an overhead of data sorting, and second an overhead of searching for cached blocks in the page cache. The overheads, however, are not significant in the sense that the processing does not take too much time if considering the benefits of the proposed technique. As evaluated with several benchmarks, the DFW enhances the performance of EXT3 journaling file system several times for highly random data workloads, especially those consisting of small files under a hundred of kilobytes.

References

1. Tweedie, S.: Journaling the Linux ext2fs filesystem. In: LinuxExpo 1998 (1998)
2. Reiser, H.: ReiserFS (2007), http://www.namesys.com
3. Sweeney, A., Doucette, D., Hu, W., Anderson, C., Nishimoto, M., Peck, G.: Scalability in the XFS file system. In: USENIX Annual Technical Conference (1996)
4. Best, Gordon, D., Haddad, I.: IBM's journaled filesystem. Linux Journal (2003)
5. Smith, K.A., Seltzer, M.I.: File System Aging–Incrasing the Relevance of File System Benchmarks. Measurement and Modeling Systems, 203–213 (1997)
6. Rosenblum, M., Ousterhout, J.: The design and implementation of a log-structured file system. ACM Trans. on Computer Systems (1992)
7. Seltzer, M., et al.: An Implementation of a Log-Structured File System for UNIX. In: Proceedings of the 1993 USENIX, San Diego, CA, pp. 307–326 (January 1993)
8. Piernas, J., Cortes, T., Garcia, J.: The Design of New Journaling File Systems: The DualFS Case. IEEE Trans. on Computers 56(2) (2007)
9. Smith, K.A., Seltzer, M.: A Comparision of FFS Disk Allocation Plolicies. In: USENIX Annual Tech. Conf. (1996)
10. Prabhakaran, V., Arpaci-Dusseau, A.C., Arpaci-Dusseau, R.H.: Analysis and Evolution of Journaling File Systems. In: USENIX Annual Technical Conference (April 2005)
11. Card, R., Ts'o, T., Tweedie, S.: Design and implementation of the second extended filesystem. In: The First Dutch Int'l Symp. on Linux (1994)
12. Ts'o, T., Tweedie, S.: Future Directions for the Ext2/3 Filesystem. In: USENIX Annual Technical Conference (June 2002)
13. Black, P.E.: Radix Sort, in Dictionary of Algorithms and Data Structures (online). National Institute of Standards and Technology, December 14 (2005)
14. Katcher, J.: PostMark: A New File System Benchmark., Technical Report TR3022, Network Appliance Inc. (October 1997)

IMS Session Management Based on Usage Control*

Giorgos Karopoulos and Fabio Martinelli

Institute of Informatics and Telematics (IIT),
National Research Council (CNR),
Via G. Moruzzi 1, 56124 Pisa, Italy
{georgios.karopoulos,Fabio.Martinelli}@iit.cnr.it

Abstract. Multimedia applications have made their way to the wireless/mobile world and this is not likely to change. However, people have not stopped using multimedia services through wired networks and this is also something that is not foreseen to change. What really is changing in the coming networks is the separation of network and service providers; this separation is creating new security challenges since the end user does not have the same trust relationships with all these providers. This paper proposes an architecture for protecting end users from untrusted and unreliable multimedia service providers in Next Generation Networks (NGNs) that utilize the IP Multimedia Subsystem (IMS) for multimedia delivery. Our proposal is based on the Usage Control (UCON) model for monitoring continuously the multimedia content delivered to the end user and ensure that it is the proper content requested by the user.

Keywords: Usage Control; UCON; IMS; NGN; multimedia; security.

1   Introduction

The next step in the networking world are the so-called Next Generation Networks (NGNs) which according to ITU-T [1] will be based on the IP protocol, support mobility but also fixed networks as well, provide unrestricted access to different service providers and utilize multiple access technologies. While this is not a complete list of NGNs characteristics, it is obvious that such a complex system which presents high heterogeneity not only at the network but at the application level as well, will also impose difficult security issues to solve. In this paper we focus on multimedia security in such an environment.

IP Multimedia Subsystem (IMS) [2] was specified by 3GPP as a subsystem that manages all multimedia sessions in 3G systems; IMS is also expected to play a central role in the NGN vision as well. Its operation is based on protocols originating from the Internet world like Session Initiation Protocol (SIP) [3] and Diameter [4] developed by IETF. One of the strengths of IMS is that it can support multiple administrative

---

* This work was carried out during the tenure of an ERCIM "Alain Bensoussan" Fellowship Programme.
  Work partially supported by EU FP7-ICT project NESSoS (Network of Excellence on Engineering Secure Future Internet Software Services and Systems) under the grant agreement n. 256980.

J.J. Park et al. (Eds.): STA 2011, CCIS 186, pp. 71–78, 2011.

domains and thus promote the convergence of networks that belong to different operators and also the deployment of independent multimedia service providers.

In NGNs there will be a distinction between network and service providers and this creates certain trust/security issues. The issue with the different providers can be better pointed out if we consider the environment in which different network and service providers will coexist in NGNs. In the first data networks or even today in many cases, usually the network provider, the one that gives access to the network level so that users can exchange data, is also a service provider, giving access to various services like voice, multimedia delivery etc. as well. This corresponds to a vertically integrated network architecture as opposed to an horizontally integrated one. As stated in ITU-T's recommendation [5] in NGNs "service-related functions are independent from underlying transport-related technologies"; this separation of services and transport in NGNs is realized with the definition of the NGN service stratum and the NGN transport stratum.

In practice, the aforementioned concepts result in a wide variety of choices for the end users. There can be overlapping networks of different link layer technologies on the same area; however, the user normally will have sign a contract with and thus trust only one network provider or a very limited number of them. The user can choose one of these network providers in order to have network access but he should also choose among numerous service providers which will not be trusted or known in many cases. The problem is that anyone can act as a service provider thus leaving the domain open for trusted as well as untrusted service providers.

In such an environment, an end user can never be sure that what he asked will be delivered to him as exactly was agreed during negotiations. Moreover, the user is under the risk of paying for receiving a service which was not what he asked for. In such cases there should be a way for confirming that the proper content was delivered to the end user and the service provider has been paid after delivering the right service.

At the moment there is no way to (either statically or continuously) determine whether (part or the whole of) the multimedia content of a session corresponds to the negotiated session characteristics or the content that the end user has requested. For example, the user requests a video of sports highlights, which of course he pays, but instead of that he receives a meaningless video stream. Another case is that the video he receives is partly what he asked for: there are some highlights as well as some other meaningless data; again, this is not what he paid for. Here we are not mostly concerned about accidental cases (however, these are also defeated by our proposal); our main focus is on cheating service providers.

The rest of the paper is organized as follows. Section II provides the necessary background by describing the main features of the Usage Control model. In Section III our proposed architecture is analyzed. Section IV presents some indicative applications that could benefit from our proposal. In Section V we present some works that we believe are related to our own, and finally Section VI provides conclusions and future work.

2   Background

Usage Control (UCON) model [6] is considered the next step in the access control world after Mandatory Access Control (MAC), Discretionary Access Control (DAC) and Role-based Access Control (RBAC). These traditional access control models deal with authorizations only at the time of access of resources. The novelty of UCON is that it does not only allow authorizations of subjects to use objects at the time of access, but also considers the continuously monitoring of the usage of resources and accordingly the authorization decisions to be taken.

UCON comprises eight components: subjects, subject attributes, objects, object attributes, rights, authorizations, obligations, and conditions. The separation of authorizations, obligations, and conditions as three distinct factors, the mutability of attributes and the continuity of enforcement makes UCON an appropriate model for supporting modern applications and systems like IMS.

3 Our Proposal

Our proposal is to use the UCON model in order to ensure for the whole lifetime of the content that the content delivered to the end user is actually the one he requested. The contribution of this work is an architecture for supporting the UCON model realization in IMS and provides the needed mechanisms for confirming that at all times the content corresponds to the user preferences and the policies he has in place. Our proposal is a service that can be offered to the end users of a network rather than a security mechanism that is dictated by the network itself to the users. They can utilize it for specific kinds of applications as we will describe later in the "Applications" Section.

One precondition for our mechanism to work properly is to have some method of describing the content prior to its delivery to the end user. This can be realized with the use of MPEG-7 standard [7]. MPEG-7 offers a very flexible model for describing content in different abstraction levels and the volume of detail is dependent on the application. Here we would like to point out that the metadata extraction methods are out of the scope of this paper; in fact, the MPEG-7 standard itself does not dictate some specific method in order to leave space for innovation.

The actual filtering of the multimedia content can be realized with the same mechanisms as in Lawful Interception (LI) [9]. The difference of our method from LI is that the former is the end user's choice while the latter is executed without the user having any knowledge of it taking place. Also, in our mechanisms the user can impose his own preferences that will be taken into account during the content filtering.

For the architecture of our scheme we follow the approach chosen by 3GPP for IMS which does not standardize specific physical nodes but functions instead. Practically this means that two or more functions can be implemented into one physical node. A simplified view of IMS architecture is depicted in Fig. 1. Here we can see the main elements of IMS which are built around Call Session Control Functions (CSCFs). The nodes presented in the figure are the Proxy-CSCF (P-CSCF), the Interrogating-CSCF (I-CSCF), and the Serving-CSCF (S-CSCF) which control the session, the Home Subscriber Server (HSS) which handles user accounts and an Application Server (AS) which provides the multimedia content. Mw, Gm, Cx, Sh and ISC represent different interfaces for the communication between the functions and the servers, which are based on SIP and Diameter protocols.

Our mechanism serves as additional functions (or modules) on the traditional 3GPP IMS architecture which can be implemented in different machines or collocated with other function/s in one machine. As shown in Fig. 2 it is positioned so that it can intercept data from either the P-CSCF or the S-CSCF or both. The choice is left to the network administrator and it is based on network configuration. Moreover, our architecture is distributed in the sense that each administrative domain can implement it irrespective of similar mechanisms of other domains, while it is not a requirement that every domain has this mechanism in place.

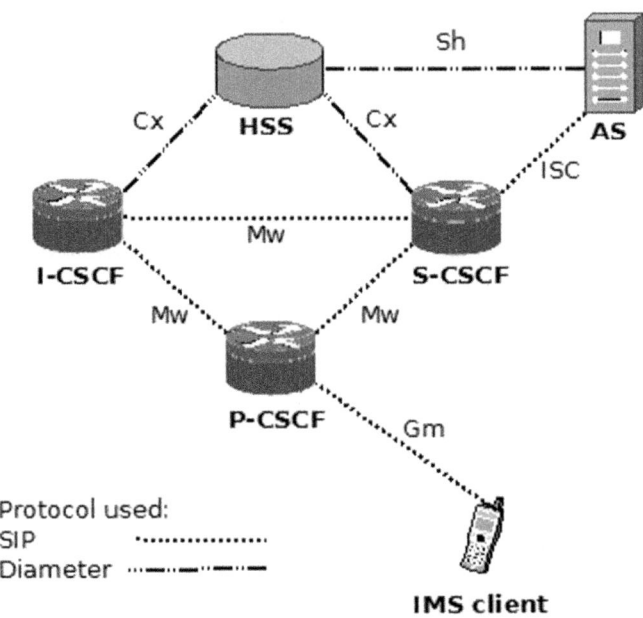

Fig. 1. Simplified IMS architecture

3.1   The Policies Module

The first module is the policies module where two kinds of policies are stored: general user policies and user policies related with the current session only. These types of policies can coexist and the policy module is the place where these policies are merged and the unified resulting policy is forwarded to the UCON module so that it can take further actions. The body of the policy describes the accepted or not accepted type of content and also the actions that the user wishes to be taken in case these requirements are not met. The aforementioned policies can be realized with XACML [8] which also allows the combination of different policies; in this context, the policies module acts as a Policy Administration Point (PAP).

General user policies describe user preferences that persist across all sessions that the user initiates. On the other hand, session related policies are valid for the current session only and can override the general policies. For example, a general user policy might dictate that no pornographic material should be delivered at all times, while a

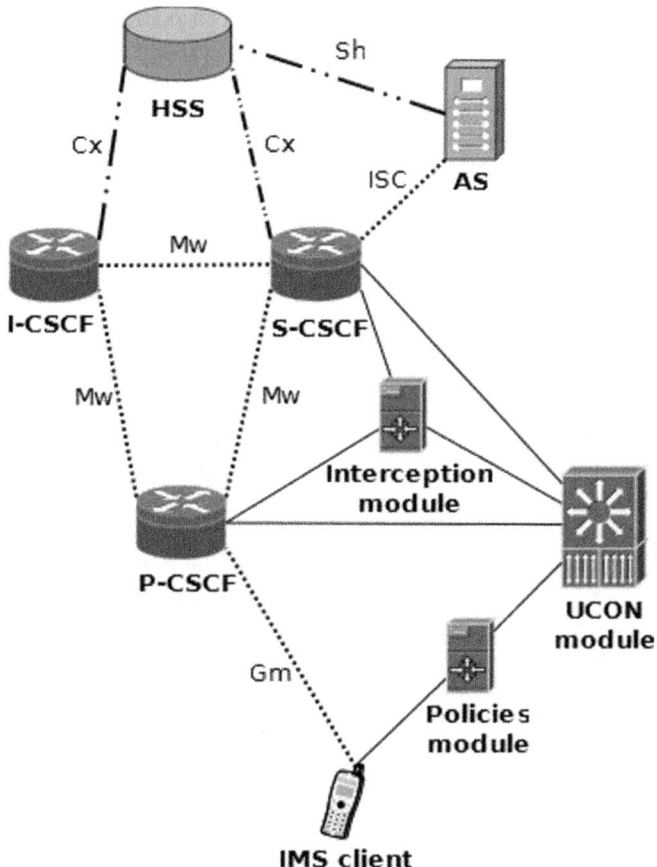

Fig. 2. Proposed architecture

session related policy might dictate that no advertorial material should be delivered as well but during this session only. Another example is a general policy which forbids multimedia that contain advertising material, but a session related policy might explicitly allow advertorial material for the current session only.

3.2 The Interception Module

The interception module is responsible for intercepting the content that the user wants to be monitored. Depending on the network configuration it can receive the content from the P-CSCF or the S-CSCF or both. Along with the content, the MPEG-7 metadata of the content are also received. The interception module does not make any decisions about policy enforcement; these are left to the UCON module. Its purpose is mainly to intercept the appropriate content and forward it to the UCON module for further processing. It should be noted here that not all content of the user is intercepted but only the content he has chosen to be monitored. Also, since constant monitoring of multimedia content is an expensive procedure in terms of resources, a sampling method could be utilized instead, for instance capturing one snapshot from a video clip every 5 sec.

As we have already discussed, there are certain similarities of our interception module to the interception mechanism of LI in NGNs since interception is common to both mechanisms. The obvious difference of our proposal is that it is a service requested by the used himself and it is not dictated by any legal entities as is the case with LI.

3.3 The UCON Module

The central building block of our mechanism is the UCON module which acts as a Policy Decision Point (PDP) according to [10]. According to the same RFC, the entities that will play the role of Policy Enforcement Points (PEPs) are the P-CSCF and/or the S-CSCF depending on the selected network configuration.

As we have already analyzed, the UCON module takes as inputs the intercepted content, the MPEG-7 metadata and the user policies. The most important point here is that the analysis of the content is continuous and the UCON module can at any given time decide the termination or the modification of the ongoing session based on the policies. More specifically, the interception data (which are one snapshot every 5 sec. in our previous example) are checked the moment they arrive, first for their consistency to the MPEG-7 metadata and then against the policies. If in any of these stages an inconsistency is found then the module forwards the appropriate actions to be taken to the P-CSCF and/or the S-CSCF according to what the policies specify.

Traditional approaches authenticate and authorize only once (in the beginning of the session) the user to have access to multimedia content and the only possibility of the latter is to "consume" the content without having any other kind of control over it apart from terminating the session. In our approach, the user authorizes a network entity which belongs to his own domain and can be considered trusted, to act on behalf of him and preserve his rights on the content against a possibly untrusted service provider. Moreover, it allows finer control over the session like modifying its characteristics instead of terminating it.

4   Applications

In this section we will present some example applications which can benefit from our proposal. The first one is an anti-SPIT (SPam over Internet Telephony) [11] mechanism. Voice over IP, and consequently multimedia services, like e-mail and other internet services are susceptible to unsolicited and unwanted communications mainly for advertorial purposes. The usual approach of anti-SPIT mechanisms is to prevent session establishment during the signaling phase. This means that once the session has been established the user must interact with the content in order to decide whether it is SPIT or not and terminate the session. The situation gets worse if the content starts as a legitimate one and ends up differently during its lifetime. In our method, which could operate in parallel with signaling prevention methods, the user has finer control over the content and his actions can be enforced automatically. For instance, the user might has multiple multimedia sessions open at the same time and not being able to review the content to decide if it is SPIT or not. Our mechanism can intercept the content and classify it as SPIT and take the proper actions which are defined by the end user in his policies. Such actions include immediate termination of the content, and modification of the session characteristics like downgrading the quality of the content in order not to waste bandwidth until the user reviews the content.

Another class of applications which could benefit from our proposed mechanism is Parental Control applications. In the Internet world this is usually implemented at the user's device as additional software. The problem in these cases is that, since the control is at the end user side, surpassing it is not impossible. For instance, changing the device used automatically renders parental control not active and this is easier when considering mobile devices where the user can use any device by just inserting his personal SIM card. One solution here is to install the Parental Control software to every possible device that will be used; however, this is not practical. In our method, Parental Control is executed in a central point so it is tied up to the actual account of the end user and not the device he uses at each time. Moreover, it can also protect minors from content that does not seem harmful or only part of it is considered harmful.

A different type of applications which follows a different logic from the previous ones which are mostly related to content filtering, is an application where the Home network of the user acts as a kind of Trusted Third Party (TTP) between the user and the content provider. As we have already described NGNs will be composed of many different network and service providers but the end user will probably have signed a contract with one of them which is the one he trusts. Thus, trying to purchase a multimedia content from a different service provider can sometimes be risky because as is the case today the content is delivered to the user after he has paid for it. By having our mechanism acting as a TTP, the content is continuously monitored and if it is not complying with the specifications then the payment is not delivered or at least there is evidence for a refund.

5 Related Work

We should note here that the authors are not aware of any previous work that adapts the UCON model to IMS or NGNs in general. The work in [12] deals with usage control of multimedia in the cloud computing paradigm; the difference from our work is that it enforces the policies of the content owner over the content consumers. In [13] the UCON model is used for the realization of a DRM application. There are also works in relevant domains like UCON on GRID systems [14] or Wireless Sensor Networks [15].

6 Conclusions and Future Work

Our work proposes a viable way of protecting end users from unknown service providers ensuring that they will only pay for the content they were initially requested.

More important, is that this is not limited at the time the user is accessing the content for the first time but there is continuous monitoring of the content.

We have left as future work issues which can further improve the extensibility of our mechanism. One such extension is the investigation of policies exchange across different administrative domains. The interest is mostly on roaming users which have their policies residing in their Home Domain and request a multimedia service from a visiting domain. Another interesting extension is the unification of user policies with policies imposed by the network; this is getting more challenging if the user is roaming to networks with different policies for multimedia use.

References

1. The International Telecommunication Union (ITU),
   `http://www.itu.int/ITU-T/studygroups/com13/ngn2004/`
   `working_definition.html`
2. 3GPP TS 23.228: IP multimedia subsystem (IMS). Version 10.2.0, Release 10 (2010)
3. Rosenberg, J., Schulzrinne, H., Camarillo, G., Johnston, A., Peterson, J., Sparks, R., Handley, M., Schooler, E.: SIP: Session Initiation Protocol. RFC 3261 (2002)
4. Calhoun, P., Loughney, J., Guttman, E., Zorn, G., Arkko, J.: Diameter Base Protocol. RFC 3588 (2003)
5. ITU-T Recommendation Y.2011: General principles and general reference model for next generation network (2004)
6. Park, J., Sandhu, R.: The UCONABC usage control model. ACM Trans. on Information and System Security (TISSEC) 7(1), 128–174 (2004)
7. ISO/IEC JTC1/SC29/WG11/N6828: MPEG-7 Overview V.10 (2004)
8. Moses, T.: eXtensible Access Control Markup Language (XACML). Version 2.0, Technical report, OASIS Standard (2005)
9. 3GPP TS 33.107: 3G Security; Lawful interception architecture and functions. Version 10.1.1, Release 10 (2010)
10. Vollbrecht, J., Farrell, S., Gommans, L., Gross, G., de Bruijn, B., de Laat, C., Holdrege, M., Spence, D.: AAA Authorization Framework. RFC 2904 (2000)
11. Rosenberg, J., Jennings, C.: The Session Initiation Protocol and Spam. RFC 5039 (2008)
12. Ali, T., Nauman, M., Hadi, F., bin Muhaya, F.: On Usage Control of Multimedia Content in and through Cloud Computing Paradigm. In: 5th International Conference on Future Information Technology (FutureTech), Busan, South Korea, pp. 1–5 (2010)
13. Ding, Y., Zou, J.: DRM Application in UCONABC. In: Advanced Software Engineering and Its Applications, Hainan Island, China, pp. 182–185 (2008)
14. Martinelli, F., Mori, P.: On usage control for GRID systems. Future Generation Computer Systems 26(7), 1032–1042 (2010)
15. Wu, J., Shimamoto, S.: Usage Control Based Security Access Scheme for Wireless Sensor Networks. In: IEEE Intern. Conf. on Communications (ICC), Cape Town, pp. 1–5 (2010)

Using Counter Cache Coherence to Improve Memory Encryptions Performance in Multiprocessor Systems[*]

Zhang Yuanyuan[1,2] and Gu Junzhong[1]

[1] East China Normal University, Department of Computer Science and Technology
200241 Shanghai, China
[2] CITI Laboratory, INSA Lyon
69621 Villeurbanne, France
{yyzhang,jzgu}@cs.ecnu.edu.cn

Abstract. When memory encryption schemes are applied in multiprocessor systems, the systems will confront new problems such as inter-processor communication overhead increasing and cache coherence protocol overhead increasing. A counter cache coherence optimization scheme AOW is proposed to improve cache hit rate. As MESI protocol which makes counter line by four states, AOW marks each counter line using three encryption states, 'Autonomy', 'Operating' and 'Waiting'. According to the simulation results, by applying AOW, memory access time decreases, and execution speed of non-AOW method improves obviously.

Keywords: Memory encryption, cache coherence, secure architecture, multiprocessor systems.

1 Introduction

Security architectures are first proposed for uniprocessor systems [1],[2]. They claimed that CPU chip is the only trusted area in system, and all other components, because the CPU chip is much more difficult to invade than others, and most data off-chip is vulnerable under physical attacks [6],[7]. Therefore, security schemes must provide both data confidentiality and integrity for data outside the CPU chip. These security goals are achieved by various memory protection methods.

Confidentiality protections in uniprocessor systems fall into two categories, direct encryption methods [1],[2] and counter mode encryption methods[3],[4]. In counter mode encryption method, each data block executes XORs with its pad generated by seed. When a block whose counter is on-chip needs to be fetched from physical memory, pad generation can be overlapped by memory access latency. Obviously, OTP (One-Time Pad generation) featured encryption has better performance, and becomes a popular method in memory encryption [4],[8],[9],[10].

Multiprocessor architecture has brought about new problems in security architecture design, e.g., establishment of shared secret among processors, confidentiality and

---
[*] This work was supported by Franco-Chinese Foundation for Basic and Applied Science (FFCSA).

J.J. Park et al. (Eds.): STA 2011, CCIS 186, pp. 79–87, 2011.

authentication of cache-to-cache bus transactions, and efficiency of caches-to-memory encryption. The former two problems are discussed in [11] and [12]. [11] described an attack model and security requirements, and proposed a brief trust architecture framework. However, the trusted area is dispersed, both in processors and north-bridge. The other problem is to securely distribute shared secrets to multiprocessors. Because the key-establishment messages are sent through inter-processor buses without confidentiality, the snoopers can easily recover the shared secret. [11] solved the above issues in their work by adding to processors a public secret key pair. Moreover, [11] guarded the clear text communication between processors in a multiprocessor environment. The primary goal of [11] is to protect cache-to-cache bus transactions, thus the caches-to-memory protection is merely introduced. When caches-to-memory encryption adopts OTP idea, the main concern will be the consistency of the pads or counters of data blocks. [11] followed the traditional cache coherency protocol for counter cache which was first proposed in [3]. In a bus-based multiprocessor system, for example, when processor A modifies block D which is shared by processor B, the counter for block D in B's counter cache is not fresh for processor B any longer. This causes B to issue another counter read thus results in nontrivial memory access latency.

In this paper, we propose a coherence protocol AOW for counter caches, in order to reduce memory access latency that is caused by reading/writing counters from/to memory. The new protocol is low-cost and easy to apply, since it is based on snoop-based cache coherence protocol slightly modification returns considerable performance improvement.

The rest of this paper is organized as follows, section 2 exhibits related work in the field; section 3 describes the attack model; our proposed scheme is introduced in section 4 and the simulation results are listed in section 5. Section 6 concludes our work.

2   Related Work

Security schemes for multiprocessor systems are much different from schemes for uniprocessor systems in many aspects: what is the trust root (in uniprocessor systems, root is usually the CPU), how to distribute shared secret information, and protection on processor-to-memory and processor-to-processor communications. [11],[12],[13] had proposed several methods to fulfill these needs.

[11] adopted cached hash tree [5] mechanisms for memory integrity verification, but it seats the hash tree root in a crypto engine in Northbridge chip which is outside the CPU chip. [11] also proposed a memory encryption method. Each crypto engine is granted a bus cycle to broadcast a random 64-bit number. Then each unit who hears the broadcast random number concatenates all the numbers including the one it broadcasted and feed them into a hash function. The hash result is truncated into a 128-bit AES session key which is to compute all the shared secrets in physical. This literature proposed an overall framework for SMP, but it lacks protection on bus transaction among processors.

[12] focused on guarding the clear text communication between processors in a multiprocessor environment. They accomplished both encryption and authentication

for bus transaction by Cipher Block Chaining mode of the advanced encryption standard (CBC-AES) to achieve low latency. [12] briefly discussed cache-to-memory protection, and it adopted OTP encryption in uniprocessor system, and the counter coherency problem was deemed as a traditional cache coherence problem.The main concern is the consistency of the counters and pads stored in on-chip counter cache in each processor, which is never evaluated in former literatures. In fact, e.g. in [12], counter cache differs from data cache, because each counter value pluses one each time when data cache line is written back to memory. Therefore, it is necessary to design a special coherence protocol for counter cache to raise the hit rate of counter cache.

3   Attack Model

As described in previous section, in uniprocessor system, the processor chip is considered to be the trust root. So does multiprocessor system also regards the CPUs are trust roots, thus on-chip information is non-extractable. We assume that attackers have the ability of both passive and active attacks on several locations as illustrated in Fig.1.

Attackers launch passive attacks, also referred to as non-invasive attacks, to eavesdrop on processor-to-processor or processor-to-memory communications. [7] introduced several non-invasive attacks, such as software attack and eavesdropping. They are destructive in two ways. Firstly, the actions might not be noticed when the secret information has been stolen, thus, the secret owner would not retrieve these exposed information. Another reason is the convenience of passive attacks, for their necessary equipment can usually be at low cost.

Active attacks include replaying old messages, snooping and modifying data in memory or on bus, which are realized by techniques such as fault generation, micro-probing and reverse engineering requiring hours or weeks in elaborating work to destroy the packaging, and requiring much more knowledge on electronic engineering and software, thus they are more difficult to launch.

4   Main Schemes

4.1   Architecture Overview

Program issuance. Each processor contains its own on-chip L1, L2 data cache and a counter cache. All processors share a small centralized main memory which would consist of several memory banks, and visit a unique memory space. Each processor maintains a pair of public and private keys. The ith processor's key pair is denoted as (k_p^i, k_s^i). One of the processors is designated as the boot processor to bring up the system, and we denote this processor as P_1 and its key pair as (k_p^1, k_s^1). The programs that are issued to such a multiprocessor system are encrypted by a symmetric key k which is then encrypted by the public key k_p^1 of P_1. The issuance process is illustrated in Fig.2.

Counter mode encryption process. In memory, each data block is assigned with a counter value which changes when it's written back from data cache to memory. It generates different seed and pads each time to sustain the freshness of encrypted data blocks. Literature [4] had proposed several efficient counter methods, such as GCM (Galois/Counter Mode) encryption, whose purpose is to shorten the encryption and authentication latency. We are focusing on how to make up for the performance lost when they are applied in multiprocessor systems. In this paper, when a data block is fetched into cache, or written back to memory, it applies its corresponding counter in counter mode encryption. The AOW counter cache coherence protocol will handle counter maintenance issues, such as fetching counter and updating its value.

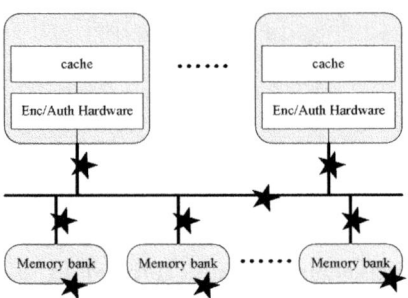

Fig. 1. Locations of attacks taking place

Data cache coherence. We adopt MESI protocol, a widely used cache coherency and memory consistency protocol, which is for a write-invalid cache in addition to the write-back memory consistence mechanism. In MESI, every data line is marked with one of the four following states coded in two additional bits: Modified (00), Exclusive (10), Shared (11) and Invalid (01).

4.2   AOW Protocol

We assume that a processor has its own on-chip counter cache and data cache. When the data block is read into data cache, its corresponding counter would be fetched into its counter cache if its counter has not been read into counter cache before, but the counter would not be replaced or written back immediately after its corresponding data line is replaced or written back.

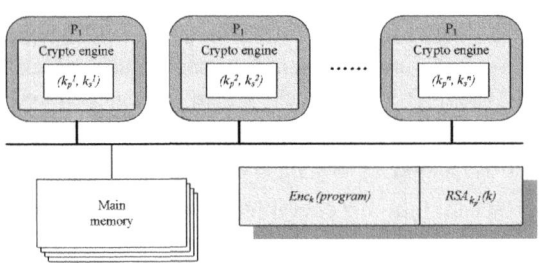

Fig. 2. Architecture Overview

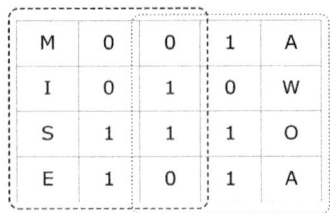

M	0	0	1	A
I	0	1	0	W
S	1	1	1	O
E	1	0	1	A

Fig. 3. States of MESI and AOW

Based on MESI, which uses two additional bits for marking the four states, we will add one more bit for counter cache coherence, see Fig.3. The first bit column implies whether this data line has the same content as its copy in memory, and the second bit column implies whether it is shared by other processors. Column one and two are dedicated to mark data line's state, and the third column implies whether the counter's corresponding data line is in data cache. It is interesting that under the agreement in above paragraph, the mutual column denotes both the data line and counter line whether they are shared by other processors. State (00) is not employed in AOW protocol, because it is covered by state Autonomy, which will be elaborated later. So, we have three states to mark on counter cache lines: Autonomy (01), Operating (11) and Waiting (10).

4.3 Operations of AOW Protocol

A snooping coherence protocol is usually implemented by incorporating a finite-state machine in each processor. When triggered by requests from the processor or the bus, the state of the line in caches will change accordingly. AOW protocol works like a write-update and write-back cache coherence protocol. In this protocol, an update to one counter cache might trigger an issue of operation "Broadcast ctr++" to other counter caches updating its copy. Different from traditional write-update protocol, AOW does not require a special bus line to broadcast updated counter value. Moreover, "Broadcast ctr++" can accomplish updating of other counter copies easier and use less cost.

Cooperating with MESI protocol, AOW establishes its three states by adding only one bit. These three states are Autonomy, Operating and Waiting.

- A - Autonomy: indicates that the counter line in counter cache is autonomic by this processor, which implies that it's not shared by other processors and its corresponding data line is in data cache.
- O - Operating: indicates that this counter is under operations of several processors. When a counter is operated, it means that it's potentially participating pad generation process in at least one processor.
- W - Waiting: indicates that this counter is right now not in pad generation process but shared by other processor, meanwhile its corresponding data line is not in data cache. So we call it in a waiting list of later pad generation process.

Fig.4 pictures a finite-state transition diagram for a single counter cache block using our AOW protocol. Detail counter cache coherence mechanism is described in Tab.1. It describes how this protocol works according to CPU requests and signals on bus. We introduce a new type of signal "ctr++", that CPU sends to bus, and a new execution "Counter + 1". Either of them will be triggered when the corresponding data line is modified. When a processor hears "ctr++", it adds 1 to corresponding counter value, and "Counter + 1" happens under some circumstances such as other counter copy being modified. Both of them are designed to keep counter value fresh. Whenever the pad generation procedure calls these counters as parameters, if the counter is in counter cache, it means this counter is fresh and ready to use.

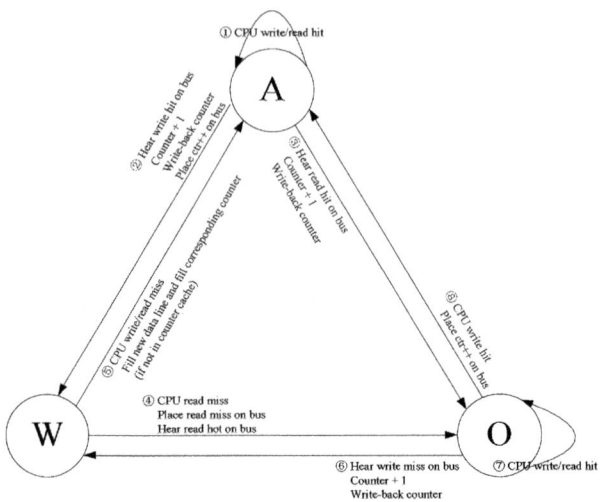

Fig. 4. Finite-state machine diagram of AOW protocol

Intuitively, AOW protocol assures that all the counters in counter cache are ready for hashing; otherwise, crypto engine has to wait for inconsistent counters to be updated, which causes considerable memory access latency. The performance promotion will be revealed later in simulation results.

Table 1. Detailed AOW protocol mechanism

No.	State transition	CPU Request(s)	Operation(s)
(1)	$A \rightarrow A$	Write hit or read hit	None.
(2)	$A \rightarrow W$	Hearing write hit	Counter + 1; Write-back this counter to memory; Broadcast ctr++.
(3)	$A \rightarrow O$	Hearing read hit	Counter + 1; Write-back this counter to memory.
(4)	$W \rightarrow O$	Read miss and hearing read hit	Fill in a new data line and its corresponding counter (if not in counter cache).
(5)	$W \rightarrow A$	Hearing write or read miss	Fill in a new data line and its corresponding counter (if not in counter cache).
(6)	$O \rightarrow W$	Hearing write hit and broadcast ctr++	Counter + 1.
(7)	$O \rightarrow O$	Read hit or hearing read hit	None.
(8)	$O \rightarrow A$	Write hit	Broadcast ctr++.

5   Experimental Evaluations

We evaluate the performance impact comparing with unoptimized DSM system with no counter cache optimization cooperating with benchmark SPLASH-2. We modeled our target SMP system by RSIM which is a fast and accurate performance evaluation of shared-memory multiprocessors. The relevant architectural features and applications used in our simulated system are listed in Tab.2.

5.1   System Performance Results

In this experiment, a basic counter encryption scheme proposed in [4] is applied. As described [4] GCM is a fine choice of block cipher mode of operation in the context, because it provides ciphertext of data blocks and their hash value almost simultaneously. On the side, when we referring to memory integrity verification, Bonsai Merkle tree [9] is a suitable base for evaluating AOW, for it is composed of counters' hash value instead of data blocks, that is a good match to AOW which is also a counter based cache coherence protocol.

Fig.5 compares the performance slowdown using GCM encryption, and GCM encryption with AOW assistance. Fig.6 reveals AOW improves performance when Bonsai Merkle tree is applied to the system. When GCM encryption and Bonsai Merkle tree algorithm integrate, the situation is more complicated, for extra transactions are necessary, e.g., when Bonsai Merkle tree requires checking a counter value which is happen to replaced from counter cache in the last operation. Therefore, the overall performance is inevitably worse than either of that shown in Fig.5 or Fig.6. When memory encryption and integrity protection both deployed in DSM, we can see form Fig.7 the overall performance improves 5% on average when DSM is assisted by AOW.

Table 2. Simulated system configuration

Parameter	Vlue
Processor clock freq.	1GHz
L1 I-cache	64KB, 2-way,32B
L1 D-cache	64KB, 2-way,32B
L1 hit latency	2 cycles
L2 Cache	64B a line, 4-way
L2 hit latency	10 cycles
Cache-to-cache latency	120 cycles
Cache-to-memory latency	180 cycles
Shared bus	3.2GB/s, 100MHz, 32B a line
AES latency	80 cycles
Hashing latency	160 cycles

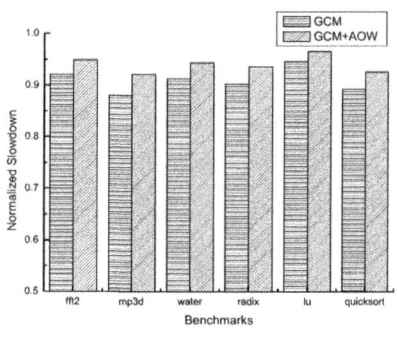

Fig. 5. Memory encryption performance

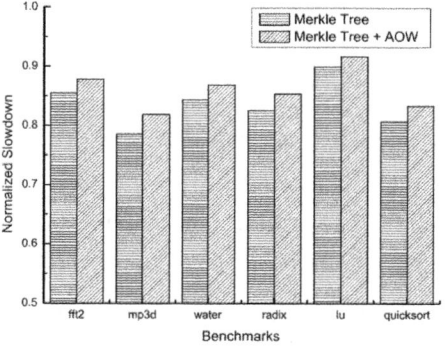

Fig. 6. Memory integrity performance

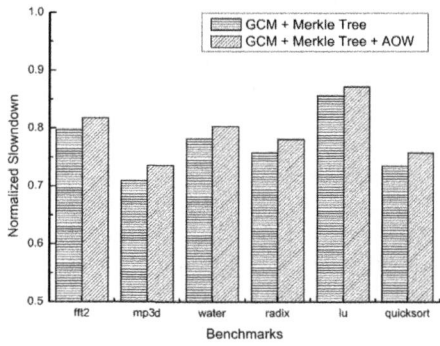

Fig. 7. Overall system performance slowdown

6   Conclusions

In this paper, we proposed a counter cache coherence protocol AOW whose main purpose is to raise the hit rate on counter cache. AOW cooperates with traditional cache coherence MESI protocol. It makes good use of the existing two flag bits of MESI, and extends its function to counter cache by adding 1 bit instead of 2 to indicate three states of a counter. Moreover, it does not introduce complex bus communications to achieve coherence. All the existing bus signals working for MESI will fulfill most of the demands of AOW. At last, the simulation results reveal it indeed improves the performance by improving the overall performance.

References

1. Lie, D., Mitchell, M., Lincoln, P., Boneh, D., Mitchell, J., Horowitz, M.: Architectural support for copy and tamper resistant software. ACM SIGARCH Computer Architecture 28, 168–177 (2000)
2. Suh, G., Clarke, D., Gassend, B., van Dijk, M., Devadas, S.: AEGIS: Architecture for tamper-evident and tamper-resistant processing. In: Proceedings of the 17 Int'l Conference on Supercomputing, San Francisco, CA, USA, pp. 160–171 (2003)
3. Yang, J., Zhang, Y., Gao, L.: Fast secure processor for inhibiting software piracy and tampering. In: The 36th Annual IEEE/ACM International Symposium on Microarchitecture (MICRO-36), San Diego, CA, US (December 2003)
4. Yan, D.Y.C., Rogers, B., Prvulovic, M.: Improving cost, performance, and security of memory encryption and authentication. In: The 33rd Annual International Symposium on Computer Architecture (ISCA 2006), Boston, MA, US, pp. 179–190 (2006)
5. Suh, G., Clarke, D., van Dijk, M., Devadas, S.: Caches and hash trees for efficient memory integrity verification. In: Proceedings of the 9th International Symposium on High-Performance Computer Architecture, Anaheim, California, USA, pp. 295–311 (February 2003)
6. Ravi, S., Raghunathan, A., Kocher, P., Hattangady, S.: Security in embedded systems: Design challenges. ACM Transactions on Embedded Computing Systems (TECS) 3(3), 461–491 (2004)
7. Skorobogatov, S.P.: Semi-invasive attacks - A new approach to hardware security analysis. Technical Report UCAM-CL-TR-630, University of Cambridge Computer Laboratory (April 2005)
8. Shi, W., Lee, H.-H.S., Ghosh, M., Lu, C., Boldyreva, A.: High Efficiency Counter Mode Security Architecture via Prediction and Precomputation. In: The Proceedings of the 32nd International Symposium on Computer Architecture, Madison, Wisconsin, pp. 14–24 (June 2005)
9. Rogers, B., Chhabra, S., Solihin, Y., Prvulovic, M.: Using Address Independent Seed Encryption and Bonsai Merkle Trees to Make Secure Processors OS- and Performance-Friendly. In: The Proceedings of the 40th Annual IEEE/ACM Symposium on Microarchitecture, MICRO (December 2007)
10. Rogers, B., Prvulovic, M., Solihin, Y.: Effective Data Protection for Distributed Shared Memory Multiprocessors. In: The Proceedings of International Conference of Parallel Architecture and Compilation Techniques (PACT), Seattle (September 2006)

11. Shi, W., Lee, H.-H.S., Ghosh, M., Lu, C.: Architectural Support for High Speed Protection of Memory Integrity and Confidentiality in Multiprocessor Systems. In: Proceedings of the International Conference on Parallel Architecture and Compilation Techniques, Antibes Juan-les-Pins, France, pp. 123–134 (September 2004)
12. Zhang, Y., Gao, L., Yang, J., Zhang, X., Gupta, R.: SENSS: Security Enhancement to Symmetric Shared Memory Multiprocessors. In: The Proceedings of the 11th International Symposium on High-Performance Computer Architecture (HPCA), Washington, DC, USA, pp. 352–362 (2005)
13. Rogers, B., Prvulovic, M., Solihin, Y.: Efficient data protection for distributed shared memory multiprocessors. In: Proceedings of the 15th international Conference on Parallel Architectures and Compilation Techniques (PACT), Seattle, Washington, USA, pp. 16–20 (September 2006)
14. Pai, V.S., Ranganathan, P., Adve, S.V.: RSIM: An Execution-Driven Simulator for ILP-Based Shared-Memory Multiprocessors and Uniprocessors. In: Proceedings of the Third Workshop on Computer Architecture Education (February 1997)

Dynamic Combinatorial Key Pre-distribution Scheme for Heterogeneous Sensor Networks

Bidi Ying[1,2], Dimitrios Makrakis[1], Hussein T. Mouftah[1], and Wenjun Lu[2]

[1] Broadband Wireless & Internetworking Research Lab,
SITE, University of Ottawa, Ottawa, Canada
[2] Zhejiang Gongshang University, Hangzhou, China
{byiung,dimitris}@site.uottawa.ca

Abstract. Previous research on sensor network security considers homogeneous sensor networks, i.e. it assumes all sensors have the same capabilities. Many schemes designed for these networks suffer from high volume of communication and/or large storage requirements. In this paper, we propose the Dynamic Combinatorial Key Pre-distribution scheme (DCKP), which differentiates between sensors in accordance to their capabilities. DCKP makes use of the Exclusion-Basis System (EBS) and sensors' location information. Performance evaluations demonstrate that DCKP is very efficient in terms of storage at a certain local connectivity, while at the same time is capable of providing better security.

Keywords: Heterogeneous sensor networks; key pre-distribution; dynamic.

1 Introduction

Many typical Wireless Sensor Networks (WSNs) are formed by the sensors themselves in order to support the communication needs of sensing devices, i.e. transfer of the collected data by sensors to specified sinks. Secure communications with WSNs are a formidable challenge (especially when the sensors are deployed in hostile environments) because of the processing, memory and energy resource limitations of the sensing devices, which do not allow use of complex encryption and security algorithms, since they will drain fast the limited energy resources of the sensing devices.

Key management is crucial to the secure operation of sensor networks. A large number of keys need to be managed in order to encrypt and authenticate the exchange of all sensitive data. There are two main types of key management schemes for sensor networks: static key management and dynamic key management. A static key management scheme performs the key management functions before or shortly after the network is deployed. However after the keys have been distributed, they cannot change. For example, key pre-distribution to sensors in static key management schemes may be performed randomly or by taking into consideration some relevant deployment information [1-2, 8]. However, rekeying is very important in terms of providing secure key management. For example, sensors may experience failure due to energy depletion, or may be compromised and exhibit anomalous behavior [3].

J.J. Park et al. (Eds.): STA 2011, CCIS 186, pp. 88–95, 2011.
© Springer-Verlag Berlin Heidelberg 2011

In such cases, we must evict these sensors from the network. When a member sensor is evicted from the network, the keys known to that member must be revoked and new keys need to be given to other sensor members in order to maintain data confidentiality. This brings us to the case of dynamic key management [4]. Younis et al. proposed SHELL [5], an EBS (g, k, p)-based scheme where nodes pre-install k keys and p rekeys. SHELL can perform location-based key assignment to minimize the number of keys revealed by capturing collocated sensors.

However, these schemes are designed for homogeneous sensor networks, and many of them suffer from impractically high cost of communication, computation, and large storage requirement, which make them impractical for use in heterogeneous sensor deployments where different sensors/groups of sensors might differ considerably in terms of stored energy, CPU power, memory size, expose to security threats. Thus developing technology that is including the heterogeneity of nodes into the design process is very important. Such technology can significantly improve network performance and security [6] for heterogeneous WSNs.

Our scheme is deciding how many keys should be deployed to a certain node by taking into consideration storage capacity, security threat level at the location of the sensor node. In the present work we define the communication models associated with a WSN consisting of two types of sensors; S-sensors and W-sensors, where S-sensors have more resource while W-sensors are weaker. We also evaluate the network connectivity versus the number of allocated keys. We continue by introducing the exclusion basis system used for random key pre-deployment. We then select the level of complexity of the EBS system by considering the resource constraints of the various sensors as well as their physical locations. Finally, we discuss how to update the keys information when sensors leave the network.

The remaining of this paper is organized as follows: an overview of dynamic key management and related work are described in section 2. Section 3 describes the exclusion basis system. In Section 4, we discuss our proposed security solution. In Section 5, we provide the validation and performance assessment of our security solution. Finally, we conclude our work in Section 6.

2   Overview of Dynamic Key Management and Related Work

The main feature of dynamic key management schemes is that they are repeating the key management process either periodically or on demand (e.g. as reaction to some nodes' compromise). After sensors are deployed, key generation and distribution might be performed, creating new keys that replace the keys assumed lost (or became known to an attacker) so that the network becomes "refreshed".

To the best of our knowledge, the work of Jolly et al. [9] is the first main contribution in the field of dynamic key pre-distribution. It is based on the identity-based symmetric keying scheme. However, the rekeying procedure is inefficient due to the higher number of messages that need to be exchanged during the key renewal process. Moharrum et.al. came up with the Exclusion Basis System (EBS)-based dynamic key management scheme [4]. However, the inability to exclude possible collusion occurring between a small number of sensors, making the proposed technology unsuitable for use with large sensor population deployments. Eltoweissy et. al. proposed the group key management scheme in which keys are distributed according to a combinatorial exclusion basis system (EBS) [10]. Each sensor is assigned k keys out of a pool of size $\{k+m\}$ keys. Once one or more sensors are captured, rekeying takes place by sending m messages containing new k keys to each of the non-evicted sensors. Although it is energy efficient in its key-updating phase, this scheme does not address collusion, which was the case with [5] as well. In order to address the collusion problem in EBS, Younis et al. proposed SHELL [5], an EBS-based scheme that performs location-based key assignment to minimize the number of keys revealed by capturing collocated sensors. These schemes rely on assuming of having homogeneous network architecture.

Heterogeneous Sensor Networks (HSNs) can significantly improve the security while maintaining reasonable levels of complexity. Thus having efficient key management schemes suitable for use in heterogeneous sensor networks is important. The scheme reported in [11] classifies sensors into I different classes, generates a set of bivariate t_i-degree polynomials for each class, and assigns the polynomial shares of these polynomials to each sensor. The scheme does not scale well to large sensor node populations. Besides, it does not provide the capability of rekeying sensors; it is a static key management scheme. Poornima et. al. [12] proposed a key management scheme for heterogeneous networks that is based on the *Chinese Remainder theorem*. The scheme is capable of handling various events, like node addition, node compromise and key refreshing. It is thus a dynamic key management scheme. However, this scheme generates higher communication overhead and computation overhead as compared to the one reported in [11].

3   Exclusion Basis Systems

An EBS is defined as a collection of **T** subsets formed by members of a certain set, with each member being different from the rest of the member of the set [7]. The definition of an EBS of **T** membership is stated as follows: let g, k and p be positive integers, such that $1<k$, $p<g$. An exclusion basis system of dimension (g, k, p), denoted by EBS (g, k, p), is the collection **T** subsets of $[1, g]=\{1,2,...,g\}$ such that for every integer $x \in [1, g]$ the following two properties hold: a) $x \leq k$ and $g \leq C_{k+p}^{k}$; b) there are exactly $(p+k)$ subsets, say A_1, A_2, ..., A_{p+k} in **T** such that $[1, g]-\{t\}=\bigcup_{i=1}^{p+k} A_i$.(That is, each element x is excluded by a union of exactly p subsets in **T**).

As an example, consider an EBS(8, 3, 2), **T** can be: **T**={ A_1={5, 6, 7, 8}, A_2={2, 3, 4, 8}, A_3={1, 3, 4, 6, 7}, A_4={1, 2, 4, 5, 7}, A_5={1, 2, 3, 5, 6, 8}}. One can verify that each integer $x \in [1,8]$ is member of exactly 5 subsets of **T** and each integer x is excluded by a union of exactly 2 subsets of **T**, as shown below:

$[1,8]-\{1\}=A_1 \cup A_2;[1,8]-\{2\}=A_1 \cup A_3; [1,8]-\{3\}=A_1 \cup A_4; [1,8]-\{4\}=A_1 \cup A_5;[1,8]-\{5\}= A_2 \cup A_3;[1,8]-\{6\}= A_2 \cup A_4; [1,8]-\{7\}= A_2 \cup A_5; [1,8]-\{8\}=A_3 \cup A_4.$

4   Dynamic Combinatorial Key Pre-distribution Scheme

4.1   System Model

We consider a HSN consisting of a command sensor and numerous sensors which are grouped into clusters. The clusters of sensors can be formed based on various criteria such as capabilities, location, communication range, etc. [6]. Each cluster is controlled by a cluster head, also known as a gateway, which can broadcast messages to all sensors in the cluster. Each gateway is assumed to be reachable by all sensors in its cluster, either directly or by multi-hopping. There are two types of sensors in a cluster: S-sensors (who have stronger storage capability) and W-sensors (who have weak storage capability). Sensors in different clusters can communicate by directly or by multi-hopping. In this paper, we assume the base station is inaccessible to attackers, both physically and electronically. We also assume all sensors and cluster leaders to be subject to such attacks. When sensors are captured, their memory can be read, erased and/or tampered with. Therefore, an adversary would know all the contents of a compromised sensor's memory. A widely accepted assumption is that an adversary will not launch an attack in the few minutes following the network's initial deployment. Thus, the network initialization will take place safely.

4.2   DCKP

In this subsection, we present an effective key management scheme for the HSN. The main idea is to pre-load only a small number of keys in each W-sensor and pre-load a relatively large number of keys in each S-sensor, since S-sensors have considerably larger storage space than W-sensors. DCKP has two phases: Initial key distribution phase, Sensor segregation phase.

1)   Initial key distribution

We define G_i as the gateway i (cluster head i). Let m_g, m_s, m_w be the number of keys stored in each G_i, each S-sensor, each W-sensor, with and $m_s > m_w$. We also define $\overline{\omega}_i$ as the population of S-sensors in cluster i (or G_i), and ω_i as the population of W-sensors in cluster i (or G_i). First we decide on the parameters (g, k, p) of an EBS by taking into consideration the number of all gateways and the maximum size of memory which stores keys for each gateway. The parameters should be satisfying the conditions $k < m_g$, and $g \leq C_{k+p}^{k}$. Gateway G_i also decides on the parameters of the EBS (g_i, k_i, p_i) according to the sensors population and the maximum number of keys fitting in the memory of a W-sensor. The parameters have to satisfy: $k_i = m_w$, $g_i = \overline{\omega}_i + \omega_i$ and $g_i \leq C_{k_i + p_i}^{k_i}$.

Then we decide on the parameters of an EBS for S-sensors as follows. Suppose that each cluster has its Physical Cluster (PC) and Upper Layer Group (ULG). PC includes as members all sensors under the control of a certain gateway. (i.e. S-sensors and W-sensors together). ULG contains as members all S-sensors within the WSN. The parameters of an EBS for ULG are constructed in two steps. a) At first, gateway $G(r_i, c_j)$ which is identified by a pair of row and column index (r_i, c_j) (see Fig. 1) forms its PC. b) At the second step, gateway $G(r_i, c_j)$ constructs its upper layer group by taking the union of PCs located inside the $t \times n$ rectangle window that is clipped from the field region such that the top-left corner of the field region. The upper layer group decides the parameters according to the population of all S-sensors in the upper layer group.

ULG_{r_i,c_j} of cluster (r_i, c_j) is constructed as:

$$ULG_{r_i,c_j} = \{\bigcup_{x,y} PC_{x,y} \mid x = i,...,i+t-1, y = j,...,j+n-1\}$$ Consider an example in Fig.1 ($t = 2, n = 2$). The first ULG_{r_1,c_1} has four clusters: PC_{r_1,c_1}, PC_{r_1,c_2}, PC_{r_2,c_1}, PC_{r_2,c_2}. Thus, The first ULG_{r_1,c_1} decides on the parameters of an EBS (g_1', k_1', p_1') for S-sensors, where $k_1' = (m_s - m_w)/(2 \times 2)$, $g_1' = \varpi_1 + \varpi_2 + \varpi_4 + \varpi_5$, $g_1' \leq C_{k_1'+p_1'}^{k_1'}$. The second ULG_{r_1,c_2} decides on the parameters of an EBS (g_2', k_2', p_2') where $k_2' = (m_s - m_w)/4$, $g_2' = \varpi_2 + \varpi_3 + \varpi_5 + \varpi_6$, $g_2' \leq C_{k_2'+p_2'}^{k_2'}$; The ULG_{r_2,c_1} decides on the parameters of an EBS (g_4', k_4', p_4') by $k_4' = (m_s - m_w)/4$, $g_4' = \varpi_4 + \varpi_5 + \varpi_7 + \varpi_8$, $g_4' \leq C_{k_4'+p_4'}^{k_4'}$; and so do other ULGs.

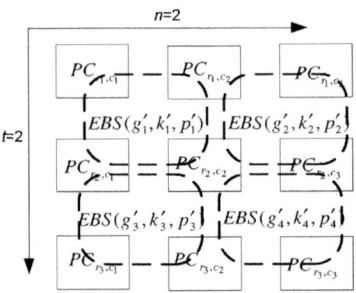

Fig. 1. Parameters of upper layer groups

Last, the command sensor designates for each cluster and generates keys (Based on an EBS (g, k, p)) for the cluster as methods in [5]. Upon generation of keys, each sensor is randomly assigned k_i keys out of $k_i + p_i$ predetermined keys according to the canonical matrix of EBS (g_i, k_i, p_i). We also randomly assign each S-sensor in the ULG k_i' keys out of $k_i' + p_i'$ predetermined keys according to the canonical matrix of EBS (g_i', k_i', p_i'). We distribute all $k_i + p_i$ or $k_i' + p_i'$ keys to each gateway (cluster) that will function as the key generation node (KGN) in the cluster or ULG to which this gateway belongs. The KGN will be used in the sensor segregation phase.

After the deployment, each sensor broadcasts information to neighbor sensors. If they have a common key, they can establish a pair-wise key based on the paper [5]. It is possible that two neighbor sensors can not find any common keys between them. In this case, they need to find a secure way to agree upon a common key.

2) Sensor segregate phase

When some sensors are compromised, we should segregate them from the network to ensure that the security of the network can be maintained. Similar to the EBS scheme described in [7] and [5], we can segregate a sensor by using the KGN to generate k new replacement keys. The new keys will be encrypted p times.

The following messages will be generated for rekeying in each cluster according to EBS (g_i, k_i, p_i):

$$E((A_{k_i+1}(E(A_1(A'_1)),...,E(A_{k_i-1}(A'_{k_i-1})),E(A_{k_i}(A'_{k_i})))))$$

$$...$$

$$E((A_{k_i+p_i}(E(A_1(A'_1)),...,E(A_{k_i-1}(A'_{k_i-1})),E(A_{k_i}(A'_{k_i})))))$$

Where $A_{k_i+1},...,A_{k_i+p_i}$ are unknown to the segregated sensor, $A_1,...,A_{k_i}$ and $A'_1,...,A'_{k_i}$ are the set of old keys and that of new keys.

Consequently, the compromised keys are replaced by the newly generated keys and only the sensors that hold the old keys can update the keys. Hence, we can segregate a compromised sensor from the network.

5 System Configuration

We use the following setup in our analysis and simulations. 1)The size of the region is 800m*800m; 2)The area is equally divided into a square of size 16=4*4; 3)Each square cluster (group) has 50 W-sensors, 5 S-sensors, one gateway, and sensors are assumed to be uniformly deployed. The communication radius of W-sensors is 40m, and the communication radius of S-sensors is 80m; 4) The size of $t \times n$ rectangle window is 2×2.

1) Connectivity

Fig. 2 shows different EBS systems affect to connectivity of one cluster. The value in Fig. 2 is average local connectivity of 16 clusters and the parameter g_i of the EBS (g_i, k_i, p_i) is 55. When the parameter k_i of the EBS (g_i, k_i, p_i) is 3, the average local connectivity will decrease with the increase of p_i, while the average local connectivity will increase with the increase of k_i at $p_i = 5$. The main reason is that the parameter k_i is the number of sensors store keys, and $C_{k_i+p_i}^{k_i}$ is the size of the key pool. If the value of $k_i / C_{k_i+p_i}^{k_i}$ is larger, the local connectivity is much larger.

Fig. 3 depicts the different EBS systems affect to the whole local connectivity. The simulation parameter EBS (g'_i, k'_i, p'_i) is EBS $(20, 3, 4)$. The whole local connectivity is 0.157 when the simulation parameter EBS (g_i, k_i, p_i) is EBS $(55, 3, 5)$ while the whole local connectivity is 0.207 when the simulation parameter EBS (g_i, k_i, p_i) is EBS $(55, 5, 5)$. It can see that the increase of the parameter k_i will increase the local connectivity.

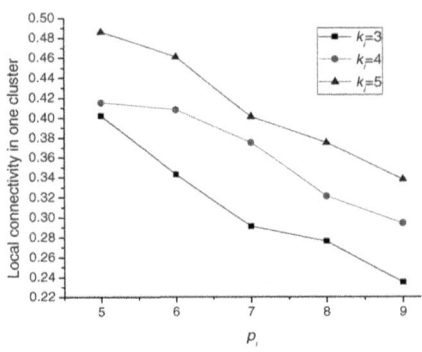 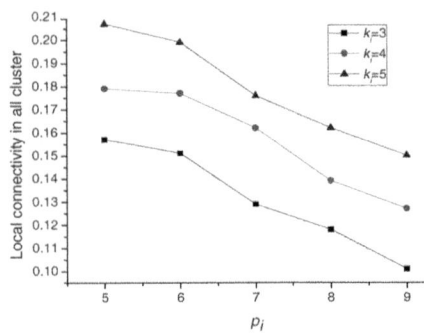

Fig. 2. Local Connectivity of one cluster   **Fig. 3.** Local Connectivity of all clusters

2) Security

Table 1 describes the fraction of communications compromised varies with the number of W-sensors compromised by the attacker. Let N_{cW} be the number of W-sensors compromised. The simulation configuration is as follows: the W-sensors compromised are in the same cluster, the parameters of EBS (g_i, k_i, p_i) is EBS (55, 3, 10), the parameters of EBS (g_i', k_i', p_i') is EBS (20, 3, 4). The values in the table1 are the average fraction of communications compromised in the whole network. From the table, we can see that the fraction of communications compromised will increase with the increase of the number of W-sensors compromised.

Table 1. Fraction of communication compromised VS Number of W-sensors compromised

		$N_{cW} =3$	$N_{cW} =4$	$N_{cW} =5$
Fraction	**of**	0.144	0.218	0.318
communications		$N_{cW} =6$	$N_{cW} =7$	$N_{cW} =8$
compromised				

Table 2 describes the number of affected sensors varies with the number of S-sensors compromised by the attacker. Let N_{cS} be the number of W-sensors compromised. The simulation configuration is as follows. The S-sensors compromised are in the same cluster, the parameters of EBS (g_i, k_i, p_i) is EBS $(55, 3, 10)$, the parameters of EBS (g_i', k_i', p_i') is EBS（ 20, 3, 4） . When the number of S-sensors compromised is 3, the number of affected W-sensors is 19 and the number of affected S-sensors is about 3.6.

Table 2. Number of affected sensors VS Number of S-sensors compromised

	1	2	3	4	5
Number of affected W-sensors	8.6	13.6	19.0	26.9	30.3
Number of affected S-sensors	0.8	2.5	3.6	4.8	5.9

6   Conclusions

In this paper, we have presented, DCKP, a dynamic combinatorial key pre-distribution scheme for heterogeneous sensor networks. DCKP is based on Exclusion Basis Systems methodology for group key management. DCKP use S-sensors' locations to decide on the parameters of an EBS for W-sensors, S-sensors, and gateways. Simulation results have demonstrated that DCKP significantly boosts the network resiliency to node capture while conservatively consuming the network's critical resources.

Acknowledgments. This work was supported by the Government of Ontario under the ORF-RE WISENSE project (3074600).

References

1. Deng, J., et al.: Multipath Key Establishment for Wireless Sensor Networks Using Just-enough Redundancy Transmission. IEEE Transaction on Dependable and Secure Computing 5(3), 177–190 (2008)
2. Simonova, K., Ling, A.C.H., Wang, X.S.: Location-aware Key Pre-distribution Scheme for Wide Area Wireless Sensor Networks. In: Proceedings of 4th ACM Workshop on Security of Ad-hoc and Sensor Networks, Alexandria, Virginia, USA, pp. 157–168 (2006)
3. Pathan, A.S.K., Hyung-Woo, L.: Security in Wireless Sensor Networks: Issues and Challenges. In: The 8th International Conference on Advanced Communication Technology, ICACT 2006, vol. 2 (2006)
4. A Study of Static versus Dynamic Keying Schemes in Sensor Networks, http://portal.acm.org/citation.cfm?id=1089976
5. Younis, M., Ghumman, K., Eltoweissy, M.: Location-aware Combinatorial Key Management Scheme for Clustered Sensor Networks. IEEE Trans. Parallel and Distrib. Sys., 865–882 (2006)
6. Yarvis, M., et al.: Exploiting Heterogeneity in Sensor Networks. In: Proceedings of the IEEE INFOCOM 2005, Miami, FL (2005)
7. Eltoweissy, M., et al.: Combinatorial Optimization of Key Management in Group Communications. Journal of Network and Systems Management: Special Issue on Network Security 12(1) (2004)
8. Eschenauer, L., Gligor, V.D.: A Key-management Scheme for Distributed Sensor Networks. In: Proceedings of 9th ACM Conference on Computer and Communication Security, pp. 41–47 (2002)
9. Jolly, G., et al.: A Low-energy Key Management Protocol for Wireless Sensor Networks. In: The Proceedings of the IEEE Symposium on Computers and Communications (ISCC 2003), Kemer Antalya, Turkey, June 30-July 3 (2003)
10. Eltoweissy, M., et al.: Group Key Management Scheme for Large-scale Wireless Sensor Network. J. Ad Hoc Networks, 796–802 (September 2005)
11. Lu, K., Qian, Y., Hu, J.C.: A Framework for Distributed Key Management Schemes in Heterogeneous Wireless Sensor Networks. In: IEEE International Performance Computing and Communications Conference, pp. 513–519 (2006)
12. Key Management Schemes for Secure Communication in Heterogeneous Sensor Networks, http://academypublisher.com/ijrte/vol01/no01/ijrte0101243247.pdf

Exclusion Based VANETs (EBV)

Ahmad A. Al-Daraiseh[1] and Mohammed A. Moharrum[2]

King Saud University
Riyadh, Kingdom of Saudi Arabia
[1] College of Computer and Information Science
[2] Center of Excellence in Information Assurance
{adaraiseh,mmorsi}@ksu.edu.sa

Abstract. Vehicular Ad hoc NETworks (VANETs) were proposed to improve driving safety. In VANETs vehicles communicate with other vehicles and with the infrastructure's Road Side Units (RSUs) to achieve this safety. 5.9 GHz band was assigned by FCC for the use of VANETs in Dedicated Short Range Communications (DSRC) [1]. VANETs' security has been a hot topic since the very first day of its announcement. While IEEE 1609.2 is setting security standards for VANETS, many researches around the world are working hard to provide an ideal system. IEEE 1609.2 chose Public Key Infrastructure (PKI) to be used in VANETs [2]. PKI comes with its inherent issues such as key management and Certificate revocation lists (CRLs) in addition to issues related to wireless networks such privacy and linkability. In this paper we propose Exclusion-Based Vanet (EBV), a novel framework based on a combination of PKI and Exclusion Based Systems (EBS) [3] to address the above issues. EBV eliminates the need for CRLs, guarantees privacy and scalability.

Keywords: VANETS, Security, EBS, Privacy, Revocation, Scalability Framework, PKI, Hybrid.

1 Introduction

Securing VANETs is a very challenging task due to conflicting interests such as privacy and linkability, in addition to size and mobility of such networks and time and hardware limitations. Despite the fact that PKI is very successful in the internet, we believe that PKI alone might not be able to fulfill all the security requirements exist in VANETs.

VANETs security involves message integrity and authentication, vehicle privacy, non-repudiation and long term linkability for investigation purposes. Moreover, all message processing needs to be almost real-time due to the fact that an old message for a safety application may lose its value after a short period of time. Considering a transmission range of 150 m (i.e. 300 diameters), heartbeat message frequency of 10Hz as suggested in [4], number of messages, CRL size and the hardware limitations, a VANET's security system must be very swift and efficient.

In this paper we propose Exclusion-Based Vanet (EBV), a framework that uses a combination of PKI and EBS to deal with VANET's security issues. In our proposed

J.J. Park et al. (Eds.): STA 2011, CCIS 186, pp. 96–104, 2011.

framework, the network architecture and key management utilize EBS. EBV's main contribution is the elimination of CRLs, vehicle privacy, long term linkability, scalability and efficiency.

The remainder of this paper is organized as follows. In section II, a discussion of the latest related work is given. In section III, EBS, EBV and EBV's phases of operation are presented. In section V, analysis is provided. In section VI, conclusions are drawn and future work is discussed.

2 Related Work

The current IEEE 1609.2 standard for secure VANETs communication proposes the use of the Elliptic Curve Digital Signature Algorithm (ECDSA) for signatures to verify messages [2]. For authentication, TESLA appears to provide an efficient alternative to signatures since it uses symmetric cryptography with delayed key disclosure to provide the necessary asymmetry to prove the sender was the source of a message. However, TESLA is vulnerable to memory-based Denial of Service attacks. A. Studer et al. [5] provides a hybrid authentication mechanism, VANETs Authentication using Signatures and TESLA++ (VAST), that combines the advantages of ECDSA signatures and TESLA++.

Prior work has shown that the verification of a single ECDSA signature requires 7ms of computation on proposed OBU hardware [6]. Several other solutions have been proposed to address security-related problems in VANETs. According to [7], these proposals can be classified into two classes: Public Key Infrastructure (PKI) and the ID-Public Key Cryptosystem (ID-PKC). PKI-based solutions use group signature, as a cryptographic basis, to achieve the security goals mentioned earlier. For efficiency and scalability reasons, researchers tried to combine PKI-based systems with other cryptographic based systems, such as ID-based cryptography. In the following sub-sections, we review literature for related work in the two classes.

2.1 PKI-Based Proposals

There have been several proposals for achieving security requirements in VANETs based on PKI. There are early schemes [8] and [9] or more advanced schemes which may be classified as either with pseudonyms [10], [11], [12], [8] or group signature [13], [14], [15], [16], [6]. Pseudonyms have been used to protect the real identity of the vehicles.

2.2 ID-PKC Proposals

Since PKI-based frameworks suffer from overhead of Certificate Revocation Lists (CRLs), other security frameworks were used. ID-Public Key Cryptosystem (ID-PKC) [5] have been introduced in [17], [16], [7], and [18]. In such cryptosystem, the user's information, such as phone number and e-mail address, can be used as his public key for verification and encryption. In other words, the ID-based cryptosystem simplifies the certificate management process.

3 The Proposed Framework

We propose EBV, a new key management framework that utilizes Exclusion-Based System [3] to provide better efficiency as well as security features. We start by providing a background about the EBS, and then we move to our proposed EBV.

3.1 The Exclusion Basis Systems (EBS)

EBS is a combinatorial framework for group key management. An EBS is defined as a collection Γ of subsets of the set of members [3]. Each subset corresponds to a key and the elements of a subset $A \in \Gamma$ are the nodes that have that key. An EBS Γ of dimension (N, k, m) represents a situation in a secure group where there are N members numbered 1 through N, and where a key server holds a distinct key for each subset in Γ. If the subset A_i is in Γ, then each of the members whose number appears in the subset A_i knows the distinct key (provided by the key server) for that subset. Furthermore, for each $t \in [0, N-1]$ there are m elements in Γ whose union is $[0, N-1] - \{t\}$. From this it follows that the key server can evict any member t, re-key, and let all remaining members know the replacement keys for the k keys they are entitled to know, by multicasting m messages encrypted by the keys corresponding to the m elements in Γ whose union is $[0, N-1] - \{t\}$.

Re-keying an EBS-based system is illustrated using the following example. Assume that there are 15 members in the group. Suppose member N_0 has been compromised. Since N_0 possesses keys K_1, K_2, K_3 and K_4 these will have to be redistributed. Except N_0 every member has at least a key in the set $(K_5 \cup K_6)$. Hence, the keys used for re-keying will be K_5 and K_6. The following messages will be generated for re-keying:

Message 1: $E (K_5 (S', E (K_1 (K_1')), E (K_2 (K_2')), E (K_3 (K_3'), E (K_4 (K_4')))))$

Message 2: $E (K_6 (S', E (K_1 (K_1')), E (K_2 (K_2')), E (K_3 (K_3'), E (K_4 (K_4')))))$,

Where $E (K_1 (K_1')) \rightarrow$ key K_1' is encrypted with key K_1 and S' is the new session key for the cluster.

The way these messages are constructed ensures that only the legitimate nodes will be able to decrypt the new keys. Thus, as a result of the above messages being broadcasted, member N_0 will be evicted and the new keys K_1', K_2', K_3' and K_4' will be made available to only those nodes that possessed keys K_1, K_2 K_3, and K_4.

3.2 The Exclusion Based VANETs (EBV)

EBV is a novel framework that utilizes EBS and PKI to create a robust, efficient and scalable security solution for VANETs. EBV hierarchy is illustrated in Fig. 1. Such hierarch consists of the following entities:

1. Global VANET Authority (GVA): a trusted party that registers and manages CVAs, run by an international cooperation.
2. Country VANET Authority (CVA): a trusted country wide authority that registers all country's RVAs, run by national DMV.

3. Regional VANET Authority (RVA): a trusted regional authority that manages an EBS system in a specific region (could be a city or a state), run by regional DMV.
4. Road Side Unit (RSU): is a node in VANETs that relays messages between vehicles and RVAs and vice versa. An RSU logs all received messages temporarily and upload to its RVA periodically. RSUs could be used to broadcast safety messages amongst many other functions. In EBV, an RSU is treated as a stationary special vehicle. RSUs located at borders (regional or country) will register in two or more RVAs.
5. Vehicles: normal vehicles and special ones (e.g. Police and emergency vehicles).

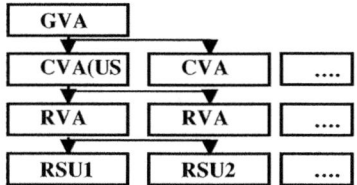

Fig. 1. Shows how EBV is structured

Before we start further description of EBV, we assume the following:

1. GVAs, CVAs and RVAs are trusted and secure entities that use PKI to securely communicate. A medium to high speed wired connection is mandated.
2. RSUs and OBUs are tamper proof.
3. RSUs are connected to RVAs with a high speed wired connection. In remote areas though, a 3G or 4G connection could be utilized.

The idea of EBV is to use EBS keys in every region. All vehicles and RSUs in a specific region will use one session key, S, to communicate. An RVA is responsible for creating the administrative keys (using EBS) and the session key. After distributing the keys to newly registered vehicles, a vehicle can use the session key to communicate with other vehicles or RSUs. GVA, CVAs and RVAs will use PKI to securely communicate with each other.

Evicting a vehicle occurs at an RVA when a vehicle misbehaves and the RVA decides that this vehicle needs to be evicted. An RVA generates new administrative keys and a new session key S`. The new session key will be broadcast to all vehicles by sending m messages to all RSUs; each contains the key encrypted with one of the m keys that the evicted vehicle does not have. RSUs will broadcast all messages. Receiving vehicles will extract session key and use to generate new administrative keys. Upon completing this process, all vehicles other than the evicted vehicle will be able to communicate using the new session key S`.

3.3 EBV Main Phases

Initialization Phase
When an RVA is deployed, it calculates a canonical matrix A with a large number of columns (i.e. larger than the number of vehicles expected in this region in the next 20 years). When choosing k and m an RVA preserves the following:

- The number of keys is kept small (i.e. k + m).
- m should be large enough (i.e. the number of vehicles an attacker needs to attack to reveal all keys of the group should be very large). Although this will increase the number of messages in case of rekeying, this should be acceptable considering that rekeying will not happen with high rate.

We propose the numbers k = 8 and m = 50. This will give us enough columns to support C(58,8) = 1916797311 vehicles. Please refer to the analysis section for more justification of the numbers we used. The RVA Then generates 58 admin keys and one common key K_{com} known to all valid vehicles.

RVA initially loads every vehicle and RSU with the following (probably during first registration/ or first registration after VANET deployment):

- ID (probably VIN number plus some random number).
- KGF a one-way trapdoor Key Generation Function that uses tow inputs to create a random number.
- S the current session key in this area.
- A set of 9 admin keys generated by RVA. RVA maps every vehicle ID to a column in the matrix A.
- A bit string of 58 bits that represents the column from Matrix A assigned to this specific vehicle.
- RVA Public key (e).

Normal Operation Phase

Every vehicle and RSU use the current session key S to securely communicate safety messages as follows:

$$E (S (message)) \tag{1}$$

The session key, S, is changed regularly to prevent statistical attacks. This could be done every few hours. The new key S' will be sent out through RSUs to all vehicles encrypted as follows:

$$E (S (E (K_{com}(S')))) \text{ signed by RVA's private key} \tag{2}$$

This way, even if the current session key was jeopardized, the new one is not. Also all vehicles will know that only an RVA could have generated this message because of the signature.

This message will be stored until the next update occurs. If a vehicle V is met with another V' that uses the previous session key S_{old}, all V has to do is to replay the session key update message.

For long term likability by authorities, every vehicle will append its ID to a time stamp, encrypt both with the RVA's public key and append to every message. This would increase the size of every message by the number of bits added. This way, only an RVA can link a message to its vehicle. This sort of signature will prevent short term linkability since the signature will be different with every message sent. Every other vehicle shouldn't decrypt the attached signature it receives. If the messages received are encrypted with S then the sender is valid.

Rekey phase

RSUs relay complaint messages to RVA. RVA may decide that a certain vehicle needs to be evicted due to large number of complaints according to a certain criteria. RVA starts a rekey process in the region, where all keys known to the evicted vehicle V_e will be modified by every other vehicle.

The process starts by RVA issuing a new session key S' and k admin keys to replace the keys the evicted vehicle has. Assuming V_e knows K_{e1} through K_{ek} and does not know K_1 through K_m, RVA generates replacement keys by repeating the following operation k times once for each key:

$$K_{ei}' = KGF (S', K_{ei}) \qquad (3)$$

Where KGF is a one-way trapdoor Key Generation Function, that uses two inputs to create a random number. RVA notifies all vehicles to replace the keys they share with V_e, by broadcasting V_e' bit-string (BSV_e) in a message composed of the following m parts:

$$part_i = K_{index}, E (K_i (S')) \qquad (4)$$

where $1 <= i <= m$, and K_{index} is the index of K_i. And the message:

$$M = E (S (\text{"rekey"}, BSV_e, part_1, part_2, ...part_m)) \qquad (5)$$

This message will be signed with RVA's private key (d), so that a vehicle V can validate the message.

Upon receiving the message, Each RSU broadcasts the message on behalf of the RVA several times separated by certain amount of time.

After verifying a received message, a vehicle uses the session key to decrypt the first level of encryption and extract BSV_e and m parts. It checks the BSV_e to see if it shares any keys with the evicted vehicle. If so, it continues to decrypt one of the m parts with K_j, any of its k keys. Once it decrypts any of the m parts, it replaces all the shared keys by executing operations similar to (3).

Every vehicle should store the rekey message it received until the next eviction or periodic change of admin keys occurs. If any vehicle V is met with another one V' that was away from the RSU broadcast and didn't get the update, V' will be using a different session key, all V has to do is replay the saved message, if V' is valid then it should be able to decrypt and replace its k keys.

Evicting a vehicle takes place only after the number of complaints against this vehicle exceeds a specific threshold. To put an evicted vehicle V_e back in the system, V_e has to visit the RVA center and have them update its keys.

4 EBV Analysis

In this section, we analyze the proposed EBV. We focus on overhead incurred over different entities, and then we analyze the choice of different parameters and its effect on efficiency as well as possible collusion. We discuss how EBV is resilient to different attacks.

4.1   Computational Overhead

Any regular vehicle maintains the k keys as well as the session key. For every message, the vehicle adds its ID plus Time Stamp encrypted with RVA public key, which consumes around 20 Bytes. In addition to this, the message body should be around 100 Bytes, which totals to 120 Bytes. It uses the session key for symmetric encryption, which is much lower than PKI from time point of view. When rekeying takes place, the rekey message will consist of 50 parts, each consisting of 7 bit index and 16 byte key a total of 844 Bytes plus 13 Bytes for the word "rekey" and BSV_e.

4.2   Proper Choice of EBS Parameters

In [19], an analysis of efficiency and collusion resilience was introduced for EBS-based schemes. Any evicted vehicles might collude together to reveal system keys before rekeying takes place. They measure c_{min}, the required number of entities that need to collude to reveal all system keys. They stated that if we select k>m, there exist two users whose collaboration might reveal all the k+m keys. And for any other values for k and m, c_{min} cannot exceed m+1. If we have c colluders, then the probability that they collectively can reveal k+m administrative keys is shown in equation (6).

$$p = \left(1 - \prod_{i=1}^{c} \frac{\binom{k+m-1}{k} - i + 1}{\binom{k+m}{k} - i + 1}\right)^{k+m} \tag{6}$$

In order to minimize such probability from one hand and to maximize the number of potential vehicles, or columns in the EBV matrix, we may select m=50 and k=8. This choice will allow the canonical matrix to include C(58,8) = 1916797311 possible vehicles per RVA, which much exceeds the 10.699 million vehicles registered in New York City in 2009 [20]. At the same time, the probability that 15 concurrently evicted vehicles may collude to reveal the administrative keys before rekeying takes place is 0.1%.

If the number of vehicles in a region approaches the number of combinations in EBV, one key could be added to m to double the number of vehicles or the region is split.

Deploying EBV incrementally can be done by having only an RVA and a few RSU. Considering that vehicles store and relay RVA's messages, EBV emphasizes V-V and relies less on R-I communication, and hence, fewer RSUs are needed upon deployment of such system.

4.3   Handling Attacks

In this section we discuss how EBV handles known attacks in VANETS.

1. *Bogus information attack:* In EBV a session key S is used to encrypt messages. This key is changed every few hours. We believe that breaking this key within few hours is highly unlikely with current hardware and techniques.
2. *Unauthorized preemption attack:* In our proposed system any special vehicle will have its ID signed by the RVA private key. RSU, traffic lights and other vehicles will be able to verify that and act accordingly.

3. *Message replay attack:* In EBV, in addition to TP OBU assumption, and frequent key update, a time stamp is attached to every message to limit that. Such attacks could also be used to flood the network: handling this could be done in the physical layer which is out of the scope of this research.

4. *Message modification attack:* If done before an event happens it becomes similar to attack No. 1, Otherwise, modifying one's log will not matter since all traffic is logged by RVAs.

5. *Impersonation attack:* In EBV, RSUs and Special vehicles are protected through their signed certificates; all other vehicles are equal so there is no point in impersonating a regular vehicle.

6. *RSU relocation attack:* In EBV, RSUs are tamper proof, attach their signature and original location to all messages, included in both the signature as well as in the message itself, when relocated it will be easily discovered.

7. *DOS:* We believe this type of attack should be handled by the lower layers and out of the scope of this research.

8. *Movement tracking:* In EBV, short term linkability is not possible due to the fact that all vehicles in a region use the same key, and attach different signatures.

9. *Impersonating an RSU:* Since an RSU in EBV is treated as a special vehicle (as far as security is concerned) RSU will have a certificate signed by the RVA's private Key, this way any vehicle can verify that the sender is indeed an RSU.

10. *Malicious vehicle:* In EBV, the only thing an RVA needs to do to link a message to its vehicle is to decrypt the second part of every message which includes an ID and TS.

11. *Brute force attack:* Changing the session key periodically and the admin keys every eviction or regularly every day may be, will make this very hard.

12. *Illusion attack:* We believe that this attack has the same effect as #1.

5 Conclusion and Future Work

Key and CRL management in VANETs is very difficult and time consuming task. While many proposed frameworks for VANETs handled some of the attacks listed, we believe they will not be adopted because any or a combination of: Large number of : certificates or pseudonyms , large computation time, large communication overhead, lack of scalability, or inability to defend some other attacks.

Our proposed framework EBV uses symmetric key for efficiency, eliminates the need for CRLs and pseudonyms, very scalable and defends against a wide range of attacks.

We believe that some more analysis and simulation is needed (especially to set timing parameters) to compare it to other frameworks, also we would like to reduce relying on TPDs. This was left for future work.

References

1. (FCC), U.F.C.C.: Standard specification for Telecommunications and Information Exchange Between Roadside and Vehicle Systems - 5 GHz Band Dedicated Short Range Communications (DSRC) Medium Access Control (MAC) and Physical Layer (PHY) Specifications. In: Book Standard specification for Telecommunications and Information Exchange Between Roadside and Vehicle Systems (September 2003)

2. IEEE: 1609.2: Trial-use standard for wireless access in vehicular environments-security services for applications and management messages. IEEE Standards 2006 (2006)
3. Eltoweissy, M., Heydari, M.H., Morales, L., Sudborough, I.H.: Combinatorial Optimization of Group Key Management. Journal of Network and Systems Management 12(1), 33–50 (2004)
4. Communications, V.S.: Vehicle safety communications project-final report (2006)
5. Studer, A., Bai, F., Bellur, B., Perrig, A.: Flexible, Extensible, and Efficient VANET authentication. In: Proc. in 6th Conference on Embedded Security in Cars, Escar (2008)
6. Raya, M., Hubaux, J.-P.: Securing vehicular ad hoc networks. Journal of Computer Security 15(1), 39–68 (2007)
7. Li, C.-T., Hwang, M.-S., Chu, Y.-P.: A secure and efficient communication scheme with authenticated key establishment and privacy preserving for vehicular ad hoc networks. Computer Communications 31(12), 2803–2814 (2008)
8. Amit Kumar, S., David, B.J.: Modeling mobility for vehicular ad-hoc networks. In: Proceedings of the 1st ACM International Workshop on Vehicular Ad Hoc Networks, Philadelphia, PA, USA (2004)
9. Sampigethaya, K., Huang, L., Li, M., Poovendran, R., Matsuura, K., Sezaki, K.: CARAVAN: Providing Location Privacy for VANET. In: Proc. 3rd International Workshop on Vehicular Ad Hoc Networks (2006)
10. Beresford, A.R., Stajano, F.: Mix zones: user privacy in location-aware services. In: Book Mix Zones: User Privacy in Location-Aware Services, pp. 127–131 (2004)
11. Gerlach, M., Guttler, F.: Privacy in VANETs using Changing Pseudonyms - Ideal and Real. In: Book Privacy in VANETs Using Changing Pseudonyms - Ideal and Real, pp. 2521–2525 (2007)
12. Philippe, G., Dan, G., Jessica, S.: Detecting and correcting malicious data in VANETs. In: Proceedings of the 1st ACM International Workshop on Vehicular Ad Hoc Networks, Philadelphia, PA, USA (2004)
13. Franklin, M., Boneh, D., Boyen, X., Shacham, H.: Short Group Signatures. In: Franklin, M. (ed.) CRYPTO 2004. LNCS, vol. 3152, pp. 41–55. Springer, Heidelberg (2004)
14. Jinhua, G., Baugh, J.P., Shengquan, W.: A Group Signature Based Secure and Privacy-Preserving Vehicular Communication Framework. In: Book A Group Signature Based Secure and Privacy-Preserving Vehicular Communication Framework, pp. 103–108 (2007)
15. Leping, H., Matsuura, K., Yamane, H., Sezaki, K.: Enhancing wireless location privacy using silent period. In: Book Enhancing Wireless Location Privacy Using Silent Period, vol. 1182, pp. 1187–1192 (2005)
16. Xiaodong, L., Rongxing, L., Chenxi, Z., Haojin, Z., Pin-Han, H., Xuemin, S.: Security in vehicular ad hoc networks. IEEE Communications Magazine 46(4), 88–95 (2008)
17. Pandurang, K., Arati, B., Wade, T.: An identity-based security framework For VANETs. In: Proceedings of the 3rd International Workshop on Vehicular Ad Hoc Networks, Los Angeles, CA, USA (2006)
18. Xiong, H., Qin, Z., Fagen, L.: Secure Vehicle-to-roadside Communication Protocol Using Certificate-based Cryptosystem. IETE Technical Review 27(3) (2010)
19. Moharrum, M., Mukkamala, R., Eltoweissy, M.: A novel collusion-resilient architecture for secure group communication in wireless ad-hoc networks. Journal of High Speed Networks 15(1), 73–92 (2006)
20. DMV, N.: Vehicle Registrations in Force. In: Book Vehicle Registrations in Force (2009)

Embedding Edit Distance to Allow Private Keyword Search in Cloud Computing

Julien Bringer and Hervé Chabanne[*]

Morpho
`surname.name@morpho.com`

Abstract. Recently, Li et al. introduced a fuzzy keyword search over encrypted data in Cloud Computing. Their approach relies on fuzzy keyword sets which are used by a symmetric searchable encryption protocol. The idea behind these fuzzy keyword sets is to index -- before the search phase -- the exact keywords but also the ones differing slightly according to a fixed bound on the tolerated edit distance. We here suggest a different construction. We exploit a classical embedding of the edit distance into the Hamming distance. This enables us to adapt results on private identification schemes to this new context. This way of doing implies more flexibility on the tolerated edit distance.

Keywords: Edit distance, Embeddings for edit distance, Private Identification schemes.

1 Introduction

Cloud Computing enables users to have access to shared resources somewhere on the Internet. At least, some storage capacities can easily be envisaged. This brings many sensitive information in the Cloud where they should stay, to preserve their confidentiality, encrypted. To look at their content remotely (and without decrypting them), some specific procedures have been developed. Searchable encryption [6] builds up an index for each keyword of interest. This way, a user can search over his encrypted data for such a keyword and retrieve the files containing it. Note that this search should be made with great care, for privacy reasons, in order for the Cloud to not be able to find out what is the underlying keyword. Symmetric Searchable Encryption (SSE) as introduced by [10] relies on symmetric encryption primitives for efficiency reasons. In [19], Li *et al.* build on SSE for a solution for fuzzy keyword search over encrypted data in Cloud Computing. The fuzziness should here be understood as minor typos introduced by users when entering the request through their keyboard. In this context, the edit distance (Levenshtein distance) is relevant to measure the strings similarity. [19] considers two different techniques: wildcard-based and gram-based techniques, for achieving fuzzy keyword search over encrypted data. These two methods build a set consisting of the searched keyword and the nearby words according to the used technique. For instance, for the keyword CASTLE, the fuzzy keyword set for wildcard-based technique contains for instance,

---

[*] Hervé Chabanne is also with Télécom ParisTech.

J.J. Park et al. (Eds.): STA 2011, CCIS 186, pp. 105–113, 2011.
© Springer-Verlag Berlin Heidelberg 2011

*ASTLE, C*STLE, ... (respectively, CSTLE, CATLE, ... for the gram-based technique) for an edit distance of 1. Our approach is somewhat different. In their works on private identification, Bringer et al. [1, 7, 8] (see also Section 3.1) actually show how to carry out fuzzy keyword search for the Hamming distance. Our idea is to combine this with a classical embedding of edit distance into the Hamming distance [21, 22] (see Section 3.2) to obtain a fuzzy keyword search for the edit distance. This way of doing has at least two advantages. Firstly, our way of proceeding does not need to a priori define the set of words which are considered as acceptable for the search. Moreover, we inherit of the security properties of [7] in their security model. Note that our proposal thus relies on an asymmetric security model. This can be seen as an asset for Cloud Computing applications. Indeed, using public-key encryption seems relevant in this context.

2 Model Presentation

2.1 Entities for the Protocol

The context is Cloud Computing where users can either store or retrieve data from the Cloud. This leads to three different entities:

- The Cloud CL which represents a single point of access to remote shared resources (i.e. a remote storage system). The Cloud is assumed to be untrusted, so we consider the content as publicly accessible to a third party and that communications in the Cloud and with users can be eavesdropped.
- The sender x sends data to be stored on the Cloud CL.
- The receiver y generates queries to the Cloud CL to obtain the results of his searches.

Note that the sender and the receiver are not necessarily the same user and it is even possible that several senders and several receivers exist and interact. This corresponds well to the Cloud Computing model.

2.2 Definition of the Primitives

In the sequel, messages are strings of length N, and $ed(m_1, m_2)$ denotes the edit distance between $m_1, m_2 \in \{0,1\}^N$, i.e. the minimum number of character insertions, deletions and substitutions needed to transform one string into the other. Note that edit distance is well defined on larger alphabet and variable length strings. The model of [7] can be extended to these cases.

Definition 1. *A $(\varepsilon, \lambda_{min}, \lambda_{max})$ -Public Key Error-Tolerant Searchable Encryption for the edit distance is obtained with the following probabilistic polynomial-time methods:*

- *KeyGen(1^ℓ) initializes the system, and generates public and private keys (pk, sk) for a security parameter ℓ. The public key pk is used to store data in the Cloud, and the secret key sk is used to retrieve information.*

- Send$_{X,CL}(m, pk)$ *is a protocol in which* X *sends to* CL *the data* $m \in \{0,1\}^N$ *to be stored in the Cloud. At the end of the protocol,* CL *has stored the message* m *at a virtual address noted* $\varphi(m)$.

- Retrieve$_{Y,CL}(m', sk)$ *is a protocol in which, given a fresh message* $m' \in \{0,1\}^N$, Y *asks for the virtual addresses of all data that are stored on* CL *and are close to* m', *with respect to the Completeness(* λ_{min} *) and Soundness(* λ_{max} *) criteria (cf. Section 2.3). This outputs a set of virtual addresses, noted* $\Phi(m')$, *where* Y *can reach the corresponding messages.*

We emphasize that the definition above is focused on the searching problem (which is the tough task here): the algorithms' outputs are the virtual addresses where the retriever Y can retrieve the messages. The messages are possibly stored encrypted via a second encryption scheme.

An important difference compared to [19] is that we do not rely on fuzzy keyword sets, we want to ensure a given tolerance (materialized by $\lambda_{min}, \lambda_{max}$). By avoiding wildcards and grams, we do not make any prior assumption on the location of the errors.

2.3   Security Requirements

Condition 1 (Completenes and Soundness). *Let* m_1, ..., $m_p \in \{0,1\}^N$ *be* p *different binary strings, and let* $m' \in \{0,1\}^N$ *be another string. Assume that, after initialization of the system, all the messages* m_i *have been stored in the Cloud* CL *with virtual addresses* $\varphi(x_i)$, *and that a user* Y *retrieved the set of virtual addresses* $\Phi(m')$ *associated to* m'.

*1. The scheme is said to be **complete**, up to a probability* $1 - \varepsilon_1$ *if*

$$\Pr_{m'}[\exists i, ed(m', m_i) \leq \lambda_{min} \& \varphi(m_i) \notin \Phi(m')] \leq \varepsilon_1$$

(i.e. that except with a small probability all close messages are retrieved during the search through a Retrieve *query).*

*2. The scheme is said to be **sound**, up to a probability* $1 - \varepsilon_2$ *if*

$$\Pr_{m'}[\exists i, d(m', m_i) > \lambda_{max} \& \varphi(m_i) \in \Phi(m')]$$

is bounded by ε_2 *(i.e. that a false positive happens only with a small probability).*

Condition 2 (Privacy). *The scheme is said to respect Sender Privacy if the advantage of any server is negligible in the* $\text{Exp}_A^{SenderPrivacy}$ *experiment, described below. Here,* A *is a malicious opponent taking the place of* CL, *and* C *is a challenger at the user side.*

$\mathrm{Exp}_A^{\mathrm{SenderPrivacy}}$

1.	(pk, sk)	$\leftarrow$	KeyGen(1^ℓ)	(C)
2.	$\{m_2,\ldots,m_\Omega\}$	$\leftarrow$	A	(A)
3.	$\varphi(m_i)$	$\leftarrow$	Send$_{C,CL}(m_i, pk)$	(C)
4.	$\{m_0, m_1\}$	$\leftarrow$	A	(A)
5.	$\varphi(m_e)$	$\leftarrow$	Send$_{C,CL}(m_e, pk)$	(C)
			$e \in_R \{0,1\}$	

6. Repeat steps$(2,3)$

7.	$e' \in \{0,1\}$	$\leftarrow$	A	(A)

The advantage of the adversary is $|\Pr[e' = e] - \frac{1}{2}|$.

Condition 3 (Privacy) *The scheme is said to respect Receiver Privacy if the advantage of the Cloud is negligible in the experiment* $\mathrm{Exp}_A^{\mathrm{ReceiverPrivacy}}$ *described below.* A *denotes the malicious opponent taking the place of* CL, *and* C *the challenger at the user side.*

$\mathrm{Exp}_A^{\mathrm{ReceiverPrivacy}}$

1.	(pk, sk)	$\leftarrow$	KeyGen(1^ℓ)	(C)
2.	$\{m_1,\ldots,m_\Omega\}$	$\leftarrow$	A	(A)
3.	$\varphi(m_i), (i \in \{1,\ldots,\Omega\})$	$\leftarrow$	Send$_{C,CL}(m_i, pk)$	(C)
4.	$\{m'_2,\ldots,m'_p\}$	$\leftarrow$	A	(A)
5.	$\Phi(m'_j), (j \in \{2,\ldots,p\})$	$\leftarrow$	Retrieve$_{C,CL}(m'_j, sk)$	(C)
6.	(m'_0, m'_1)	$\leftarrow$	A	(A)
7.	$\Phi(m'_e)$	$\leftarrow$	Retrieve$_{C,CL}(m'_e, sk)$	(C)
			$e \in_R \{0,1\}$	

8. Repeat steps$(4,5)$

9.	$e' \in \{0,1\}$	$\leftarrow$	A	(A)

The advantage of the adversary is $|\Pr[e' = e] - \frac{1}{2}|$.

3 Useful Technical Tools

3.1 Private Identification Schemes

The principle of a private identification scheme is to manage nearest neighbor search in the encrypted domain. The two main sub-problems are the Approximate Nearest Neighbor (ANN) problem and Searchable Encryption

The Approximate Nearest Neighbor (ANN) problem is defined as follows: Let P be a set of points in a metric space (E, d_E). For an input $x \in E$ and $\varepsilon \geq 0$, find a point $p_x \in$ P such that $d_E(x, p_x) \leq (1+\varepsilon) \min_{p \in P} d_E(x, p)$.

This is an approximation of the Nearest Neighbor problem as the exact case is hard to solve in large dimension spaces. Several algorithms for the ANN problem have been proposed [25] and the basic principle is to rely on sketching methods which output shorter vectors with increased stability and which enable to simplify the search: P is preprocessed with such sketching to end-up with a look-up table of short vectors on which the search can be realized quickly through counting the number of the exact or almost exact matches. Sketching needs there to guarantee that two close inputs would give with a good probability the same short vector. Examples of sketching methods are numerous for vector space (with Hamming distance or Euclidean distance) [2, 17, 18, 26]; for instance random projections on small subspace. In the private identification schemes [1, 7, 8], the authors suggest to use a construction exploited in [16] for iris biometry. This is adapted to binary vectors with Hamming distance comparison. The sketching functions are restriction of n bits vectors over $r \ll n$ of their coordinates to obtain r bits vectors:

Definition 2. *Let* $\mathsf{F} = (f_1, \ldots, f_\mu)$ *be a family of function from* $\{0,1\}^n$ *to* $\{0,1\}^r$ *such that for* $x \in \{0,1\}^n$, *we have for all* $i \in \{1, \ldots, \mu\}$, $f_i(x) = (x_{i_1}, \ldots, x_{i_r})$. *We say that* F *is a sketching family for the Hamming distance from dimension* n *to dimension* r.

With a sketching family where all functions are independent and if we assume that the inputs are uniformly distributed, the probability to obtain the same output with two distinct inputs can be estimated as follows.

$$\forall x, x' \in \{0,1\}^n \begin{cases} Pr_{f \in \mathsf{F}}[f(x) = f(x') | d(x, x') < \lambda_1] > (1 - \frac{\lambda_1}{n})^r \\ Pr_{f \in \mathsf{F}}[f(x) = f(x') | d(x, x') > \lambda_2] < (1 - \frac{\lambda_2}{n})^r \end{cases}$$

In our construction, we rely on this idea for Hamming distance approximation combined with the embedding method from [21, 22] of edit distance into the Hamming space.

As far privacy and security are concerned, private identification schemes are based on searchable encryption principle. The main goal of searchable encryption [5, 10] is to store messages into an encrypted database while still enabling to search the messages related to some keywords. A general solution to design a searchable encryption scheme is to associate a message to a set of keywords and to consider each keyword as a virtual address where the receiver can recover a link toward the associated messages. To manage all these relations in an efficient way, we follow [3, 6, 14] by using Bloom filters. Bloom filter [4] is a notion used in membership checking applications to reduce the memory cost of the data storage. We use an extension of this notion called *Bloom filters with storage*. It enables to store identifiers of elements in each array.

Definition 3 (Bloom Filter with Storage, [6]). *Let* S *be a finite subset of a space* E *and a set of identifiers associated to* S. *For a family of* v *(independent and random) hash functions* $\mathsf{H} = \{h_1, \ldots, h_v\}$, *with each* $h_i : E \to \{1, \ldots, k\}$, *a* (v, k)-*Bloom Filter with Storage for indexation of* S *is* H, *together with the array* $(t_1, \ldots, t_k)$, *defined recursively as:* 1. $\forall i \in \{1, \ldots, k\}$, $t_i \leftarrow \emptyset$, 2. $\forall x \in \mathsf{S}$, $\forall j \in \{1, \ldots, v\}$, $t_{h_j(x)} \leftarrow t_{h_j(x)} \cup \{Id(x)\}$ *where* $Id(x)$ *is the identifier of* x.

In other words, the array is empty at the beginning and for each element $x \in S$, we add the identifier $Id(x)$ of x at the cells indexed by $h_1(x), \ldots, h_v(x)$. To recover the identifiers associated to an element y, we compute $T(y) = \bigcap_{j=1}^{v} t_{h_j(y)}$.

3.2 Edit Distance Approximation

Our construction is based on the embedding of edit distance into Hamming distance designed in [22]. Let (E_1, d_{E_1}) and (E_2, d_{E_2}) be two metric spaces. An embedding $\psi : (E_1, d_{E_1}) \rightarrow (E_2, d_{E_2})$ has a distortion c if for all $(x, y) \in E_1$,

$$c^{-1} \times d_{E_1}(x, y) \leq d_{E_2}(\psi(x), \psi(y)) \leq c \times d_{E_1}(x, y)$$

[22] proves that $\{0,1\}^N$ with edit distance can be embedded into ℓ_1 with small distortion $2^{O(\sqrt{\log_2 N \log_2 \log_2 N})}$ and then shows from a previous work [18] how to end up efficiently into the Hamming space. More precisely:

Lemma 1 ([22]). *There exists a probabilistic polynomial time algorithm π and constants $c_1, c_2 > 0$ that, for every $N \in \mathbb{N}$, for every $4^{-N} \gg \delta > 0$, and for all $x \in \{0,1\}^N$, computes $\pi(x) \in \ell_1^{c_2(N^2 \log_2(N/\delta))}$ and such that for all $(x, y) \in \{0,1\}^N$, with probability at least $1 - \delta$,*

$$2^{-c_1(\sqrt{\log_2 N \log_2 \log_2 N})} ed(x, y) \leq L_1(\pi(x), \pi(y)) \leq 2^{c_1(\sqrt{\log_2 N \log_2 \log_2 N})} ed(x, y)$$

where L_1 denotes the distance L_1.

Based on [18], the authors then show that there exist $0 < \alpha < \beta < c_2$ and an embedding ψ from $\{0,1\}^N$ with edit distance ed to $\{0,1\}^{c_2(\log_2(1/\delta))}$ with Hamming distance HD that computes $\psi(x) = \psi(x; t)$ for every $t \in \mathbb{N}$ and such that with probability at least $1 - \delta$:

- If $ed(x, y) \leq t$, then $HD(\psi(x), \psi(y)) \leq \alpha \log_2(1/\delta)$.
- If $ed(x, y) \geq 2^{c_1(\sqrt{\log_2 N \log_2 \log_2 N})} t$ then $HD(\psi(x), \psi(y)) \geq \beta \log_2(1/\delta)$.

4   Our Construction

4.1   Technical Description

Setup. Let $\{0,1\}^N$ be equipped with the edit distance. Let ψ be the embedding of $(\{0,1\}^N, ed)$ into $(\{0,1\}^{c_2(\log_2(1/\delta))}, HD)$. Let $\mathsf{F} = (f_1, \ldots, f_\mu)$ be a sketching family for the Hamming distance from dimension $c_2(\log_2(1/\delta))$ to a dimension r. Let

$(H, (t_1, \ldots, t_k))$, with $H = \{h_1, \ldots, h_v\}$, and $h_i : \{1, \ldots, \mu\} \times \{0,1\}^r \rightarrow \{1, \ldots, k\}$, be a (v, k)-*Bloom Filter with Storage*. Let $(\text{Gen}, \text{Enc}, \text{Dec})$ be a semantically secure (IND-CPA, [15]) public key cryptosystem, let Query_{DB}^{PIR} be the retrieve query from a database DB of a Private Information Retrieval protocol and let $\text{Update}_{DB}^{PIS}(val, i)$ be the write query into a database DB (that adds val to the i-th field) of a Private Information Storage protocol.

A Private Information Retrieval (PIR) [11] protocol enables to retrieve a specific block from a database without letting the database learn anything about the query and the answer (i.e. neither the index of the block nor the value of the block). This is done through a method $\text{Query}_{DB}^{PIR}(i)$, that allows a user to recover the element stored at index i in DB by running the PIR protocol. A Private Information Storage (PIS) protocol [23] enables to write information in a database while preventing the database from learning information on what is being stored (neither the value of the data, nor the index of the location where the data is being stored). Such a protocol provides a method $\text{Update}_{DB}^{PIS}(val, index)$, which takes as input an element and a database index, and puts the value val into the database entry $index$.

KeyGen(1^ℓ) *The function takes a security parameter ℓ as input and uses* **Gen** *to generate a public and private key pair (pk, sk). It also initializes the Bloom filter array, $(t_1, \ldots, t_k) \leftarrow (\varnothing, \ldots, \varnothing)$, and provides it to the Cloud.*

Send$_{X,CL}(m, pk)$ *To send a message to* CL, *a user* x *executes the following algorithm.*

1. x sends $\text{Enc}(m, pk)$ to CL which will give him back a virtual address $\varphi(m)$.

2. x computes the embedding $\psi(m)$ and for all $i \in \{1, \ldots, \mu\}$, $f_i \circ \psi(m)$ and for all $j \in \{1, \ldots, v\}$, x asks to CL to update the Bloom filter array through queries $\text{Update}_{CL}^{PIS}\big(\text{Enc}(\varphi(m), pk), h_j(i \| f_i \circ \psi(m))\big)$ in order to add the identifier into the cell $t_{h_j(i \| f_i \circ \psi(m))}$.

For privacy concerns, x will also complete the Bloom filter array with random data in order to get the same number l of elements for all cells $t_1, \ldots, t_k$. At the end of the algorithm, CL has stored the message m at a virtual address noted $\varphi(m)$ and the Bloom filter structure has been filled of encrypted identifiers via indexation by several sketches that enable to search with approximate data.

Retrieve$_{Y,CL}(m', sk)$ *To retrieve a message in* CL, *a user* Y *proceeds as follows.*

1. For all $i \in \{1, \ldots, \mu\}$ and for all $j \in \{1, \ldots, v\}$, Y computes $\alpha_{i,j} = h_j(i \| f_i \circ \psi(m))$.

2. Y executes $\text{Query}_{CL}^{PIR}(\alpha_{i,j})$ to retrieve the content of the cells $t_{\alpha_{i,j}}$ from the Bloom filters stored into CL.

3. Y decrypts the content of the cells with $\text{Dec}(., sk)$ and for $i \in \{1, \ldots, \mu\}$
   - Y computes the intersection of all the decrypted version of the cells
     $t_{\alpha_{i,1}}, \ldots, t_{\alpha_{i,v}}$.
   - If $\varphi(m)$ is in this intersection, this means that Y most probably found a match
     $$f_i \circ \psi(m) = f_i \circ \psi(m')$$
4. Y counts the number of times an identifier is retrieved in such intersections
   $\cap_{j=1}^{v} t_{\alpha_{i,j}}$ (for $i \in \{1, \ldots, \mu\}$).
5. Y selects all the identifier which are retrieved above some threshold τ. This leads
   to the result $\Phi(m') = \{\varphi(m_{i_1}), \ldots, \varphi(m_{i_\gamma})\}$ of the execution of Retrieve

4.2 Security Properties

Lemma 2 (Completeness). *The scheme is complete up to a probability* $1 - \varepsilon_1$ *with*
$\varepsilon_1 \leq 1 - (1 - \frac{\alpha}{c_2})^{r\tau}$. *More precisely,* $\varepsilon_1 \approx \sum_{i=0}^{\tau-1} \binom{\mu}{i} (1 - (1 - \frac{\alpha}{c_2})^r)^{\mu-i} (1 - \frac{\alpha}{c_2})^{ri}$.

Lemma 3 (Soundness). *With* $\lambda_{max} = 2^{c_1(\sqrt{\log_2 N \log_2 \log_2 N})} \lambda_{min}$ *and provided that Bloom
filter functions from* H *behave like pseudo-random functions from* $\{1, \ldots, \mu\} \times \{0,1\}^r$
to $\{1, \ldots, k\}$, *then the scheme is sound up to a probability* $1 - \varepsilon_2$, *with*
$\varepsilon_2 \approx \left((1 - \frac{\beta}{c_2})^r (1 - \frac{1}{k^v}) + \frac{1}{k^v} \right)^\tau$

Lemma 4 (Sender Privacy). *Assume that the PIS protocol achieves PIS User
Privacy, the scheme ensures Sender Privacy.*

Lemma 5 (Receiver Privacy). *Assume that the PIR protocol ensures PIR User
Privacy, then the scheme ensures Receiver Privacy.*

References

[1] Adjedj, M., Bringer, J., Chabanne, H., Kindarji, B.: Biometric identification over
    encrypted data made feasible. In: Prakash, A., Sen Gupta, I. (eds.) ICISS 2009. LNCS,
    vol. 5905, pp. 86–100. Springer, Heidelberg (2009)
[2] Andoni, A., Piotr, I.: Near-optimal hashing algorithms for approximate nearest neighbor
    in high dimensions. Commun. ACM 51(1), 117–122 (2008)
[3] Bethencourt, J., Song, D.X., Waters, B.: New Constructions and Practical Applications
    for Private Stream Searching (Extended Abstract). In: IEEE Symposium on Security and
    Privacy, pp. 132–139 (2006)
[4] Bloom, B.H.: Space/Time Trade-offs in Hash Coding with Allowable Errors. Commun.
    ACM 13(7), 422–426 (1970)
[5] Boneh, D., Di Crescenzo, G., Ostrovsky, R., Persiano, G.: Public Key Encryption with
    Keyword Search. In: Cachin, C., Camenisch, J.L. (eds.) EUROCRYPT 2004. LNCS,
    vol. 3027, pp. 506–522. Springer, Heidelberg (2004)

[6]   Boneh, D., Kushilevitz, E., Ostrovsky, R., Skeith III, W.E.: Public Key Encryption That Allows PIR Queries. In: Menezes, A. (ed.) CRYPTO 2007. LNCS, vol. 4622, pp. 50–67. Springer, Heidelberg (2007)

[7]   Bringer, J., Chabanne, H., Kindarji, B.: Error-Tolerant Searchable Encryption. In: IEEE ICC 2009 CISS (2009)

[8]   Bringer, J., Chabanne, H., Kindarji, B.: Identification with Encrypted Biometric Data. Security Comm. Networks (2010) (to appear)

[9]   Chor, B., Kushilevitz, E., Goldreich, O., Sudan, M.: Private Information Retrieval. J. ACM 45(6), 965–981 (1998)

[10] Curtmola, R., Garay, J.A., Kamara, S., Ostrovsky, R.: Searchable Symmetric Encryption: Improved Definitions and Efficient Constructions. In: CCS 2006: Proceedings of the 13th ACM Conference on Computer and Communications Security, pp. 79–88. ACM, New York (2006)

[11] Gasarch, W.I.: A Survey on Private Information Retrieval

[12] Gentry, C., Ramzan, Z.: Single-Database Private Information Retrieval with Constant Communication Rate. In: Caires, L., Italiano, G.F., Monteiro, L., Palamidessi, C., Yung, M. (eds.) ICALP 2005. LNCS, vol. 3580, pp. 803–815. Springer, Heidelberg (2005)

[13] Gertner, Y., Ishai, Y., Kushilevitz, E., Malkin, T.: Protecting Data Privacy in Private Information Retrieval Schemes. In: STOC, pp. 151–160 (1998)

[14] Goh, E.-J.: Secure Indexes. Cryptology ePrint Archive, Report 2003/216 (2003)

[15] Goldwasser, S., Micali, S.: Probabilistic Encryption. J. Comput. Syst. Sci. 28(2), 270–299 (1984)

[16] Hao, F., Daugman, J., Zielinski, P.: A Fast Search Algorithm for a Large Fuzzy Database. IEEE Transactions on Information Forensics and Security 3(2), 203–212 (2008)

[17] Kirsch, A., Mitzenmacher, M.: Distance-Sensitive Bloom Filters. Algorithm Engineering & Experiments (2006)

[18] Kushilevitz, E., Ostrovsky, R., Rabani, Y.: Efficient Search for Approximate Nearest Neighbor in High Dimensional Spaces. In: Symposium on the Theory Of Computing, pp. 614–623 (1998)

[19] Li, J., Wang, Q., Wang, C., Cao, N., Ren, K., Lou, W.: Enabling Efficient Fuzzy Keyword Search over Encrypted Data in Cloud Computing. Cryptology ePrint Archive, Report 2009/593 (2009)

[20] Lipmaa, H.: An Oblivious Transfer Protocol with Log-Squared Communication. In: Zhou, J., López, J., Deng, R.H., Bao, F. (eds.) ISC 2005. LNCS, vol. 3650, pp. 314–328. Springer, Heidelberg (2005)

[21] Ostrovsky, R., Rabani, Y.: Low distortion embeddings for edit distance. J. ACM 54(5) (2007)

[22] Ostrovsky, R., Rabani, Y.: Low distortion embeddings for edit distance. In: STOC, pp. 218–224 (2005)

[23] Ostrovsky, R., Shoup, V.: Private Information Storage (Extended Abstract). In: STOC, pp. 294–303 (1997)

[24] Ostrovsky, R., Skeith III, W.E.: Algebraic Lower Bounds for Computing on Encrypted Data. Cryptology ePrint Archive, Report 2007/064 (2007)

[25] Piotr, I.: Nearest neighbors in high-dimensional spaces. In: Goodman, J.E., O'Rourke, J. (eds.) Handbook of Discrete and Computational Geometry, 2nd edn., ch. 39. CRC Press, Boca Raton (2004)

[26] Piotr, I., Rajeev, M.: Approximate Nearest Neighbors: Towards Removing the Curse of Dimensionality. In: Symposium on the Theory of Computing, pp. 604–613 (1998)

Efficient Secret Sharing Schemes

Chunli Lv[1,2], Xiaoqi Jia[3], Jingqiang Lin[1], Jiwu Jing[1],
Lijun Tian[2], and Mingli Sun[2]

[1] State Key Laboratory of Information Security,
Graduate University of Chinese Academy of Sciences
[2] College of Information and Electrical Engineering, China Agricultural University
[3] State Key Laboratory of Information Security,
Institute of Software, Chinese Academy of Sciences

Abstract. We propose a new XOR-based (k, n) threshold secret SSS, where the secret is a binary string and only XOR operations are used to make shares and recover the secret. Moreover, it is easy to extend our scheme to a multi-secret sharing scheme. When k is closer to n, the computation costs are much lower than existing XOR-based schemes in both distribution and recovery phases. In our scheme, using more shares ($\geq k$) will accelerate the recovery speed.

1 Introduction

The Secret Sharing Scheme (SSS) is an important tool for secure key management systems and distributed file systems with high data confidentiality and availability. The fundamental approach of SSS was proposed independently by Blakley [5] and Shamir [15] in 1979. Since then lots of work has been put into the investigation of such schemes [1][9][12][16][2][3][7] [6].

Like Shamir's scheme, most of these SSSs are computed over finite fields in which there are four operations, namely addition, subtraction, multiplication and division. However, in some applications, for example, when the low-cost and low energy RFID tags require to implement a secret sharing scheme [11][8], we need more simple and efficient schemes. Using XOR-based SSS would further reduce the number of gates and save cost for RFID because of XOR being the the simplest instructor (the number of gates is small).

In order to improve the efficiency of SSS, Karnin et al.[9] considered (k, L, n) multi-secret SSS, where there are L secrets $S_j (0 \leq j \leq L - 1)$ to be shared, and it is required that: (**C4**) any group of at least k participants can recover all the L secrets S_j, i.e., the Shannon's conditional entropy $H(S_j | any\ k\ shares) = 0$; (**C5**) any group of fewer than k participants cannot obtain any information about any particular secret, i.e., $H(S_j | any\ k - 1\ shares) = H(S_j)$. It has the advantage of allowing L independent secrets (or a large secret is divided into L sub-secrets) to be protected with the same amount of data as is usually needed to protect one secret by itself. There are lots of works focusing on such multi-secret SSSs [12] [17]. Like single-secret SSS, most of these multi-secret SSSs are also computed over finite fields, which cause relatively heavy computation costs if being used in RFID systems or storage applications.

J.J. Park et al. (Eds.): STA 2011, CCIS 186, pp. 114–121, 2011.

In this paper, we propose a new (k, n)-threshold SSS. Our contributions are summarized as follows.

- We give a new (k, n) threshold secret SSS, where the secret is a binary string and only XOR operations are used to make shares and recover the secret. It is easy to extend our scheme to a (k, L, n) multi-secret sharing scheme.
- When k is closer to n, the computation costs are much lower than existing XOR-based schemes in both distribution and recovery phases. In our scheme, using more shares ($\geq k$) will accelerate the recovery speed. In real world, there are often more than k shares available to recover the secret.

2   Preliminaries

We introduce some mathematical results, which are very important in understanding our schemes. Let the matrix $\widetilde{E}_{p-1}^m (0 \leq m \leq p - 1) = [e_{i,j}]_{(p-1) \times (p-1)}$ be defined over the finite field $GF(2)$ as

$$e_{i,j} = \begin{cases} 1 & for\ i = (j + m)\ mod\ p \\ 0 & otherwise. \end{cases}$$

For example, when $p = 5$

$$\widetilde{E}_4 = \begin{bmatrix} 0&0&0&0 \\ 1&0&0&0 \\ 0&1&0&0 \\ 0&0&1&0 \end{bmatrix} \widetilde{E}_4^2 = \begin{bmatrix} 0&0&0&1 \\ 0&0&0&0 \\ 1&0&0&0 \\ 0&1&0&0 \end{bmatrix} \widetilde{E}_4^3 = \begin{bmatrix} 0&0&1&0 \\ 0&0&0&1 \\ 0&0&0&0 \\ 1&0&0&0 \end{bmatrix} \widetilde{E}_4^4 = \begin{bmatrix} 0&1&0&0 \\ 0&0&1&0 \\ 0&0&0&1 \\ 0&0&0&0 \end{bmatrix} I_4 = \widetilde{E}_4^5 = \begin{bmatrix} 1&0&0&0 \\ 0&1&0&0 \\ 0&0&1&0 \\ 0&0&0&1 \end{bmatrix}$$

$$(1)$$

Let $M_{k \times n}$ be a *Vandermonde-like* matrix based on $\widetilde{\alpha} = \widetilde{E}_{p-1}$.

$$M_{k \times n} = \begin{bmatrix} I & I & \cdots & I \\ I & \widetilde{\alpha}^1 & \cdots & \widetilde{\alpha}^{n-1} \\ \vdots & \vdots & \ddots & \vdots \\ I & \widetilde{\alpha}^{(k-1)} & \cdots & \widetilde{\alpha}^{(k-1)(n-1)} \end{bmatrix} (k \leq n \leq p)$$

$$(2)$$

$M_{k \times n}$ is a $k(p - 1) \times n(p - 1)$ binary matrix which can be regarded as a $k \times n$ block matrix. Each block-column contains $(p-1)$ columns, while each block-row contains $(p - 1)$ rows.

Theorem 1. *Any k block-columns from $M_{k \times n}$ are linear independent and form a full rank matrix which has multiplication inverse over $GF(2)$.*

Proof See Appendix

Next, let G be the Abelian group $(\{0, 1\}^d, \oplus)$ (here, d is the length of the string), i.e., (BinaryString,XOR). Now we define vector space $G^{p-1} = \underbrace{G \times \cdots \times G}_{p-1}$.

where the scalar operation is over the field $GF(2)$. Elements $\overrightarrow{g}$ of G^{p-1} are represented as $[g_0, \cdots, g_{p-2}]$, where $g_i \in G$. The unity element is $[0^d, \cdots, 0^d]$. Addition in G^{p-1} is defined as

$$[g_0, \cdots, g_{p-2}] + [g_0', \cdots, g_{p-2}'] = [g_0 \oplus g_0', \cdots, g_{p-2} \oplus g_{p-2}']$$

Obviously, $(\overrightarrow{g}, +)$ is an Abelian group. The scalar operation over $GF(2)$ is defined as follows,

$$1 \times g_i = g_i \times 1 = g_i \qquad and \qquad 0 \times g_i = g_i \times 0 = 0^d \tag{3}$$

For the sake of convenience, let $\widetilde{\alpha}^m = \widetilde{E}_{p-1}^m (0 \leq m \leq p-1)$ (When $p = 5$, it is shown by Equation (1)). It is easy to see

$$\widetilde{\alpha} \times \overrightarrow{g} = \widetilde{E}_{p-1} \times \overrightarrow{g} = \widetilde{E}_{p-1} \times [g_0, \cdots, g_{p-2}] = [0, g_0, \cdots, g_{p-3}] \tag{4}$$

and

$$\widetilde{\alpha}^m \times [g_0, \cdots, g_{p-2}] = \widetilde{E}_{p-1}^m \times [g_0, \cdots, g_{p-2}]$$
$$= [\underbrace{g_{p-m}, \cdots, g_{p-2}, 0}_{m}, g_0, \cdots, g_{p-2-m}] \tag{5}$$

3   Our Secret Sharing Scheme

In this section, we directly propose a (k, L, n) multi-secret SSS $(1 \leq L \leq k \leq n)$. Obviously, the scheme is a single-secret scheme when $L = 1$. When $L > k$, our multi-secret sharing scheme also works if there $L - k$ shares are public in the $(L, L, n + L - k)$ multi-secret scheme. Here we focus on $1 \leq L \leq k$ cases.

Notations and Definitions. Any secret is a binary string which can be equally divided into several blocks. Therefore, we use the following notations and definitions to describe the secrets:

- G be the Abelian group $(\{0,1\}^d, \oplus)$ and d is the length of the string.
- p is a prime number such that $p \geq n + L$.
- $\overrightarrow{s}_j \in G^{p-1} (0 \leq j \leq L - 1)$ denotes the L secrets. Therefore, each secret $\overrightarrow{s}_j = [s_{0,j}, s_{1,j}, \cdots, s_{p-2,j}]$ can be regarded as a vector $\in G^{p-1}$ and each size of $s_{i,j}$ is d.
- $|X|$ denotes the size of X, therefore, $|s_{i,j}| = d, |\overrightarrow{s}_j| = d(p-1)$.

3.1   Distribution Algorithm

Our (k, L, n)-threshold scheme requires the dealer to do next 6 steps to make shares:

1. Find a prime p $(\geq n + L)$.
2. Generate $(k - L)(p - 1)$ random values $r_{i,j} \in (G = \{0,1\}^d)$. Let $\overrightarrow{c}_j = [r_{0,j}, r_{1,j}, \cdots, r_{p-2,j}](0 \leq i \leq p - 2, 0 \leq j \leq k - L - 1)$. So $\overrightarrow{c}_j \in (G^{p-1} = \{0,1\}^{d(p-1)})$.
3. Make $M_{(n+L-k)\times(n+L)}$ by Equation (2).
4. Solve following equations:

$$[\underbrace{\underbrace{\overrightarrow{c}_0, \cdots, \overrightarrow{c}_{k-L-1}}_{The\ k-L\ random\ values}, \underbrace{\overrightarrow{c}_{k-L}, \cdots, \overrightarrow{c}_{n-1}}_{To\ be\ computed}, \underbrace{\overrightarrow{s}_0, \cdots \overrightarrow{s}_{L-1}}_{The\ L\ secrets}}_{The\ n\ shares}] \times M_{(n+L-k)\times(n+L)}^T = \overrightarrow{0}$$

$$\tag{6}$$

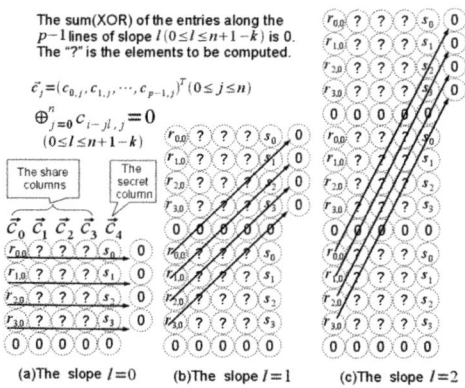

Fig. 1. Geometric Presentation of Distribution. There is a $p \times (n + L)$ array where each element $\in G = \{0,1\}^d$ and all elements in the last row are imaginary 0^d. The right L columns are L secrets and the left n columns are the n shares. As shown by the parts a, b and c in the Figure, the relation between the n shares and L secrets is that the sum (XOR) of the entries (elements in the array) along the $p-1$ lines of slope $l(0 \le l \le n + L - k - 1)$ are 0^d. The part b and c are heaped up by part a.

where $(\vec{c}_{k-L}, \cdots, \vec{c}_{n-1})$ are the shares to be computed.

5. Compute $(\vec{c}_{k-L}, \vec{c}_{k-L+1}, \cdots, \vec{c}_{n-1})$.
6. Finally, send the n shares $\vec{c}_0, \vec{c}_1, \cdots, \vec{c}_{n-1}$ to n participants through secure channels.

Its Geometric Presentation. Based on the Equation (6) (4) (5), we get the geometric presentation. As shown in the Figure 1(a), the dealer first puts the L secret $\vec{s}_j = (s_{0,j}, s_{1,j}, \cdots, s_{p-1,j})$ $(0 \le j \le L - 1)$ into the right L columns and puts the $k - L$ random vectors $\vec{c}_j = (r_{0,j}, r_{1,j}, \cdots, r_{p-2,j})$ $(0 \le j \le k - L - 1)$ into the left $k - L$ columns. The relation between the n shares and L secrets is that the sum (XOR) of the entries (elements in the array) along the $p - 1$ lines of slope $l(0 \le l \le n + L - k - 1)$ are 0^d. According to the relation between the shares and the secrets, the dealer computes the middle $n + L - k$ columns $(\vec{c}_{k-L}, \vec{c}_{k-L+1}, \cdots, \vec{c}_{n-1})$ and gets all the n shares.

3.2 Recovery Algorithm

The recovery algorithm is naturally same as the distribution algorithm. Briefly, it requires us to do the following steps to recover the L secrets after we collect $w(\ge k)$ shares: use the same matrix $M_{(n+L-k)\times(n+L)}$ as in distribution, then put $w(\ge k)$ shares into the Equation (6) and compute unknown values $(\vec{s}_0, \cdots \vec{s}_{L-1})$ which are the L secrets. It is easy to see that using more shares $(\ge k)$, will enhance the recovery speed.

3.3   Evaluation of Efficiency

Computational complexity. Due to limited space, we directly give the final results, and we will put the details analysis in the extended version. Our distribution algorithm requires at most

$$O((n + L - k)^2 p) \cdot |\vec{s_j}|$$

bitwise XOR operations to make n shares. The recovery algorithm is naturally same as the distribution algorithm, but only the L secrets $(\vec{c}_n, \vec{c}_{n+1}, \cdots, \vec{c}_{n+L-1})$ need to be computed. Furthermore, using more shares $(w \geq k)$ will faster the recovery speed. The most of bitwise XOR operations to be required in the recovery algorithm with w shares is

$$O(L(n + L - w)p) \cdot |\vec{s_j}|$$

bitwise XOR operations.

3.4   The Scheme Is Perfect Security

From the Equation (6), it is easy to see that our scheme can be regard as a linear code over the group G. According to Lemma 1, any k block-rows from $\widetilde{M}_{n \times k}$ form a full rank matrix over $GF(2)$, therefore, this code is linear Maximum Distance Separable code [13]. It is well known that Any linear MDS code yields a perfect secret sharing scheme. The connection between coding and secret sharing having been made by Massey [14] in particular and by others such as Blakley [4], Karnin [9]. Therefore, out scheme is perfect security.

4   Related Works

Although there are also some secret sharing schemes which could use only XOR operations [3][7][6], they are not ideal schemes, in which the size of each share is much larger than that of the secret. Moreover, some of them are not practical when k, n are large. For example, computational complexity of [7] is $O(Combination(n-1, k-1))$. Recently, Kurihara et al. [10] also presented a fast (k, n)-threshold SSS. However, compared to our SSS, there are several shortcomings which cannot be neglected in Kurihara's schemes: (**1**) Their scheme is not fit for being extended to multi-secret sharing scheme, note that their scheme can be extended to a weak ramp scheme whose security property is same as Yamamoto's ramp scheme based on Shamir's scheme. However, the ramp scheme based on Shamir's scheme is not always multi-secret sharing schemes [17]. (**2**) When k is closer to n, the computation costs in their scheme become heavier for both making shares and recovering the secret. (**3**) In their scheme, more shares $(\geq k)$ cannot help to reduce the computational cost of recovery. However, in real world, there are often more than k shares available to recover the secret.

5   Conclusion

In this paper, we propose (k, n)-threshold secret sharing schemes which requires XOR operations to make shares and recover the secret. It is easy to extend our scheme to a (k, L, n) multi-secret sharing scheme. We show that our scheme is very efficient. Moreover, when k is closer to n, the computation costs are much lower than existing XOR-based schemes in both distribution and recovery phases. In our scheme, using more shares $(\geq k)$ will accelerate the recovery speed. In real world, there are often more than k shares available to recover the secret. It is fit for such applications as RFID systems and storage systems.

Acknowledgment

We want to thank many anonymous reviewers for their great help to this paper. This work is supported by Natural Science Foundation of China (Grant No.70890084/G021102 and Grant No.61073179) and Knowledge Innovation Program of the Chinese Academy of Sciences (Grant No.YYYJ-1013).

References

1. Asmuth, C., Bloom, J.: A modular approach to key safeguarding. IEEE Transactions on Information Theory 29(2), 208–210 (1983)
2. Bai., L.: A strong ramp secret sharing scheme using matrix projection. In: Proceedings of the 2006 International Symposium on a World of Wireless, pp. 652–656 (2006)
3. Benaloh, J.C., Leichter, J.: Generalized Secret Sharing and Monotone Functions. In: Goldwasser, S. (ed.) CRYPTO 1988. LNCS, vol. 403, pp. 27–35. Springer, Heidelberg (1990)
4. Blakley, G., Kabatianski, G.: Ideal perfect threshold schemes and mds codes. p. 488
5. Blakley, G.R.: Safeguarding cryptographic keys. In: Proc. AFIPS 1979 National Computer Conference, AFIPS, pp. 313–317 (1979)
6. Desmedt, Y.G., Frankel, Y.: Perfect homomorphic zero-knowledge threshold schemes over any finite abelian group. SIAM J. Discret. Math. 7(4), 667–679 (1994)
7. Ito, M., Saito, A., Nishizeki, T.: Secret sharing schemes realizing general access structures. In: Proceedings of the IEEE Global Communication Conference, pp. 99–102
8. Kapoor, H., Huang, D.: Secret-sharing based secure communication protocols for passive rfids. In: Global Telecommunications Conference, GLOBECOM 2009, pp. 1–6. IEEE, Los Alamitos (2009)
9. Karnin, E.D., Member, S., Greene, J.W., Member, S., Hellman, M.E.: On secret sharing systems. IEEE Transactions on Information Theory 29, 35–41 (1983)
10. Kurihara, J., Kiyomoto, S., Fukushima, K., Tanaka, T.: A new (k,n)-threshold secret sharing scheme and its extension. In: Wu, T.-C., Lei, C.-L., Rijmen, V., Lee, D.-T. (eds.) ISC 2008. LNCS, vol. 5222, pp. 455–470. Springer, Heidelberg (2008)
11. Langheinrich, M., Marti, R.: Practical minimalist cryptography for rfid privacy. IEEE Systems Journal, Special Issue on RFID Technology 1(2), 115–128 (2007)

12. Chien, H.Y., Jan, J.K., Teng, Y.M.: A practical (t,n) multi-secret sharing scheme. IEICE Trans. on Fundamentals 12, 2762–2765 (2000)
13. MacWilliams, F.J., Sloane, N.J.A.: The Theory of Error-Correcting Codes. North-Holland, Amsterdam (1977)
14. Massey, J.L.: Minimal codewords and secret sharing. In: Proceedings of the 6th Joint Swedish-Russian International Workshop on Information Theory, pp. 276–279 (1993)
15. Shamir, A.: How to share a secret? Communication of the ACM 22, 612–613 (1979)
16. Wu, T., He, W.: A geometric approach for sharing secrets. Computers and Security 14(11), 135–145 (1995)
17. Yamamoto, H.: Secret sharing system using (k, l, n) threshold scheme. Electronics and Communications in Japan (Part I: Communications) 69, 46–54 (1986)

Appendix

Let p be an odd prime, and the matirx $E_{p-1}^m (0 \leq m \leq p-1) = [e_{i,j}]_{(p-1) \times (p-1)}$ is defined over the finite field $GF(2)$ as

$$e_{i,j} = \begin{cases} 1 & for \ j = p - m \ mod \ p \\ 1 & for \ i = (j + m) \ mod \ p \\ 0 & otherwise. \end{cases}$$

It can be easily verified that $\{I_{p-1}, E_{p-1}, E_{p-1}^2, \cdots, E_{p-1}^{p-1}\}$ form an Abelian group with matrix multiplication over the finite field $GF(2)$. The unity element is I_{p-1}, i.e., identity matrix. Therefore, $E_{p-1}^i \times E_{p-1}^j = E_{p-1}^j \times E_{p-1}^i = E_{p-1}^{i+j}$ and $E_{p-1}^0 = E_{p-1}^p = I_{p-1}, E_{p-1}^{-1} = E_{p-1}^{p-1}$.

Lemma 1. *For any prime p and $m(0 \leq m \leq p-1)$, the determinant of E_{p-1}^m is 1 over $GF(2)$, i.e., $det(E_{p-1}^m) = 1$ over $GF(2)$.*

Proof. Obviously, $det(I_{p-1}) = 1, det(E_{p-1}) = 1$, therefore, $det(E_{p-1}^m) = 1^m = 1$.

Lemma 2. *For any prime p and $m(1 \leq m \leq p-1)$, the determinant of $I_{p-1} - E_{p-1}^m$ is 1 over $GF(2)$, i.e., $det(I_{p-1} - E_{p-1}^m) = 1$ over $GF(2)$. Moreover, $det(E_{p-1}^l - E_{p-1}^m) = 1$ over $GF(2)$ for $(l \neq m \ mod \ p)$.*

Proof. As shown by Equation (7), For any $(I_{p-1} - E_{p-1}^m)$ for $(1 \leq m \leq p-1)$, there is one and only one "0" in the diagonal elements. We add all other rows to the line which the "0" is in, then the "0" becomes "1", and other elements of the line become "0"s. Therefore, according to the basic definition of determinant, we get $det(I_{p-1} - E_{p-1}) = 1$, $det(I_{p-1} - E_{p-1}^2) = 1$. By the similar method, we get $det(I_{p-1} - E_{p-1}^m) = 1$ $(m \neq 0 \ mod \ p)$. Obviously, $det(E_{p-1}^l - E_{p-1}^m) = det(E_{p-1}^l \times (I_{p-1} - E_{p-1}^{m-l})) = det(E_{p-1}^l) \times det(I_{p-1} - E_{p-1}^{m-l}) = 1$ for $(l \neq m \ mod \ p)$.

$$det(I_4 - E_4) = \left| \begin{bmatrix} 1&0&0&1 \\ 1&1&0&1 \\ 0&1&1&1 \\ 0&0&1&0 \end{bmatrix} \right| = \left| \begin{bmatrix} 1&0&0&1 \\ 1&1&0&1 \\ 0&1&1&1 \\ 0&0&0&1 \end{bmatrix} \right| = 1;$$

$$det(I_4 - E_4^2) = \left| \begin{bmatrix} 1&0&1&1 \\ 0&1&1&0 \\ 1&0&0&0 \\ 0&1&1&1 \end{bmatrix} \right| = \left| \begin{bmatrix} 1&0&1&1 \\ 0&1&1&0 \\ 0&0&1&0 \\ 0&1&1&1 \end{bmatrix} \right| = (-1)^{2 \times 3} \times 1 \times \left| \begin{bmatrix} 1&0&1 \\ 0&1&0 \\ 0&1&1 \end{bmatrix} \right| = 1;$$

(7)

Let $V_{k \times k}$ be a Vandermonde matrix based on $\alpha = E_{p-1}$.

Lemma 3. *The determinant of $V_{k \times k}$ is $\prod\limits_{i > j} det(\alpha^{t_i} - \alpha^{t_j}) = 1$ over $GF(2)$.*

Let $\pi_{p-1}, \tau_{p-1}, O_{p-1}$ be three $p-1 \times p-1$ matrices which are defined over $GF(2)$ as follows

$$\pi_{p-1} = (e_{i,j})_{p-1 \times p-1} = \begin{cases} 0 & for\ i = j \\ 1 & otherwise. \end{cases} ; \qquad \tau_{p-1} = (e_{i,j})_{p-1 \times p-1} = 1;$$

$$O_{p-1} = (e_{i,j})_{p-1 \times p-1} = 0.$$

If no confusion arises, we use I, π, τ and O in place of the $I_{p-1}, \pi_{p-1}, \tau_{p-1}$ and O_{p-1}, respectively.

Lemma 4. *Obviously, the determinant of π is 1, i.e., $det(\pi) = 1$ over $GF(2)$.*

Proof of Theorem 1
Any k block-columns from $M_{k \times n}$ form a *Vandermonde-like* matrix $\widetilde{V}_{k \times k}$.

Lemma 5. $det(\widetilde{V}_{k \times k}) = 1$ *over the $GF(2)$.*

Proof. Let $\Gamma_{k \times k}$ be a $k \times k$ blocks matrix as follow

$$\Gamma_{k \times k} = \begin{bmatrix} I & O & O & \cdots & O \\ \tau & \pi & O & \cdots & O \\ \tau & O & \pi & \cdots & O \\ \vdots & \vdots & \vdots & \ddots & \vdots \\ \tau & O & O & \cdots & \pi \end{bmatrix} \quad (k \leq n \leq p) \tag{8}$$

it is easy to see that for any k

$$\Gamma_{k \times k} \times \widetilde{V}_{k \times k} = V_{k \times k} \Rightarrow det(\Gamma_{k \times k}) \times det(\widetilde{V}_{k \times k}) = det(V_{k \times k})$$
$$\Rightarrow 1 \times det(\widetilde{V}_{k \times k}) = 1 \Rightarrow det(\widetilde{V}_{k \times k}) = 1 \tag{9}$$

Since, $det(\widetilde{V}_{k \times k}) = 1$ over $GF(2)$, any k block-columns from $M_{k \times n}$ are linear independent and form a full rank matrix which has multiplication inverse over $GF(2)$.

Two Dimensional PalmPhasor Enhanced by Multi-orientation Score Level Fusion

Lu Leng[1], Jiashu Zhang[1], Gao Chen[1], Muhammad Khurram Khan[2], and Ping Bai[1]

[1] Sichuan Province Key Lab of Signal and Information Processing, Southwest Jiaotong University, Chengdu Sichuan 610031, P.R. China
lenglu@126.com, jszhang@home.swjtu.edu.cn
[2] Center of Excellence in Information Assurance, King Saud University, Riyadh, Saudi Arabia
mkhurram@ksu.edu.sa

Abstract. The security and protection of biometric template has been the bottleneck of its applications due to permanent appearance of biometrics. Texture codes are important approaches for palmprint recognition; unfortunately, there is no ideal cancelable scheme for palmprint coding until now. We propose a novel cancelable palmprint template, called "PalmPhasor", which is a set of binary code fusing the user-specific tokenised pseudo-random number (PRN) and multi-orientation texture features of PalmCodes. PalmPhasor is extended from one dimension to two dimensions to reduce computational complexity. Two dimensional (2D) PalmPhasor in row orientation has better performance than one dimensional (1D) PalmPhasor. Furthermore, 2D PalmPhasor fuses multi-orientation texture features in score level to enhance recognition performance. Besides, the number of orientations of texture features for fusion is also discussed in this paper. The experimental results on PolyU palmprint database show the feasibility and efficiency of 2D PalmPhasor enhanced by multi-orientation score level fusion.

Keywords: 2D PalmPhasor, Multi-orientation score level fusion, BioPhasor, Cancelable palmprint template, Biometric security.

1 Introduction

Biometrics characteristics are immutable. When biometrics are compromised, user can't revoked and reissue their biometric templates. Besides, one biometric template of the same user may be stored and shared in various databases with more and more biometric systems appearing in our daily life, which imperils biometric security and users' privacy. Some biometric protection schemes were proposed. Khan and Zhang employed information hiding techniques to protect biometrics [1,2], but the biometric template must be extracted and restored at the authentication end, that is, the biometric template is not secure at matching phase. Li and Zhang employed biometric protection schemes based on encryption technique without decryption at the authentication end [3,4], but their schemes are invertible.

"Cancelable Biometrics" schemes for biometric protection and security should meet four objectives, including diversity, revocability/reusability, non-invertibility

J.J. Park et al. (Eds.): STA 2011, CCIS 186, pp. 122–129, 2011.

and performance. Unfortunately, it is hard to meet the four objects at the same time. Teoh et al. designed a representative cancelable biometric, named BioHashing [5], which achieved a zero false acceptance rate, but the performance rests mainly on users' tokens, in other words, biometrics play an unimportant role in BioHashing [6]. To solve the defects of BioHashing, Teoh et al. used nonlinear operation in BioPhasor instead of linear operation in BioHashing and obtained the desired results [7]. Furthermore, they develop a 2^N discretisation of BioPhasor based on users' specific statistical data [8]. However, the user's identity is usually not known before recognition, so the technique of users-dependent quantization or thresholding has limited application scope. The conflict between the security and performance is not compromised satisfactorily until now, so most current studies focus on how to reduce the performance degrading due to non-invertibility.

Palmprint has been used more and more widely due to its superiority over other biometrics [9-10], so it is necessary to study the scheme of cancelable biometric for palmprint protection. PalmHashing is a palmprint template protection scheme based on BioHashing [11], so PalmHashing has the same fatal drawback as BioHashing. Kong and Zhang proposed three measures for secure palmprint identification [12], but their measures are invertible. Leng and Zhang proposed a novel cancelable PalmCode generated from randomized Gabor filters [13], but the performance is only approximate to that of PalmCode.

In this paper, BioPhasor framework is employed to PalmCode [14] directly to constitute "PalmPhasor". The performance of PalmPhasor is not good, so one dimensional (1D) PalmPhasor is extended to two dimensional (2D) PalmPhasor to reduce computational complexity and enhance recognition performance. To furthermore overcome the performance degrading due to non-invertibility, 2D PalmPhasor fuses multi-orientation texture features of PalmCodes in score level. The performance of the proposed scheme is compared with PalmCode and Binary Orientation Co-occurrence Vector (BOCV) that is a state-of-the-art coding approach for palmprint identification [15]. Besides, the number of multi-orientation texture features of PalmCodes is also discussed in this paper.

2   Proposed Methodology

2.1   PalmPhasor

BioPhasor can be directly employed to generate cancelable PalmPhasor based on PalmCode feature according to the following steps.

Step 1. The original images of palmprint are filtered by Gabor filter to extract PalmCode texture. The real part and imaginary part of the result after Gabor filtering are both down-sampled to the size of 32×32, thus the size of texture feature is 32×64=2048. Reshape the feature matrix to a vector $x \in R^n$ where n=2048.

Step 2. Use token to generate a set of PRN $\{r_i \in R^n \mid i = 1, 2, ..., m\}$. For the comparison with other approaches and different experimental conditions, m is set to be 1024. The basis is transformed into an orthonormal set of r, $\{r_{\perp i} \in R^n \mid i = 1, 2, ..., m\}$, by Gram-Schmidt process.

Step 3. Mix x with $r_{\perp i}$ to form complex number $\left\{ z_i = x + r_{\perp i} j \in C^n \mid i = 1, 2, ..., n \right\}$ and calculate their complex arguments

$$\left\{ \varphi_i = \arg(z_i) \in R^n \mid i = 1, 2, ..., n \right\} \tag{1}$$

Step 4. Average the complex arguments

$$\left\{ \overline{\varphi}_j = \frac{1}{n} \sum_{i=1}^{n} \varphi_i \in R^m \mid j = 1, 2, ..., m \right\} \tag{2}$$

Step 5. Quantize the average argument $\overline{\varphi}_j$ and reshape the result to the matrix whose size is 32×32 to generate PalmPhasor template. Quantization is carried out to divide the complex plane into two sectors. $\overline{\varphi}_j$ is converted into one bit by

$$b_j = \begin{cases} 0, \text{ if } 0 < \overline{\varphi}_j < \pi \\ 1, \text{ if } -\pi < \overline{\varphi}_j \leq 0 \end{cases} \tag{3}$$

Step 6. The normalized Hamming distance can be measure the similarity of two cancelable templates of PalmPhasor P and Q by

$$D = \frac{\sum\limits_{i=1}^{M} \sum\limits_{j=1}^{N} P_{ij} \cap Q_{ij}}{M \times N} \tag{4}$$

where $M=N=32$. PalmPhasor, as cancelable palmprint template, can be used cross many databases due to its cancelable ability.

2.2   2D PalmPhasor

The length of texture feature vector is 2048 and the size of PRN matrix is 2048×1024, hence the computational complexity is too large. To reduce time cost, 1D PalmPhasor is extended to 2D PalmPhasor. Each row of the texture feature matrix is implemented by 1D PalmPhasor, respectively. There is no need to reshape feature matrix to feature vector. 2D PalmPhasor is generated according to the following steps.

Step 1. Extract texture feature of PalmCode. The size of texture feature matrix is 32×64. $\left\{ x_k \in R^n \mid k = 1, 2, ..., 32, n = 64 \right\}$ is the vector in Row k of the feature matrix.

Step 2. Use token to generate a set of PRN $\left\{ r_{ki} \in R^n \mid i = 1, 2, ..., m, k = 1, 2, ..., 32 \right\}$. For the comparison with other approaches and different experimental conditions, m is set to be 32. The basis is transformed into an orthonormal set of r, $\left\{ r_{\perp ki} \in R^n \mid i = 1, 2, ..., m, k = 1, 2, ..., 32 \right\}$, by Gram-Schmidt process.

Step 3. Mix x_k with $r_{\perp ki}$ to form complex number $\left\{ z_{ki} = x_k + r_{\perp ki} j \in C^n \mid i = 1, 2, ..., n, k = 1, 2, ..., 32 \right\}$ and calculate their complex arguments

$$\left\{ \varphi_{ki} = \arg(z_{ki}) \in R^n \mid i = 1, 2, ..., n, k = 1, 2, ..., 32 \right\} \quad (5)$$

Step 4. Average the complex arguments

$$\left\{ \overline{\varphi}_{kj} = \frac{1}{n} \sum_{i=1}^{n} \varphi_{ki} \in R^m \mid j = 1, 2, ..., m, k = 1, 2, ..., 32 \right\} \quad (6)$$

where $n = 64, m = 32, m \leq n$.

Step 5. Quantize the average argument $\overline{\varphi}_{kj}$ by equation (3) in Section 2.1.

Step 6. The same as Section 2.1

The computational complexity of 2D PalmPhasor is lower than that of 1D PalmPhasor; while the recognition performance of 2D PalmPhasor is better than that of 1D PalmPhasor. The experimental results will be given in Section 3.

2.3   2D PalmPhasor Enhanced by Multi-orientation Score Level Fusion

Although BioPhasor has better performance than BioHash, it also inevitably degrades the performance in the stolen-token scenario. Multi-orientation texture features of PalmCodes are fused in score level to enhance the performance of PalmPhasor. Texture feature extracted by Gabor filters along many orientations are implemented by 2D PalmPhasor and the matching scores are fused by sum operation. The matching score is rewritten as

$$D = \frac{\sum_{i=1}^{M} \sum_{j=1}^{N} \sum_{\tau=1}^{L} P_{ij}^{\tau} \cap Q_{ij}^{\tau}}{M \times N \times L} \quad (7)$$

where τ denotes the orientation index, L denotes the number of orientations.

3   Experiments and Discussions

The PolyU Palmprint Database was employed to test our scheme. This database contains 7,752 grayscale images captured from 386 different palms by a CCD-based device. The size of the images in the database is 384×284. All images were preprocessed and central 128×128 part of the image was cropped to represent the whole palmprint.

Four objectives are used to evaluate the performance of the proposed scheme.

(1) Performance: The best scenario is that the imposters can't steal the genuine token; while the worst scenario is that the imposters always steal the genuine token successfully. Fig. 1 (a) and (b) show the receiver operator characteristic (ROC) curves of 1D/2D PalmPhasors generated along four orientations and their fusion of score level in the worst scenario, respectively. ROCs of 2D PalmPhasors are higher than those of 1D PalmPhasors along the same orientations. The performance of 1D or 2D PalmPhasor enhanced by multi-orientation score level fusion is commonly better than that of the PalmPhasor generated along single orientation.

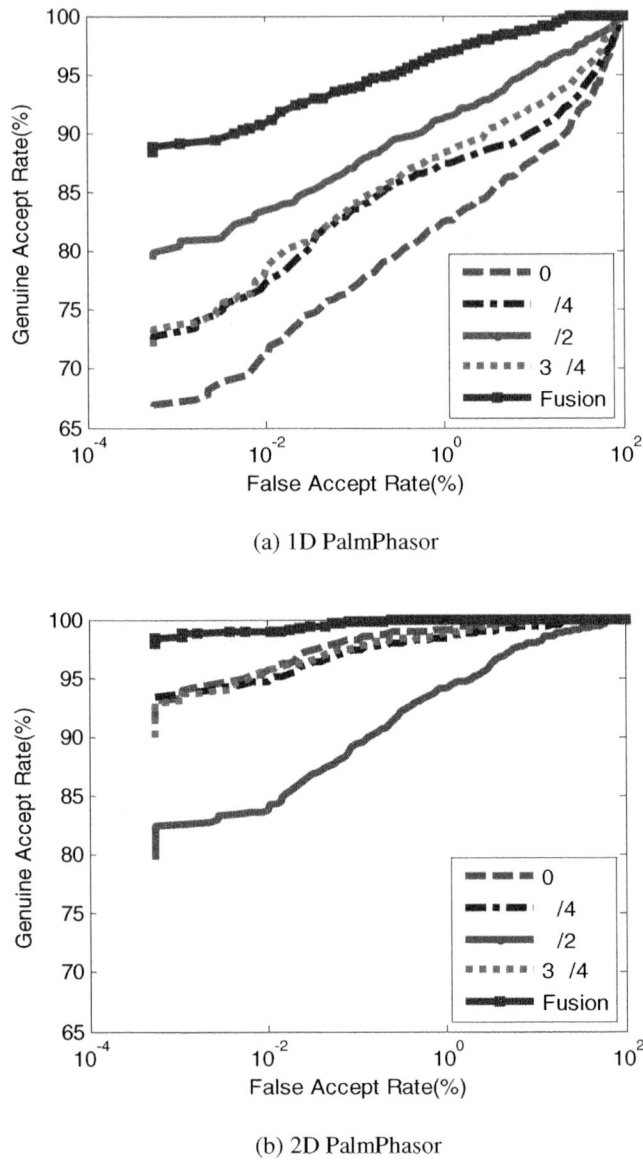

(a) 1D PalmPhasor

(b) 2D PalmPhasor

Fig. 1. PalmPhasor along 4 orientations and their fusion

Fig. 2 shows the comparison among PalmCode, BOCV (state-of-the-art) and 2D PalmPhasors (2/4/6 orientations fusion). The experiments in the worst scenario (stolen-token) and the best scenario are both tested. 2D PalmPhasors (4/6 orientations fusion) in the best scenario have desired performance. 2D PalmPhasors (4/6 orientations fusion) in the worst scenario have better performance than that of

PalmCode. 2D PalmPhasors (2 orientations fusion) has not good verification ability. Although 2D PalmPhasor (6 orientations fusion) has nice performance, its computational complexity is large. From the above discussion, 2D PalmPhasor (4 orientations fusion) is appropriate for cancelable palmprint protection.

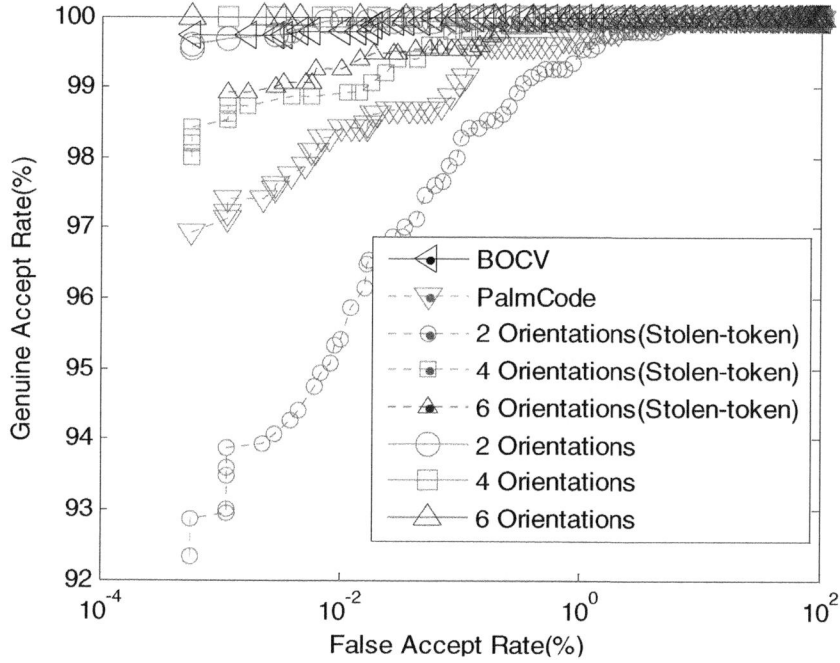

Fig. 2. Comparison of ROCs

Table 1 lists the time cost of Gram-Schmidt process and the generation of 1D PalmPhasor and 2D PalmPhasor for each palmprint sample. 2D PalmPhasor has much less time cost than 1D PalmPhasor.

Table 1. Comparison of time cost

/second	1D PalmPhasor	2D PalmPhasor	/second	1D PalmPhasor	2D PalmPhasor
Gram-Schmidt	16.5997	0.0030	Template Generation	0.4553	0.0035
Multiple	1	32	Multiple	1	32
Total	16.5997	0.0928	Total	0.4553	0.1105

(2) Diversity: Each user has his own token to generate PRN. Multiple protected templates from the same original template can be generated by mixed with various PRNs that are generated from various tokens. Thus different cancelable PalmPhasor templates can be used across various applications.

(3) Revocability/Reusability: The cancelable property of PalmPhasor should be evaluated whether a PalmPhasor mixed by PRN A and a PalmPhasor mixed by PRN B with the same palmprint. In our scheme, if one user changes his/her own token, about half elements of PalmPhasor template alter. The cancelable property of PalmPhasor prevents the old template from falling into the region of acceptance of the updated template, hence PRN refreshment is equivalent to issue a new template.

(4) Non-invertibility: Consider the scenario φ_i and r are both known when r is used once. The PalmPhasor elements $\varphi_j = \frac{1}{n}\sum_{i=1}^{n}\arctan\frac{r_{i,j}}{x_i}, j=1,2,...,m$ form m system of equations where $r_i \perp r_j$ for $i \neq j$ and $r_i \neq r_j$. n numbers are unknown, but there are only m equations, so the system of equations has infinite number of solutions. x can't be recovered by φ_i and r if r is used once. The proof of the scenario when r is used many times can be found in [8].

4   Conclusions

PalmPhasor is a novel cancelable palmprint template generated from texture features of PalmCode. 2D PalmPhasor, the extended form of 1D PalmPhasor, reduces computational complexity and performance degrading due to non-invertibility. Furthermore, we proposed a framework of 2D PalmPhasor enhanced by score level fusion of multi-orientation texture features of PalmCodes. The number of the orientations for score level fusion is discussed and proved that 2D PalmPhasor enhanced by score level fusion of four orientations is an effective and secure cancelable scheme for palmprint protection and security.

Acknowledgments. The authors would like to express their sincere thanks to the Biometric Research Center at the Hong Kong Polytechnic University for providing us the Palmprint Database. The authors would also like to thank the associate editor and anonymous reviewers for their comments, which significantly helped to improve this paper.

This work was partially supported by National Science Foundation of P. R. China (Grant: 60971104), Research Fund for the Doctoral Program of Higher Education of China (Grant: 20090184110008), Sichuan Youth Science & Technology Foundation (Grant: 09ZQ026-091), Open Research Foundation of Chongqing Key Laboratory of Signal and Information Processing, Chongqing University of Posts and Telecommunications (Grant: CQSIP-2009-01), Fundamental Research Funds for the Central Universities (Grant: SWJTU09ZT16), and Science & Technology Key Plan Project of Chengdu (Grant: 10GGYB649GX-023).

References

1. Khan, M.K., Zhang, J.S., Tian, L.: Chaotic Secure Content-based Hidden Transmission of Biometric Templates. Chaos, Solitons & Fractals 32, 1749–1759 (2007)
2. Khan, M.K., Xie, L., Zhang, J.S.: Chaos and NDFT-based Concealing of Fingerprint-biometric Data into Audio Signals for Trustworthy Person Authentication. Dig. Sign. Proc. 20, 179–190 (2010)

3. Li, H.J., Zhang, J.S., Zhang, Z.T.: Generating Cancelable Palmprint Templates via Coupled Onlinear Dynamic Filters and Multiple Orientation Palmcodes. Inf. Sci. 180, 3876–3893 (2010)
4. Li, H.J., Zhang, J.S.: A Novel Chaotic Stream Cipher and Its Application to Palmprint Template Protection. Chinese Physics B 19, 040505-1–040505-10 (2010)
5. Teoh, A.B.J., Ngo, D.C.L., Goh, A.: BioHashing: Two Factor Authentication Featuring Fingerprint Data and Tokenised Random Number. Patt. Recogn. 37, 2245–2255 (2004)
6. Kong, A., Cheung, K.H., Zhang, D.: An Analysis of BioHashing and Its Variants. Patt. Recogn. 39, 1359–1368 (2006)
7. Teoh, A.B.J., Ngo, D.C.L.: Biophasor: Token Supplemented Cancellable Biometrics. In: 9th International Conference on Control, Automation, Robotics and Vision, ICARCV, pp. 1–5 (2006)
8. Teoh, A.B.J., Toh, K.A.: 2^N Discretisation of BioPhasor in Cancellable Biometrics. In: Lee, S.-W., Li, S.Z. (eds.) ICB 2007. LNCS, vol. 4642, pp. 435–444. Springer, Heidelberg (2007)
9. Leng, L., Zhang, J.S., Xu, J., Khan, M.K., Alghathbar, K.: Dynamic Weighted Discrimination Power Analysis in DCT Domain for Face and Palmprint Recognition. In: International Conference on Information and Communication Technology Convergence, pp. 467–471 (2010)
10. Leng, L., Zhang, J.S., Khan, M.K., Chen, X., Alghathbar, K.: Dynamic Weighted Discrimination Power Analysis: a Novel Approach for Face and Palmprint Recognition in DCT Domain. Int. J. Phys. Sci. 5, 2543–2554 (2010)
11. Connie, T., Teoh, A.B.J., Goh, M., Ngo, D.C.L.: PalmHashing: a Novel Approach for Cancelable Biometrics. Inf. Proc. Lett. 93, 1–5 (2005)
12. Kong, A., Zhang, D., Kamel, M.: Three Measures for Secure Palmprint Identification. Patt. Recogn. 41, 1329–1337 (2008)
13. Leng, L., Zhang, J.S., Khan, M.K., Chen, X., Ji, M., Alghathbar, K.: Cancelable PalmCode Generated from Randomized Gabor Filters for Palmprint Template Protection. Sci. Res. Ess. 6, 784–792 (2011)
14. Zhang, D., Kong, W.K., You, J., Wong, M.: On-line Palmprint Identification. IEEE Trans. Patt. Anal. Mach. Intell. 25, 1041–1050 (2003)
15. Guo, Z.H., Zhang, D., Zhang, L., et al.: Palmprint Verification Using Binary Orientation Co-occurrence Vector. Patt. Recogn. Lett. 30, 1219–1227 (2009)

Improved Steganographic Embedding Exploiting Modification Direction in Multimedia Communications

Cheonshik Kim[1], Dongkyoo Shin[1], Dongil Shin[1], and Xinpeng Zhang[2]

[1] Dept. of Computer Engineering, Sejong University 98 Gunja-Dong,
Gwangjin-Gu, Seoul, 143-747, Korea
mipsan@paran.com, {shindk,dshin}@sejong.ac.kr
[2] School of Communication and Information Engineering, Shanghai University,
Shanghai 200072, China
xzhang@shu.edu.cn

Abstract. Steganography provides secure communications over the Internet with a cover image. However, it is difficult to transfer many messages with small-sized images. We have improved EMD (Exploiting Modification Direction), proposed by Zhang and Wang, to solve this problem. In this paper, we have developed a $(2^{n+2}-1)$-*ary* scheme. Our scheme shows a higher embedding rate, $R=\log_2(2^{n+2}-1)/n$, which is greater than that of the EMD scheme, because the EMD scheme embedding rate is $R=\log_2(2n+1)/n$, for $n>=2$. The experimental results show that our scheme is able to embed twice as many secret bits in multimedia communications compared to the existing EMD embedding method. Our method has low complexity and achieves higher embedding performance with good perceptual quality against the earlier arts. An experiment verified our proposed data hiding method in multimedia communications.

Keywords: Steganography, data hiding, EMD, secret communications, multimedia communications.

1   Introduction

Almost every one of us has heard a friend complaining that his email account has been hacked. Alternatively, it may have happened to you. The truth is that exposure to hacking of you yahoo messenger or any other kind of email supplier account has become quite a problem to users. Hacking MSN password accounts is no longer the realm of professionals. Thanks to the widespread use of the internet, any cyber-terrorist can learn the required tricks to master the art of hacking email passwords. He only needs to make a basic search with keywords, such as hacking yahoo passwords, msn hacking programs, hacking yahoo mail, hotmail hacking programs or even something as simple as hotmail hacking guide. All of that is out there, ready to be learned.

Thus, researchers have investigated steganography for personal safety communications with various multimedia, such as audio, text and images. Steganography is the art and science of hiding communications.

J.J. Park et al. (Eds.): STA 2011, CCIS 186, pp. 130–138, 2011.
© Springer-Verlag Berlin Heidelberg 2011

A steganographic system thus embeds hidden content in unremarkable cover media, so as not to arouse an eavesdropper's suspicion. Sender and receivers agree on a steganographic protocol system to communicate. This needs both parties need to know how a message is encoded in the cover medium. For example, Alice creates a new image with messages. Alice sends an image to Bob. When Bob receives the image, he uses the shared secret message. However, statistical analysis may reveal the presence of a hidden message in cover medium. Thus, the cover image with a message should be able to resist such an attack to safely communicate.

But, it is not difficult to avoid detectable traces, as image quality is in inverse proportion to the modification of an image. Therefore, to increase the security of an image in multimedia communications, the amount of hidden data or modification of an image needs to be reduced [1], [2]. There are two main issues [3], [4], [5] in steganography: First, creating stego images must be imperceptible to protect secret messages without detection or extraction. In order to preserve, an image with secret image require high quality of an image. A second important issue is embedding capacity. There are a few schemes to provide high capacity in an image. According to implementation of steganography, there are two categories, which are spatial domain and frequency domain method [6].

First, secret hidden messages are hidden in the spatial domain of a host image. This method is embedded into the pixels of the host image directly. Usually, this can be hidden by replacing the rightmost four the least significant bits per pixel in LSB substitution schemes [7], [8], [9]. Second, the discrete cosines transform (DCT) [10] or the discrete wavelet transform (DWT) [11] is used to transform pixel values. Zhang and Wang [12] proposed steganography to embed a secret message in an image in a $(2n+1)$-ary notation system. They use a $(2n+1)$-ary notational system, where n is the numbering of the pixel to carry one digit. The embedding rate of the secret message in an image is $R = (\log_2(2n+1)) = n$.

That is, it is about 1.161 bpp (bits per pixels) when $n = 2$. In Chin-Feng Lee's [13] method the capacity steadily increases as m increased and the dB value decreases as m increases. This method used a virtual hyper cube to hide a message in an image; this was created by a random number. In fact, it is impossible to change virtual pixels. Thus, the modification value must be stored in a pair-pixel. This paper introduces a new method improving Zhang and Wang's embedding method (called EMD), especially in embedding capacity with high image quality, it is about 46 dB.

We use a $(2^{n+2}-1)$-ary notational system in our proposed method that encodes a stream of bits with a cover pixel. The embedding rate of our method is double that of the EMD method, when $n = 2$. Moreover, the quality of the stego image is very high and there is no problem in security. Therefore, our proposed scheme is a novel steganography scheme in which the image's quality and capacity are balanced to increase capacity in a cover image.

2   EMD Embedding Method

EMD [12] is a novel method to hide data in an image with schemes of modification directions. This method carried a over 3 bits with n cover pixels, when $n \geq 2$. $(g_1, g_2, ..., g_n)$ is a group of pixels. Using this method, n pixels are used to carry one secret digit in the $(2n+1)$-*ary* notational system. Especially, in this method only one pixel is incremented or decremented by 1 in a group of pixels. A vector $(g_1, g_2,..., g_n)$ in n-dimensional space is indicated with its f value, which is calculated by the Eq. (1):

$$f(g_1, g_2,..., g_n) = \left[\sum_{i=1}^{n} (g_i \bullet i) \right] \bmod (2n+1) \tag{1}$$

No modification is needed if a secret digit d equals the extraction function of the original pixel-group. Secret data: $d \neq f$, calculate $s = d - f \bmod (2n+1)$. If s is no more than n, increase the value of g_s by 1, otherwise, decrease the value of $g2n + 1 - s$ by 1.

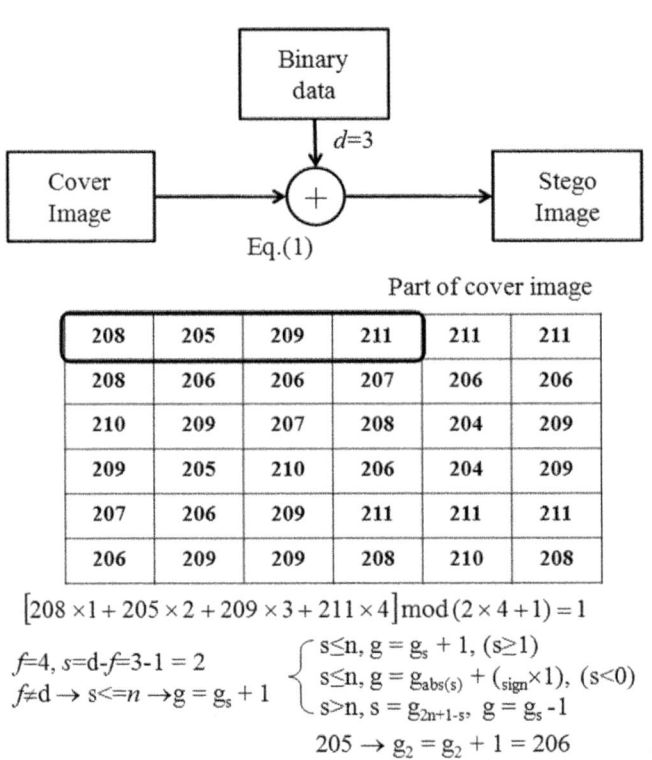

$$[208 \times 1 + 205 \times 2 + 209 \times 3 + 211 \times 4] \bmod (2 \times 4 + 1) = 1$$

$f=4, s=d-f=3-1 = 2$
$f \neq d \rightarrow s <= n \rightarrow g = g_s + 1$
$\begin{cases} s \leq n, g = g_s + 1, (s \geq 1) \\ s \leq n, g = g_{abs(s)} + (_{sign} \times 1), (s<0) \\ s > n, s = g_{2n+1-s}, g = g_s - 1 \end{cases}$
$205 \rightarrow g_2 = g_2 + 1 = 206$

Fig. 1. EMD Encoding procedure

Example 1: [208 205 209 211], $n = 4, f = 1$. Let $d = 3$. Since $s = 2$, an encoder would increase the gray value of the first pixel by 1 to produce the stego-pixels [208 206 209 211]. At the decoder, $f = 3$. The decoder can extract secret message 3. The detailed explanation can be seen in Fig.1.

Example 2: [137 139 141 140], $n = 4, f = 3$. Let $d = 0$. Since s = 6, an encoder would decrease the gray value of the third pixel by 1 to produce the stego-pixels [137 139 140 140]. At the decoder, $f = 0$. The decoder can extract secret message 0.

In fact, the EMD embedding scheme provides a very good stego image quality with the PSNR value greater than 52 dB and the embedding capacity is 1.16 bpp when $n = 2$. However, it is not appropriate to send a big message to a receiver. This requires that the capacity of an image is increased.

3   The Proposed Scheme

In this section, we shall present the proposed steganography scheme based on a $(2^{n+2}-1)$-ary notational system in a group of pixels. Our scheme is composed of the embedding and extracting procedure, described below. This paper proposes a novel steganographic embedding method that fully exploits the modification directions. In this method, modifications in different directions are used to represent distinctive secret data, leading to a higher embedding efficiency.

3.1   The Embedding Procedure

In the EMD method, just one bit is increased or decreased in a group of pixels. Therefore, we have an idea from those viewpoints that it is possible to increase or decrease by a maximum of four bits in a group of pixels with a high stego image. We formulated the concept of Eq.2 to hide the more secret bit than that of the EMD method. b_i uses embedding and extracting secret data in function f as a weighted sum modulo $(2^{n+2}-1)$. n is a group of pixels. In the case of $n=2$, b_i is [1, 3, 6, 9, 12,..., $(n-1)\times3$]. Table 1 is used for encoding in our proposed $(2^{n+2}-1)$-ary system. s uses encoding to make $d = f$, and it is composed of three types. If $d \geq f$, calculate $d - f$, and if $d < f$ and $n > 2$, calculate $(2^{n+2} - 1)$-$|d$-$f|$, and if $d < f$ and $n = 2$, calculate $(2^{n+2} - 1)$-$|d$-$f|$. After finding the value s from equation (4), apply equation (5) to a group of pixels.

$$f(g_1, g_2,..., g_n) = \left[\sum_{i=1}^{n}(g_i \bullet b_i)\right] \mod (2^{n+2} - 1) \tag{2}$$

where,

$$[b_1, b_2,..., b_n] = \{[1, 3, 6, 9,..., (n-1)\times3, \; n \geq 2 \tag{3}$$

and

$$s = \begin{cases} d - f & if \; d \geq f \\ (2^{n+2} - 1) - |d - f| & if \; d < f \; and \; n \geq 2 \end{cases} \tag{4}$$

$$g = g + g_s \tag{5}$$

Example 3: We will explain the embedding procedure with an example. For a group of pixels, vector g = [10 5 3]. If the extraction function value is f and the value to hide is d, we need to find a suitable g to make $f = d$. For example, let n be 3. The numbers generated by the basis vector [1 3 6] are shown in Table 2.

Step1: It is necessary to calculate the f value with a three pair of g and basis vector [1 3 6]. f is 13 as Eq.2.

Step2: If you want to hide decimal digit 5 into g, what you need to do first is to compute the value g_s with Eq.4. After calculation, the result is -8. In this case, d is less than or equal f. i.e., we calculate s= $(2^{n+2}-1)-|d - f|$. That is, s is 7.

Step3: Look up s=7 from Table 1 using the index and find the row of 7, which is [1 0 1] starting with the first and last value of the pixel value vector that should be increased by 1. Therefore, g_s is [1 0 1]. It is referenced by s. So, the result of a group of pixels becomes [11 5 4].

Table 1 is used to reference s encode and decode using Eq.2. We need to expand the EMD method.

Table 1. A basis vector [1, 3, 6] when n is 3

index	1	3	6
0	0	0	0
1	1	0	0
2	-1	1	0
3	0	1	0
4	1	1	0
5	-1	0	1
6	0	0	1
7	1	0	1
8	-1	1	1
9	0	1	1
10	1	1	1
11	2	1	1
12	0	0	2
13	1	0	2
14	-1	1	2
15	0	1	2
16	0	-1	-2
17	1	-1	-2
18	-1	0	-2
19	0	0	-2
20	-2	-1	-1
21	-1	-1	-1
22	0	-1	-1
23	1	-1	-1
24	-1	0	-1
25	0	0	-1
26	1	0	-1
27	-1	-1	0
28	0	-1	0
29	1	-1	0
30	-1	0	0

3.2   The Extracting Procedure

The decoding procedure is very simple, because you have only to know the f value as in Eq.2 with a group of pixels. That is, f is an embed bit in a pixel-group.

Example 4: Consider a pixel-group [253 203 250] with n = 3 and f = 7. We assume a secret digit is 4, s is 12. The s value can be calculated by Eq.4. The next step is to reference s from Table 1, and apply referenced values to a group of pixel value vectors $g = [253\ 203\ 252]$. The decoding process is very simple. That is, we apply Eq.2 to a group of pixels, $g = [254\ 203\ 252]$. Therefore, we will find $f = 4$, and digit 4 is extracted successfully from the group of pixels $[253\ 203\ 252]$.

Step1: First, we must calculate f with Eq.2 and the basis vector $[1\ 3\ 6]$. In this case, we can extract $f = 7$ in the $(2^{n+2}-1)$-*ary* system.

Step2: For a secret digit 4, we need to find the s value from Eq.4. It is easy to extract the s value from $(2^{n+2}-1)$-|d-f|, that is, $s = 12$.

Step3: Look up Table 1 and find s from the row, which is $[0\ 0\ 2]$ stating that the last value of the pixel value vector should be increased by 2. Therefore, the changed pixel value vector becomes $[253\ 203\ 252]$. In the case of an overflow or underflow, (g_1, g_2, g_3) has to be adjusted to the appropriate values. The rules are in Eq.6 and Eq.7

$$if\ g_s > 255, \qquad g = g_s - (2^{n+2} - 1) \tag{6}$$

$$if\ g_s < 0, \qquad g = g_s + (2^{n+2} - 1) \tag{7}$$

Step4: A receiver is needed to calculate f with Eq.2 to find the message from the stego-image. No extra calculation is needed, so it is a very simple algorithm. In this case, f is 4.

4   Experimental Results

The purpose of our scheme is to embed data into a cover image for secret communications. This requires the proposed method to have high capacity and good image quality. We experimented with some grayscale image and compared them to other methods, such as EMD [12] and Lee's method [13], to show the performance of the proposed method. The secret data used in this experiment use the MATLAB function rand () to generate a pseudo random number, rounded to $(2^{n+2}-1)$-*ary* number to generate a payload. Then, we apply the EMD [12] and proposed scheme to test images, including the University of Southern California [17].

In general, the evaluation of data hiding performance depends on the visual quality of the stego image and data hiding capacity. Hence, data hiding capacity is a crucial issue to consider in evaluating the performance of data hiding methodologies. Data hiding capacity is defined as the amount of data that can be hidden under the cover image. The capacity of EMD is $R = \log_2(2n+1)/n$, where n is a group of pixel numbers and $n \geq 2$, which has the best embedding rate R of $(\log_2(5))/2=1.161$, when n is set to be 2.

In the proposed method, $R = \log_2(2^{n+2}-1)/n$, where $n = 2$, which has also the best embedding rate R of $\log_2(15) = 1.9534$, which is about two times than that of the EMD method. Fig.2 compares the embedding rate for EMD [12] embedding and the proposed methods. The simulation reveals the capacity of our scheme is better than that of the EMD scheme.

Lee's method [13] is to use a virtual hypercube as a random number to increase capacity in an image. This method only stores $g_{2n} +1 - s$ value in a pair pixel. Thus, a group of pixels do not modify from Eq.1. p_m is a local range in a pair of pixels, where s is stored. When p_m is 3, the capacity of data hiding is less than that of EMD. This is why we do not compare it to the proposed method.

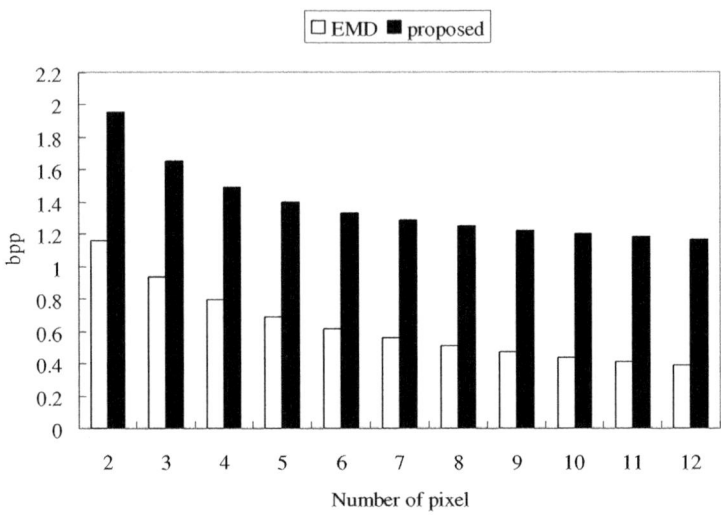

Fig. 2. Comparison of capacity rate between proposed and EMD

We experiment with nine grayscale images, such as Lena, Baboon, Elaine, Airplane, Pepper, Goldhill, Barbara, Boat and Zela, as cover-images. Their size is 512×512 pixels.

In our proposed method, the embedding rate $R = (\log_2(15))/2 = 1.9534$. This is a greater payload than that of EMD. In the real experiment, we hide 516,823 bits in the cover image and the proposed method is higher capacity than that of Lee's method [13]. Furthermore, our method is better than Lee's [13] method, because it does not always flipping four bits in a group of pixels. Sometimes, there is no flipping bit in a group of pixels. Conversely, Lee's method always flips three bits, when p_m is three. Thus, this method is a not a complete method to use in the aspect of optimization. In the case of less optimization, it can be possible to allow a statistical analysis attack. Therefore, Lee's method [13] does not conceal the secret message in a stego image from the steganographic technique [14]. The average PSNR value of our proposed method is about 48.2797 *dB*. In fact, our method is not as good quality as that of EMD. However, 48.2797 *dB* are a high quality image, so it can resist steganalysis detection using a human visual system. Thus, it is acceptable to use a carrier for secret communications. Table 2 shows the comparison PSNR between our proposed method and Lee's method when $n = 3$. As you can see Table 2, our proposed method is very good PSNR against that of Lee's method.

Table 2. The PSNR of nine test cover images when $n = 3$

Test Image	Proposed Method	Lee's method [13]
Lena	48.2765	46.5777
Baboon	48.2768	46.5613
Tiffany	48.2877	46.5953
Airplane	48.2887	46.5626
Pepper	48.3869	48.2887
Goldhill	48.2805	46.5894
Barbara	48.2738	46.5681
Boat	48.2749	46.5371
Zelda	48.2717	46.5827

5   Conclusion

Secret communications over the Internet have become an issue of communication fields, because it is not easy to protect a secret message from hackers and attackers. Steganography provided a secure safety channel for communications. Thus, researchers developed various stegnography schemes. However, there are a few methods to provide high capacity of secret messages and good quality of an image. Therefore, we improved a steganography of EMD [12] scheme. Our proposed scheme provided a $\log_2(2^{n+2} -1)$-*ary* system, so that our method has better capacity than that of EMD [12]. Lee's method [13] has lower image quality than our method.

Acknowledgement

This work was supported by the Industrial Strategic technology development program (10011346, Development of Intelligent Human Interface Terminal and Context-Awareness Gateway) funded by the Ministry of Knowledge Economy (MKE, Korea)

References

1. Wang, H., Wang, S.: Cyber warfare:steganography vs. steganalysis. Communication of the ACM 47(10), 76–82 (2004)
2. Goljan, M., Hogea, D., Soukal, D.: Quantitative Steganalysis of Digital Images: Estimating the Secret Message Length. ACM Multimedia Systems Journal, Special Issue on Multimedia Security 9(3), 288–302 (2003)
3. Katzenbeisser, S., Petitcolas, F.A.P. (eds.): Information Hiding Techniques for Steganography and Digital Watermarking. Artech House Books, Boston (2000) ISBN I-58053-35-4

4. Westfeld, A.: F5-A steganographic algorithm. In: Moskowitz, I.S. (ed.) IH 2001. LNCS, vol. 2137, pp. 289–302. Springer, Heidelberg (2001)
5. Provos, N., Honeyman, P.: Hide and Seek: An Introduction to Steganography. IEEE Security and Privacy 1(3), 32–44 (2003)
6. Yua, Y.-H., Changa, C.-C., Hub, Y.-C.: Hiding secret data in images via predictive coding. Pattern Recognition 38(5), 691–705 (2005)
7. Mielikainen, J.: LSB matching revisited. IEEE Signal Processing Letters 13(5), 285–287 (2006)
8. Chan, C.-K., Cheng, L.M.: Hiding data in images by simple LSB substitution. Pattern Recognition 37(3), 469–474 (2004)
9. Lin, I.-C., Lin, Y.-B., Wang, C.-M.: Hiding data in spatial domain images with distortion tolerance. Computer Standards and Interfaces 31(2), 458–464 (2009)
10. Chang, C.C., Chen, T.S., Chung, L.Z.: A steganographic method based upon JPEG and quantization table modification. Information Sciences-Informatics and Computer Science 141(1-2), 123–138 (2002)
11. Spauldinga, J., Noda, H., Shirazib, M.N., Kawaguchia, E.: BPCS steganography using EZW lossy compressed images. Pattern Recognition Letters 23(13), 1579–1587 (2002)
12. Zhang, X., Wang, S.: Efficient Steganographic Embedding by Exploiting Modification Direction. IEEE Communications Letters 10(11), 781–783 (2006)
13. Lee, C.-F., Chang, C.-C., Wang, K.-H.: An improvement of EMD embedding method for large payloads by pixel segmentation strategy. Image and Vision Computing 26(12), 1670–1676 (2008)
14. Fridrich, J., Goljan, M., Du, R.: Detecting LSB steganography in color, and gray-scale images. IEEE Trans. Multimedia 8, 22–28 (2001)
15. Westfe3d, A., Pfitzmann, A.: Attacks on Steganographic Syste. In: Proc. 3rd Information Hiding Workshops, Dresden, Germany, September 28-October 1, pp. 61–75 (1999)
16. Goljan, M., Soukal, D.: Higher-Order Statistical Steganalysis of Palette Images. In: Proc. SPIE, Electronic Imaging, Security, Steganography, Watermarking of Multimedia Contents V, Santa Clara, California, pp. 178–190 (2003)
17. http://sipi.usc.edu/database/

An Ontology Based Information Security Requirements Engineering Framework

Azeddine Chikh[1], Muhammad Abulaish[2,*],
Syed Irfan Nabi[2,3], and Khaled Alghathbar[1,2]

[1] College of Computer and Information Sciences, King Saud University Riyadh, KSA
az_chikh@ksu.edu.sa
[2] Centre of Excellence in Information Assurance, King Saud University Riyadh, KSA
{mAbulaish,syedIrfan,kAlghathbar}@ksu.edu.sa
[3] Faculty of Computer Science, Institute of Business Administration, Karachi, Pakistan

Abstract. Software Requirement Specification (SRS) is frequently evolving to reflect requirements change during project development. Therefore, it needs enhancement to facilitate its authoring and reuse. This paper proposes a framework for building a part of SRS related to information security requirements (ISRs) using ontologies. Such a framework allows ensuring ISRs traceability and reuse. The framework uses three kinds of generic ontologies as a solution to this problem – software requirement ontology, application domain ontology, information security ontology. We propose to enhance SRS by associating the ISR with specific entities within ontologies. We aim to facilitate a semantic-based interpretation of ISRs by restricting their interpretation through the three previous ontologies. Semantic form is used to improve our ability to create, manage, and maintain ISRs. We anticipate that the proposed framework would be very helpful for requirements engineers to create and understand the ISRs.

Keywords: Information security, software requirements engineering, Software requirements specification.

1 Introduction

Due to increasing popularity and development of domain-specific ontologies there is an increasing effort of research dedicated to applying ontologies in software engineering and in its subset software requirements engineering (SRE) [1,2,5-7]. But, much of the research efforts have concentrated upon ontologies representing requirements models in general and a little effort has been made to address specific areas such as information security requirements (ISRs) engineering. Since it is such an important sub-area for many modern information systems and involves a complex set of concepts of its own, we see this as a shortcoming and the present research work, which could be considered as another labor of this trend, aims to apply ontologies to eliciting and managing ISRs. Authors in [8], believe that information security (IS)

---

* Corresponding author. On leave from Jamia Millia Islamia (A Central University), New Delhi, India.

J.J. Park et al. (Eds.): STA 2011, CCIS 186, pp. 139–146, 2011.

poses challenges to SRE that exceed those posed by other non-functional requirements, and so they elevate it to be a research hotspot. In order to tackle these challenges we advocate the idea that ontologies can be used to annotate ISRs content, thus providing them with semantics.

In recent past, a small number of research works have been directed towards using ontologies in ISR engineering. In [5], Asheras *et al.* have proposed an ontology-based framework for representing and reusing security requirements based on risk analysis. A risk analysis ontology and a requirement ontology are developed and combined. It aims to represent reusable security requirements formally. Similarly, Lee *et al.* [18] have presented a novel technique from SRE and knowledge engineering for systematically extracting, modeling, and analyzing ISRs and related concepts from multiple enforced regulatory documents. They apply a methodology to build problem domain ontology from regulatory documents enforced by the Department of Defense Information Technology Security Certification and Accreditation Process.

In this paper, we propose the design of an ontology-based Information Security Requirements engineering framework which supports analysts in building and managing their ISRs. The proposed framework allows analysts to reuse existing IS knowledge in building new ISRs. The fundamental challenge for our framework is the management of ISR knowledge. While IS ontologies and requirements ontologies already exist, to the best of our knowledge, no methods have been proposed to map existing knowledge and best-practices guidelines on ISR to those existing ontologies.

The remainder of the paper is organized as follows. Section 2 presents a brief overview of SRE. It also presents the role of ontologies and IS in SRE. In section 3, we present the ISRs framework that integrates IS, SR, and application domain ontologies to annotate the domain knowledge resources for building new ISRs. Finally, section 4 draw conclusions and suggest future perspectives.

2   Software Requirements Engineering

SRE is a sub-category of requirements engineering that deals with the elicitation, analysis, specification, and validation of requirements for software [10] and it is critical for successful software development. SR are growing in importance as a means for the customer to know in advance what solution he/she will get.

The software requirement specification (SRS) is an official statement of what the system developers should implement. It should include both the user requirements for a system and a detailed specification of the system requirements [9]. A different understanding of the concepts involved may lead to an ambiguous, incomplete specification and major rework after system implementation [1]. Accordingly, it is important to assure that all analysts and stakeholders in the analysis phase have a shared understanding of the application domain. Even when users can express their needs, analysts find it difficult to write them accurately. The result is that the real demands and the written requirements don't match [9]. The nature of SRE involves capturing knowledge from many sources. Ontologies can be used for both, to describe requirements specification [8,9] and formally represent requirements content. Ontologies seem to be well suited for an evolutionary approach to the specification of requirements and domain knowledge [4]. In addition, ontologies can be used to support requirements management and traceability [3].

2.1 Software Requirements Engineering Ontology

The SRE ontology we have selected to be part of our framework has been proposed by [7] and named SWORE - SoftWiki Ontology for Requirements Engineering. SoftWiki (Distributed, End-user Centered Requirements Engineering for Evolutionary Software Development) is to support the collaboration of all stakeholders in software development processes in particular with respect to SR. Potentially very large and spatially distributed user groups shall be enabled to collect, semantically enrich, classify and aggregate SR. The rationale is to provide a semantic structure, which will capture requirements relevant information and enables interlinking of this information with domain and application specific vocabularies.

Figure 1 visualizes the core of the SWORE ontology, which was developed in accordance with standards of the requirements engineering community [11]. Central to this ontology are the classes – Stakeholder and Abstract Requirement along with property details. Abstract requirements have the subclasses – Goal, Scenario, and Requirement each of which are defined by stakeholders and can be detailed by other abstract requirements. This enables the specification of abstract requirements at different levels of granularity. The collaborative aspects of requirements engineering are emphasized by integrating discussions amongst the stakeholders and voting in the model. In the requirement engineering process this documentation is often relevant for future decisions. [7].

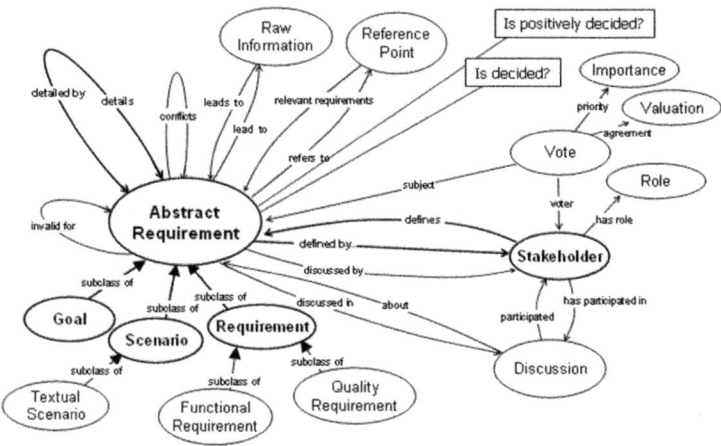

Fig. 1. Visualisation of the SWORE Ontology Core [7]

2.2 Information Security in Software Requirements Engineering

Information security requirements (ISRs) include the types and levels of protection necessary for equipment, data, information, applications, and facilities to meet security policy. Specifically, ISR are identified by risk analysis – the systematic use of information to identify sources and to estimate the risk. Risk analysis is one of the three sources identified by the security standard ISO 27002 (Code of Practice for IS

Management) to identify ISRs [12]. The other two sources are related to the legal, regulatory and contractual requirements of an organization and to the principles, objectives and business requirements for information processing that an organization has developed to support its operations [5].

Navigating the large number of existing dedicated standards for IS for building a new ISRs present a challenge to costumers. Some authors typically find, in reviewing requirements documents, that ISRs, when they exist, are likely to be incomplete or are in a section by themselves and have been copied from a generic list of security features. The requirements elicitation and analysis that are needed to get a better set of ISRs seldom take place. A systematic approach to security requirements engineering will help to avoid the problem of generic lists of features and to take into account the attacker perspective [13]. A number of authors highlighted the needs of an ontology for a security community [14]. Authors in [15] ask the following research question: "To what extent can the IS domain knowledge, including concepts and relations which are required by common IS risk management methodologies, be modeled formally? Which source can be used to enrich the knowledge model with concrete and widely accepted IS knowledge?"

2.3 Ontologies in Information Security

The security ontology we have selected to be part of our framework has been proposed by [15] and based on the security relationship model described in the National Institute of Standards and Technology Special Publication 800-12 [16]. Figure 2 shows the high-level concepts and corresponding relations of this ontology. A threat gives rise to follow-up threats, represents a potential danger to the organization's assets and affects specific security attributes (e.g. confidentiality, integrity, and/or availability) as soon as it exploits a vulnerability in the form of a physical, technical, or administrative weakness, and it causes damage to certain assets. Additionally, each threat is described by potential threat origins (human or natural origin) and threat sources (accidental or deliberate source). For each

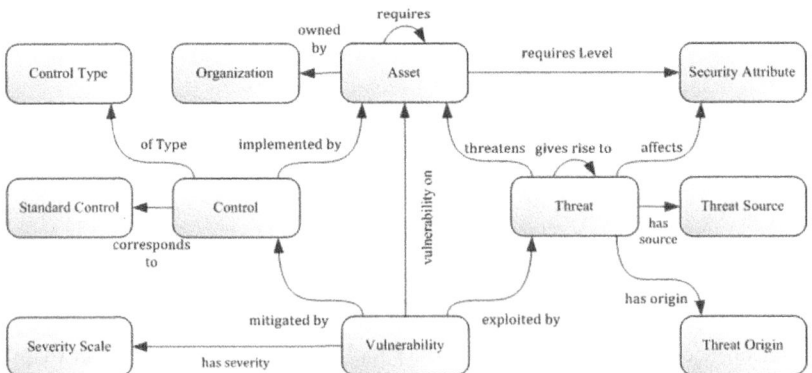

Fig. 2. A sample security ontology proposed in [15]

vulnerability a severity value and the asset on which the vulnerability could be exploited is assigned. Controls have to be implemented to mitigate an identified vulnerability and to protect the respective assets by preventive, corrective, deterrent, recovery, or detective measures (control type). Each control is implemented as asset concept, or as combinations thereof. Controls are derived from and correspond to best-practice and IS standard controls [15].

3 Proposed Ontology Based ISRs Engineering Framework

In this section, we discuss the proposed ontology-based information security requirements engineering framework that can present to the readers (end-users, stakeholders, analysts, designers and developers) an integrated view of the knowledge and best practices related to ISRs within a given software development project. Indeed, the readers of the user requirements, such as end-users, are not habitually concerned with how the system will be implemented. But, the readers of the system requirements, such as designers and developers, need to know more precisely what the system will do because they are concerned with how it will support the domain user tasks. The proposed ontology-based ISRs engineering framework is based on the organization of knowledge in three complementary domains – application, SRE, and IS. The functional details of the major components of the framework are explained as following:

Domain Ontologies containing domain-related concepts and relationships in a structured and machine-interpretable format are used to annotate domain resources. Corresponding to the three above-mentioned domains, we have considered three different ontologies – Software Requirements Ontology (SRO), Information Security Ontology (ISO), and Application Domain Ontology (ADO). We advocate the idea that ontologies can be used to describe ISRs, thus providing them with a new dimension of content reusability. These ontologies are further discussed in the following paragraphs:

SRO encompasses the whole set of SRE concepts. It covers many possibilities – requirements on various levels from goal-level to design-level, different requirements styles from plain texts to diagrams, and from data requirements to quality requirements, many techniques and methods from elicitation and analysis to validation and verification [17]. We have selected as SRO the SWORE ontology (SoftWiki Ontology for Requirements Engineering) in [7].

ISO provides the semantic concepts based on some IS standard such as ISO/IEC_JTC1, and their relationships to other concepts, defined in a subset of the IS domain. We have selected as ISO the security ontology proposed by Fenz & Ekelhart [15] and based on the security relationship model described in the National Institute of Standards and Technology Special Publication 800-12 [16].

ADO involves understanding the application domain (library, human resources, finances, sales, etc.). In order to enable effective ISRs understanding we have to further enhance semantics of their content. Therefore, we recommend that they should be further enhanced by providing application domain ontology based annotations of their content. Many specific application domain ontologies exist on the Web that can be found using the Swoogle[1] – a semantic web search engine.

Knowledge Resources correspond to the three above-mentioned domains – SR resources, IS resources, and application domain resources. These resources represent every document or reference useful in the corresponding domain. This includes theoretical as well as practical knowledge (best practices) in the domain. The framework allows indexing, using and reusing of knowledge resources in different software development projects, based on concepts from the former ontologies.

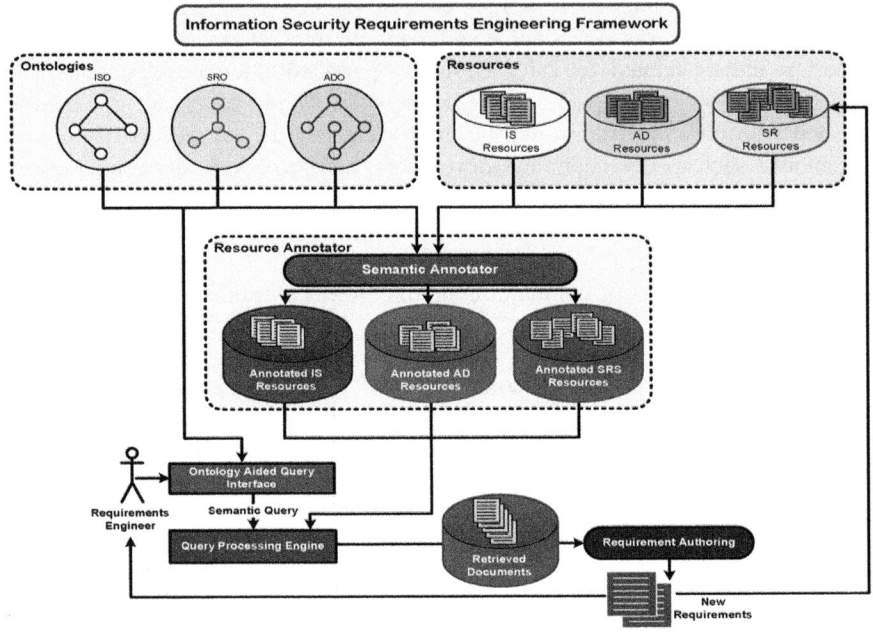

Fig. 3. Ontology-based Information Security Requirements engineering framework

Semantic Annotator : Annotation (also called tagging) is a process that associates names, attributes, comments, or descriptions to a document or to a selected part in it [19]. It provides additional information (metadata) about an existing piece of data. Compared to tagging, which speeds up searching and helps you find relevant and precise information, Semantic Annotation enriches the unstructured or semi-structured data with a context that is further linked to the structured knowledge of a domain and it allows results that are not explicitly related to the original search. Thus, semantic annotation adds diversity and richness to the search process. Semantic Annotation helps to bridge the ambiguity of the natural language when expressing notions and their computational representation in a formal language. By telling a

---

[1] http://swoogle.umbc.edu/

computer how data items are related and how these relations can be evaluated automatically, it becomes possible to process complex filter and search operations. For this purpose, the semantic annotator module exploits the concepts and relationships stored in ontologies and annotate the resources with them. Thus, this module outputs annotated knowledge resources in which relevant components are tagged with ontological concepts.

Semantic Query Processor makes the proposed framework capable to process users (requirements engineers) queries over annotated knowledge resources. The query processor has an ontology-guided query interface that helps users to formulate queries using ontological concepts at different levels of specificities. The output of the query interface sub-module is a semantic query which is passed to the query processing engine to get relevant documents from annotated knowledge resources.

Requirement Authoring takes the retrieved knowledge resources by semantic query processor as input and analyze (reuse) them to build new requirements. The new requirements are present to the users (requirements engineers) and also added in the software requirements resources for future use.

4   Conclusion

In this paper, we have presented an ontology-based information security requirements engineering framework which can facilitates the requirements engineers to create and understand the information security requirements after analyzing domain resources annotated with ontological concepts. The novelty of the proposed framework to unify software requirements, information security, and application domain ontologies to annotate domain knowledge resources. The annotated resources are then analyzed by the semantic query processor to identify new requirements. Presently, we are developing a prototype of the proposed framework to analyze its effectiveness for real-life applications.

References

1. Happel, H.J., Seedorf, S.: Applications of Ontologies in Software Engineering. In: Proceedings of the International Workshop on Semantic Web Enabled Software Engineering, SWESE (2006)
2. Decker, B., Rech, J., Ras, E., Klein, B., Hoecht, C.: Self Organized Reuse of Software Engineering Knowledge Supported by Semantic Wikis. In: Proceedings of the Workshop on Semantic Web Enabled Software Engineering (SWESE) (November 2005)
3. Ayank, V., Kositsyna, N., Austin, M.: Requirements Engineering and the Semantic Web, Representation, Management, and Validation of Requirements and System-Level Architectures. Technical Report, Part II, TR 2004-14, University of Maryland (2004)
4. Wouters, B., Deridder, D., Van Paesschen, E.: The Use of Ontologies as a Backbone for Use Case Management. In: Proceedings of the European Conference on Object-Oriented Programming (ECOOP), Workshop: Objects and Classifications, A Natural Convergence (2000)

5. Asheras, J., Valencia-García, R., Fernández-Breis, J.T., Toval, A.: Modelling Reusable Security Requirements based on an Ontology Framework. Journal of Research and Practice in Information Technology 41(2) (May 2009)
6. Kaiya, H., Saeki, M.: Using Domain Ontology as Domain Knowledge for Requirements Elicitation. In: Proceedings of the IEEE International Requirement Engineering Conference, pp. 186–195 (2006)
7. Yanwu, Y., Xia, F., Zhang, W., Xiao, X., Li, Y., Li, X.: Towards Semantic Requirement Engineering, Semantic Computing and Systems. In: IEEE International Workshop on Semantic Computing and Systems, pp. 67–71 (2008)
8. Cheng, B.H.C., Atlee, J.M.: Research Directions in Requirements Engineering. In: Future of Software Engineering (FOSE), in ICSE, pp. 285–303. IEEE Computer Society, Minneapolis (2007)
9. Sommerville, I.: Software Engineering. Pearson Education, London (2011)
10. Bourque, P., Dupuis, R. (eds.): Guide to the Software Engineering Body of Knowledge. IEEE Computer Society, Los Alamitos (2004)
11. Pohl, K.: Requirements Engineering - Grundlagen, Prinzipien, Techniken. Dpunkt Verlag (2007)
12. ISO27002, ISO/IEC 17799-27002 Code of Practice for Information Security Management (2005)
13. Mead, N.R.: Security Requirements Engineering (2006),
    `https://buildsecurityin.us-cert.gov/bsi/articles/`
    `best-practices/requirements/243-BSI.html`
14. Tsoumas, B., Gritzalis, D.: Towards an Ontology based Security Management. In: Proceedings of the 20th International Conference on Advanced Information Networking and Applications. IEEE Computer Society, Los Alamitos (2006)
15. Fenz, S., Ekelhart, A.: Formalizing information security knowledge. In: Proceedings of the ACM Symposium on Information, Computer and Communications Security (2009)
16. IST. An Introduction to Computer Security – The NIST Handbook. Technical report, NIST (National Institute of Standards and Technology) (October 1995); Special Publication 800-12
17. Lauesen, S.: Software Requirements - Styles and Techniques. Addison-Wesley, Reading (2002)
18. Lee, S.-W., Gandhi, R., Muthurajan, D., Yavagal, D., Ahn, G.-J.: Building Problem Domain Ontology from Security Requirements in Regulatory Documents. In: Proceedings of the International Workshop on Software Engineering for Secure Systems (2006)
19. Popov, B., Kiryakov, A., Ognyanoff, D., Manov, D., Kirilov, A.: KIM – A Semantic Platform for Information Extraction and Retrieval. Journal of Natural Language Engineering 10(3-4), 375–392 (2004)

Simulating Malicious Users in a Software Reputation System

Anton Borg, Martin Boldt, and Bengt Carlsson

Blekinge Institute of Technology, 37141 Karlskrona, Sweden
{anton.borg,martin.boldt,bengt.carlsson}@bth.se

Abstract. Today, computer users have trouble in separating malicious and legitimate software. Traditional countermeasures such as anti-virus tools mainly protect against truly malicious programs, but the situation is complicated due to a "grey-zone" of questionable programs that are difficult to classify. We therefore suggest a software reputation system (SRS) to help computer users in separating legitimate software from its counterparts. In this paper we simulate the usage of a SRS to investigate the effects that malicious users have on the system. Our results show that malicious users will have little impact on the overall system, if kept within 10% of the population. However, a coordinated attack against a selected subset of the applications may distort the reputation of these applications. The results also show that there are ways to detect attack attempts in an early stage. Our conclusion is that a SRS could be used as a decision support system to protect against questionable software.

Keywords: Software reputation system, simulation, reputation system attacks.

1 Introduction

Among the vast horde of software available to the users today, the user is expected to differentiate between various types of software. For example, the user is supposed to be able to recognize software that bundle other programs in order to exploit the user. These programs are often of a dubious nature, monitoring the users habits and selling the information to third parties, alternatively displaying various advertisements that correspond to the users interests [14]. The nature of these programs often makes them fall under categories such as spyware or adware [5].

As the legal status of these programs differ between different juridical territories, these programs fall in a legal grey-zone and as a result the anti-virus industry has hesitated to remove them[1]. Regardless of this, there still exist tools that operate in a manner similar to anti-virus programs available, commonly known as anti-spyware programs. However, there are two main problems with these applications. First, due to the legal status of the programs in question, there is a concern that antispyware programs, because of pressure from software developers, will catch not all dubious applications. Second, many of today's anti-spyware programs are such that they will

---

[1] http://www.benedelman.org/spyware/

J.J. Park et al. (Eds.): STA 2011, CCIS 186, pp. 147–156, 2011.
© Springer-Verlag Berlin Heidelberg 2011

only remove already installed spyware, failing to prevent new spyware from installing. Thus the damage might already be done when anti-spyware applications detect the spyware.

We have proposed using a software reputation system (SRS) as a complement to traditional anti-spyware tools, in order to mitigate several of the questioned aspects of the traditional approach [2][3]. The idea behind SRS is that users should provide ratings of programs that they use, thus providing a collaborative platform for judging applications whilst also removing the legal pressure that traditional anti-spyware developers are subject to. The users will, when trying to install applications be presented with information on how other users have rated the program in question, i.e. providing a preventive mean of allowing informed user decisions. This would provide a mean of preventing the damage done by spyware, as opposed to trying to clean up afterwards.

In this paper we rely on a custom-made simulator for simulating the use of a SRS with users entering and leaving the community dynamically. In this setting we investigate the effects of having a portion of the user-base participating in an attack on a small number of the applications, where they try to maximize different variables for distorting the rating within the SRS. We investigate both the effects on the overall system and for the targeted software programs.

In section 2 we present the related work, which in section 3 is followed by the background of the study. In section 4 we present the simulator and how the experiment was designed. In section 5 the results from the simulation are shown. The results are discussed in section 6 and conclusions are presented in section 7.

2   Related Work

Reputation and recommender systems have increased in popularity since their introduction in the early 1990s, much due to the rapid spread of Internet connectivity. One of the earliest systems was GroupLens that were presented in 1994 by Resnick et al. [12], which enabled automatic filtering of newsgroup content based on the community users' feedback.

Reputation systems and recommender systems are related to each other, but the main difference is that reputation systems take explicit ratings from the users [9]; while recommender systems instead rely on events such as previous purchases of some goods, e.g. books [13]. A well known example of a reputation system is the Internet Movie Database, IMDb, that compile overall movie scores from individual community users' movie ratings. One example of a recommender system is Amazon.com that recommend potentially interesting goods to customers based on for instance previous purchases.

Reputation systems are vulnerable to attack from stakeholders that have much to gain if being able to tweak such systems. As a result there exists several attacks, which Marmol and Perez elaborate on [10]. The attacks range from individual to collaborative in nature, which attack either the whole system or a subset thereof. Some attacks also include camouflaging techniques based on for instance oscillating or random behaviours that allow the malicious users to behave trustworthy except during brief raids. For each attack Marmol and Perez present the cost and detectability, and a conclusion is that an attacker that can cope with medium to high costs can generate attacks with low detectability.

Another taxonomy of the attacks within reputation systems are presented by Hoffman et al. [6], and one conclusion they draw is that it is the open nature of reputation systems that allow for various attacks, which are hard to defend against. Reputation systems are vulnerable to these attacks according to Hoffman et al.:

- Self-promoting, attackers falsely manipulate their own reputation by increasing it.
- Whitewashing, attackers abuse the system but manage to escape the consequences, e.g. by resetting their reputation through some system vulnerability or by rejoining with a new identity.
- Slandering, attackers manipulate the reputation of a victim by reporting false data to lower the victim's reputation.
- Orchestrated, attackers apply several of the above mentioned attack techniques in a sophisticated attack.
- Sybil, a single attacker manage to create a large number of sybil identities within the community that each represent one vote, i.e. allowing the attacker to have several votes.
- Denial of service, attackers manage to subvert the underlying mechanisms of the reputation system.

Both Hoffman and Marmol Perez also present defence strategies as a way to defend against the mentioned attacks. Such defence strategies are composed by a number of techniques, such as heuristics, statistics, randomization and cryptography. One example of an effective defence strategy that is used to protect against file pollution in file-sharing networks is Credence [15], which make use of heuristics, statistics, and cryptography.

Finally, Josang and Golbeck stress the importance of robustness in reputation systems, and they also present some insights about the problems involved in developing a standardized test environment for evaluating all different types of reputation systems [8].

3 Background

In a previous study we investigated the feasibility of a software reputation system in regards to the individual trust factor of users as well as the accuracy of the system given the environment [2]. We found that using user-based trust factors allows separation between different user groups based on their experience, i.e. accuracy in rating software. The individual trust factors reward users with more experience, resulting in an overall stable system.

The previous study was done by implementing a simulator that incorporated user models with different skill levels, which allowed us to simulate various scenarios. In this study we will investigate the effect from malicious user within a SRS. Also, unlike the previous study, users are allowed to enter and terminate their participation within the system, i.e. we are simulating a dynamic system. These scenarios are further explained in section 4 and the simulator is thoroughly explained in [2].

One important difference between a SRS and for instance IMDb is the time constraints imposed on SRS, i.e. the occurrence of an erroneous rating would potentially trick users into installing spyware or keep them from installing clean software were the former having more impact. This could be done by faking a large number of community users that provide erroneous ratings on a single program, i.e. a Sybil attack that result in the rating of the program being altered to the liking of the attacker.

3.1 Simulator Tool

We have in our simulator divided users into different groups consisting of expert, average and novice, where the first group is most likely to vote correctly and the last is least likely. This is done in order to simulate a difference in knowledge between users. These users can rate a program on a 10-graded rating scale.

In order to differentiate different users based on knowledge, each user has a trust factor, which affects the impact of the vote. Every user has an initial trust factor of 1.0 and the factor can never be lower than that. In order to measure the accuracy we randomize a value for each application in the simulator to act as the "correct rating", which we evaluate against. The deviation between the correct rating and the end result we named evaluation score (ES). The trust factor is changed based on the vote cast, e.g. if a user cast a vote that is deemed "good", i.e. the user's vote is within 1 step from the current arithmetic average rating of the software object rated, then the trust factor is increased by a pre decided change factor. However, if the vote is deemed erroneous, i.e. the user votes outside the allotted steps, the trust factor is lowered by an equivalent amount. Thus users, who over time provide more accurate votes, have a bigger impact on the system than an unskilled user.

In previous simulations we found that using an exponential change factor of 1.25 together with a maximum trust factor limit of 1000 is to be preferred. This change factor was found to best differentiate between users, as well as producing an end result within one ES step from an ideal reputation system. The maximum trust factor of 1000 is set in order to prevent individual users from having too much impact.

We have made three improvements of our simulator compared to the previous study. First, we have implemented support for users leaving and entering the SRS during the simulation, i.e. using a non-static user base. This is what we call user change rate. In order to simulate this, we have designated a certain amount of users to be replaced every cycle in the simulation. However, to keep the conformity of the different user groups we have chosen to limit our simulation in the aspect that the number of users leaving the system is equivalent to the number of users entering the system. A subset of the users is randomly selected in the beginning of each simulation cycle, proportionally across the three different user groups. For the selected users, we simply reset their vote counters, i.e. the number of votes cast, and the trust factor, making the user object return to the state it was in when it was created. Of course, this will not affect any of the votes already cast by these users.

The second simulator improvement is that the users now choose which software objects to rate randomly according to a zipf-distribution with a skew of 0.9 [1]. As a result, 10% of the simulated software objects are more popular than the rest, i.e. are more popular and therefore also more likely to receive user ratings. The zipf-distribution was chosen because it has proven to be valid for popularity distribution in other computer science settings as well as various real world distributions [11][4][1].

The third improvement is the introduction of malicious users into the population, as we need to investigate how a SRS behaves when subjected to attacks. This is something that we have seen happen in several real world reputation systems [6], and as a result we need to investigate how a SRS behaves when subjected to attacks. The implementation of the malicious users is done as subgroups of the existing users groups. When voting maliciously, these users will vote as far from the software objects average rating as possible. The malicious users do not always vote maliciously, in an attempt to increase their reputation and impact within the SRS. That is why each malicious user is assigned a trigger chance, i.e. the probability of casting a malicious vote. However, all votes from malicious users target the same subset of software object.

It should also be noted that a user could be marked as both changeable and malicious, so some overlap will most likely occur. That means that some of the malicious users are also likely to be leaving and entering the system users, and as a result will be subject to their profile being reset.

4   Experiment Settings

The simulator we use is meant to reflect how software reputation system works, more importantly how one can with the aid of a reputation system decide if an application is to be considered good or bad. What we want to find out in this study is one of the problems with a collaborative rating system. What happens if a group of users votes bad out of ignorance, in which case the user can be considered a novice, or if a user votes bad out of malicious intent, in which case the user can be considered a malicious user. How do the system react when a portion of the user base vote maliciously, e.g. when an Orchestrated attack is carried out?

In all simulations presented in this work we have a total of 10,000 software programs and 100,000 users, casting a total of 9,600,000 votes, with experts being the smallest group at 9.4%, average group at 27.1%, and the novice group at 63.5%, based on the results in the following survey [7].

We use a user change rate of 1%, which means that for instance 94 expert users (1% of 9400) are replaced on average every cycle in the simulation. This results in an overall retention rate of approximately 37%, which corresponds to statistics from the early use of other social networks such as Facebook and Twitter[2].

4.1   Malicious Users

In order to estimate how well a software reputation system handles malicious users, we have chosen to simulate such scenarios. We simulate scenarios with the following three different constellations where 0.1%, 1% and 10% of the total number of users

---

[2] http://blog.nielsen.com/nielsenwire/online_mobile/
twitter- quitters-post-roadblock-to-long-term-growth/

are being malicious, i.e. 100, 1000 and 10000 distinct users. All malicious users are distributed among the three user groups (expert, average and novice) based on their proportions.

Our attack scenarios can be said to mimic an orchestrated or slandering attack, i.e. a group of users intently using the same behaviour in order to influence the system [8], as well as a Sybil attack. In this case the influence is of a malicious nature since the users wants to alter the ES for a subset of targeted software objects. In our scenarios 1% (or 100) of the total number of software objects are targeted by the attacks. These software objects are also chosen randomly in accordance with the popularity distribution.

The malicious users in our scenarios are designed to be sleepers, i.e. they will appear to be normal users while building up their trust factor, and thus their influence, in the community before turning malicious. A user's trigger chance determines the possibility to cast a malicious vote, if too high the user will never gain enough influence in the SRS to affect its ratings, but on the other hand if too low there will simply not be enough malicious votes to affect the SRS. We therefore simulate four different scenarios that use the following trigger chances 25, 12.5, 6.25 and 3.125%.

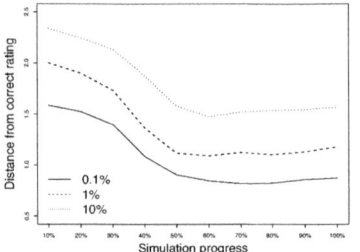
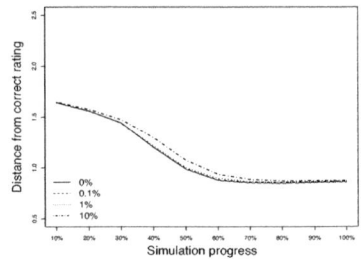

(a) Three different scenarios with varying number of malicious users targeting the same set of 100 software programs

b) Overall system accuracy based on four scenarios with different trigger chances and a population of 1% malicious users

Fig. 1. The impact of malicious users attacking the targeted list of software and the overall system

5   Results

In the following section we present the results from our simulated scenarios with malicious users. We have found that the introduction of user change rate have a subtle effect on the system. Comparing the baseline of 1% user change rate with no change rate at all (that is a static user base) the results were found to be approximately the same.

5.1   Malicious Users

Figure 1(a) shows the results of malicious users attacking a small group of 100 programs. Every vote cast by the malicious users have a 12.5% chance of being malicious. The results for 1% malicious users show a deviation of approximately 2.0 ES from correct value in the beginning of the simulation. However, the ES quickly decreases and halfway, i.e. after 50% of the total number of votes has been cast, it has reached an ES of approximately 1.0 since the non-malicious users have built up their trust factor. Then, in the second half of the simulation there is a slight increase of ES as expert users begin to reach the maximum trust factor limit, i.e. their influence can not grow any further. As can be seen in Figure 1(a) there is a noticeable difference when comparing 1% malicious users with a population of instead 0.1%, which starts at an ES of 1.6 and reach 0.9 halfway through. However, in the latter scenario there is only a very subtle increase of the ES in the second half of the simulation.

When comparing the effect malicious users have on the overall system, as seen in Figure 1(b), the malicious users do not have any noticeable affect on the overall SRS with a malicious population of 1.0% or less. For the scenario with a population of 10% malicious users there is at most only a slight difference of approximately 0.1 ES. However, even this minor difference vanish in the second half of the simulation as the increased impact of the regular users catch up.

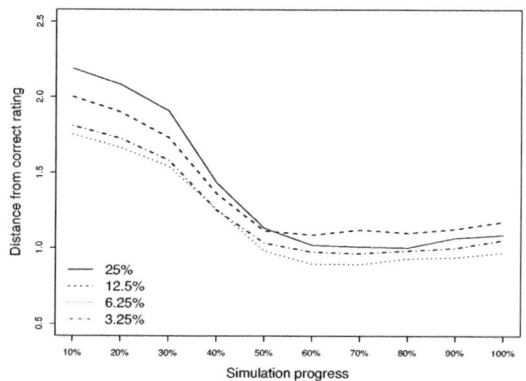

Fig. 2. The effects of various chances of voting malicious with 1% malicious users targeting a subset of software

In another scenario we investigate how different trigger chances of the malicious users affect the success of the attack. Figure 2 shows the ES for the 100 targeted software programs, when a population of 1% of malicious users make use of four different trigger chances. Our results show that even though there is a high chance of malicious voting taking place, the system is capable of suppressing the malicious votes, i.e. such user behaviour stick out and is therefore possible to detect and maybe also address.

Our data also shows that we can detect the occurrence of such an attack by looking at the sum of the trust factors for any program and comparing them to other applications. The trust factor sum for an attacked program in such a scenario is, on average, quite a lot larger than for programs in general. In some cases up to 20-30 times larger. These tendencies can be seen early in the simulation progress, and is therefore a promising approach to detecting attacks.

Finally we made a comparison how the simulated reputation system using trust factors for all users would compare with a simpler reputation system where all users are given the same impact, i.e. a system that calculates the software ratings as simple arithmetic mean based on all votes. In such a system the overall system accuracy would be 1.7 ES throughout the whole simulation, which could be compared with the SRS that stabilizes at about 1.0 ES as shown in Figure 1(b). That is approximately a 70% improvement of accuracy once the SRS has stabilized. When only considering the attacked software programs, the ES are 1.7, 2.0 and 2.6 for 0.1, 1 and 10% malicious users respectively, i.e. also considerable improvements.

6 Discussion

The proposed simulated reputation system involves an environment of rated programs with varying popularity and with a differentiation of votes given by the users depending on their skills. More exactly we used a zipf-distribution and an exponentially increased trust factor with an upper bound of 1000 initial votes. Furthermore, a dynamic population of differently skilled users determine the accuracy within the reputation system. As a result, the trust factor allows an initially small amount of expert votes to later on outperform the votes from a far larger group consisting of for instance novice and malicious users. On the other hand, an expert leaving the reputation system will be replaced by another expert starting with an initial trust factor of 1.0, i.e. most probably a larger decrease of the trust factor than for an average or a novice user. The different parameters used in the simulation were either based on external scientific sources or by testing different variables, e.g. varying the trigger chance for malicious users.

Malicious users were introduced and by using a coordinated attack it is possible to substantially influence the rating of a selected subset of applications available in a SRS. The ES of the targeted software decreases in the middle of the simulation (between 30 and 60%) as seen in Figure 1(a). This is explained by a proportional larger impact from malicious users in the beginning of the simulation (around 0-30%) in combination with continuously increasing trust factors for non-malicious users. If a deviation of ±1 ES (or 10% on a 10 graded rating scale) in rating accuracy is regarded as acceptable, then the SRS can withstand around 1% malicious users focusing their combined attack on a small subset of all available programs. However, when instead looking at the overall system accuracy the SRS can withstand even more than 10% malicious users while still keeping an accuracy of ±1 ES.

A SRS may be highly vulnerable to various attacks, which makes detection of attack attempts an important topic. An attack scenario with 1% malicious users attacking a limited number of 100 programs was also simulated. These malicious users adopt successful strategies in order to increase their trust factor before voting maliciously, i.e. improving their reputation by voting as ordinary novice, average or expert users at all other occasions. A favourable malicious strategy should get both a fast response and a fairly high evaluation score when voting on the attacked programs, i.e. limit the number of votes given in order to accumulate the trust factor. Looking at Figure 2 we see the result of four different strategies consisting of voting malicious on average 25% to 3.125% of given votes. These results show that the system stabilizes halfway into the simulation and in the second half there is only a slight increase in the overall ES. An attacker would probably consider the case with a trigger chance of 12.5% to be the "best" attack strategy due to the overall high ES. An important note here is that the users in an SRS does not have to know what trust factor they are currently holding, which would make it harder for malicious users to find the most suitable trigger chance for the attack.

Malicious users can be counteracted in two ways, either automatically based on the trust factors within the reputation system, or calculate the distance between the logged votes and the average rating of the program, where a long distance could indicate an attack. The final measure to protect the reputation system could be to temporarily freeze the programs that are under attack, i.e. not to register any new votes for these programs over some limited period of time. However, it should be noted that these indications not always point out an attack, and should therefore be used more as a warning system that requires for instance a moderator to look into the program in question. Given these circumstances, reputation systems can withstand severe collaborative attacks from a fairly high proportion of malicious users.

7 Conclusion and Future Work

A dynamic reputation system involving different skilled users was simulated. Malicious users were introduced and by using a coordinated attack it was possible to substantially influence the rating of a selected subset of the applications. The malicious strategies simulated included both scenarios that prioritized a fast response as well as an optimal damage to the attacked programs.

Since any reputation system is open for attacks from unscrupulous users it is important to implement measures to mitigate such effects. Our simulated reputation system that is based on individual trust factors shows an increased overall accuracy of approximately 70% compared to an ordinary reputation system using no trust factors at all, i.e. where every user have the same impact. In addition to this we also conclude two ways of detecting attack attempts. First by monitoring the trust factor sum for programs, where increased sums of up to 20-30 times the average could indicate an attack. Secondly, by measuring the distance between users votes and the average rating for software. Potential response measures could be to either silently reject ratings from suspected malicious users, or to temporarily freeze the programs that are under attack while manual investigation is conducted. Based on these measures it is our conclusion that a software reputation system can withstand severe collaborative attacks from a fairly high proportion of malicious users.

References

1. Adamic, L.A., Huberman, B.A.: Zipf's law and the internet. Glottometrics 3, 143–150 (2002)
2. Boldt, M., Borg, A., Carlsson, B.: On the simulation of a software reputation system. In: ARES 2010 International Conference on Availability, Reliability, and Security 2010, pp. 333–340 (2010)
3. Boldt, M., Carlsson, B., Larsson, T., Lindén, N.: Preventing privacy-invasive software using collaborative reputation systems. In: Jonker, W., Petković, M. (eds.) SDM 2007. LNCS, vol. 4721, pp. 142–157. Springer, Heidelberg (2007)

4. Breslau, L., Cao, P., Fan, L., Phillips, G., Shenker, S.: Web caching and zipf-like distributions: Evidence and implications. In: Proceedings of Eighteenth Annual Joint Conference of the IEEE Computer and Communications Societies, INFOCOM 1999. IEEE, Los Alamitos (January 1999)
5. Good, N., Dhamija, R., Grossklags, J., Thaw, D., Aronowitz, S., Mulligan, D., Konstan, J.: Stopping spyware at the gate: a user study of privacy, notice and spyware. In: Proceedings of the 2005 Symposium on Usable Privacy and Security, p. 52 (2005)
6. Hoffman, K., Zage, D., Nita-Rotaru, C.: A survey of attack and defense techniques for reputation systems. ACM Computing Surveys (January 2008)
7. Horrigan, J.: Pew internet & americal life project: A typology of information and communication technology users (May 2007),
   http://www.pewinternet.org/Reports/2007/ATypology-of-Information-and-Communication-Technology-Users.aspx
8. Jøsang, A., Golbeck, J.: Challenges for robust of trust and reputation systems. In: 5th International Workshop on Security and Trust Management (STM 2009) (September 2009)
9. Josang, A., Ismail, R., Boyd, C.: A survey of trust and reputation systems for online service provision. Decision Support Systems 43(2), 618–644 (2007)
10. Marmol, F., Pérez, G.: Security threats scenarios in trust and reputation models for distributed systems. Computers & Security (January 2009)
11. Pitkow, J.: Summary of www characterizations. World Wide Web (January 1999)
12. Resnick, P., Iacovou, N., Suchak, M.: Grouplens: an open architecture for collaborative filtering of netnews. In: Proceedings of the 1994 ACM Conference on Computer Supported Cooperative Work (January 1994)
13. Resnick, P., Varian, H.: Recommender systems. Communications of the ACM (January 1997)
14. Sipior, J., Ward, B., Roselli, G.: A united states perspective on the ethical and legal issues of spyware. In: Kishino, F., Kitamura, Y., Kato, H., Nagata, N. (eds.) ICEC 2005. LNCS, vol. 3711. Springer, Heidelberg (2005)
15. Walsh, K., Sirer, E.G.: walsh. In: 3rd Symposium on Networked Systems Design & Implementation, pp. 1–14 (April 2006)

Weak Keys of the Block Cipher SEED-192
for Related-Key Differential Attacks

Jongsung Kim[1,*], Jong Hyuk Park[2], and Young-Gon Kim[1,**]

[1] Division of e-Business, Kyungnam University
449 Woryeong-dong, Masan, Changwon, Korea
{jongsungk,ygking}@kyungnam.ac.kr
[2] Department of Computer Science and Engineering,
Seoul National University of Science and Technology
172 Gongreung 2-dong, Nowon-gu, Seoul, Korea
jhpark1@seoultech.ac.kr

Abstract. In this paper, we analyze the block cipher SEED-192 which is an extended version of the ISO/IEC block cipher SEED. According to the result of this paper, there exist weak keys in 8 out of 20 rounds of SEED-192 against related-key differential attacks. This is the first cryptanalytic result for the key schedule of SEED-192.

Keywords: block cipher, SEED-192, weak keys, related-key differential/rectangle/boomerang.

1 Introduction

Recently, SEED-192 was developed [1], which is an extended version of the ISO/IEC block cipher SEED [2]. This extended cipher has the same encryption/decryption process as the 16-round original SEED, while it has 20 rounds in total and applies different rules in the key schedule. The key schedule of SEED-192 is similar to that of SEED; it is implemented on-the-fly and uses 6 registers for the 192-bit key storage. However, till now, there has no cryptanalytic result for the key schedule of SEED-192.

In this paper, we examine the security of SEED-192 by using its key schedule. In our analysis, we observe that reduced-round SEED-192 has various weak keys; related-key differential attacks compromise various weak keys for reduced 8 rounds. For details, see Table 1.

This paper is organized as follows: in section 2, we describe the block cipher SEED-192 with its key schedule. Section 3 introduces how to extract weak keys of SEED-192, and section 4 concludes this paper.

---

* First Author: Jongsung Kim
** Corresponding Author.

J.J. Park et al. (Eds.): STA 2011, CCIS 186, pp. 157–163, 2011.
© Springer-Verlag Berlin Heidelberg 2011

Table 1. Weak keys of reduced-round SEED-192

# rounds	# weak keys	Attack method
8 (1~8 rounds)	2^{122}	Related-key differential attack
8 (9~16 rounds)	2^{123}	Related-key differential attack
8 (3~10 rounds)	2^{123}	Related-key differential attack
8 (11~18 rounds)	2^{119}	Related-key differential attack

2   Description of SEED-192

In this section, we describe the encryption algorithm of SEED-192 with its key schedule (the decryption algorithm of SEED-192 is omitted, as it is just a reverse function of the encryption algorithm).

2.1   Encryption Algorithm

The high-level structure of the encryption algorithm is a Feistel structure which is shown in Figure 1. It accepts a 128-bit plaintext (L^0, R^0) and a 192-bit key K, and outputs a 128-bit ciphertext (L^{20}, R^{20}) after it runs 20 rounds in total.

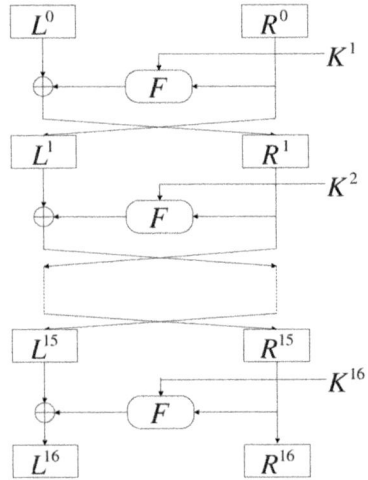

Fig. 1. Structure of SEED-192

We use the following notation.

o $a \boxplus b$: $a + b$ mod 2^{32}

o $X^{<<<s}(X^{>>>s})$: circular rotation of X with s bits to the left (to the right)

o (L^i, R^i) : 128-bit output of round i

o $K^i=(K_0^i,K_1^i)$: 64-bit round key for round i

o KC_i : round constant used in round $i+1$ of the key schedule

The F function accepts 64-bit (C,D) and round key $K^i=(K_0^i,K_1^i)$, and outputs 64-bit (C',D'), where i is the round number. Furthermore, the G function, which is used in the F function, accepts 32-bit and outputs 32-bit. We omit a detailed description of the F and G functions, as our attacks do not use them.

2.2   Key Schedule

The key schedule of SEED-192 accepts 192-bit key K, and then generates 20 round keys. First, the key K is divided into 6 32-bit registers A, B, C, D, E, F: $K=A\backslash\backslash B\backslash\backslash C\backslash\backslash D\backslash\backslash E\backslash\backslash F$. The round key $K^i=(K_0^i,K_1^i)$ used in round i is generated as in Figure 2. The circular rotation rot is used as 9, 8, 12, alternatively, per 2 rounds.

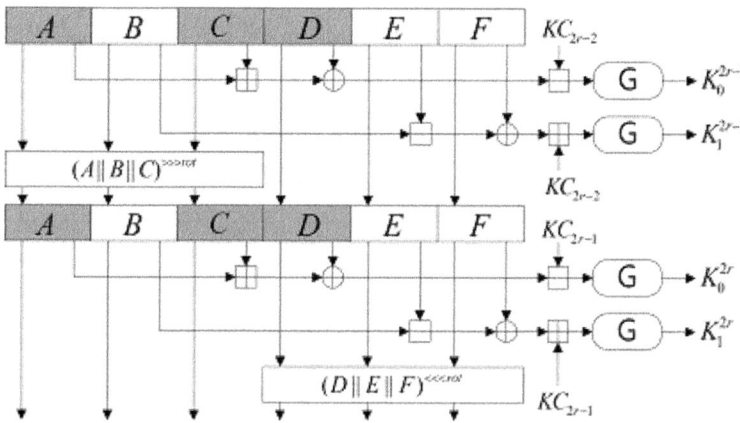

Fig. 2. Key schedule of SEED-192

3   Weak Keys of Reduced-Round SEED-192

The weak-key attack [3] and the related-key attack [4] are both the cryptanalytic tools to use key schedules. If a block cipher uses a weak key, then its security is less than when it uses other keys. According to [3], IDEA has various weak keys to compromise the boomerang attack. The related-key attack is a type of differential cryptanlaysis which applies to block ciphers with related keys, and thus we consider the related-key differential attack as the related-key attack. Moreover, the related-key attack using weak-key classes has been introduced in [5].

In this section, we present weak keys of reduced-round SEED-192 using the related-key differential attack.

The following is the notation which is used throughout this section.

o ΔX: Bitwise XOR difference for register X $(X=A, B, C, D, E$ or $F)$

o x_i : i-th bit of register X ($i=0,1,\ldots,31$: x_0 is the most right bit which is the smallest value in X, and x_{31} is the most left bit which is the largest value in X)

o $\Delta X = e^{i,j}$: i-th and j-th bits of ΔX are both 1 and the other bits are all 0

In order to generate a round key, the key schedule of SEED-192 applies two G functions at the last stage. In this round key generation, we focus on the input and the output for the second G function; its input is $((B-E) \hat{\oplus} F)+Cst$, where Cst is a constant value.

Property 1. If $\Delta B=0$, $B=2^{32}-1$ and $\Delta E=\Delta F$, then $\Delta(B-E)= \Delta E$ and $\Delta((B-E) \hat{\oplus} F)$ $= \Delta E \hat{\oplus} \Delta F =0$. It follows that the output of the second G function is 0, that is, $\Delta G(((B-E) \hat{\oplus} F)+Cst)=0$.

Futhermore, the rotation amounts for $(A\backslash\backslash B\backslash\backslash C)$ and $(D\backslash E\backslash\backslash F)$ in the key schedule are 9, 8, 12, alternatively, and thus their accumulated rotation amounts are the following Property 2.

Property 2. The accumulated rotation amounts in the key schedule are as follows:

r	Accumlated rotaion amounts of $(A\backslash\backslash B\backslash\backslash C)$ in the r-round key generation	Accumlated rotaion amounts of $(D\backslash E\backslash\backslash F)$ in the r-round key generation
1	0	0
2	9	0
3	9	9
4	17	9
5	17	17
6	29	17
7	29	29
8	38	29
9	38	38
10	46	38
11	46	46
12	58	46
13	58	58
14	67	58
15	67	67
16	75	67
17	75	75
18	87	75
19	87	87
20	0	87

Properties 1 and 2 lead to the following property of the key schedule of SEED-192.

Proposition 1. *If the key* $K=A\backslash\backslash B\backslash\backslash C\backslash D\backslash\backslash E\backslash\backslash F$ *and its related key* $K'=A'\backslash\backslash B'\backslash\backslash C'\backslash\backslash D'\backslash\backslash E'\backslash\backslash F'$ *have difference* $\Delta K=0\backslash/0\backslash\backslash 0\backslash\backslash 0\backslash\backslash \Omega \backslash\backslash \Omega$ *(* $\Omega \in S$, $S=\{e^0,e^1,e^2,e^{0,1},e^{0,2},e^{1,2},e^{0,1,2}\}$*) and* $A=B=2^{32}-1$, $c_0=c_1=c_2=c_3=c_4=c_5=1$, *then from the first round key to the eighth round key have all 0 differences, that is,* $\Delta K^1=\Delta K^2=\cdots=\Delta K^8=0$.

(Proof) Proposition 1 is proven by showing that the G functions used in the round key generation for rounds 1-8 have all zero input differences. By the assumption, it is easy to know that $\Delta A=\Delta B=\Delta C=\Delta D$, $\Delta E=\Delta F=\Omega$, and by Property 2, we know that the accumulated rotation amount of $D\backslash\backslash E\backslash\backslash F$ is not larger than 30 for rounds 1-8. It follows that the first G functions for rounds 1-8 have all zero input differences. Moreover, the registers which are used in the input of the second G function in the round key generation are B, E, F, and, $\Delta E=\Delta F$ is in the set S. As stated earlier, the accumulated rotation amount of $D\backslash\backslash E\backslash\backslash F$ is not larger than 30 for rounds 1-8, and thus the bits whose difference is 1 in ΔE, ΔF are still in the same registers E, F till round 8. As the input of the second G function is $(B-E)\hat{=}F$ except for the constant, by the Property 1, the input difference to the second G function is 0 if the difference $B-E$ is equal to the difference F. $A=B=2^{32}-1$, $c_0=c_1=c_2=c_3=c_4=c_5=1$ leads to the register B to be $2^{32}-1$ for rounds 1-8, and $\Delta E=\Delta F=\Omega$. It follows that the input difference to the second G function is 0 for each of rounds 1-8. Therefore, $\Delta K^1=\Delta K^2=\cdots=\Delta K^8=0$. ∎

Using Proposition 1 we have the following 8-round related-key differential with probability 1 for rounds 1-8 of SEED-192 .

Theorem 1. [8-round related-key differential for rounds 1-8] *If the key* $K=A\backslash\backslash B\backslash\backslash C\backslash D\backslash\backslash E\backslash\backslash F$ *and its related key* $K'=A'\backslash\backslash B'\backslash\backslash C'\backslash\backslash D'\backslash\backslash E'\backslash\backslash F'$ *have difference* $\Delta K=0\backslash/0\backslash\backslash 0\backslash\backslash 0\backslash\backslash \Omega \backslash\backslash \Omega$ *(* $\Omega \in S$, $S=\{e^0,e^1,e^2,e^{0,1},e^{0,2},e^{1,2},e^{0,1,2}\}$*) and* $A=B=2^{32}-1$, $c_0=c_1=c_2=c_3=c_4=c_5=1$, *then there exists an 8-round related-key differential* $0\rightarrow 0$ *with probability 1 for rounds 1-8 of SEED-192.*

(Proof) By Proposition 1, we have $\Delta K^1=\Delta K^2=\cdots=\Delta K^8=0$. Therefore, if the plaintext difference is 0, then the output difference after 8 rounds still remains 0. ∎

Theorem 1 shows that SEED-192 has 2^{122} weak keys for which rounds 1-8 are vulnerable to the related-key differential attack.

Similarly, we can find another 8-round related-key differential for rounds 9-16 of SEED-192.

Proposition 2. *If the key* $K=A\backslash\backslash B\backslash\backslash C\backslash D\backslash\backslash E\backslash\backslash F$ *and its related key* $K'=A'\backslash\backslash B'\backslash\backslash C'\backslash\backslash D'\backslash\backslash E'\backslash\backslash F'$ *have difference* $\Delta K=0\backslash/0\backslash\backslash 0\backslash\backslash \Omega'\backslash\backslash \Omega'//0$ *(* $\Omega' \in T$, $T=\{e^{26},e^{27},e^{28},e^{26,27},e^{26,28},e^{27,28},e^{26,27,28}\}$*) and* $a_6=a_7=\cdots=a_{31}=b_0=b_1=\cdots=b_{10}=1$, $C=2^{32}-1$, *then from the ninth round key to the sixteenth round key have all 0 differences, that is,* $\Delta K^9=\Delta K^{10}=\cdots=\Delta K^{16}=0$.

(Proof) In order to generate the ninth round key, registers $(A//B//C)^{>>>38}$ and $(D//E//F)^{<<<38}$ are used. If $\Delta D = \Delta E \subseteq T$ and $\Delta F = 0$, then $(D//E//F)^{<<<38} = 0 \| \Omega // \Omega$ ($\Omega \subseteq S$; refer to Proposition 1 for the set S). Furthermore, $a_6 = a_7 = \cdots = a_{31} = b_0 = b_1 = \cdots = b_{10} = 1$, $C = 2^{32}-1$ are transformed to $A = B = 2^{32}-1$, $c_0 = c_1 = c_2 = c_3 = c_4 = 1$ after 8 rounds (note that registers $A//B//C$ are transformed to $(A//B//C)^{>>>38}$ after 8 rounds). Therefore, the proof of Proposition 1 leads to $\Delta K^9 = \Delta K^{10} = \cdots = \Delta K^{16} = 0$ (note that the reason why the condition for c_5 of Property 1 is excluded is that rounds 9-16 use the rotation amounts 8, 12, 9, 8, while rounds 1-8 do the rotation amounts 9, 8, 12, 9). ∎

Using Proposition 2 we have the following 8-round related-key differential with probability 1 for rounds 9-16 of SEED-192.

Theorem 2. [8-round related-key differential for rounds 9-16] *If the key $K = A\backslash\backslash B\backslash\backslash C\backslash\backslash D\backslash\backslash E\backslash\backslash F$ and its related key $K' = A'\backslash\backslash B'\backslash\backslash C'\backslash\backslash D'\backslash\backslash E'\backslash\backslash F'$ have difference $\Delta K = 0\backslash/0\backslash\backslash 0\backslash\backslash \Omega '\backslash\backslash \Omega '//0$ ($\Omega ' \subseteq T$, $T = \{e^{26}, e^{27}, e^{28}, e^{26,27}, e^{26,28}, e^{27,28}, e^{26,27,28}\}$) and $a_6 = a_7 = \cdots = a_{31} = b_0 = b_1 = \cdots = b_{10} = 1$, $C = 2^{32}-1$, then there exists an 8-round related-key differential $0 \to 0$ with probability 1 for rounds 9-16 of SEED-192.*

(Proof) By Proposition 2, we have $\Delta K^9 = \Delta K^{10} = \cdots = \Delta K^{16} = 0$. Therefore, if the input difference of round 9 is 0, then the output difference of round 16 still remains 0. ∎

Theorem 2 shows that SEED-192 has 2^{123} weak keys for which rounds 9-16 are vulnerable to the related-key differential attack.

Similarly, we can also make 8-round related-key differentials for other rounds of SEED-192 which use other weak keys. The proofs of the following propositions and theorems are omitted, as they are similar to the above ones.

Proposition 3. *If the key $K = A\backslash\backslash B\backslash\backslash C\backslash\backslash D\backslash\backslash E\backslash\backslash F$ and its related key $K' = A'\backslash\backslash B'\backslash\backslash C'\backslash\backslash D'\backslash\backslash E'\backslash\backslash F'$ have difference $\Delta K = 0\backslash/0\backslash\backslash 0\backslash\backslash \Psi \backslash\backslash 0\backslash\backslash \Psi$ ($\Psi \subseteq U$, $U = \{e^{23}, e^{24}, e^{25}, e^{23,24}, e^{23,25}, e^{24,25}, e^{23,24,25}\}$) and $A = 2^{32}-1$, $b_9 = b_{10} = \cdots = b_{31} = c_0 = c_1 = \cdots = c_{13} = 1$, then from the third round key to the tenth round key have all 0 differences, that is, $\Delta K^3 = \Delta K^4 = \cdots = \Delta K^{10} = 0$.*

Theorem 3. [8-round related-key differential for rounds 3-10] *If the key $K = A\backslash\backslash B\backslash\backslash C\backslash\backslash D\backslash\backslash E\backslash\backslash F$ and its related key $K' = A'\backslash\backslash B'\backslash\backslash C'\backslash\backslash D'\backslash\backslash E'\backslash\backslash F'$ have difference $\Delta K = 0\backslash/0\backslash\backslash 0\backslash\backslash \Psi \backslash\backslash 0\backslash\backslash \Psi$ ($\Psi \subseteq U$, $U = \{e^{23}, e^{24}, e^{25}, e^{23,24}, e^{23,25}, e^{24,25}, e^{23,24,25}\}$) and $A = 2^{32}-1$, $b_9 = b_{10} = \cdots = b_{31} = c_0 = c_1 = \cdots = c_{13} = 1$, then there exists an 8-round related-key differential $0 \to 0$ with probability 1 for rounds 3-10 of SEED-192.*

Proposition 4. *If the key $K = A\backslash\backslash B\backslash\backslash C\backslash\backslash D\backslash\backslash E\backslash\backslash F$ and its related key $K' = A'\backslash\backslash B'\backslash\backslash C'\backslash\backslash D'\backslash\backslash E'\backslash\backslash F'$ have difference $\Delta K = 0\backslash/0\backslash\backslash 0\backslash\backslash \Psi '\| \Psi '\|0$ ($\Psi ' \subseteq V$, $V = \{e^{18}, e^{19}, e^{20}, e^{18,19}, e^{18,20}, e^{19,20}, e^{18,19,20}\}$) and $a_{14} = a_{15} = \cdots = a_{31} = b_0 = b_1 = \cdots = b_{22} = 1$, $C = 2^{32}-1$, then from the eleventh round key to the eighteenth round key have all zero differences, that is, $\Delta K^{11} = \Delta K^{12} = \cdots = \Delta K^{18} = 0$..*

Theorem 4. [8-round related-key differential for rounds 11-18] *If the key* $K=A\backslash\backslash B\backslash\backslash C\backslash\backslash D\backslash\backslash E\backslash\backslash F$ *and its related key* $K'=A'\backslash\backslash B'\backslash\backslash C'\backslash\backslash D'\backslash\backslash E'\backslash\backslash F'$ *have difference* $\Delta K=0\backslash/0\backslash\backslash 0\backslash\backslash \Psi'\|\Psi'\|0$ ($\Psi' \in V$, $V=\{e^{18},e^{19},e^{20},e^{18,19}, e^{18,20}, e^{19,20}, e^{18,19,20}\}$) *and* $a_{14}=a_{15}=\cdots=a_{31}=b_0=b_1=\cdots=b_{22}=1$, $C=2^{32}-1$, *then there exists an 8-round related-key differential* $0\to 0$ *with probability 1 for rounds 11-18 of SEED-192.*

Theorem 3 (resp., Theorem 4) shows that SEED-192 has 2^{123} weak keys (resp., 2^{119} weak keys) for which rounds 3-10 (rounds 11-18) are vulnerable to the related-key differential attack.

4   Conclusions

In this paper, we have evaluated the security of the key schedule of SEED-192. According to the result of the paper, SEED-192 has $2^{119}{\sim}2^{123}$ weak keys for which reduced 8 rounds are vulnerable to the related-key differential attack. This is the first cryptanalytic result for the key schedule of SEED-192.

Acknowledgments. This work was supported by Kyungnam University Research Fund, 2011.

References

1. Korea Internet Security Agency (KISA), Development of the block cipher SEED-192/256 (2008)
2. Korea Internet Security Agency (KISA), Development and analysis of the 128-bit block cipher algorithm SEED (2003)
3. Biryukov, A., Nakahara Jr, J., Preneel, B., Vandewalle, J.: New Weak-Key Classes of IDEA. In: Deng, R.H., Qing, S., Bao, F., Zhou, J. (eds.) ICICS 2002. LNCS, vol. 2513, pp. 315–326. Springer, Heidelberg (2002)
4. Biham, E.: New Types of Cryptanalytic Attacks Using Related Keys. Journal of Cryptology 7(4), 229–246 (1994)
5. Lee, E., Kim, J., Hong, D., Lee, C., Sung, J., Hong, S.: Weak-Key Classes of 7-Round MISTY 1 and 2 for Related-Key Amplified Boomerang Attacks. IEICE Transactions on Fundamentals of Electronics, Communications and Computer Sciences E91-A(2), 642–649 (2008)

The Method of Database Server Detection and Investigation in the Enterprise Environment

Namheun Son[1], Keun-gi Lee[1], SangJun Jeon[1], Hyunji Chung[1],
Sangjin Lee[1], and Changhoon Lee[2]

[1] Center for Information Security Technologies
Korea University, Seoul, Korea
{pida2,lifetop,heros86,foryou7187,sangjin}@korea.ac.kr
[2] Hanshin University, Osan, Korea
chlee@hs.ac.kr

Abstract. When a forensic investigation is carried out in the enterprise
environment, most of the important data is stored in database servers, and data
stored in them are very important elements for a forensic investigation. As for
database servers with such data stored, there are over 10 various kinds, such as
SQL Server, Mysql and Oracle. All the methods of investigating a database
system are important, but this study suggests a single methodology likely to
investigate all the database systems while considering the common
characteristics of database system. A method of detecting a server, data
acquiring and investigating data in the server can be usefully used for such an
investigation in the enterprise environment. Therefore, such a methodology will
be explained through a way of carrying out a forensic investigation on SQL
Server Database of Microsoft Corporation.

Keywords: forensic, enterprise, database server, network topology.

1 Introduction

In general, one of the most well-known forensic methods is to carry out a forensic
investigation on a personal PC. When a forensic investigation is carried out in an actual
enterprise environment, however, it shouldn't be overlooked that there exist various
different systems, such as a business-use system simply performing job tasks and a
database system playing a role in storing data. Especially, since most of the data for a
company is stored in its data system, investigating such a system through this method
will help acquire a great deal of meaningful data in terms of forensics. Therefore, it is
very important to adopt a forensic investigation method for database systems.[1]

There are various different kinds of database systems, such as SQL Server, Mysql,
Oracle, Sybase Anywhere, Postgresql, DB2, Sybase ASE and Informix. Besides, there
exist a variety of accounting-specialized programs using a database system, such as
Neo Plus I/II, Neo I PLUS and Neo I CUBE in Korea. There exist some difference in
each database system, but all the database systems basically have common
characteristics.

J.J. Park et al. (Eds.): STA 2011, CCIS 186, pp. 164–171, 2011.
© Springer-Verlag Berlin Heidelberg 2011

Due to such a variety of database systems, it is important to choose a proper investigation method for each database system. Before investigation methods are discussed for each unique database system, however, it is needed to suggest a single comprehensive investigation method by using the common characteristics of database systems. Not only does it help choose an investigation method proper for each database system, but it can be effectively used in investigating the enterprise environment, although investigators don't know all the investigation methods for each database system.

Thus, by using the common characteristics all the database systems have, this study intends to suggest an all-round investigation method, based on which it will also help perform a prompt and accurate forensic investigation on the enterprise environment.

In Chapter 2, the existing researches having been conducted so far will be discussed, and in Chapter 3, discussions will be made about how to detect and investigate a database server. In Chapter 4, through the method suggested in Chapter 3, it will be examined how investigation and analysis are efficiently carried out by targeting SQL Server, the database system of Microsoft Corporation. And then, further studies in this field will be mentioned, while this paper is being concluded.

2   Related Work

In this chapter, researches related to database systems will be discussed.

Kyriacos E. Pavlou said about how to investigate data manipulated in the database system, especially suggesting an algorithm likely to find out information about who manipulated the data as well as the fact the data was manipulated.[2]

Keun Gi Lee mentioned the importance of investigating database systems, while suggesting a method of detecting a database system concealed. Besides, he also suggested another method of detecting the server running a database system. Those methods of detecting such a server function as an important element in this paper.[3]

Jisung Han discussed how to acquire information about connection to a database system with agent tools, such as Mysql Query Browser, SQL Gate for MSSQL and Toad for Oracle, which queries the database, or where the database system is installed. Information about the database system accessed also includes important particulars, such as IP of the server, service port numbers, account names, server names and passwords.[4]

So far, researches in this field have been basically conducted on methods of detecting information concealed inside the database system, seeking servers where database systems are installed or acquiring information about a particular server. In this paper, however, it is examined how a forensic investigation should be carried out on database systems in an actual enterprise environment.

3   Process of Investigation

To perform an efficient investigation on database systems in the enterprise environment, the investigation can be largely divided into three stages, such as server detection, data collection and inquiry into data collected. The stage of server detection deals with a method of detecting the server running a database system, and the stage of data collection discusses a method of collecting data by accessing to the system directly or remotely when the database system is detected. Finally, the stage of investigation suggests a method of using the data, acquired in the stage of collection, at an investigator's computer.

3.1   Server Detection

In case that the internal system of a company is investigated, since there are various systems to examine as an investigation target, and the investigation should be done within a time limit, it is hard to judge what system should be first selected and checked into. In such a case, it is required to grasp the overall network circumstance inside a company as soon as possible, so it is important to acquire the network topology inside the company. To acquire the network topology, detecting server-group systems and the host system will be the main purpose most of all, and especially this paper focuses on detecting the database server where data is stored.

What should be done to collect database data most of all is also to work on checking whether or not a database server exists. As a method of detecting a database server, it is required to check the kind of a database system, its version, IP and service port number with such a network scanning tool as 'Nmap'.[5] Since the enterprise environment varies in every company, and there are various different kinds of database systems all over the world, there may be some cases that a server cannot be found with the existing network scanning tools. In such a case, adding a method of detecting the relevant server to the network scanning tools or creating a network scanning tool to detect it directly should be considered in applying it to an actual investigation. Prior to carrying out an investigation by using scanning tools, it is very important to have interviews with the company staff member in charge of the system. In the stage of interview, it is likely to additionally grasp server locations and accounting information besides basic information such as IP of the database server and service port numbers. Actually, there exists a possibility that more information can be acquired from database servers through this method than scanning tools.

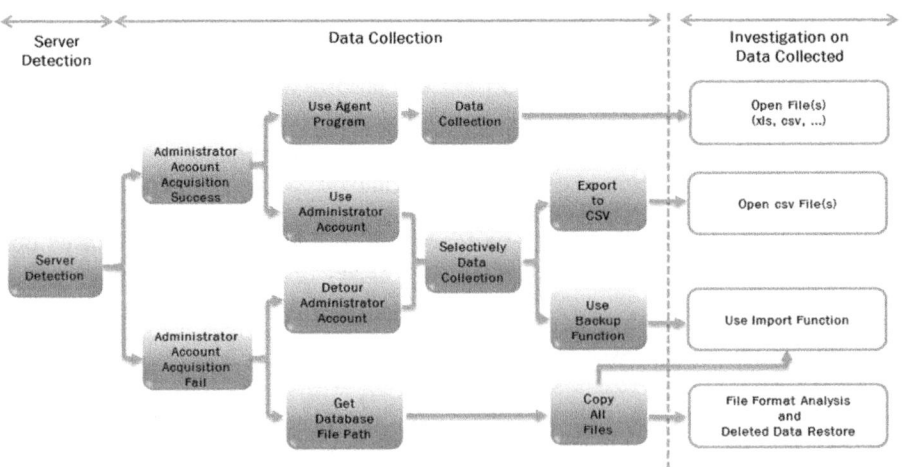

Fig. 1. Process of Investigation

3.2   Data Collection

The stage of collecting data can be largely divided into a stage of selectively collecting files and a stage of collecting the entire files, depending on whether account information is acquired in the stage of interview, or whether there exists a method of making a detour to the administration authority of a database system investigated.

If information about the administration account is acquired from the stage of interview or with the information stored in a database agent, it is possible to selectively collect data only wanted, by directly using the administration account at the relevant database server. Selective collection means to collect data by selecting the entire database, a specific database, a specific table of the database or a specific column of the table. The reason why data should be selectively collected is that it takes too long to collect the entire since data stored in a database system under the enterprise environment. Moreover, only if the entire data were acquired, the data would be too much to carry out an analysis, while the efficiency of an investigation could get lower in general. For selective collection, it is needed to create dump files by using basic back-up commands equipped in the database system, or output into CSV(comma separated value) files by using specific commands. On the other hand, in case that approaching a server directly is not allowed, it is needed to access it by using a database agent (such as SQLGate and Toad), likely to help approach the database remotely, and then collect data by outputting into such files as txt, xls, html(Hypertext Markup Language) and CSV through the data collection function provided by the agent.

If it is failed to acquire information about the administration account either in the stage of interview or with the information stored in the database agent, the administration authority should be acquired by using a method of making a detour at the relevant server, and then selective collection can be performed in the same way as mentioned earlier.

The method of making a detour to the administration account doesn't support all the database systems. In such a case, by finding the path locating a database file where data is actually stored, the database file can be acquired at the server so that it may be examined at an investigator's computer. The database file acquired can be used by being imported to the investigator's computer.

3.3   Investigation on Data Collected

How to investigate data collected can vary, depending on a method of collecting data, and methods of investigating data can be largely divided into three kinds, such as investigating data collected by using an agent remotely, investigating data collected by using back-up commands and investigating data collected by using the entire files.

Data collected by using an agent remotely can be read and investigated right away since it is in such patterns as txt, xls, html and CSV.

Data collected by using back-up commands at the server can be investigated at an investigator's computer by using the same commands since it supports the restoration command for each database system. For such a case, a server program fit for the relevant database version should be installed at an investigator's computer in advance. In case that data is selectively collected as a CSV file, the data can be examined by reading CSV files.

The remaining case except ones above is that database files are acquired, and such a case can be largely divided into two kinds.

One case is that database files are used by being imported from the database system (such as SQL Server and SQLAnywhere), and the other case is that database file format is analyzed. Data can be examined by being extracted on the foundation of the file format analyzed. Besides, when the file format is completely analyzed, it is possible to restore data deleted, which makes it possible to acquire much more data than the existing method. SQLite, a light-weight database, has been researched with such a method at present.[6]

4   Example of Investigation

In this chapter, whether the method suggested in Chapter 3 can be really used for a forensic investigation on database systems is actually proved by being applied to SQL Server 2005 of Microsoft Corporation.

4.1   Server Detection

SQL Server can be detected by using a port-scan tool named 'Zenmap(Namp)'.

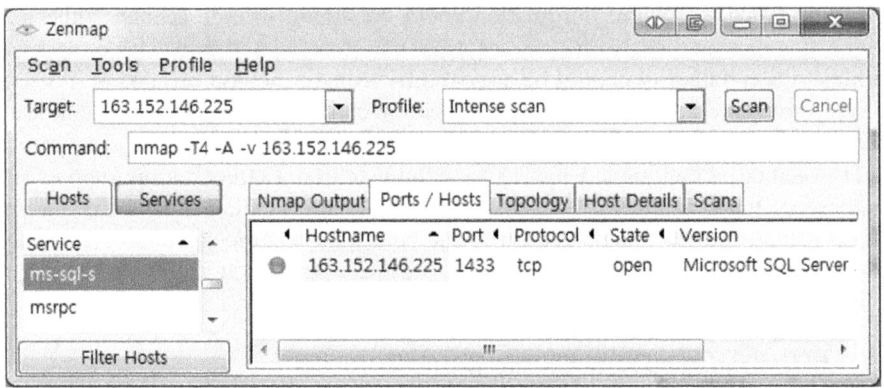

Fig. 2. Server Detecting using Zenmap(Nmap)

4.2   Data Collection

The installation path should be checked by referring to registry values in the following table. At this point, careful attention should be paid since SQL Server may have a different path according to its different version.

To acquire the entire database files, it is needed to grasp their location. Exploring {%SQLPath%}\Data paths through registry values and SQLPath helps detect database files (mdf) and log files (ldf). However, in case that mdf and ldf files are used be being imported from another database, their paths can be checked in the administration menu.

Files can be acquired by exploring the path of database files as checked above. When database files (mdf) and log files (ldf) are acquired, SQL Server can be used at an investigator's system in the same environment as that of the system investigated, without information about the administration account.

However, since it is impossible to access database files in process of use, it is natural that they cannot be acquired. Although those files can be acquired by accessing them through the file system, they are still in process of running, which makes it hard to acquire files in a normal state. For such a reason, any service in process of operation should be stopped before files are acquired. Service can be stopped by executing 'Service' in the control panel and selecting the name of the relevant service corresponding to the database.

When database files are acquired in a normal way, the contents of database should be output into CSV files that have readability and are easy to use. Administration tools will be used to output into CSV files. Unlike other database systems, SQL Server doesn't need an additional administration account on the side of the server. Instead, when 'localhost (127.0.0.1)' and 'windows authentication' are selected by executing the administration tool, it is accessed. When access to the administration tool is completed, a database wanted will be selected, and then a table wanted can be selected as well. Afterwards, a query wanted can be executed, and by selecting the entire breakdown performed, 'file export' can be executed to output into CSV files.

Table 1. Registry Path and Key

Version	Registry Path	Key
SQL Server 2000	HKLM\SOFTWARE\Microsoft\ MSSQLServer\Setup	SQLDataRoot
		SQLPath
SQL Server 2005	HKLM\SOFTWARE\Microsoft\ Microsoft SQL Server\MSSQL1.\ Setup\SQLPath	SQLProgramDir
		SQLPath
SQL Server 2008	HKLM\SOFTWARE\Microsoft\ Microsoft SQL Server\ MSSQL10.MSSQLSERVER\Setup	SQLProgramDir
		SQLPath

Table 2. Service Name

Version	Service Name
SQL Server 2000	MSSQLSERVER
SQL Server 2005	SQL Server(MSSQLSERVER)
SQL Server 2008	

Table 3. Name of Administrator Tool

Version	Name of Administrator Tool
SQL Server 2000	SQL Query Analyzer
SQL Server 2005	SQL Server Management Studio
SQL Server 2008	

4.3   Investigation on Data Collected

SQL Server can be used by importing database files. In case that the entire database files and logs (mdf and ldf) are acquired, it can be imported by using administration tools. 'Import' can be added by selecting 'mdf' with the function of 'Attach' in the administration tool. At this point, what should be careful is to make sure that 'ldf' files corresponding to 'mdf' files exist in the same folder.

After data is imported, the rest of analysis will be carried out in the same way as that for the existing SQL Server.

In case that CSV files are acquired through selective collection, an investigation can be performed by reading the files.

5   Conclusion and Future Work

When a forensic investigation is carried out in the enterprise environment, most data is stored in the database, and there exist over 10 kinds of database systems. In regard to the database system that is an important element for enterprise forensic investigations, therefore, this study suggested an investigation methodology likely to deal with all kinds of database systems, while putting emphasis on the necessity of an investigation methodology. Actually, while data collection and analysis were being conducted on SQL Server of Microsoft Corporation by using such a methodology, it was found that such a methodology can be used for actual forensic investigation in the enterprise environment. On the basis of those findings, a further study will be carried out on investigation methods for each kind of a database system. In addition, by detecting a database server and using an investigation method proper for the relevant database system, integrated database system investigation tools will be implemented, which are likely to automatically collect and analyze data. Using such an integrated automatic analysis tool will make efficient use of investigations on database systems in an actual enterprise environment.

Acknowledgments. This research was supported by Bio R&D program through the National Research Foundation of Korea funded by the Ministry of Education, Science and Technology (20100020634).

And This research was supported by Basic Science Research Program through the National Research Foundation of Korea(NRF) funded by the Ministry of Education, Science and Technology(grant number 2010-0005571).

References

1. Miklau, G., Levine, B., Stahlberg, P.: Securing history: Privacy and accountability in database systems,
   `http://www.cs.umass.edu/~miklau/pubs/cidr2007/`
   `miklau07securing.pdf`
2. Pavlou, K.E., Snodgrass, R.T.: Forensic analysis of database tampering. ACM Transaction on Database Systems 33 (November 2008)
3. Lee, K., Choi, J., Lim, K., Lee, S., Lee, S.: Novel methodologies to detect covert databases. ICIC International 6, 1–10 (2010)
4. Han, J., Lee, K., Choi, J., Lim, K., Lee, S.: Analysis of Connection Information for Database Server Detection. IEEE Computer & Science 2, 550–554 (2010)
5. `http://www.nmap.org`
6. Jeon, S., Bang, J., Byun, K., Lee, S.: Recovery Method of Deleted Record for SQLite Database. In: WCC 2010, vol. 3, pp. 64–71 (December 2010)

Sensitive Privacy Data Acquisition in the iPhone for Digital Forensic Analysis

Jinhyung Jung, Chorong Jeong, Keunduk Byun, and Sangjin Lee

Center for Information Security Technologies, Digital Forensic Research Center,
Korea University Seoul, Korea
{blueliony,cutycom_,gdfriend,sangjin}@korea.ac.kr

Abstract. As a diverse range of smartphones has been recently developed, the use of smartphones is being dramatically increased. The use of smartphones allowed many tasks to be done at smartphones, which used to require the use of computers. Especially, along with the increase in smartphone use, the users of SNS (Social Network Service) also have been sharply increased. The SNS saves a variety of information such as exchanged pictures and videos, voice mails or location sharing, chat history, etc. as well as simple user data, so that the acquisition of data that are useful in the aspect of digital forensic is achievable. This thesis reviews the types of SNS that are available for the iPhone, a recent example of highly used smartphones, and studies the data to be collected by client and the analysis methods accordingly.

Keywords: iPhone; SNS; Smartphone forensic.

1 Introduction

Portable mobile devices save the data that are more private to the users than PC's because PC's are usually more limited and less flexible in their usage, considering the lifestyles of the users. The call history, the text messages and other relevant data provide information about whom they talked to or exchanged the text messages with, and allow the investigators to collect the data such as contact lists or future schedules.

In 2010, various domestic smartphones came into wide use following the wide spread of the iPhone imported to Korea at the end of 2009, so the overall share of smartphones was increased in the entire mobile phone market. Especially, the SNS's such as Twitter or Facebook that were mainly used at PC's only were adapted to smartphones, which led to the even more increase of SNS users. Especially, the SNS's save the pictures and videos shared between the users, location information, group chatting and chat histories, etc. and this feature of SNS allows for the investigator to collect more user data than at the existing mobile devices. This research reviews the types of SNS clients available for iPhone by limiting the subject of research to the iPhone; figures out what data are available to be collected and suggests the methods of SNS data utilization for digital forensic investigations, based on the collected data.

J.J. Park et al. (Eds.): STA 2011, CCIS 186, pp. 172–186, 2011.
© Springer-Verlag Berlin Heidelberg 2011

1.1   SNS Utilization and Types of Clients

The SNS's (Social Network Services) can be used also at client programs specifically designed for these services besides at the existing web browsers. According to "Survey on Internet usage in Korea" by KISA (Korea Internet & Security Agency), 65.7% of Internet users use the SNS's [1]. Additionally, the number of current users in 2011 must have increased. Table 1 represents the changes made in the numbers of visitors for each type of SNS, investigated by Metrix, an Internet research institution, in October 2010 [2]. As the result of conducting an investigation to five leading domestic and international SNS clients, especially Twitter and Facebook showed a remarkable growth. This thesis reviews the data acquisition and analysis methods for a total of eight SNS clients including the smartphone version of NateOn securing a high number of domestic users, the KakaoTalk and the newly provided Daum MyPeople such as Yozm with various services supported besides the five clients listed below.

Table 1. SNS's Visitors & Pageviews 1 Year Compared Trends

Growth		Cyworld	Me2day	SNS Yozm	Twitter	Facebook
2009	Visitors	22,079	2,046	-	1,379	984
	Page View	11,792,018	49,606	-	9,302	15,878
2010	Visitors	24,653	3,964	2,119	8,654	7,380
	Page View	9,211,123	30,767	7,594	175,576	259,243
Growth	Visitors	11.7%	93.7%	N/A	527.7%	649.9%
	Page View	-21.9%	-38.0%	N/A	1,787.5%	1,583.8%
	Since	1999. 9	2007. 2	2010. 2	2006. 7	2004. 2

2   iPhone SNS Data Acquisition Methods

The methods to acquisition the SNS data installed at an iPhone are largely classified into two. The first is applicable to Jailbreaked iPhones and the second is to acquisition the information using the backup data.

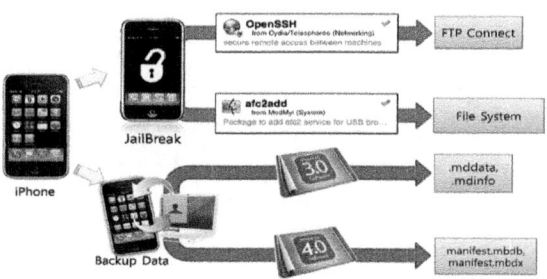

Fig. 1. iPhone Data Acquisition Concepts

Jailbreak is a method to release the security features of the iPhone, and with a Jailbreaked iPhone, it permits a direct approach to the inside data. When Jailbreak is not applied, the inside data can be backed up at a PC using iTunes, a synchronizing program between an iPhone and a PC. By analyzing these backup data, the SNS data can be collected [3].

2.1 SNS Data Acquisition for Jailbreaked iPhone

If the iPhone obtained as a proof is Jailbreaked, the inside data can be acquisitioned by using the programs such as iFunbox [4], DiskAid [5], etc. and by directly approaching the file system of the iPhone.

2.2 SNS Data Acquisition with Backup Data

For usual iPhones, SNS data can be extracted by backing up inside data using the iTunes, a synchronizing program provided by Apple Inc. The saving method of backup data differs depending on the provided version of iOS, the firmware of iPhone. Although actually saved data are same, the Metadata referred to, for the purpose of extracting data, show differences. At iOS 3.x version, a .mddata extension is generated at an actual data file, paired up with a Metadata file with a same file name and a .mdinfo extension to create each backup file.

However, from the 4.x version, all information on the backup file is saved as a pair of files, manifest.mbdx and manifest.mbdb.

Generation of Backup data. Only the method of indicating data has been changed along with each version of iOS, but the file name of the actual data has not been changed and remains same. The applications and inside data are largely classified by eight domains. "AppDomain", "HomeDomain", "KeychainDomain", "ManagedPreferencesDomain", "MediaDomain", "RootDomain", "SystemPreferencesDomain" and "WirelessDomain", and the SHA1 hash values including these domain names and the path names of respective data become the file names of backup data [6]. At the iOS 3.x version, the Meta information of the backup file is saved at a .mdinfo file and has a plist structure which is a supported saving format for Apple. As an abbreviation for Property-List, each key exits in a similar manner to the XML format, and the value matched with the individual key is provided in the format, or the value alone is provided in another format [7].

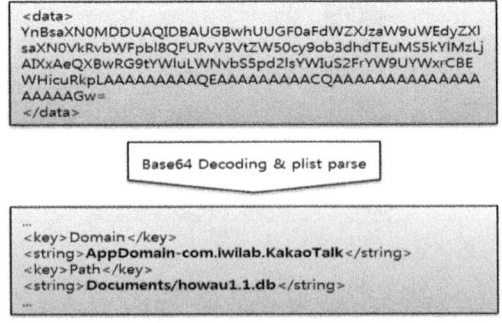

Fig. 2. Backup Metadata Analysis of iOS 3.x

The <data> object of the plist file format is saved, as the original data is encoded as Base64. And, if the <data> value of mdinfo file is decoded, again a separate plist file appears and the actual path of the backup data and the domain information are saved at this file.

When obtaining the SHA1 hash value by combining the domain and the path information with a hyphen after the decoding process, the following result appears.

AppDomain-com.iwilab.KakaoTalk-Documents/howau1.1.db → (SHA1 Hash) AD407D8E15291C0B18EAB85881DAA731A04F19F8.

At the iOS 4.x version, the system called .mdinfo where the Meta information is saved by respective backup data disappears and the Meta information of entire backup data is managed through the two files; manifest.mbdb and manifest.mbdx. Because only the method of managing the original information of backup data is changed and the method of converting the file name of the data remains as same as the iOS 3.x version, the file names of the backup data do not vary with the used version. This applies same to the case of iPhone 3GS and iPhone 4. The backup data do not form a tree structure by each application as the inside structure of the Jailbreaked iPhone and all backup data are saved in a single folder. Therefore, the data for respective SNS clients must be determined by analyzing the Meta file of each iOS version.

MobileSyncBrowser analyzes the data that are backed up through the iTunes; classifies them into each folder to present them[8].

3   Acquisition and Analysis of Sensitive Data

In this chapter, the available data that are useful in the aspect of digital forensic are reviewed under each client category. Also, the data path to approach the designated data and each file name were organized according to the data acquisition method. The data path is a path from the route of each application and the backup file name is given, based on the backup data of the iOS 4.x version. Also, in the cases of using the 3.x version, the file having the same file name with .mddata extension becomes the data file.

3.1   SNS's Client-Specific Data Acquisition

Cyworld. Cyworld is an application to use a mini homepage service in Korea and support the users to manage their Il-Chon list (a friend list) and view the uploaded pictures and the guestbook.

Table 2. Acquisition Data & Path of Cyworld

Data Types		Path / Backup File Name
User Info	JB	Library/preferences/com.nate.minihompy.plist
	Backup	cc1993f656f199b44f3b015c80fcf3d7d24817a2
Friend List		Documents/MiniHompy/[TID]
Picture/Media		Documents/MiniHompy/[TID]/*

For the management of the Cyworld data, a folder is generated as a TID value which is a genuine number for a private user, the viewed data of the visited mini homepage are saved and normally, only the image information is saved.

Me2Day. Me2Day is a SNS managed by NHN; the message history is not saved, but the picture and the information of the searched users are saved.

Table 3. Acquisition Data & Path of Me2Day

Data Types		Path / Backup File Name
User Info	JB	Library/Preferences/com.nhncorp.me2DAY.plist
	Backup	f1012cea6e78e3f3ae241faa16d1c5eec895df40
List of Search friend / Picture		tmp/me2DAY/profileImage/me2day.net/images/user/[ID]/*.cache

Me2day does not save the friend list separately, but saves the searched friend list at the information file or a temporary file. When the program is updated, some of information disappears from the saved data file, and the cache file where the image of registered friend gets also deleted

Daum Yozm. Yozm is one kind of SNS's operated by Daum, and recently, Daum also lanched a service called MyPeople. Yozm saves the friend list and the message as a database file. However, for the friend list, it does not save the entire user list but saves the data only when recent messages are registered, and the profile image URL of the corresponding user gets saved at the DB.

Table 4. Acquisition Data & Path of Daum Yozm

Data Types		Path / Backup File Name
User Info	JB	Library/Preferences/net.daum.yozm.plis
	Backup	e82b91a282f74efafef591e53ce100f6e25b2dda
Friend List	JB	Documents/Yomamte.sql
	Backup	406cefcc95c117b83780a57ca58e0682d9bfe4c7
Message	JB	Documents/Yomamte.sql [message]
	Backup	406cefcc95c117b83780a57ca58e0682d9bfe4c7
Picture/Media		Library/Caches/ImageCache/*

For the picture file of ImageCache, the image of recently received information and other relevant information of the user are saved.

Twitter. Twitter is one of the leading SNS's at the international scene along with Facebook.

Table 5. Acquisition Data & Path of Twitter

Data Types		Path / Backup File Name
User Info	JB	Documents/com.atebits.tweetie.application-state/app.state
	Backup	eb8899d553cf563080453f9a366600de1dcf6286
Mention/DM		Documents/com.atebits.tweetie.streams/[32bytes characters]
All Messages		Documents/com.atebits.tweetie.streams/[32bytes characters]
Picture/Media		Library/Caches/com.atebits.tweetie.profile-images/*

A concept of 'follow' wich acquaintances and other users is adopted to exchange messages, and these messages are saved as a plist structure.

Due to the nature of Twitter messages, the DM (Direct Message), supporting the function of private message exchange, and the Mention data, the open conversation between the friends are saved, separately from the other messages. Also, all profile images are saved regardless of the following or follower situation.

Facebook. Facebook was established by Mark Zuckerberg while he was attending Harvard University in the United States and its users in Korea has dramatically increased along with the Twitter users since the Korean encoding service had been supported. Facebook saves the chat histories and the friend list in a database file format.

Each file in the Three20 folder has a length of 32 bytes, and the chat histories are also saved in a XML file format with the photo data.

Table 6. Acquisition Data & Path of Facebook

Data Types		Path / Backup File Name
User Info	JB	Library/Preferences/com.facebook.Facebook.plist
	Backup	384eb9e62ba50d7f3a21d9224123db62879ef423
Friend List	JB	Documents/friends.db
	Backup	6639cb6a02f32e0203851f25465ffb89ca8ae3fa
Picture/Media		Library/Caches/Three20/*

NateOn UC. NateOn UC is a client program for smartphones of a leading messenger service in Korea, NateOn UC can connect the user to the Cyworld. Using a smarthone, the users exchange private messages and chat with their registered friends. However, the information of exchanged messages using smartphones is also saved at the server in the same manner with the NateOn for PC, so that the direct verifications at smartphones cannot be supported.

Table 7. Acquisition Data & Path of NatOn UC

Data Types		Path / Backup File Name
User Info	JB	Library/Preferences/com.nate.nateon.plist
	Backup	575308d6756147c7cbc5994ef765ce8aa746bc6b
Friend List	JB	Documents/UC.db
	Backup	2945a0d8601dbfcd4fc184384c0453c0e050cc4c

NateOn UC does not save the private messages or chat contexts, but saves the user information and the friends list in detail. For the user information, the account with its auto log-in set up and the synchronization time are saved, and for the friend list, all of Cyworld information, phone number, E-mail, etc. are saved.

KakaoTalk. KakaoTalk is a SNS developed and served in Korea, provided only for smartphones such as iPhones, and it has secured a large number of domestic users.

KakaoTalk saves all infromation of the friend list, the exchanged messages and the group chatting. Facebook pictures as well as KakaoTalk image data is stored in the Three20 folder.

Table 8. Acquisition Data & Path of KakaoTalk

Data Types		Path / Backup File Name
User Info	JB	Library/Preferences/com.iwlab.KakaoTalk.plist
	Backup	4903197cb3ac6b15b086afe9e437472614ef29e1
Friend List	JB	Documents/Talk.sqlite
	Backup	d5bd128369e2a96f96e3314450a8955363f66035
Message	JB	Documents/Talk.sqlite
	Backup	d5bd128369e2a96f96e3314450a8955363f66035
Picture/Media		Library/Caches/Three20/[32bytes characters]

MyPeople. MyPeople is a SNS newly provided by Daum. Voice messages are supported and the GPS information can be shared by a location sharing service utilizing Duam Map application. MyPeople also saves a range of information and especially, it is verified that the contact list of an iPhone is saved as a separate plist file. Also, the MyPeople user list and the user list registered at Favorite are separately managed at the iPhone contact list.

Table 9. Acquisition Data & Path of MyPeople

Data Types		Path / Backup File Name
User Info	JB	Library/Preferences/net.daum.air21.plist
	Backup	45f054b67052e4637ee0908bbd969566e4bbb989
Friend List	JB	Documents/myPeopleList.archive
	Backup	ba08e750aa66a337c820dff7f33e391ab8471cc9
Message	JB	Documents/Air21-0.1.2.sqlite
	Backup	ff97a3423571c6785a9fe2dc945f59ee16fb552b
Contacts	JB	Documents/allContactsList.archive
	Backup	305584c73efa66f168bf6105bf3c372a87f1f23c
Picture/Media		Documents/*.png
Voice Message		Documents/*.m4a

3.2   SNS Acquisition Data Classification

The collectable types of data and the saving location of the file were reviewed for each client in the prior section. In this section, we will look into what types of data that are meaningful for actual digital forensic analysis and the information that are helpful for the investigation are available.

User Information. User information refers to data such as account information necessary for a log-in to use the designated client, E-mail, phone number, etc. The format of user inforamtion saved for each client differs, however if collecting these account and relative informatoin, even the account information used at other web services or SNS clients can be inferred, also.

(Fig. 3) shows the user information saved at NateOn UC. As the log-in ID and password, E-mail account and other information are saved as a plaintext format, their actual values are verifiable.

Fig. 3. User Information of NateOn UC

Because the ID and the Password are exposed, logging in to other clients that are similar to the saved E-mail account can be attempted, as well as logging in to NateOn UC.

Friend list and Messages. The friend list and the message histories are similar to the contact list or the SMS messages found on existing mobile devices, and the information on whom they exchanged messages with through which SMS client can be obtained. Especially, because some clients save the profile images when saving the friend list, the appearances of the acquaintances can be verified.

As NateOn UC saves the TID value of Cyworld at the friend list, the address of connected homepage is searchable, also.

If inserting the CyworldCmn field value into the TID value of the URL, the Cyworld url of the acquaintance is obtained. KakaoTalk manages the chat histories through the chat_id, so in the case of multi chats, the entire list of participated users is saved, which allows the investigator to understand the relationships between the acquaintances.

At the members field, the nicknames, the contact information and other relevant data of all users participated when the initial chatting group was created are saved.

All SNS clients except Twitter owing to the large data is stored using SQLite3 DB format.

R.	id	title			members	active_member...	last...	I...	last_message
					Click here to define a filter				
19	24638117	명			[{"type":2,"directChatId":2463 [3579879]	1976	<		아 근다이 ㅋ
20	25391533	어	누르		[{"type":2,"directChatId":2539 [3659442]	1902	<		난 오늘 소맥이 먹고팠는뎅
21	25429670	강			[{"type":2,"directChatId":2542 [1624831]	8976	<		네 날 찜겠습니다
22	25862553	정			[{"type":2,"directChatId":2586 [3193845]	1676	<		다행.. 저 주황 넘온거 같더
23	25907408	우	강토	가	[{"type":1,"directChatId":2590 [3689421]	2129	<		그래. 쉬어랑!*^o^*
24	28323473	건	형		[{"type":2,"directChatId":2832 [69786]	-7363	<		인제 할라구요 ㅋ

Fig. 4. Chat Messages of KakaoTalk

Multimedia Data. Since the corresponding GPS information is included at the pictures taken with an iPhone as a default setting, the locations of the pictures taken can be obtained. However, when the data are shared through a client, even the basic EXIF data as well as the GPS informatoin are excluded from the saving process or changed into a separate image format such as PNG, regardless of inclusion of the GPS information.

Therefore, it is hard to capture the location of the pictures taken by the GPS information available at the image. But, the shared images are not affected even when the pictures at the iPhone are deleted, because an iPhone separately saves the image data for each client.

Besides the photos, the recorded videos can be also shared with acquaintances through a SNS client, and these are also saved separately from the videos on the iPhone. The videos on the iPhone are saved in a MOV format, which is a multi-media format for Apple Quicktime. And, the client saved in a same format does exist; however, sometimes they are saved in an MPEG video format such as m4v.

Lastly, there are voice data. The recorded voices using the voice mail function at MyPeople can be transferred to the receivers. The voice messages can be recorded for 30 seconds in the maximum and the data are saved in an m4a file format which is one of the MPEG audio formats.

Others. Besides the data classification mentioned above, the recent SNS can share other data. A location sharing function is also provided at MyPeople of Daum. This location sharing information displays the corresponding location on the Daum Map and allows the users to transfer the information through emails or to other smartphone users. The location sharing function does not have a specific format but saves the URL information containing the corresponding GPS coordinates at the chat history database.

Fig. 5. Share the Location of MyPeople

4   Digital Forensic Analysis for Sensitive Data

In Section 3.2, the large classification of the collected data is reviewed. In this section, the efficient data analysis method for digital forensic investigations is suggested by analyzing the relationships within the data saved by each client.

4.1   Data Relationship Analysis by SNS's Client

Cyworld. Cyworld does not save information other than photo data. The data are classified under the each folder of the photos and even when all folders of the users who visisted the homepage are opened for the public access, the information does not get saved unless it is already viewed. The structure is shown in (Fig. 6).

At the path of Documents/MiniHompy shown at Table 2, a list of folders is visible as 8-digit numbers, and the values that these numbers imply are the TID values, the genuine values of the users registered at Cyworld. The TID value can be used to connect to the MiniHompy of the corresponding user, using the following URL.

http://minihp.cyworld.com/pims/main/pims_main.asp?tid=**TID2**

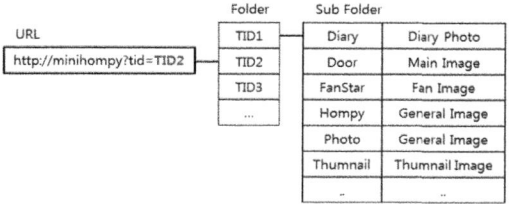

Fig. 6. Data Strucutre of Cyworld

Under the subcategories of each TID folder, only the viewed images are saved among the pictures uploaded at Main Picture, Diary, Photos, etc.

Daum Yozm. There exists an Yomamte.sql file at Daum Yozm, and it manages the attached images or the message histories with the registered friends. The structure of Yomamte.sql file is as following.

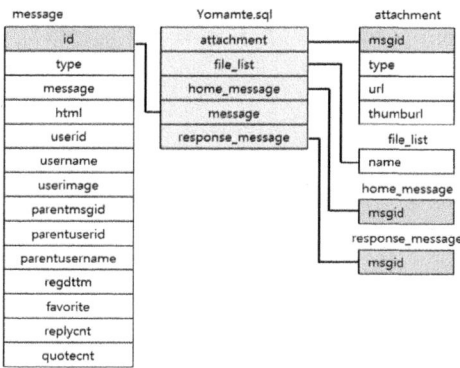

Fig. 7. Database Structure of Daum Yozm

The database of Yomamte.sql is consisted of five tables such attachment, file_list, etc. and each table except the file_list table contains a common msgid value. Through this msgid value, the relationship between the tables can be discovered. The message whose ID value is "17957326" contains an attached image URL, "http://cfile187.uf.daum.net/image/15302D054CD7935C2BE3C1" at the same msgid row of the attached table.

Twitter. Twitter does not manage the data as a database file. So the data is not systematically. The messages and the chat histories of Twitter saved into a total of three plist files. The app.state file, a user information file, of Table 5 contains the information of the user who is using the client.

Also, the recent message exchanged with other users and the Direct Message are also saved, but their formats do not support the structure of the Key and the Value, and saved as an independent string.

All messages and chat histories are not saved at an app.state file. There exists a format in that the file saving the timeline only, which is the entire message history, and a format saving the Direct Message or the chat exchanged only with the friends. In this case, if reviewing the two NS.String Key values within the app.state file, the plist file format is used as a saving method identically with the app.state file.

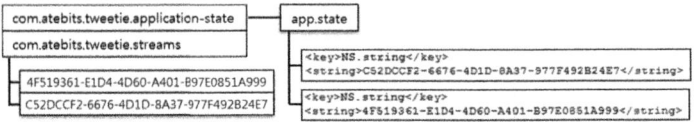

Fig. 8. Relation App.state with other files

Facebook. Facebook does not save chat histories or messages, but manages the friend list using a database file called friends.db, which is consisted of the two tables, so called, "meta" and "friend".

Only the information about the version is listed at the Meta table, and the friend list is saved at the friend table. The name and the profile image URL are known, but the e-mail address and the phone number are saved as plaintexts so they are hard to be read.

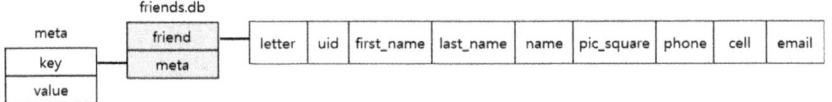

Fig. 9. Database Structure of Facebook

However, many files with 32 byte length strings are created within the Library/Cache/Three20 folder, and files such as JPG, GIF, PNG, XML, etc. are mixed and saved. They are the list of the temporary cache files created using Facebook and the posted texts and the profile information are saved at the XML file. The posted texts are saved including the messages and the comments between the <stream_post> and </stream_post> tag, and if they are the posts by the registered friends, the relationship with the users who post the texts can be discovered by using the <actor_id> value and comparing it with uid value at the friend table. However, since this temporary file does not get backed up, it is collectable only at the Jailbreaked iPhones.

NateOn UC. NateOn creates a database file when updated to the UC version and manages the friend list through it. It is consisted of a total of six tables; it saves the contact list of NateOn and creates a separate table with E-mails and phone numbers.

The values saved at each table are matched through the ClientId value, and because the UID is a changeable value, it can be referred. As discussed above, Cyworld provides the mini homepage address of the corresponding user, using the TID value, and the value of CyworldCmn column is as same as the TID value.

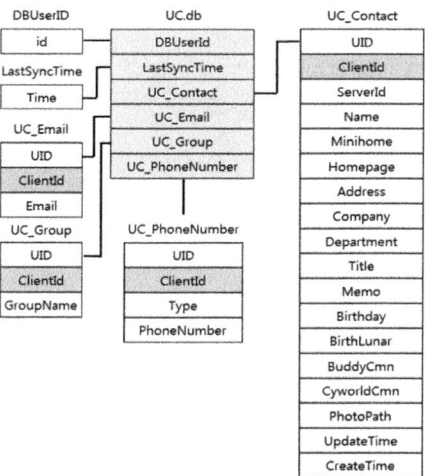

Fig. 10. Database Structure of NateOn UC

KakaoTalk. KakaoTalk saves a lot of information through a database file. The same colored columns of (Fig. 11) mean the same values, and the relationships between each table can be prehensible.

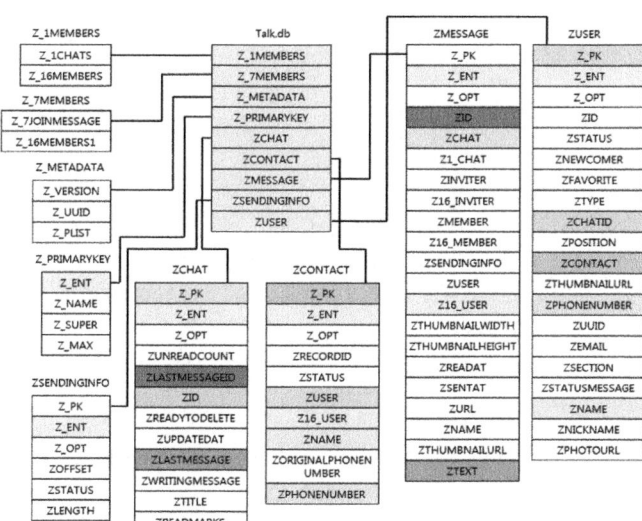

Fig. 11. Database Structure of KakaoTalk

ZCONTACT is not visible on an actual client, but is a table containing the contact information of an iPhone, and ZUSER is the list of users who are using KakaoTalk at the contact information of the iPhone. KakaoTalk marks the friends who were registered before but changed the contact information later as invalid friends. Even when the user deletes these invalid friends from the list, the ZUSER table still contains the remained records.

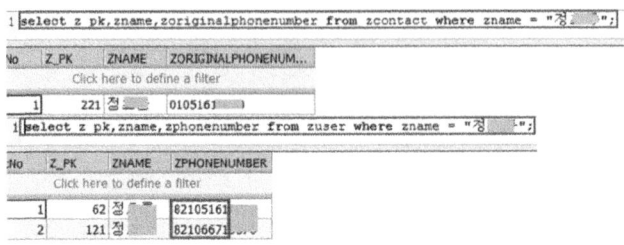

Fig. 12. Trace Phone-Number Changes in ZUSER table

The ZCHAT table and the ZMESSAGE table are the concept in that the chatting room and the chatted messages are separated to be saved. The ZLASTMESSAGE value of the ZCHAT table is a column matched to one of various ZTEXT values of the ZMESSAGE table. If wanting to know a specific chat history among the messages of the ZMESSAGE table, can be used as a query below.

SELECT ZTEXT, ZSENTAT FROM ZMESSAGE WHERE ZCHAT = "##";

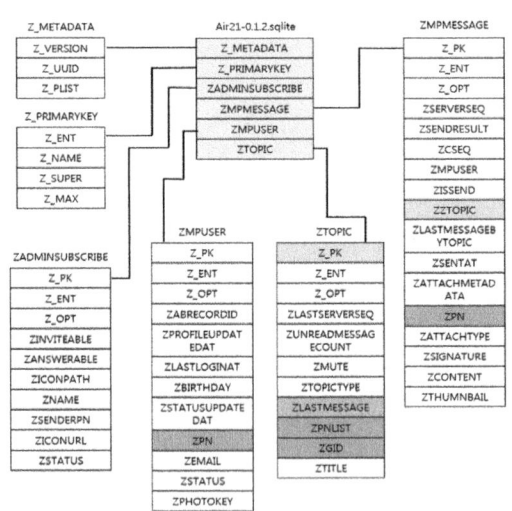

Fig. 13. Database Structure of MyPeople

MyPeople. MyPeople also has a similar structure with that of KakaoTalk, which is a characteristic appeared when modeling the database using the iOS SDK and has the similar column name with the same table name [9]. The database structure of MyPeople is not complicated compared to its provided functions. Also when saving files, all files are simultaneously saved at the folder shared with the corresponding database file.

The main functions supported at MyPeople include location sharing, voice message, free voice talk which is added after the recent update, and other services. All information about whether each function is used or not is saved at the ZMPMESSAGE table, and recorded vocie files, downloaded pictures and videos are all saved in the Document folder.

MyPeople manages the chatting room, which is a similar concept with the KakaoTalk, using the ZTOPIC table. The message transferred by the operator has a separate ZADMINSUBSCRIBE table, and the chat history can be viewed using the ZMPMESSAGE, and the chat parties and the friend list came be viewed using the ZPN column, which is the mobile phone number.

As shown in (Fig. 5), MyPeople's location sharing service with GPS information can be found directly via the Web. It does not save the current location but the desired location, marks on the map and transfers the values of the coordinates to the receiver. Storage form of "Location share" and "Free call" is displayed into ZMPMESSAGE table within the database file, whether in the use of each function.

5   Conclusion and Future Works

The increase in Smartphone usage has a very close relationship with the increase in the number of SNS users.

Not only their high portability, but also their inexpensive fees, compared to the existing SMS's or MMS's to share the data, and a good range of available data rate fee plan allowed the SNS's to form a high percentage of contact or conversation methods between the users along with the high usage rate of the mobile Internet.

This thesis reviews the SNS client types and the data acquisition and analyzing methods of iPhone that have been secured a large number of users in the domestic. If collecting SNS information, more detailed information on the user and the social and human relations with the user's acquaintances can be efficiently analyzed. Especially, an alternative to assemble the relevant data and columns was suggested from the analysis of the collected files and the relationship between the tables at the database.

The use of SNS increasing and an analysis of SNS in the digital forensics are becoming more important. In this paper, the literature on this basis could be.

Acknowledgments. This work was supported by the IT R&D program of MKE/KEIT [10035157, Development of Digital Forensic Technologies for Real-Time Analysis].

References

1. Survey on the Internet Usage in Korea, Statistics report, Korea Internet Security Agency (2010)
2. SNS's Visitors & Pageviews 1 year compared trends, Metrix,
   http://www.metrix.co.kr

3. iPhone & iPod Touch: About Backup, Apple,
   http://support.apple.com/kb/HT1766
4. i-FunBox, iFunBox.com Team, http://www.i-funbox.com
5. DiskAid, DIGIDNA, http://www.digidna.net
6. Adam, C.: iPhone Forensics, sans iPhone (2010)
7. Property List Programming Guide, Apple,
   http://developer.apple.com/library/ios/documentation/
   Cocoa/Conceptual/PropertyLists
8. Cordero, V.S.: Mobile Sync. Browser, http://mobilesyncbrowser.com
9. Core Data Tutorial for iOS, Apple,
   http://developer.apple.com/library/ios/documentation/
   DataManagement/Conceptual/iPhoneCoreData01

An Efficient Processing Scheme for Continuous Queries Involving RFID and Sensor Data Streams

Jeongwoo Park[1], Kwangjae Lee[1], Wooseok Ryu[1], Joonho Kwon[2], and Bonghee Hong[1]

[1] Dept. of Computer Engineering
[2] Institute of Logistics Information Technology
Pusan National University
Busan, Republic of Korea
{pjw1129,lkwangjae,wsryu,jhkwon,bhhong}@Pusan.ac.kr

Abstract. RFID technology is being applied to the wide field of distributions and logistics for item-level tracking of tagged goods. Recently, spoilage and abnormalities of product in Blood Supply Chain (BSC), Cold Chain Management (CCM) and Hazardous Materials (HAZMAT) Management become issues. To monitor item's health status is as a crucial issue as to keep track of the item. By augmenting passive RFID tags with sensor nodes, we can easily extend existing RFID systems and reduce operational cost. However, this approach will suffer from high overhead for joining two streaming data in real time. To address this problem, we propose a scheme for continuous query processing to monitor sensing information of tagged items in real-time. It makes integrated stream data from each stream data. And we summarize integrated stream data using MBR, and we make summarized data. It requires comparing the summarized data with registered queries. Finally, we do query processing between integrated stream data and matched query. Experimental results show that our method can handle both RFID tag data and sensing information efficiently.

Keywords: RFID; logistics distribution.

1 Introduction

RFID technology is a method to recognize product information with data transmission between electronic tags and a reader by radio frequency. Although traditional bar code systems need a direct contact between a barcode reader and an object, an RFID reader is capable to read RFID tags without a physical contact. Thus, RFID is expected to be a next generation technology that replaces the old system.

RFID tags can be divided into two categories: passive tags and active tags. A passive has no battery and only small memory, but it is relatively cheap. An active tag has an on-board battery for more functionality, but it is considerably more expensive. Thus, most of the existing RFID technologies in SCM (Supply Chain Management) use only passive tags for the simple identification information of goods[1].

However, some applications in BSC, CCM and HAZMAT demand for monitoring of environmental changes of each item such as temperature, humidity, and so on.

J.J. Park et al. (Eds.): STA 2011, CCIS 186, pp. 187–192, 2011.
© Springer-Verlag Berlin Heidelberg 2011

In this case, the passive tag is not suitable because it only provides static information. An active tag is not suitable due to the high cost for implementing. We believe that augmenting passive tags with sensor nodes can be the most efficient candidate for three reasons: (1) providing dynamic information, (2) for easier extending of existing RFID systems and (3) the cheaper cost than using active tags.

A data stream is a real-time, continuous, ordered (by arrival time or timestamp) and unbounded sequence of items [3,4,5]. Data generated by our target application is a perfect example of a data stream.

However, our target application makes two data streams: a data stream from RFID tags and a data stream from sensor nodes. The existing RFID middleware system is designed to simply process continuous queries on RFID data stream only. Therefore, for the processing query that both sensor type and RFID type in single system, we need to join two different types of data streams.

In the data stream management systems, there exist lots of studies for efficient processing of joining two data streams based on the sliding window [6,7,8]. However, these approaches are two general and do not consider the specific characteristics of augmenting RFID tags with sensor nodes.

In this paper, to address this problem, we propose a scheme for continuous query processing to monitor sensing information of tagged items in real-time. It makes integrated stream data from each stream data. And we summarize integrated stream data using MBR, and we make summarized data. It requires comparing the summarized data with registered queries. Finally, we do query processing between integrated stream data and matched query. Using the proposed scheme, we can efficiently process a join between two different types of continuous stream data.

The rest of the paper is organized as follows. In Section 2, presents target environment and defines problem. To solve it, we propose our scheme for query processing in Section 3. We show the performance evaluation our approach with existing in Section 4. We make a conclusion in Section 5.

2   Problem Definition

In this section, we shall explain a logistics system which is a target environment of our method. Then, we present the environment configuration and the characteristics of data generated during shipping and transportation. Finally, we describe the problem when we process the created data by the continuous query.

2.1   Target Environment

In the existing logistics environment, using only identification information of RFID tags, goods and inventory control is supported. However, identification information is not only necessary, but status information also is essential for safe distribution in a circumstance such as distribution/management of blood, fresh products, valuable groceries, and dangerous cargo.

In the application environment, we can collect we can collect identification data of goods and sensing data in a vehicle when the vehicle is moving. The devices used under this environment are passive RFID tags and sensor nodes on the vehicle. Although these devices have already been used, we need a novel technique to monitor status of goods in shipping in real-time using those devices.

2.2   Generated data in Target Environment

The sensor nodes on the vehicle collect sensing data such as the temperature, the humidity, etc, and the data is transmitted by a PDA or a smart phone. The collected data is sent to the middleware through the CDMA network in real-time. The sensing data is in the type of Continuous Event, and contains the sensor ID (SID), the sensor location, the sensor type, a sensor value, and sensing time. It can present status data of goods accordingly.

The stream data created in the target environment can be divided into two as shown above. The middleware processes the stream data as continuous queries registered by the user. The system can perform one time query or continuous query from a user or an application program, using general DSMS. A query required by the target environment wants to see the status of the product in real-time.

2.3   Problem in RFID and Sensing Data Processing

The existing RFID middleware processes only a query about RFID stream data as shown in Figure 1(a). As mentioned earlier, however, a complex event is required during logistics transportation, shown in Figure 1(b). To generate composite event, we need to join two stream data at real-time.

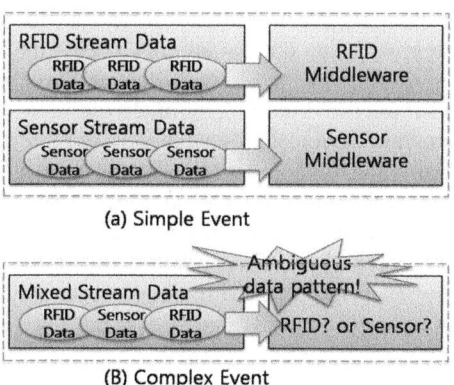

(a) Simple Event

(B) Complex Event

Fig. 1. Problem of Generated Data

As it is true that stream data is generated endlessly, the data processed have to be restricted by the idea of sliding window[3,4,5].

Under the environment in this paper, however, the stream data is created in the type of two basic tables. Also the type and the time of data are different. RFID data is generated at a specific time, not at regular intervals, whereas sensing data is created regularly. It is not suitable to process those stream data with the sliding window technique within a restricted time.

3   An Efficient Processing Scheme for Continuous Queries

In this section, we suggest the continuous query processing method based on integrated data from logistics transportation.

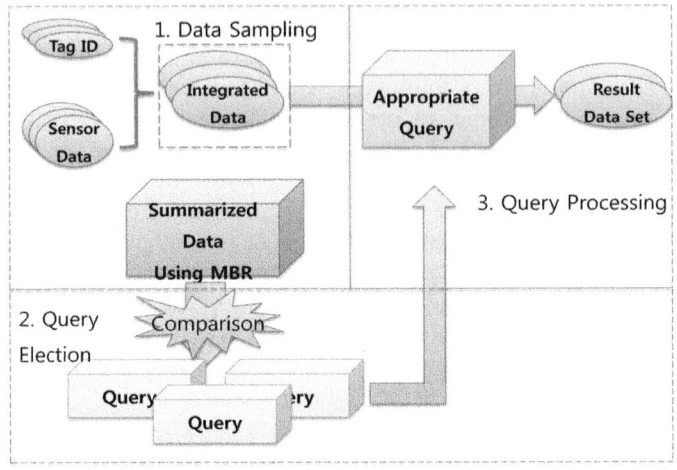

Fig. 2. Processing Scheme for Continuous queries

First of all, we make an integrated data using comparison that made between the location parameters of data on sensor table and an RFID stream data, when the stream data is created. An integrated data consist another stream data, integrated stream data. For search appropriate queries, we need to make sample data from integrated stream data. We define it as summarized data. A summarized data is result of MBR process using integrated stream data`s each attributes.

Using a summarized data, we compare between a registered query on system and summarized data to search for queries corresponding to data.

Appropriate queries are determined using the summarized integrated data. As the integrated data is processed with MBR, the data is not suitable to process the selected queries. Thus, it requires original stream data before that is summarized. Using appropriate queries and source of integrated stream data, we can make result of query processing.

4   Evaluation

In this section, we will present the results of some experiments to verify the effectiveness of the proposed method.

Table 1. Data Set for Experiment

Data Set	D1	D2	D3	D4
No. of vehicle	5	10	20	40

We generate the virtual data and prepare continuous query. Table 1 describes four data sets for our experiments. "No. of Vehicle" denotes the number of vehicle varying from 3 to 20. In our setting, each vehicle has 1000 RFID tags.

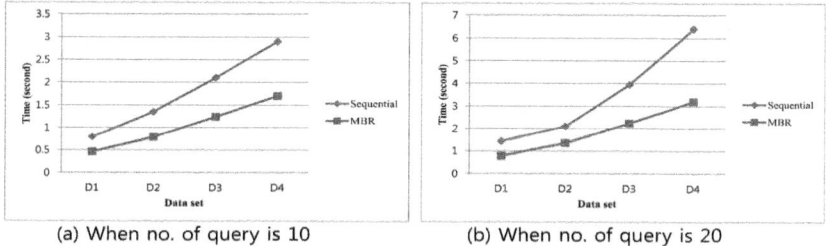

(a) When no. of query is 10   (b) When no. of query is 20

Fig. 3. Experimental Results

For instance, the data set 'D1' is a situation which includes 5 vehicles and 3000 tags. For each data set, we have run 10 or 20 queries over the data which is collected from several vehicles. Figure 8 shows the experimental results. As the number of vehicle increases, the gaps in time between sequential method and our method increase.

5 Conclusion and Future Work

In this paper, we propose an efficient query processing method on an RFID system in which passive RFID tags are augmented with sensor nodes. In this case, we need a join between two data streams: a data stream from RFID tags and a data stream from sensor nodes. Since the generated time and the type of each data do not match, it is impossible to apply the sliding window-based join approach. Thus, we assume that data is analyzed by transportation stages, and a composite event (integrated RFID and sensor data) is generated from the transportation. This composite event may cause a system overload when processing a query because the events must be processed in order in the existing RFID systems. To solve this problem, we suggest a scheme for continuous query processing which uses a minimum bounding rectangle (MBR). First, we estimate the minimum and the maximum values of all attributes in queries and create a multidimensional rectangle with the estimated values. Instead of comparing all the data with queries, we only compare the rectangle with selected queries to determine the satisfied queries. Then, we refine the candidate queries.

As a future work, we plan to carry out experiments with a variety of real-world data to show feasibility of our proposed method.

Acknowledgements

This work was supported by the grant No. B0009720 from the Regional Technology Innovation Program of the Ministry of Knowledge Economy (MKE).

References

1. EPCglobal, The EPCglobal Architecture Framework. EPCglobal Inc. (2005)
2. Jedermann, R., Ruiz-Garcia, L., Lang, W.: Spatial temperature profiling by semi-passive RFID loggers for perishable food transportation. Computers and Electronics in Agriculture, 1–10 (2008)
3. Babcock, B., et al.: Models and Issues in Data Stream Systems. In: Proc. the 21st ACM SIGACT-SIGMOD-SIGART Symp. on Principles of Database Systems (PODS), Madison, Wisconsin, pp. 1–16 (June 2002)
4. Golab, L., Ozsu, M.T.: Issues in Data Stream Management. ACM SIGMOD Record 32(2), 5–14 (2003)
5. Motwani, R., et al.: Query Processing, Approximation, and Resource Management in a Data Stream Management System. In: Proc. the First Biennial Conf. on Innovative Data Systems Research, Asiloma, California, pp. 245–256 (January 2003)
6. Chandrasekaran, S., Franklin, M.J.: Streaming queries over streaming data. In: Proc. of the VLDB Conference (2002)
7. Kang, J., Naughton, J.F., Viglas, S.D.: Evaluation window joins over unbounded stream. In: ICDE (February 2003)
8. Madden, S., Shah, M., Hellerstein, J., Raman, V.: Continuously adaptive continuous queries over streams. In: Proc. of the SIGMOD Conference (June 2002)

Smart Warehouse Modeling Using Re-recording Methodology with Sensor Tag

Gwangsoo Lee[1], Wooseok Ryu[1], Bonghee Hong[1], and Joonho Kwon[2]

[1] Dept. of Computer Engineering
[2] Institute of Logistics Information Technology
Pusan National University
Busan, Republic of Korea
{ntctomy,wsryu,bhhong,jhkwon}@pusan.ac.kr

Abstract. As the recent growth of RFID technologies, a goal of productivity has been achieved in various industry areas where the technologies are used. With this change, a number of RFID logistics systems have been studied, and various standard systems also have been proposed. However, in the storage stage as a part of logistics process, the environmental characteristics on goods, i.e. the sensor technology is not studied to put together with. A system in which status information is processed with the existing sensor nodes has been developed a lot. But in the sensor node system, the nodes are put on specific locations, and the sensor sends sensing information on a large space. Thus, the system is inappropriate for that environment that a temperature-sensitive product has to be checked thoroughly down to a tiny section. To solve this problem, as a part of the smart logistics system, the smart storage modeling technology with sensor tags used is suggested in this paper. With the suggested technology, the space limit problem of sensor node based storage will be solved.

Keywords: Sensor tag, Warehouse, RFID.

1 Introduction

Recently, related to IT Convergence, in port, motor, manufacturing, medicine and other industrial areas, RFID technologies are applied. With this change, not only productivity, but the logistics system also is improved. As the logistics system grows, the storage technology as a part of the system has been also improved. Furthermore, sensor information application with RFID is studied in progress to keep a product the best condition in a distribution stage.

In an effective distribution and logistics service, the core part can be the warehouse management. With this, studies on RFID storage technology for fast checking goods in-and-out and inventory have reached at the very high level [1]. Yet study on the RFID smart storage technology status with which information for preservation can be identified concurrently is not sufficient.

There is a system in which sensor nodes and passive tags are applied with the existing smart storage technology. This system has two defeats: First, it has the space limit problem of sensor nodes. As sensor data from a warehouse has a certain range

J.J. Park et al. (Eds.): STA 2011, CCIS 186, pp. 193–200, 2011.

on a particular sector in the stages, it is not good for temperature-sensitive products; secondly, from the point of data processing, an RFID reader and sensor nodes are put in a different time-space from each other. As each of the devices has an independent data processor, different types of data are generated. To bind these, the common location/temporal argument are necessary, and it costs a lot.

To overcome the problem of the existing system, it is considerable to use sensor tags on each item rather than passive tags. But it is not suitable, because a sensor tag is more expensive than a passive tag. And the battery longs shortly, therefore the tag replacement costs a lot. In this paper, about a storage where RFID and status information is needed, an effective smart storage modeling technology is suggested in the aspects of the cost and the function.

In Section 2, as a related study, the existing RFID storage, DBMS, sensor tag memory space are introduced. In Section 3, the target environment is described in detail. In Section 4, a problem on the target environment is issued, and the solution is proposed in the following Section. Finally in Section 6, the conclusion of this paper and the future works are described.

2 Related Work

2.1 Logistic Warehouse with RFID

RFID technology is that information of RFID tag attached on a product is identified wirelessly using radio frequency, and the collected information is stored and processed. An RFID system consists of a tag, a reader, the middleware, and the application service platform. This kind of RFID application technologies are used in various distribution environments.[2]

RFID based distribution storage system is as shown in Fig.1. Firstly the RFID reader on the gate identifies tags on goods. The identified information is filtered on repeated events through the real-time RFID processor, and then generates the report about it. The report is stored into the database in the end.

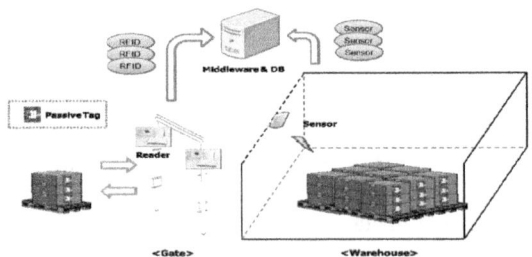

Fig. 1. Logistic warehouse with RFID

When a sensor node is added to the existing system, the status accuracy is not guaranteed that indirect sensing information from the storage is mapped on each item with RFID tag information, and the status accuracy of a sensing information-sensitive product is not reliable. As RFID data processor and sensor processor independently exist, binding and joining sensor information and RFID identification information cost a lot.

2.2 Memory Space of Sensor Tag

A sensor tag is a special tag with sensor function that a general tag has only identification information. It varies 900 MHz half-passive sensor tag and 2.4 GHz/433MHz active sensor tag, etc. In the real world, a half-passive sensor tag is preferred, due to its low cost.

The half-passive tag is available to process sensor data based on ECPglobal Class1 Gen2 protocol, which is the existing passive method. Also along Gen2 Tag standard, the memory Bank area consists of TID, USER Memory. EPC, Reserved Memory.

In Fig. 2, as an example for the memory Bank of sensor tag, A927 memory structure of Caen is shown. As illustrated in the picture, the memory of sensor tag has its logging area in User Memory area. So it has bigger User Memory area than general tags. To store data, the sensor uses TID memory. To manage with a fixed address, memory location is mapped by SAM. And data stored in the sensor forms the type of binary.

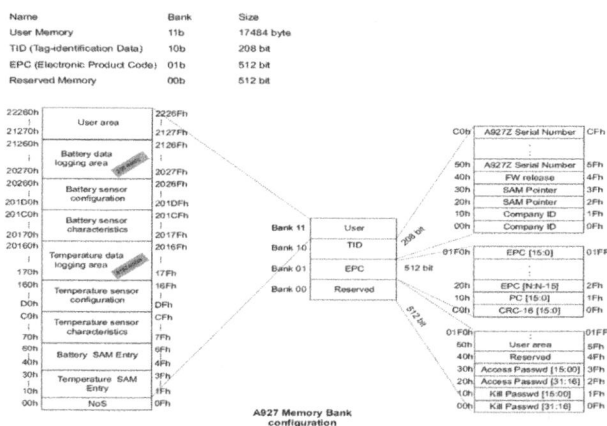

Fig. 2. Sensor Tag Memory Structure (Caen)

3 Target Environment

The target environment is low-temperature storage in APC (Agricultural Products Processing Center) where food products stay long. APC is a scaled and modernized center for mass supply of fresh products directly from the producing places to large distribution chains. In the center, the fresh goods are sorted, stored, packed and sold by needs: the products stay in the center longer than any other place before packed or sold. Thus, in the low-temperature storage, a system is necessary in which the temperature remains stable so that food products are freshly stored.

In the existing low-temperature storage as Fig. 3, an RFID reader is placed on the outer gate and reads identification information of tags on goods. The temperature sensor is put on the upper place of the inner gate, and it senses at a regular interval to control the indoor temperature. In the storage, there are the gate controller, the humidity sensor, the cooling controller, the cooler, the monitoring system, and the monitoring terminals for food products to keep fresh.

The gate controller is on the front gate of the storage and set up the cooling status for food storage when the goods in. The humidity sensor is put on the upper inside of the gate and sensing the temperature and the humidity. The cooler lowers the inside temperature of the storage. The cooling controller automatically detects the temperature difference between the cooler and the sensor on the gate, and controls the temperature of the cooler to keep cooling. The monitoring system and the monitoring terminal are a system to monitor the current humidity statement in the storage through the controller.

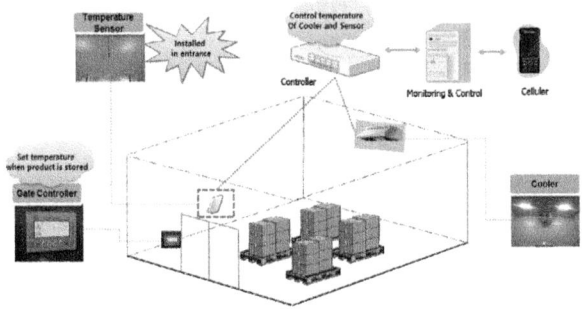

Fig. 3. Warehouse system in APC

In the existing storage system, the mechanism to process events on RFID and sensing information is shown in Fig. 3. Sensor events and RFID events are independent events generated from different locations from each other. Firstly, an RFID event created on the gate is stored into the database. Therefore this becomes a historical event. Secondly a sensor data from the storage inside is a real time event. To process these data of which the special and temporal attributes are different, a stream processor is used as illustrated in Fig. 3.

4   Problem Definition

In this Section, it is described that two defeats from when a sensor node mentioned in the target environment is used and a problem arising from when a sensor tag is used to solve those two defeats.

4.1   Temperature Deflection in APC

In the low-temperature storage, the temperature inside is checked with only one humidity sensor on the upper inside place of the gate. As goods come in and out

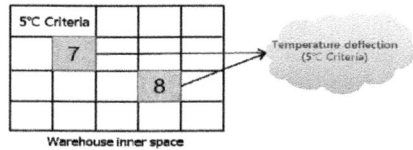

Fig. 4. Temperature deflection

often, the temperature difference is significant around the gate. Therefore, the extreme condition can be checked with the sensor on the gate. [3]

However, in the actual storage as in Fig. 4, the product temperature and the air circulation are the main factors making the temperature difference.

In the low-temperature storage, there is a system in which the sensor checks the highest temperature in the storage and compares it with the cooler's temperature to control the cooler, so that the temperature inside keeps stable. However, this kind of systems does not guarantee that the temperature in every section of the storage is identical and remains unchanged. The temperature in a particular sector increases by the product temperature; the cooler sends the cold air, but it does not guarantee that the temperature is constant in all the areas. If the air circulation is insufficient, some products freezes and some are spoiled. As the existing sensing technique cannot detect the detailed temperature statement, these problems will not be solved.

4.2 Unreachable RFID Reader Range

To solve the accuracy problem on the temperature measurement mentioned previously, suppose that sensor tags are put on each pallet. Technically we can assume that identification and sensing information on every single product, due to the sensor tags on all the pallets.

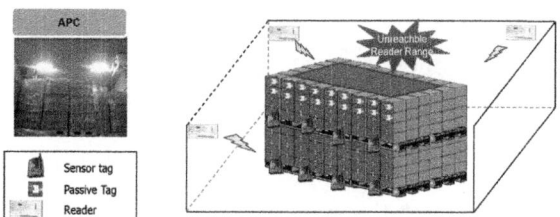

Fig. 5. Unreachable RFID reader range

However, in Fig. 5, there are blind spots in the reader range on products stacked in the storage. In particular, when an item is surrounded by other goods, its sensor tag cannot be read, and it fails to get sensor information from the item.[3]

4.3 Approximate Join of Sensor and Tag Event

In a system in which the existing sensor node is used, to join sensor data with tag data, the attribute of event time on the database table should be the standard to be processed. However sensor node and reader are independent devices, so sensor data and tag event information of the reader are bound by the time slices or the approximate time: as the amount of data increases, the accuracy and efficiency of the join decrease and the data processing cost increases.

5 Solution

In this Section, to solve the previously mentioned precision problem on sensor information of the existing sensor node based distribution storage, the blind spot problem on reader range when a sensor tag is used, the smart storage modeling with the clone technique between sensor tags is suggested.

The main mechanism of the smart storage modeling is recording and deleting EPC codes of passive tags on User Bank of sensor tags using RFID reader. And the modeling consists of 4 stages: warehousing, stack, unstuck, and delivery.

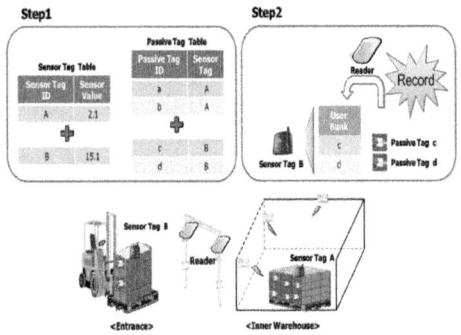

Fig. 6. Warehousing Process

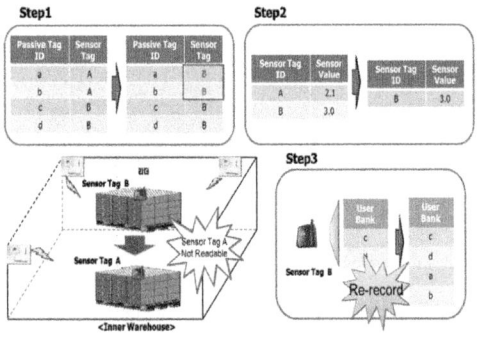

Fig. 7. Stack Process

Firstly, the stage of warehousing is as in Fig. 6. Passive tags are attached onto each box on a pallet, and a sensor tag is put on the top. The sensor tag is on the top is so that the reader can easily read a tag. The reader on the gate reads both of the sensor tag and the passive tag. Tag data is sent to the stream data processor, and then the database performs Aggregation operation to insert the new sensor tag record into the sensor tag table as well as passive tag record into the passive tag table. Finally, to get RFID information in real-time in the storage, the passive tag is recorded onto User Bank of Sensor tag.

Secondly the stage of stack is as in Fig. 7. Generally when pallet B is stacked onto pallet A, the reader cannot read the sensor tag of pallet A. Consequently sensor information about passive tag of sensor tag A is no more generated. The real-time information is also not created. To solve this problem, passive re-recording method between sensor tags based on database updates is used. As aforementioned, when pallet A is no longer identified because of pallet B stacked on it, sensor tag attribute with the value A on passive tag table in the database is updated to the value B, and then the record with the value A in the sensor tag table is deleted. Finally records with the value B are re-recorded to UserID of sensor tag. By this, RFID reader in the storage can read all the data of the passive tags perpendicular to sensor tag B as well as sensor information.

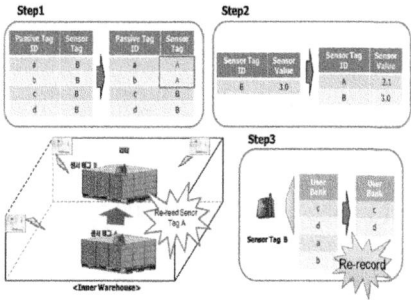

Fig. 8. Unstuck Process

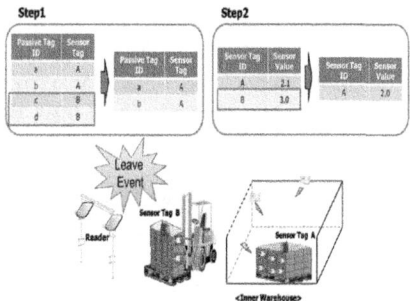

Fig. 9. Delivery Process

Thirdly, the stage of unstuck is as in Fig. 8. The processes of this stage simply go in the reverse order of the stack stage. First of all, when goods unstacked, the reader reads sensor tag A and data about Passive Tag1~3. And then, sensor tag is recorded onto sensor tag table in the database. The attribute value of passive tag is updated to A again.

Finally, the stage of delivery is as in Fig. 9. This stage is also very simple. As the reader is only one, it is regarded that a duplicated event means a product goes out. Therefore the corresponding sensor tag records and passive tag records in the database are deleted.

6 Conclusion

In this paper, the smart storage system is suggested that passive tag recording Methodology on sensor tags is used in the system. We can solve the problems of the RFID storage where the existing sensor node is used to sensor-sensitive products, i.e. real-time object information identification/verification, and the detailed sensor information obtaining problem in the storage sector.

However, in this storage, as passive tag's sensor Tag attribute has to be updated in the stack/unstuck stages; the cost of operation in the database is high. When reading, data of passive tag recorded in User Bank of sensor tag is read as bulk data, so the cost of real-time data processing is high.

A study on indexing method of DB and effective real-time data processing mechanism is necessary in future.

Acknowledgements

This work was supported by the grant No. B0009720 from the Regional Technology Innovation Program of the Ministry of Knowledge Economy (MKE).

References

1. Zhen, T., Zhu, Y., Zhang, Q.: A RFID Logistics Resource Management system for the Warehouses. Environmental Science and Information Application Technology 2, 63 (2009)
2. Yan, B., Chen, Y., Meng, X.: RFID Technology Applied in Warehouse Management System. Computing, Communication, Control, and Management 3, 363 (2008)
3. Connolly, C.: Warehouse management technologies. Sensor Review 28(2) (2008)
4. Flexible tag microlab development: Gas sensors integration in RFID flexible tags for food logistic 2; May, P., Ehrlich, H.C., Steinke, T.: ZIB Structure Prediction Pipeline: Composing a Complex Biological Workflow Through Web Services. In: Nagel, W.E., Walter, W.V., Lehner, W. (eds.) Euro-Par 2006. LNCS, vol. 4128, pp. 1148–1158. Springer, Heidelberg (2006)
5. Jeon, S., Choi, M., Kim, G., Hong, B.: Localization of Pallets based on Passive RFID Tags. In: The 7th International Conference on Information Technology New Generations, ITNG 2010 (2010)

SIMOnt: A Security Information Management Ontology Framework

Muhammad Abulaish[1,*], Syed Irfan Nabi[1,3],
Khaled Alghathbar[1], and Azeddine Chikh[2]

[1] Centre of Excellence in Information Assurance, King Saud University Riyadh, KSA
{mAbulaish,kAlghathbar}@ksu.edu.sa
[2] College of Computer Science and Information Systems, King Saud University Riyadh, KSA
az_chikh@ksu.edu.sa
[3] Faculty of Computer Science, Institute of Business Administration, Karachi, Pakistan
snabi@iba.edu.pk

Abstract. In this paper, we have proposed the design of a Security Information Management Ontology (SIMOnto) framework, which utilizes natural language processing and statistical analysis to mine an exhaustive list of concepts and their relationships in an automatic way. Concepts are extracted using TF-IDF and LSA techniques whereas, relations between them are mined using semantic and co-occurrence based analyses. The mined concepts and relations are presented to domain experts for validation before creation of ontology using Protégé.

Keywords: Information security, Knowledge management, Ontology engineering, Ontology learning, Natural language processing.

1 Introduction

Due to existence of network-centric security environment, automatic discovery of resources and the ability to share information and services across different domains are some of the basic important requirements. The first step in fulfilling these requirements is to markup the security-related resources with various metadata in a well-understood and consistent manner [8]. Such annotations will enable resources to be machine-readable and machine-understandable. Using metadata to find distributed resources that meet one's functional requirements is only the first step. Resource requestors may have additional requirements such as security, survivability, or quality of service (QoS) specifications. For example, they may require resources to possess a certain military classification level, to originate from trusted sources, or to be handled according to a specified privacy policy. Therefore, resources need to be sufficiently annotated with security-related metadata so that they can be correctly discovered, compared, and invoked according to security as well as functional requirements of the requestor.

However, the resources are generally written using natural languages which are unstructured in nature. Given the inherent nuances of natural languages and the unstructured nature of text documents, domain knowledge plays a crucial role in

---

* Corresponding author.

J.J. Park et al. (Eds.): STA 2011, CCIS 186, pp. 201–208, 2011.
© Springer-Verlag Berlin Heidelberg 2011

improving the quality of text information retrieval. Ontology is a knowledge-management structure that represents domain knowledge in a structured and machine-interpretable form. It is increasingly being accepted as the key technology wherein key concepts and their inter-relationships are stored to provide a shared and common understanding of a domain across applications and hence ideally suited to aid in context analysis tasks. The use of ontological models to access and integrate large knowledge repositories in a principled way has an enormous potential to enrich and make accessible unprecedented amount of knowledge for reasoning [7].

One of the hurdles affecting the design for an exhaustive domain ontology is the absence of an unambiguous list of values that may be used to define concepts and relationships. Since, concept definitions need not be exhaustive as new or modified definitions of concepts may emerge, one of the ways to deal with this problem is to integrate ontology learning and enhancement process with text information retrieval based applications. This can help in learning and enhancing existing ontologies effectively within the rigid structural definition. This technique is suitable for learning concepts automatically from underlying resources and therefore sheds off a definite hurdle that acts as a major bottleneck for designing any ontology-based application. This can also take care of a fast-changing world, where areas of interest, vocabulary everything changes at a very rapid rate. Due to the dynamic nature of the security-related document repository, any agent or system designed for reasoning with these concepts should be able to adapt to changes and an ontology should be upgradeable with information extracted through text mining in the domain.

In this paper, we have proposed the design of a text mining framework to create a Security Information Management Ontology (SIMOnt). SIMOnt organizes security concepts and their inter-relationships in a structured and machine-readable format that can be used to annotate security resources in a consistent and effective manner. Starting with a seed ontology, the system extracts feasible concepts and their relationships in an automatic way from underlying text documents. This takes care of a fast-changing world, where areas of interest, vocabulary everything changes at a very rapid rate. The system is also equipped with an ontology enhancing mechanism, which enriches existing concepts and relationships extracted from resource documents after domain expert validation. Marking up security aspects of resources is a crucial step toward deploying a secure Service Oriented Architecture (SOA) system. Although, a number of researchers have noticed the need for security annotation of services and proposed a set of security-related ontologies, these ontologies lack the ability to express certain important security concepts, contain unnecessary concepts, and are organized in a non-intuitive way [9].

The rest of the paper is organized as follows. Section 2 presents a review of related work on ontology engineering and learning from text documents. Section 3 proposed the architectural and functional detail of the proposed SIMOnto (Security Information Management Ontology) framework. In section 4, we discuss the experimental setup and evaluation results. Finally, section 5 concludes the paper with future directions.

2   Related Works

Ontology learning is an area that has fascinated many researchers since last decade. Traditionally ontology development is a time consuming process that is not very conducive to changes in the domain knowledge and is not error-free; therefore, numerous frameworks and methodologies have been proposed to reduce the effort and resources required to develop ontology and provide more accurate results.

Luong *et al.* [1] have developed a framework for ontology development using text mining technique on web documents crawled in a focused way. Starting with a manually-created seed ontology, they have proposed the use of Support Vector Machine (SVM) to identify relevant documents for text mining process. Although, the proposed framework is fully automatic, they recommend for the domain experts intervention for improved overall performance. Lenci *et al.* [2] have also proposed a semi-automatic ontology extraction system from text documents. They have used NLP-based hybrid method that bring together linguistic and statistical techniques such that domain terminologies are extracted linguistically while the acquired terms are organized into proto-conceptual structures using NLP. Jiang and Tan [3] have presented an automatic domain ontology learning system that combines both statistical and lexico-syntactic features present in the contemporary systems and uses NLP tools for full text parsing and Parts-Of-Speech (POS) analysis. They have also designed rule-based algorithms to extract both taxonomical and non taxonomical relations. Nie and Zhou [4] have developed a domain-adaptable ontology learning system that uses an automatic seed concept learning by taking an overview of the domain material based on frequency. These core concepts are used to learn new concepts. Parkin et al. [5] have experimented with ontology development for information security based on associating infrastructure properties with human behavior to find the effects of information security controls on human behavior. The approach may be used to better manage information security by predict human behavior.

As can be seen from the literatures discussed above that one of the key issues that is still unresolved is filtering the domain specific terms (representing concepts) and their inter-relationship in an automatic way and therefore sheds off a definite hurdle that acts as a major bottleneck for designing domain ontologies. Further, it can also be observed that most of the authors recommend human intervention at concept validation level to preserve only relevant concepts and relationship rather than preserving everything identified by the system as feasible concepts – as ontology is not a data store rather a knowledge management tool.

3   Proposed SIMOnt Framework

Figure 1 presents the SIMOnt framework proposed for creating security information management ontology. Starting with seed ontology concepts, the system identifies relevant documents on the Web and crawls them on local machine. Thereafter, the documents are processed for cleaning, chunking, and parsing using a statistical parser. The outputs generated by parser are further analyzed to extract concepts and their relationships which are incorporated in seed ontology under expert supervision. The proposed framework follows the iterative process to learn concepts and relationships and continues until there is no change in the underlying ontology. This takes care of a fast-changing world, where areas of interest, vocabulary everything changes at a very rapid rate. The major modules of the framework are – *web crawler*, *document processor*, and *knowledge miner*. The functional details of these modules are discussed in the following sub-sections.

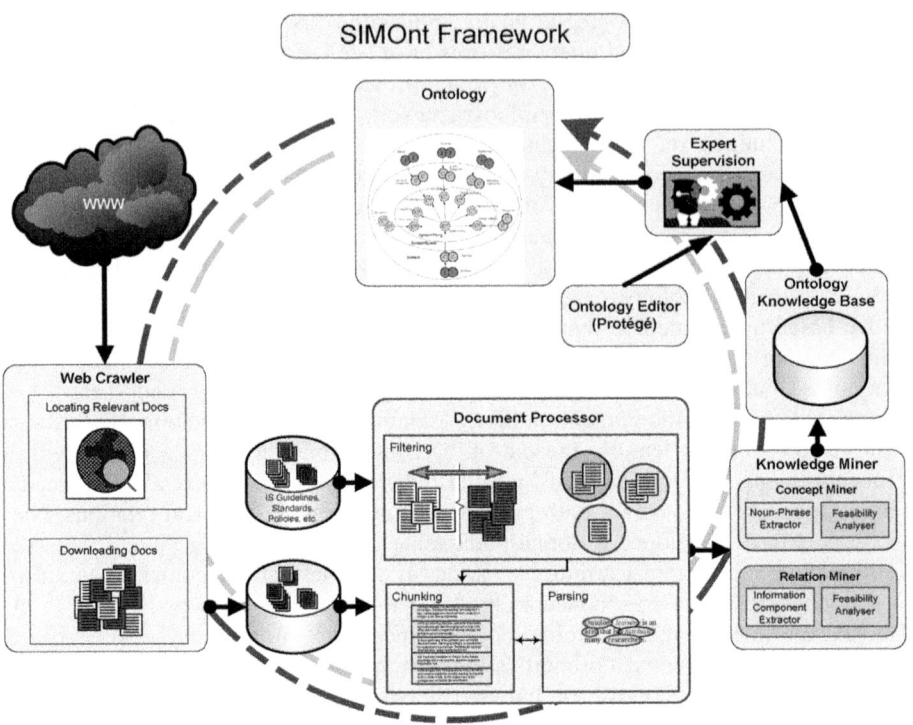

Fig. 1. Design of SIMOnt Framework

3.1   Web Crawler and Document Processor

Since a document containing security-related information can be a text document (stored as txt, doc, or pdf files) or a webpage residing on the World Wide Web (WWW), the framework is integrated with a web crawler to crawl relevant web pages from WWW. The web crawler uses the ontological concepts and relations to identify the relevant web pages on WWW and store them on local machine for further processing by document processor to mine new concepts and relations.

The document processor fetches the text documents from local database repository and filters the unwanted texts from them. For example, in case of web pages the HTML tags are filtered out. Similarly, since we are concerned only with textual contents, all the images and their labels are excluded while converting pdf documents into text documents. After filtering process, the documents are divided into record-size chunks which boundaries are decided by the paragraph marks. Finally, the submitted to the Parts-Of-Speech (POS) analyzer which assigns POS tags to every word in a sentence, where a tag reflects the syntactic category of the word. The POS tags are useful to identify the grammatical structure of sentences like noun and verb phrases and their inter-relationships.

3.2 Knowledge Miner

The knowledge miner accepts phrase structure trees output by document processor as input and analyzes them to identify candidate constituents for knowledge-base. The candidate constituents are then analyzed using Latent Semantic Analysis (LSA) technique to compile a list of feasible concepts. Thereafter, the tree is again analyzed to identify relationships between concept-pairs.

3.2.1 Concept Miner

For candidate concepts, we consider only those internal NP (noun phrase) nodes in phrase structure tree whose child nodes appear as a leaf node. If a node NP has single child node tagged as *noun* it is extracted as *term* otherwise, string concatenation is applied to club the child nodes, tagged as *noun* or *adjective*, together and it is identified as *phrase*. The lists of terms and phrases are compiled separately for the purpose of feasibility analysis using LSA. After compiling the lists, the terms having a match in the list of stop-words are filtered out and phrases starting or ending with stop-words are cleaned. For remaining phrases we calculate their weight using term frequency (*tf*) and inverse document frequency (*idf*) in each document of the corpus. The weight of a phrase p_i in j^{th} document, $\omega(p_{i,j})$, is calculated using equations 1 and 2 where, $tf(p_{i,j})$ is the number of times p_i occurs in j^{th} document. $|D|$ is the total number of documents in the corpus, and $|\{d_j : p_i \in d_j\}|$ is the number of documents where p_i appears. While counting frequency of a term or phrase they are stemmed using Porter's stemmer. All those phrases having normalized average weight over all documents above a threshold are retained for feasibility analysis using LSA.

$$\omega(p_{i,j}) = tf(p_{i,j}) \times idf(p_i) \tag{1}$$

$$idf(p_i) = \log\left(\frac{|D|}{\left|\left\{d_j : p_i \in d_j\right\}\right|}\right) \tag{2}$$

$$(p_{i,j}) = \begin{cases} idf(t_i), & \text{if } i = j \text{ and } j \leq m \\ idf(t_i), & \text{if } j > m \text{ and } t_i \text{ is a substring of the phrase} \\ 0, & \text{otherwise} \end{cases} \tag{3}$$

LSA is a technique which is used to analyze relationships between a set of documents and the terms they contain by producing a set of concepts related to the documents and terms [6]. For LSA each document d is represented as a feature vector $\vec{d} = (w_{t_1}, \cdots, w_{t_m})$, where m is the number of terms, and w_{t_i} is the weight of term t_i in document d calculated using equation 1. Feature vector for each document in the corpus is used to generate *term-document* matrix A by composing feature vectors of all the documents in the corpus. In this matrix, a column vector represents a document and a row vector represents a term as document's feature. In matrix A all column vectors are normalized so that their length is 1. Thereafter, Singular Value Decomposition (SVD) is applied on A which breaks it into three matrices U, S, and V such that $A = USV^T$. SVD translates the term and document vectors into a concept space. The first r columns of U (where r is $A's$ rank) form an orthogonal basis for the matrix $A's$ term space. Therefore, basis vectors, which are column vectors in U, represent abstract terms of corresponding document. In practice, it is not possible to take all r abstract terms. Therefore we take a threshold value, θ, and find the number of singular values (say k) in matrix S that is higher than this θ. Then, we use U_k, which consists of first k columns of U as shown in figure 3(e), to obtain k most important terms for the document corpus. At the time of identification of important terms and phrases we consider only magnitude therefore we take absolute value of U_k. Since the column vectors in U represent the importance of the terms for the document corpus, we also use U to evaluate the importance of phrases. For this, we construct a matrix P of order $m \times (m+p)$, where m and p represent the number of terms and phrases respectively. In matrix P, each row represents a term and columns represent terms as well phrases. Elements of matrix P are computed using equation 3. Like term-document matrix A, the column vector lengths in P are also normalized to 1. Thereafter, the matrix $abs(U_k^T)$ is multiplied with P to get matrix M which represents the importance of terms and phrases. In matrix M, the highest value in each row is identified and the corresponding term or phrase is extracted as feasible key concept.

3.2.2 Relation Miner

Once the list of feasible concepts is compiled, it is presented to the domain expert for validation. The human intervention is suggested just to ensure that ontology is not a generally data store rather a knowledge management tool. For each pair of validated concepts, we mine two different types of relations – structural relations and generic relations. The structural relations (IS-A, HAS-PART, etc.) are also called conceptual-semantic and lexical relations and extracted using WordNet, which is a large lexical database of English words. In WordNet, nouns, verbs, adjectives and adverbs are grouped into sets of cognitive synonyms (synsets), each expressing a distinct concept. Synsets are interlinked by means of conceptual-semantic and lexical relations. The generic relations are extracted using co-occurrence based analysis.

4   Experimental Evaluation

In this section, we present the experimental details and performance evaluation results of the proposed SIMOnt framework. For performance evaluation a prototype model of SIMOnt is implemented using Java programming language. The prototype uses a number of in-built tools for different purposes. For example, it uses Stanford Parser for POS analysis and phrase structure tree creation. Similarly, it uses Porter Stemmer to stem the phrases while counting their frequencies, checking string containments, etc.

The performance of the framework is analyzed by taking into account the performance of the knowledge miner. The quality of knowledge mining can be measured by comparing its information extraction accuracy against human curation.

Since, our intention was to study the applicability of the knowledge extraction from unstructured texts related to information security, we considered "the standard of good practice for information security" document which has been produced by the Information Security Forum (ISF). ISF is an international association of over 300 organizations which fund and co-operate in the development of a practical research programme in information security. As the ISF's document contains 372 pages and available as a pdf file, first it is converted into text file. Thereafter, it is divided into 4881 smaller files on the basis of paragraph markers and stored separately. The knowledge mining algorithm is applied on these files and the list of extracted concepts having relevance value (obtained through LSA) greater than or equal to a given threshold is presented for evaluation. We manually inspected these documents to build a complete compilation of all concepts to be extracted. Since, the number of documents are large, we have applied sampling to evaluate the results manually. The performance of this module is computed using standard measures of *precision* and *recall*, which are defined in equation 4 & 5 respectively. In these equations, *TP* indicates *true positive* which is defined as the number of correct concepts the system identifies as correct, *FP* indicates *false positive* which is defined as the number of incorrect concepts the system falsely identifies as correct, and the *FN* indicates *false negatives* which is the number of correct concepts the system fails to identify as correct.

$$precision = \frac{TP}{TP + FP} \tag{4}$$

$$recall = \frac{TP}{TP + FN} \tag{5}$$

The precision value of the system reflects its capability to identify a concept relevant to the domain. The precision of the proposed system is found to be 72.2%, which needs improvement. The precision value can be improved by tightening the rule set and enhancing the list of stop words. Recall value reflects the capability of the system to locate all instances of a concept within the corpus. The recall value of the knowledge miner module is 93.8%.

5   Conclusion and Future Works

In this paper, we have proposed the design of a text mining based Security Information Management Ontology (SIMOnt) framework. Starting with a seed ontology, SIMOnt retrieves relevant documents and applies natural language processing and statistical techniques to extract concepts and relationships from them. The mined concepts and relationships are then used to enhance the underlying ontology under expert supervision. For ontology editing, we have used protégé 4.1. Presently, we are enhancing the relation-mining technique to consider more complex relations that do not necessarily appear with relating concept-pair. We are also enhancing the framework to facilitate automatic annotation of resources using ontological concepts and answer security-related queries over them.

References

1. Luong, H.P., Gauch, S., Wang, Q.: Ontology Learning Through Focused Crawling and Information Extraction. In: Proceedings of the 2009 International Conference on Knowledge and Systems Engineering, pp. 106–112. IEEE Computer Society, Los Alamitos (2009), doi:10.1109/KSE.2009.28
2. Lenci, A., Montemagni, S., Pirrelli, V., Venturi, G.: Ontology learning from Italian legal texts. In: Proceeding of the 2009 Conference on Law, Ontologies and the Semantic Web: Channelling the Legal Information Flood, pp. 75–94. IOS Press, Amsterdam (2009)
3. Jiang, X., Tan, A.: CRCTOL: A semantic-based domain ontology learning system. J. Am. Soc. Inf. Sci. Technol. 61(1), 150–168 (2010), doi:10.1002/asi.v61:1
4. Nie, X., Zhou, J.: A Domain Adaptive Ontology Learning Framework. In: IEEE International Conference on Networking, Sensing and Control, ICNSC 2008, pp. 1726–1729 (2008)
5. Parkin, S.E., Moorsel, A.V., Coles, R.: An information security ontology incorporating human-behavioural implications. In: Proceedings of the 2nd International Conference on Security of Information and Networks, pp. 46–55. ACM, Famagusta (2009)
6. Landauer, T., Foltz, P., Laham, D.: Introduction to Latent Semantic Analysis. Discourse Processes 25, 259–284 (1998)
7. Fensel, D., Horrocks, I., Harmelen, F., van, M.D.L., Patel-Schneider, P.: OIL: Ontology Infrastructure to Enable the Semantic Web. IEEE Intelligent Systems 16(2), 38–45 (2001)
8. Kim, A., Luo, J., Kang, M.: Security Ontology for Annotating Resources, August 31. Naval Research Lab., Washington DC (2005)
9. Denker, G., Kagal, L., Finin, T., Paolucci, M., Sycara, K.: Security for DAML Web Services: Annotation and Matchmaking. In: Proc. of the 2nd International Semantic Web Conference (ISWC 2003), Sanibel Island, Florida (2003)

Using Bloom Filters for Mining Top-k Frequent Itemsets in Data Streams

Younghee Kim, Kyungsoo Cho, Jaeyeol Yoon, Ieejoon Kim, and Ungmo Kim

School of Information and Communication Engineering, Sungkyunkwan University,
300 Chunchun-dong, Suwon, Gyeonggi-Do, 440-746, Korea
younghees@gmail.com, kisschks@hotmail.com,
{vntlffl,uk3080789}@naver.com, umkim@ece.skku.ac.kr

Abstract. In this paper, we study the problem of finding the top-k most frequent itemsets in data streams. To only mine top-k restricted to the sub-domains of the workspace or the result of some query. Most previous algorithms are clearly not suitable for this problem with limited memory, such as for instance, an allocated for each stream summary. Therefore, we propose that in order to solve memory efficiency for mining frequent itemsets from massively and speedy a data stream. Our algorithm is used to a bloom filter structure, named MineTop-k, which permit the efficient computation and maintenance of the results. We show that our approach is memory-efficient method for the top-k problem.

Keywords: Data Stream, Top-k Frequent Itemsets, Bloom Filter, Data Mining.

1 Introduction

The most basic problem on a data stream is that of the finding the most frequently occurring items in the stream [1] [2]. Recently, researchers started working on novel algorithms for analyzing data streams. Problems studied in this context include approximate frequency moments, differences, distinct values estimation, bit counting, duplicate detection, approximate quantiles, histograms, wavelet based aggregate queries, frequent elements and top-k queries. Most previous studies require the specification of a *min_support* threshold that is to extract frequent itemsets from input dataset. To the data mining problem of computing all itemsets with frequency above a fixed threshold, the algorithm is must scan the entire dataset more than once and the dataset does not fit completely in main memory. Therefore, for large datasets the mining of top-k frequent itemsets becomes computationally needy [3] [4] [5]. Here the parameter k allows, in practice, for a better control on the output size. Wang *et al.* propose changing the task of mining frequent itemsets satisfying the *min_support* threshold to mining top-k frequent closed itemsets of minimum length *min_l*, where k is a user-desired number of frequent closed itemsets to be mined, top-k refers to the k most frequent closed itemsets, and *min_l* (where $min_l \geq 0$) is the minimal length of closed itemsets [6]. Vasusevan *et al.* is

J.J. Park et al. (Eds.): STA 2011, CCIS 186, pp. 209–216, 2011.
© Springer-Verlag Berlin Heidelberg 2011

used to extracting, for a fixed parameter $0 < \varepsilon < 1$, an approximation of the top-k frequent items from a sequence of items, which contains no item whose actual frequency is less than $f_K - \varepsilon$, where f_K is the actual frequency of the k-th most frequent item [7]. The problems of approximately finding frequent items and top-k elements are closely related. Finding top-k items in data streams means finding k items whose frequency are larger than other items in data stream. These techniques can be classified into counter-based and sampling-based techniques. Pietracaprina *et al.* present novel results on the effectiveness of sampling for mining top-k frequent itemsets from a transactional dataset. The author proves an upper bound t on the sample size which guarantees, with probability at least $1-\delta$, that a ε-approximation to the top-k frequent itemsets of size up to w is discovered. They also show that for $w \in O(1)$ the upper bound t is tight, within constant factors, by arguing the existence of a dataset for which a random sample of size $O(t)$ would not provide the required ε-approximation with sufficiently high probability [8]. In this paper, we studies counter based on finding top-k frequent itemsets using the extended bloom filter structure in stream environments. Typically, stream-oriented algorithms usually maintain all the data in memory to avoid the expensive overhead of disk I/Os. We propose algorithms that incrementally maintain the top-k items and monitor the updating streams continuously. In addition, our techniques utilize to improve space and time efficiency for finding frequent itemsets from data streams. The rest of the paper is organized as follows. Section 2 reviews the related work on top-k and computation model. Section 3 describes the proposed method. Section 4 described to build the frequent itemsets tree based on monitoring top-k items. Section 5 analyzes the proven space bound for the guaranteed solution. Section 6 concludes the paper with directions for future work.

2   Problem Statement

2.1   Bloom Filter

The bloom filter is a space-efficient probabilistic data structure that is used to test whether an element is a member of a set. A bloom filter is a bit array of m bits, there must also be k different hash functions defined [9]. Let set $S=\{x_1, x_2, ..., x_n\}$ be with n elements from a universe $\mathcal{U}$. It uses a set $\mathcal{H}(x)$ of k uniform and independent hash functions to map the universe $\mathcal{U}$ to the bit address space $[1, m]$.

$$\mathcal{H}(x)=\{h_i(x)|1 \leq h_i(x) \leq m, \; 1 \leq i \leq k\} \tag{1}$$

Definition 1. Given any element x, to check whether x is in S, one only needs to test whether $\mathcal{B}[\mathcal{H}(x)] = 1$. If no, then x is said to be out of S. $\mathcal{B}[\mathcal{H}(x)]$ is defined as the follows. *For all* $x \in \mathcal{U}$, $\mathcal{B}[\mathcal{H}(x)] \equiv \{\mathcal{B}[\mathcal{H}(x)] \mid 1 \leq i \leq k\}$.

For instance, a bit vector $\mathcal{B}$ represents the set $\{x, y, z\}$ using a bloom filter $\mathcal{B}$ shown as fig1. Initially, all the bits in $\mathcal{B}$ are set to '0'. Then for each $x, y,$ and $z \in S$, an operation of setting $\mathcal{B}[\mathcal{H}(x)]$ is performed.

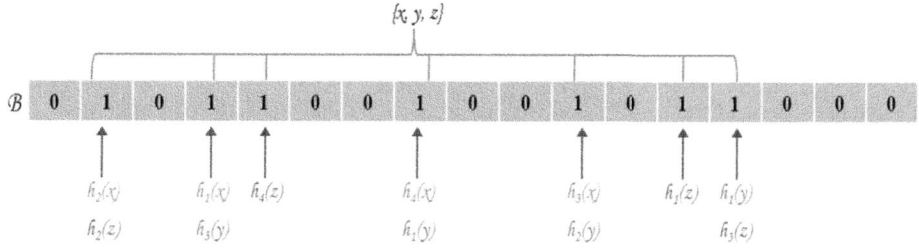

Fig. 1. Bloom Filter ($m=17$, $k=4$)

2.2   Top-*k* Frequent Itemsets

Let $S = q_1, q_2, \ldots, q_n$ be a data stream, where each $q_i \in I = \{i_1, i_2, \ldots, i_m\}$ and $n = |S|$. A frequent item, f_i, is an element whose frequency, in a stream S whose current size is N, exceeds a user specified support $\lceil \varnothing N \rceil$, where $0 \leq \varnothing \leq 1$; whereas the top-*k* itemsets are the *k* items with highest frequencies.

Definition 2. Given a length of the stream size N, the count of itemset I and the frequency of I in a stream S is defined as the follows.

$$Frequency(I, S) = \frac{count(I, S)}{N} \tag{2}$$

We consider two issues of the problems of finding frequent itemsets. Both the frequent items and the top-*k* query is an essential prerequisite for the generalized problem of finding top-*k* frequent itemsets in data stream. For instant, the FindCandidateTop (S, k, l) problem is to keep a uniform random sample of the elements stored as a list of items plus a counter for each item. The result is a list of *l* items from S such that the *k* most frequent items occur in the list. The kth most frequent item has almost the same frequency as the $l+1^{st}$ most frequent item. In sampling algorithm, if s is the size of the sample, to ensure that an item with frequency f_k appears in the sample, we need to set $\frac{s}{m}$, to be $\frac{s}{m} > O(\frac{\log n}{n_k})$, thus $s > O(\frac{\log n}{f_k})$, and gives a solution to FindCandidateTop(S, k, $O(\frac{\log n}{f_k})$). The FindApproxTop(S, k, ϵ) is a more practical approximation for the top-*k* problem. The sketch-based *CountSketch* algorithm proposed the FindApproxTop(S, k, ϵ) problem. The output is a list of *k* items from S such that every item i in the list has $n_i > (1-\epsilon)n_k$, where ϵ is a user-defined error, and $n_1 \geq n_2 \ldots \geq n_{|A|}$, such that f_k is the item with the kth rank. While the counter-based algorithm, for a given k, with $1 \leq k \leq n$, denote $f_s^{(k)} = f_s(i_k)$, and define the set of top-*k* frequent itemsets.

$$Topk(S, k, I) = \{(I, f_s(i_k)) : i_k \in I, \quad f_s(i_k) \geq f_s^{(k)}\} \tag{3}$$

Where the Top*k*(S, k, I)   is the top-*k* frequent itemset in data stream S.

3   Counting Bloom Filter Based Top-*k* Items

In this section, we propose a counting bloom filter based technique for solving top-*k* items in a data stream. The underlying idea is to maintain the frequencies of the significant items with the counting bloom filter structure. There are three aspects to the problem that what can gather statistics about computational power and storage, and guarantees about quality of results. The storage space available to the process is limited, but all activity used counters must fit in a small memory in order to keep up with the data stream. The process is limited to having at most *m* active counters at any time. The counters are updated in a way that accurately estimates the frequencies of the significant items, and a small quantity data structure is utilized to keep the items sorted by their estimated frequencies. We can make a final pass to choose the top-*k* frequencies for a desired value of *k*. In general, there is a one pass algorithm using *m* counters that determines a set of at most *m* values including all that occur strictly more than $\frac{n}{(m+1)}$ times in an input stream of length *n*.

3.1   Counting Bloom Filter Summary

Counting filters provide a way to implement a delete operation an element stored in the filter. Whenever a counting bloom filter adds or deletes an element, it increments or decrements the counters corresponding to the *k* hash values. The insert operation is extended to increment the value of the arrays and the delete operation is obviously consists of decrementing the value of each of the respective arrays. When an element is added into the stream, the counters for the corresponding bits are incremented as a counter increases from 0 to 1 or drops from 1 to 0, the corresponding bit is set to 1 or 0, and a record is added to the summary list remembering the updates.

We denote the counter at the ith position in the data structures as c_i. The counter c_i estimates the frequency f_i, of some item q_i in data stream. A frequent items, Q_i, with rank *i*, that should be accommodated in the ith counter. The counter actually only stores how much larger it is compared to the next smallest counter. If the item, Q_i, i^{th} position in the data structure has the right item, then the item with the ith rank and $q_i = Q_i$. The data structure is a linked list, ordered by counter value. The algorithm is described in Fig 2.

```
Algorithm STREAM-COUNT
1. Initialize the counters to zero, stream S
2. For each item in the data stream
     (a) If the item qi is monitored, let ci be the counter
         of qi and increment the counter.
     (b) If the item qi is not monitored, replace ci be the
         count of recent item with equal the counter of
         current qi and detach qi from the count buffer.
```

Fig. 2. Stream Counting Algorithm

The algorithm for stream counting using the count buffer required to effectively memory space. To demonstrate our algorithm effectiveness, consider any item q_i that occurs $f_i > \frac{n}{(m+1)}$. If q_i is occurred f_i when all other candidate items are full with other count values then q_i's counter is incremented $f_i + \alpha > \frac{n}{(m+1)}$. Thus, we can associate k occurrences of other frequencies along with the occurrence of q_i, for a total of $k+1$ unique location in the input stream. Our algorithm thus identifies at most k candidates for having appeared more than $\frac{n}{(m+1)}$.

Example 1. Assuming $k=3$, and $I = \{A, B, C, D\}$. The data stream S is consecutively occurrence with *ABBCDC*. As Fig 3(a), the data stream $S=AB$ will yield the stream summary structure, after the count buffer accommodate the observed items. The value of the count buffer is the same as the counters' value of all of its items. When another item B arrives, a new count buffer is created with value 2, and item B is attached to it, as shown in Fig 3 (b). As Fig 3(c), when item C arrives, if the item has a value equal to the new value of the item, then the item is attached to in the child list of this list. When item D arrives, the item store buffer is full and the item has a value equal to the new value of the item, A, is replaced by D. Finally, top-*3* items are shown in fig 3(e).

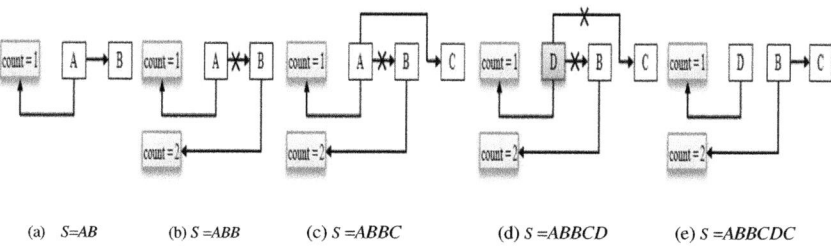

(a) *S=AB*   (b) *S =ABB*   (c) *S =ABBC*   (d) *S =ABBCD*   (e) *S =ABBCDC*

Fig. 3. Top-3 Counter Stream Summary Structure

4   Mine of Frequent Itemsets

In the previous frequent itemsets mining, the minimum support threshold is used for reducing the generation of candidate frequent itemsets. To mine top-k frequent itemsets timely, our approach is to build the frequent itemsets tree based on monitoring top-k items. This approach is done in two steps, where each step requires a one I/O scan of the data streams. Step one is the construction of the frequent itemsets tree based monitored top-k items and step two is the actual mining for these data structures. Then we can mine minimizing the candidacy node generation and the constrained top-k frequent itemsets.

4.1   Construction of the Frequent Itemset Tree

To illustrate the construction of the tree, we will explain step by step the process of creating tree in Fig 4. A first initial scan of the data streams identifies the top-3 items.

This step starts by counting the items appearing in the data streams. We use an example with the transactions shown in table of Fig 4. After scan from TID_1 to TID_3 on the dataset, the top3-items generated {A:3, E:2, B:2} and removes all non-top3 items {D, G, C, H}. The transactions are sorted according to generate the top-3 summary structure. This ordered transaction generates the first path of the frequent itemsets tree with counter link. The same procedure is executed for the TID_4, which yields the stream summary structure, after the count buffer accommodates the observed items {A, B, C, D}. The item E is not occurred, then the value of the count buffer of item E is 2 and set $\varepsilon = -1$.   For item E, with value (count buffer value – ε) such as $2 - \varepsilon = 0$, then the item E is removed to the tree. When another item C arrives, the item store buffer is full and the item has a value equal to the new value of the item, a new count buffer is created with value 1. After then another item D arrives, the item store buffer is full and the item has a value equal to the new value of the item, C, is replaced by D. Finally, we can create the tree with the three of the buffer. Our goal is to propose an algorithm that directly to generate only the actual top-3 frequent itemsets without candidate generation using the monitored top-3 items. The results of the top-3 frequent itemsets is {A}, {AB}, and {AE}.

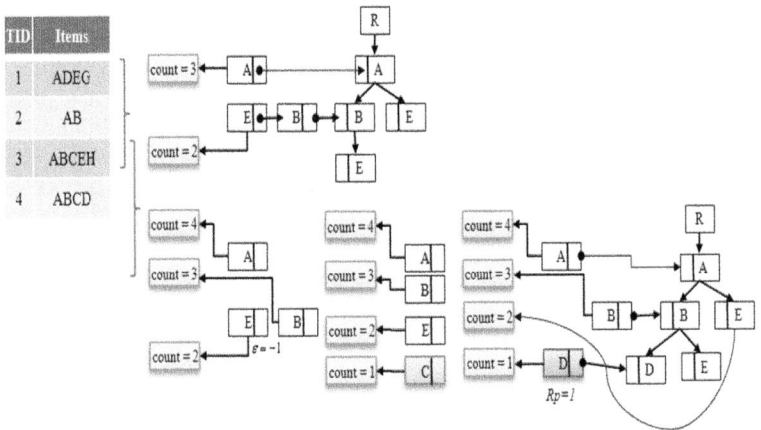

Fig. 4. Mine Frequent Itemset Tree

4.2   Mining Top-K Frequent Itemsets

To mine the top-k itemsets, a set of k items can produce 2^k-1 itemsets, from which only the top-k itemsets are chosen. In dense datasets contain long itemsets particularly, a quite small number of items are generates top-k frequent itemsets. The algorithm MineTop-k is given in Fig 5. The algorithm consists of three loops. The first loop is outputs the candidate top-k items from stream summary data structure. The summary data structure ensures constant time retrieval of the number of k items. All items with the same counter value are linked together in a linked list and can be sequentially traversed as a sorted list. At the end of the loop, top-k candidates are checked that exceed the overestimate counter of the $k+1$ item. These generated top-k items are used in constructing the prefix-tree. In the second loop, the first prefix-tree is built for item as it is the largest count value in the counter buffer. A child node of the tree is a smaller value than the parent node. The last loop performs a mining top-k frequent itemsets after prefix tree has been built. The condition k=*full* is checked, after the routine traverses the tree from the top to the bottom. It presents exactly k frequent items where k is a user specified number.

```
Algorithm: MineTop-k( DS, integer  k)
begin
  read DS;
  cᵢ ← fᵢ(qᵢ);
  construct count-list(cᵢ (qᵢ));
      for i = 1 … k {
            output Qᵢ ;
            if ( (i > k+1) && ( fᵢ(qᵢ₊₁) = = fᵢ(qᵢ)) )
                output Qᵢ₊₁;
  }//end for
  while (count-list) {
            built prefix-tree;
  }//end while
      for i = 1 … k {
          Search breath-first(tree);
      output ∪top-k (Fi);
  }// end for
```

Fig. 5. Top-k Frequent Itemsets Mining Algorithm

5   Analysis

For the top-k items, it is impossible in general to report the most common category in one pass using less than $\Theta(n)$ storage. We provide the first proven space bound for the guaranteed solution of the exact top-k problem, for data streams. For each n item, we assign the m counters to monitor the first m distinct items that appear in the data stream. Then the item is being monitored, increment the appropriate counter. For the each item return the k distinct items with the largest counts, for the desired value of k.

Theorem 1. To calculate the exact frequent items, it use only $\min(|A|, \frac{N}{F_k})$ counters. We have to make sure that the difference between F_k and F_{k+1} is more than F_{max}, for all monitored top-k items.

Proof. The least frequent items that is monitored, F_l, it is true that $F_{max} \leq \frac{N-\sum_{i\leq l}(F_i - F_{max})}{m}$. By the same token, $F_{l+1} \leq F_{max}$, it follows that $F_{l+1} \leq \frac{N-\sum_{i\leq l}F_i}{m-l}$. Hence, we can establish a bound on the space needed for the exact solution of the frequent items that $\min(|A|, O(k^2\ln(|A|)))$.

Definition 3. We define X as a frequent itemset over data stream, that given a support threshold, $\sigma(0 < \sigma \leq 1)$. If $X \geq \sigma$, X is a top-k frequent itemsets if there exists no more than k-1 frequent itemsets which support count is higher than support of X.

6   Conclusion

We propose algorithms that incrementally maintain the top-k items and practically interesting problem, mining top-k frequent itemsets. The underlying idea is to maintain the frequencies of the significant items and can gather statistics about computational power and storage, and guarantees about quality of results. We can make a final pass to choose the top-k frequencies for a desired value of k. In general, there is a one pass algorithm using m counters that determines a set of at most m values including all that occur strictly more than $\frac{n}{(m+1)}$ times in an input stream of length n. In addition, our techniques utilize to improve space and time efficiency for finding frequent itemsets from data streams.

References

1. Charikar, M., Chen, K., Farach-Colton, M.: Finding Frequent Items in Data Streams. Theoretical Computer Science 312(1), 3–15 (2004)
2. Cormode, G., Korn, F., Muthukrishnan, S., Srivastava, D.: Finding Hierarchical Heavy Hitters in Data Streams. In: Proceedings of the 29th VLDB Conference, Berlin, Germany, pp. 464–475 (2003)
3. Metwally, A., Agrawal, D., Abbadi, A.E.: Efficient computation of frequent and top-k elements in data streams. In: Eiter, T., Libkin, L. (eds.) ICDT 2005. LNCS, vol. 3363, pp. 398–412. Springer, Heidelberg (2005)
4. Theobald, M., Weikum, G., Schenkel, R.: Top-k Query Evaluation with Probabilistic Guarantees. In: Proceedings of the 30th VLDB Conference, Toronto, Canada, pp. 648–659 (2004)
5. Zhang, X., Peng, H.: A Sliding-Window Approach for Finding Top-k Frequent Itemsets from Uncertain Streams. In: Li, Q., Feng, L., Pei, J., Wang, S.X., Zhou, X., Zhu, Q.-M. (eds.) APWeb/WAIM 2009. LNCS, vol. 5446, pp. 597–603. Springer, Heidelberg (2009)
6. Wang, J., Han, J.: TFP: An Efficient Algorithm for Mining Top-K Frequent Closed Itemsets. IEEE Transactions on Knowledge and Data Engineering 17(5), 652–664 (2005)
7. Vasudevan, D., Vjnović, M.: Ranking through Random Sampling (2009) (manuscript)
8. Pietracaprina, A., Vandin, F.: Efficient Incremental Mining of Top-K Frequent Closed Itemsets. In: Corruble, V., Takeda, M., Suzuki, E. (eds.) DS 2007. LNCS (LNAI), vol. 4755, pp. 275–280. Springer, Heidelberg (2007)
9. Zhu, Y., Jiang, H.: False Rate Analysis of Bloom Filter Replicas in Distributed Systems. In: Proceeding of the 2006 International Conference on Parallel Processing, pp. 255–262 (2006)
10. Fan, L., Cao, P., Almeida, J., Broder, Z.A.: Summary cache: a scalable wide-area web cache sharing protocol. In: Proceeding of the ACM SIGCOMM 1998 Conference on Applications, Technologies, Architectures, and Protocols for Computer Communication, pp. 254–265. ACM Press, New York (1998)
11. Han, J., Wang, J., Lu, Y., Tzvetkov, P.: Mining top-k frequent closed patterns without minimum support. In: proceedings of IEEE ICDM Conference on Data Mining, pp. 211–218 (2000)
12. Quang, T.M., Oyanagi, S., Yamazaki, K.: ExMiner: An Efficient Algorithm for Mining Top-K Frequent Patterns. In: Li, X., Zaïane, O.R., Li, Z.-h. (eds.) ADMA 2006. LNCS (LNAI), vol. 4093, pp. 436–447. Springer, Heidelberg (2006)

An RSN Tool : A Test Dataset Generator for Evaluating RFID Middleware[*]

Wooseok Ryu[1], Joonho Kwon[2], and Bonghee Hong[1]

[1] Dept. of Computer Engineering
[2] Institute of Logistics Information Technology,
Pusan National University, Busan, Republic of Korea
{wsryu,jhkwon,bhhong}@pusan.ac.kr

Abstract. Evaluation of RFID middleware is a complex process due to its cost for constructing a test bed involving RFID readers and tags. An input dataset of the RFID middleware is a tag event stream from connected readers. A randomly generated dataset can be considered for stress testing, but this cannot guarantee whether the middleware can provide correct answers on given dataset. To enable this, the dataset should be meaningful to represent tags' activities based on business rules. This paper presents an RSN Tool which generates semantic datasets based on tags' behavior. The basic idea is to virtualize RFID environments in a point of business processes. To do this, the RSN Tool provides a modeling of real world RFID environments using graph representations, and execution mechanisms of tags' movements under several business rules. The experimental result shows that the RSN Tool can create a semantic valid dataset which reflects tags' behavior.

Keywords: Middleware Evaluation, Test Dataset, RFID Middleware.

1 Introduction

Radio Frequency Identification (RFID) is a leading technology in ubiquitous computing by means of automatic and wireless identification [1]. RFID technology enables capturing of real world behavior by identifying, tracking, and monitoring tagged physical objects [2]. With its inherent advantages, RFID has been adopted in variety of business areas, such as supply-chain management, manufacturing process management, and asset management [3].

An RFID system consists of three components: tag, reader, and middleware. An RFID tag can be attached to any item and enables unique identification of the item by a tag ID. RFID readers are usually installed at business locations such as gate and door to identify tags within its RF-field. The purpose of RFID middleware is to capture business information from mass of tag events generated by RFID readers. Similar to the stream data management system, the RFID middleware filters a tag

---

[*] "This work was supported by the grant of the Korean Ministry of Education, Science and Technology" (The Regional Core Research Program/Institute of Logistics Information Technology).

J.J. Park et al. (Eds.): STA 2011, CCIS 186, pp. 217–224, 2011.
© Springer-Verlag Berlin Heidelberg 2011

event stream and collects user-requested events only. As one of core components in RFID systems, the performance of the middleware needs to be carefully evaluated under various business environments.

To evaluate RFID middleware, it is necessary to acquire a tag event stream which is a test dataset for RFID middleware. Several approaches are discussed to generate the stream by means of emulating RFID readers [4][5]. The paper [4] defined several performance parameters for RFID middleware such as tag throughput and response time, and presented a reader emulator which generates random tag data to evaluate the parameters. Several reader emulators are presented in [5] to evaluate functionality of the middleware. Although the emulation approach enables stress testing of the middleware using huge stream of data, it is not possible to evaluate correctness of RFID middleware because the data do not include any business semantic.

It is obvious that semantic validity should be provided in the tag event to evaluate correctness of RFID middleware using meaningful queries [6]. The best way to solve this problem is to construct a real RFID test bed based on real RFID-enabled business environments. However, this approach is not common because of its huge cost involving capital, personnel and time [3]. It is necessary to develop a simulation mechanism of RFID environments to generate a semantic tag event stream.

In this paper, we present an RFID Simulation Network Tool (RSN Tool) to generate a semantically valid test dataset by means of virtualizing RFID environments. To do this, this paper presents an RFID Simulation Network (RSN) which is a graph representation of RFID environments to capture business activities of tags. To provide semantic validity of the tag event stream, this paper presents a mechanism for executing tags' movement based on business rules such as group movement.

The main contributions of this work include development of complete mechanisms to provide semantic validity of generated tag event stream, and evaluation of the RSN Tool to verify usability of the tool. Using the RSN Tool, correctness of RFID middleware can be easily evaluated under various virtual environments.

The remainder of this paper is as follows. Section 2 presents the RSN to virtualize an RFID environment. In Section 3, we describe execution mechanisms for executing the RSN and generating a semantic tag event stream. Implementation the RSN Tool is discussed in Section 4. In Section 5, expressive power of the RSN tool is evaluated using experiments. We conclude our work in Section 6.

2   Representation of RFID Environment

In the RSN Tool, an RFID Environment is represented using an RFID Simulation Network (RSN) which is based on the Petri net. An RSN consists of four components : reader, process, arc and tag. Detailed descriptions of each component are discussed as follows:

- Reader : A reader is a one type of nodes representing a physical RFID reader which identifies tag's identifiers within RF-field of the reader.

- Process : A process is the other type of nodes which represents a business process where RF-field from readers are not reachable. The process is placed between two or more readers and takes a role of the bridge between them. The process typically represents geographical locations or business status of the tag. Examples of the process include room, warehouse, shipped, transporting and so on.

- Arc : An arc connects two types of nodes. The arc represents a route of tags' movement. An arc can connect a reader with a process only. It mean that no arc can connect two readers or two processes.

- Tag : A tag represents a passive RFID tag. A tag may reside in a reader or a process. A tag is represented as a 2-tuple $t_i=(rid, ts)$ where rid is a reader ID and ts is an arrival time of t_i in rid. The tag moves to other nodes by passing arcs connected to the node under business rules.

An example of the RSN is shown in Fig. 1. In the figure, readers are marked using circles, and processes use rectangles. 6 tags are initially located at r_1. If the RSN executes, the tags move to the other nodes using several execution mechanisms of each node. Detailed descriptions of the tags' movements are discussed in next section.

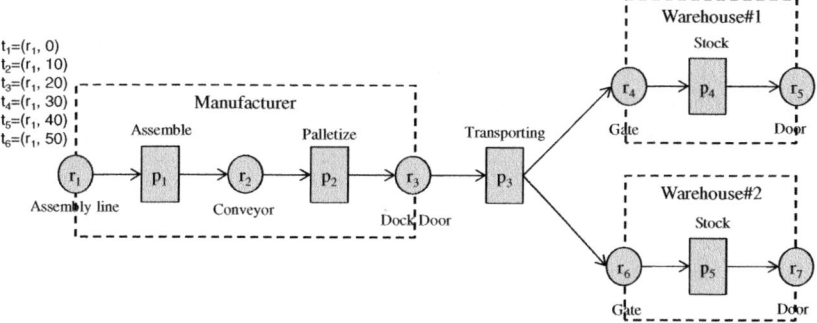

Fig. 1. An RSN example describing a simplified production management

3 Execution Mechanisms of the RSN Tool

3.1 Movement of Tags Based on Business Rules

There are several cases of tags' movements in the RFID environment. Tags can be traversed to other readers sequentially, or a set of tags can form a group which moves together. For example, a set of tagged items can be loaded on a pallet, and then the pallet traverses several readers. Obviously, the tags can be grouped together or separated from the group dynamically. To represent such business activities, we define some attributes for describing the movement of tags as follows:

- Movement Time (*time*) : This is an attribute of a node to define visiting time in the node. If a tag stays in a node for a specified *time*, the tag moves to the other node connected from the node. It represents timed-behavior of business processes such as movement of tags using conveyors or vehicles. In case of a reader, it represents a staying time in the RF-field of the reader. In case of a process, it represents a consumed time during in the process. For example, assume that $r_1.time$ in Fig. 1 is set to 20 seconds. Then, t_1 will enter r_1 at 0 second and leave r_1 at 20 seconds.

- Group Size (*groupSize*) : This is an attribute of a process to define the cardinality of a tag group in the process. It represents packing processes or palletizing processes that require movements of a tag group. If the number of tags reaches the *groupSize*, then the tags can move to the next node. For example, assume that p_2.*groupSize* in Fig. 1 is 3. Then, three tags should always move from p_2 to r_3 at the same time.

- Split Interval (*splitInterval*) : This is an attribute of a process to define a separation time interval of a tag group. A set of tags always traverses several nodes together once they are grouped together. The *splitInterval* attribute can describe a separation of tags in the group. If *splitInterval* is specified in a process, grouped tags in the process move to the next node one by one at every *splitInterval* times. Unpacking process can be expressed using this attribute. For example, assume that three tags enter p_4 at the same time and p_4.*splitInterval* is 5seconds. Then, three tags move to r_5 one by one at every 5 seconds.

Using above three attributes, the RSN can determine which tag should be moved at which time. In addition, the RSN also need to determine to which node the tag should move. If the number of next nodes of a node is more than one, it is required to choose a single target node to move. For example in Fig. 1, since a process node p_3 has two outgoing arcs, tags in p_3 can move to either r_4 or r_6. To handle this, the RSN Tool defines a distribution function which determines the target node of the tag's movement.

```
Algorithm ExecuteTagsMovement (node, currentTime)
 1   node is a Node of the RSN
 2   currentTime is current execution time of the RSN
 3   Begin
 4     // The first-round Loop :
 5     // choose tags to be grouped together and calculate last arrival time
 6     tagGroup = {}        // an empty array of tags
 7     for each tag in node
 8       if tag.ts + node.time <= currentTime then
 9       begin
10         tagGroup.add (tag);
11         lastArrivalTime = tag.ts;
12         if tagGroup.size() == node.groupSize then
13           break;
14       end if
15     next
16
17     // Determine whether the size of the group
18     if tagGroup.size() < node.groupSize then
19       End;
20
21     // Determine whether the tag can be split at currentTime
22     if (node.splitInterval != 0) then
23       if (currentTime - node.time - lastArrivalTime) % node.splitDuration != 0 then
24         End;
25
26     // The second-round Loop :
27     // Move tags to the next node
28     nextNode = node.getNextNode(tagGroup);
29     for each tag in tagGroup
30       MoveTag(tag, nextNode);
31     next
32   End
```

Fig. 2. Algorithms for tags' movements

Figure 2 describes an *ExecuteTagsMovement* algorithm for a node to execute tag movements using above attributes. In the first loop, a set of tags is chosen to make a group. In the algorithm, there is an assumption that tags in a node are sorted in an increasing order of their arrival times (*ts*). A last arrival time is calculated to evaluate that the tags can be moved by *splitInterval*. The *getNextNode* function is a distribution function discussed above. The implementation of the *getNextNode* function can be a round-robin function, a probability function, or other distribution function regarding tags' ID. By including the distribution function, a full movement rule for the tag in the RSN can be described.

3.2   Generation of a Test Dataset

Output dataset of the RSN Tool is an ordered list of generated tag events with ascending order of time. We define a tag event as a 3-tuple $e_i=<rid, tid, ts>$ where *rid* is an identifier of a reader, *tid* is an identifier of a tag, and *ts* is a timestamp indicating when e_i is generated.

Generation of tag events are performed by each reader node. To imitate physical behavior of RFID readers, we define an attribute named *readCycle* representing a read cycle of RFID reader. A read cycle is an atomic interval of a reader to acquire tag IDs of all tags within the reader's RF-field [7]. At every time interval defined in *readCycle*, the reader node monitors incoming tags and also outgoing tags. When a *readCycle* elapses, the reader summarizes a set of tags that have stayed during the interval and generates tag events for the tags.

4   Implementation of the RSN Tool

The RSN tool is implemented using Java platform, standard edition 6.0. Main components of the RSN Tool consist of user-interface, RSN Manager, RSN Executor, and Loggers. The RSN Manager maintains an RSN for representing an RFID environment. The RSN Executor executes the RSN and generates a tag event stream. The logger records the events and sends them to the RFID middleware. Main Features of the RSN Tool is as follows:

- Creation of an RSN : This provides creation of an RSN using several drawing tools. All attributes discussed in Section 3 can be configured using the tool.

- Simulation of an RSN : This can execute an RSN and displays execution logs in a separated window. A stepwise execution of the RSN is also provided. The execution can be paused at any time to check immediate results of the execution.

- Emulation of RFID Readers : The current version of the RSN Tool supports connection with the LIT ALE Manager [8] by emulating reader protocol [7].

A snapshot of an execution of the RSN tool is shown in Fig. 3. An RSN described in Fig. 1 is edited in a main window, and toolboxes are at the left side of the window. A configuration window of a reader r_1 is also shown in which all attributes are configured with tag information.

222   W. Ryu, J. Kwon, and B. Hong

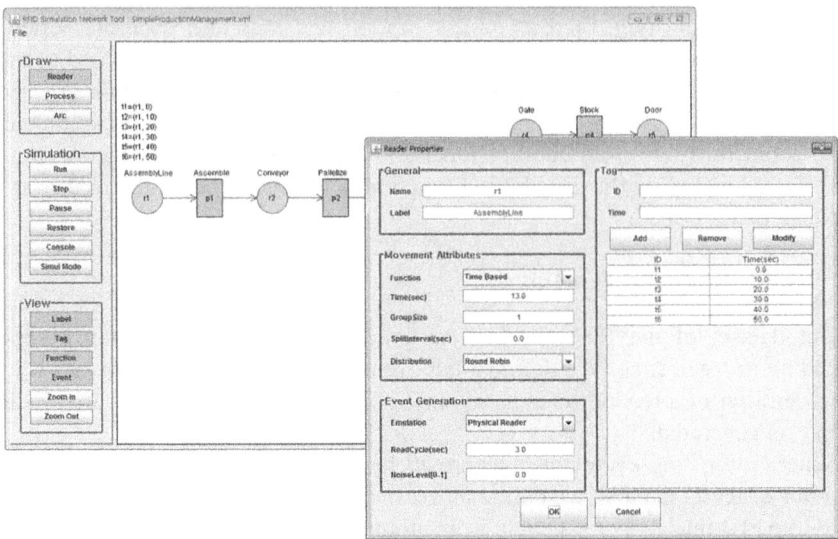

Fig. 3. A snapshot of the RSN Tool

5   Evaluation Results

To verify usability of the RSN Tool, we analyze an execution result whether the tool can represent business activities specified by several attributes. In this experiment, we use an RSN described in Fig. 1. Configurations of each node's attribute are summarized in Table 1. As p_3 has two output nodes, we apply a round-robin function in the $p_3.getNextNode$. Total 20 tags are used for the execution. The initial location of tags is r_1 and ts of the tags increases by 5 seconds from 0.

Table 1. Configuration of attributes for each node of the RSN in Fig. 1

Attributes	Configuration
time	13 seconds to all readers, 20 seconds to all processes.
groupSize	4 to p_2, 1 to other nodes.
splitInterval	10 seconds to p_4 and 20 seconds to p_5.
readCycle	3 seconds to all readers.

Figure 4 shows a traversal time of each tag to seven readers. In Fig. 4 (a), four tags are sequentially identified by r_1 and r_2. The result shows that r_3 identifies $t_1 \sim t_4$ tags at the same time. This suggests that $p_2.groupSize$ aggregates four tags in a single group. The result also shows that the tags are sequentially identified by r_5 again because of $p_4.splitInterval$. Comparing Fig. 4 (a) with (b), $t_1 \sim t_4$ are identified at r_4 and r_5, while $t_5 \sim t_8$ are identified at r_6 and r_7. This suggests that $p_3.getNextNode$ distributes incoming tags to either r_4 or r_6. The result also shows that the time interval of tags' identification at r_5 (Fig. 4 (a)) is different from the interval at r_7 (Fig. 4 (b)) because of differences between $p_4.splitInterval$ and $p_5.splitInterval$.

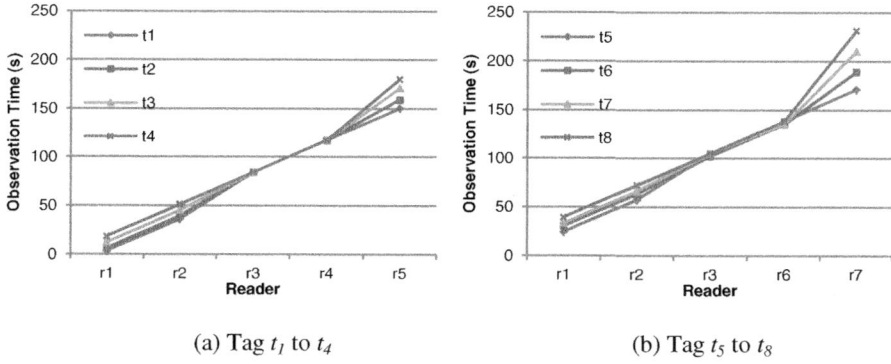

(a) Tag t_1 to t_4 (b) Tag t_5 to t_8

Fig. 4. Traversal time of the tags to seven readers

Figure 5 shows the observation time of 20 tags at seven readers. All tags are identified sequentially by r_1 and r_2, but the tags are grouped by 4 when they are identified by r_3. As a result, r_3 shows a stair-shape line in the figure. They are split again and sequentially identified by either r_5 or r_7. This suggests that the RSN Tool can correctly represent tags' movement behavior by following several business rules discussed in Section 3.

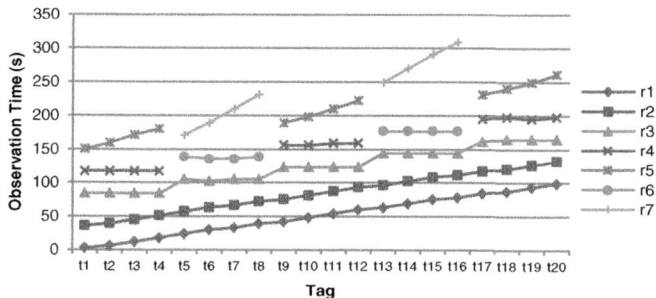

Fig. 5. The observation time of each tag at seven readers

6   Conclusion

In this paper, we have proposed an input dataset generator for the RFID middleware. As an input dataset, the tag event stream should have business semantics to evaluate correctness of the middleware. The semantic can be captured by investigating tag movements among several RFID readers based on business rules, not by simple random generation. To provide semantic validity of the tag event stream, the proposed RSN Tool presents a modeling mechanism of real-world RFID environments using graph representations and execution mechanisms for movements of tags following business rules. This paper also verified the semantic of generated tag events by several experiments. With help of the RSN Tool, we can evaluate the RFID middleware whether the middleware can report correct answers on given meaningful queries. Future works include reader emulations for benchmarking existing RFID middlewares as well as fine revisions for free distributions.

References

1. Want, R.: An Introduction to RFID Technology. IEEE Pervasive Computing 5(1), 25–33 (2006)
2. Wang, F., Liu, S., Liu, P., Bai, Y.: Bridging Physical and Virtual Worlds: Complex Event Processing for RFID Data Streams. In: Ioannidis, Y., Scholl, M.H., Schmidt, J.W., Matthes, F., Hatzopoulos, M., Böhm, K., Kemper, A., Grust, T., Böhm, C. (eds.) EDBT 2006. LNCS, vol. 3896, pp. 588–607. Springer, Heidelberg (2006)
3. Banks, J., Hanny, D., Pachano, M., Thompson, L.: RFID Applied. John Wiley & Sons, New Jersey (2007)
4. Lee, J., Kim, N.: Performance Test Tool for RFID Middleware: Parameters, Design, Implementation, and Features. In: 8th International Conference on Advanced Communication Technology, pp. 149–152 (2006)
5. Rifidi Toolkit, http://www.rifidi.org/documentation_toolkit.html
6. Arasu, A., Cherniack, M., Galvez, E., Maier, D., Maskey, A.S., Ryvkina, E., Stonebraker, M., Tibbetts, R.: Linear Road: A Stream Data Management Benchmark. In: Proceedings of the 30th VLDB Conference, pp. 480–491 (2004)
7. EPCglobal Inc.: The Reader Protocol version 1.1 Ratified Standard (2006)
8. Wang, Q., Ryu, W., Kim, S., Hong, B.: Demonstration of an RFID middleware: LIT ALE manager. In: Proceeding of 18th ACM Conference on Information and Knowledge Management, pp. 2071–2072. ACM Press, New York (2009)

Design and Implementation of a Virtual Reader for Emulation of RFID Physical Reader

Jiwan Lee, Jekwan Park, Wooseok Ryu, Bonghee Hong, and Joonho Kwon

Dept. of Computer Engineering
Institute of Logistics Information Technology
Pusan National University
Busan, Republic of Korea
{wldhks85,Jekwan,wsryu,bhhong,jhkwon}@pusan.ac.kr

Abstract. Recently, RFID technology has become one of essential technologies, which applies to a wide area of applications such as logistic, manufacture and pharmacy. Testing of RFID middleware is a critical process to increase stability of RFID system. As it requires much money to use a real RFID reader, a virtual reader to emulate an RFID reader is necessary. To emulate a physical reader, it is necessary to consider the reader's operational characteristics as well as protocol-level emulation. In this paper, we propose a mechanism for a virtual RFID reader which closely emulates an RFID reader by considering communicational characteristics between the reader and RFID tags. To do this, we analyze characteristics of RF communications and parameterize them. Based on the parameters, we present a mechanism for the virtual reader. The experimental results show that our approach can emulate more similar to RFID physical reader using set parameters.

Keywords: virtual reader; RFID reader; RFID middleware; test.

1   Introduction

Radio Frequency Identification (RFID), which automatically identifies product has become the key technology in ubiquitous computing environment. EPCglobal[1] establishes hardware & software standard[2,3,4] of RFID infrastructure for wide uses of RFID systems in industry.

Generally, RFID system consists of RFID tag which stored electronic code for identifying product, RFID reader which reads tag information from RFID tag, and RFID middleware [5] which collects RFID data and responses a result of user queries. Numerous RFID readers transmit a huge stream of tag identifications to the middleware. Performance of RFID middleware is critical because it should correctly process the stream. For example, A large retailer annually handles 60 billion items[6]. It means that about 1900 items should be processed per second. Therefore, the RFID middleware needs to be tested in such harsh environments to ensure performance of the middleware.

Generation of the data using real readers causes a lost of money as to test RFID middleware. Therefore, it is common approach to emulate RFID physical reader for

J.J. Park et al. (Eds.): STA 2011, CCIS 186, pp. 225–230, 2011.

the testing. However, A previous research for emulating RFID physical reader do not consider constraint of reader such as read fail in real environment. It was only functional emulation[7,8,9] which emulate reader protocols to verify functional correctness. To provide the proper emulation of the RFID reader, the emulation should include various exceptions that commonly occur in RFID reader. These exceptions are mainly communicational characteristics from RF communication. Without considering them, we cannot test the middleware whether or not the middleware can handle exceptional data and process the event stream correctly.

In this paper, we propose a virtual reader which emulates RFID reader by imitating the reader's various operational characteristics. Our approach is to parameterize real reader's activities by considering characteristics of RF communication between RFID reader and RFID tags. As a result, this paper proposes two parameters: ReadCycle which is a time period of reader's interaction and ReadFailRatio which is probability of reading failure, we propose an event generation mechanism which emulates RFID readers more accurately. We also perform an experimental study that our approach can emulate RFID reader more similarly using the parameters.

The rest of the paper is organized. In Section 2, we discuss the related work on RFID reader. In Section 3, we propose an idea of virtual reader. Section 4, we shows the experiment of result and suggest design and implementation. Summary and future works are presented in Section 5.

2   Related Work

RFID reader needs to be emulated for testing of RFID middleware. Previous researches of reader emulation[7,8,9] have purposed simply to transfer Electronic Product Code(EPC) to the RFID middleware.

Rifidi Emulator is a program that emulates reader protocol[9]. There is related work to builds a virtual store by using Rifidi Emulator. This study introduces a characteristic of reader for emulating reader. It is as follow: every RFID reader has an IP address and a specific port. The reader works like a server. It puts on the socket the information about a tag, which will be read by the application client. Another previous research for emulating RFID physical reader is handling the functional factor of physical reader. It is not suitability to test RFID middleware because RFID physical reader may be occurred that an error to read tags since the surrounding environment. Therefore, it is need to be considering functional error such as read fail and splatter read because RFID middleware must be tested when exceptions occur from physical reader.

3   Virtual Reader Emulation

In this section, we propose an idea of virtual reader which closely emulates an RFID reader. We define parameters through the analysis of characteristics of RF communication in section 3.1. We propose an event generation mechanism of virtual reader in section 3.2.

3.1 Patten Analysis of Physical Reader

In this section, we define parameters to emulate RFID reader. To do this, we first analyze RF communication. RF communication is used to communicate between RFID reader and tags. An RFID reader transmits RF signals and receives backscattered signals from tags in a read cycle. The read cycle is a period of time to read tag data from RFID reader.

RF communication has some feature. If tags were covered with some object, RFID reader cannot read the tag data perfectly. For example, there are three boxes attached RFID tags. We assume that the tag is attached on the surface of the box. And the surface is far from RFID reader. At that time, the reader fails to read tags because the box jams the RF signal. It is called reading failure. In the Fig 1, some reading failures exist in read cycles.

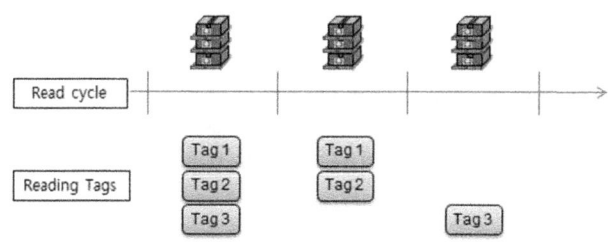

Fig. 1. Example of read failures

Therefore, we define three kinds of parameters for emulating of RFID physical reader as described in Table 1. The detailed descriptions of each parameter are as follows.

Table 1. Parameter of Virtual Reader

Virtual Reader Parameters	Description
Read Cycle : R_c	Tag information acquisition period from reader
Read Fail ratio : R_f	Probability of the reading failure about tag information

- Read Cycle : Read cycle(R_c) is period of time to read tag data from RFID reader. Read cycle is changeable by environment using RF technology. For quickly reporting, read cycle should reduce period of time. We represent milliseconds for read cycle like 1000ms.
- Read Fail Ratio : Read Fail ratio(R_f) is probability of read failure by read cycle. RFID physical reader may occur to a reading fail by both moving time of tag and interference. For example, if there are 100 tags and this parameter is 10%, the reader fails to read tags of 0 to 10.

3.2 Event Generation Mechanism of Virtual Reader

Event generation mechanism of virtual reader is reading a RFID tag using proposed parameter. RFID tags are input data of the virtual reader. The tag has Electronic Product Code(EPC) for identification product. There are typical EPCs like GID-96 and SGTIN-96. They have common values consisting of company code, item code and serial code. The EPCs tags are granted sequentially by serial or random numbers.

The virtual reader generates event data using parameter to emulate RFID reader. Generation steps are described as follows:

- Define read cycle
- Define parameter
- Define the number of tag
- Process reading tags using the parameter

It is an essential to design an event process mechanism for parameters. We propose an algorithm to process parameters to generate events. This algorithm determines whether the reader should read tag or not. The algorithm receives input parameters of tags and Read Fail ratio. After that, it checks the available value. If value is available then ReadingRatio for each tag generates a random value. If the generated value is higher than Read Fail ratio read, then tag is successful read. Otherwise, it is read to fail. The returned value is a list of successful tag reading. Fig 3. shows the algorithm to apply read fail parameter.

```
1 BEGIN
2 INPUTDATA := Tags, MissedReadingRatio
3      IF MissedReadingRatio is available THEN
4          LOOP from 0 to Tags.count
5              Tag := Tags[LOOP.count]
6              ReadingRatio := RandomRatio()
7              IF ReadingRatio > MissedReadingRatio THEN
8                  TEMP_Tags.append(Tag)
9          END LOOP
10     ELSE IF
11         TEMP_Tags := Tags
12 OUTPUTDATA := TEMP_Tags
13 END
```

Fig. 2. Algorithm to apply parameter for read fail ratio

4 Implementation and Performance Evaluation

4.1 Design and Implementation

We have design a virtual reader to emulate RFID physical reader. The virtual reader system consists of virtual reader manager, virtual tag manager. The virtual reader manager has virtual readers. Each virtual reader has the common parameters which are read cycle and reader fail ratio. We propose the architecture of virtual reader in Fig 4. And we implement the virtual reader system based on JAVA(jdk 1.6.0.2). This system work on a computer using WindowsXP Pro.SP3 with core2quad 2.4Ghz CPU, 2Gb RAM.

4.2 Performance Evaluation

To evaluate performance of system we proposed, we perform experiments to evaluate parameter of virtual reader. We also perform comparing with RFID physical reader alien9900.

Firstly, we evaluate our virtual reader whether the parameters work correctly. Fixed conditions are 100 virtual tags and 1000ms reader cycle. Variable conditions are read fail ration and splatter read ratio. We increase these variable conditions from 5% to 25% at interval of 5%. Fig. 3-(a) shows the experimental results for parameters. An expected result is made by calculation. It means that if there are 100 tags in RFID reader sight, then the reader can read 95 tags when read fail ratio is 5%. This experiment shows approximate result between expected result and emulation result.

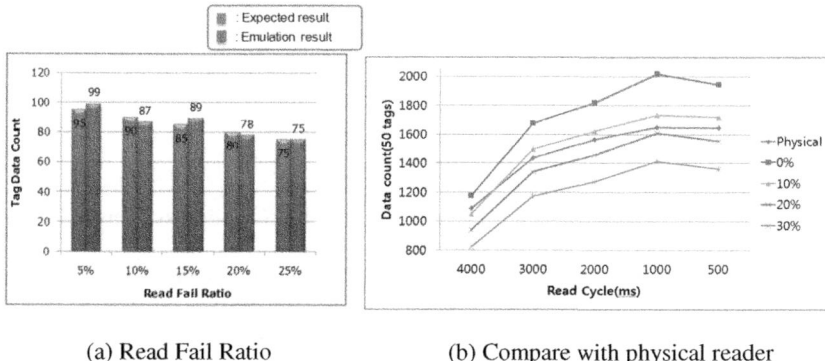

(a) Read Fail Ratio   (b) Compare with physical reader

Fig. 3. Result of Read Fail Ratio

Secondly, we perform experiment to compare the generated data from the virtual reader with RFID reader alien9900. We use 50 tags, and compared with physical reader by using read fail ratio from 30% to 0% for this experiment. We collect tag data during 100sec by varying read cycle from 4000ms to 500ms. We expect that the number of tag data will be 1250 when the read cycle is 4000ms. Similarly, 10,000 tags will be generated when the read cycle is 500ms. As a result of the experiment, the physical reader needs least read cycle to read tags. The read cycle of the reader is required approximately 2 seconds to read tags. Also, we found read fail ratio as 10% by analysis 50 tags. Fig. 3-(b) shows that the virtual reader can closely emulate physical reader by read fail ratio approximately 10%.

5 Conclusion and Future Work

Emulation of RFID physical reader is essential to reduce cost for testing RFID middleware. However, simple protocol-level emulation does not express characteristics of RFID reader. The simple emulator cannot provide testing of RFID middleware in various exceptional cases.

In this paper, we propose a virtual reader which closely emulates real reader's operational mechanisms. To do this, we analyze characteristics of RF communication between RFID reader and RFID tags, such as reading failure and presented a virtual reader which emulates these characteristics. We also performed experiments for evaluating the proposed virtual reader. The result shows that the presented virtual reader generates similar data compared with physical RFID reader. The future work need to closely emulate a RFID physical reader based on proposed parameter of virtual reader.

Acknowledgements

This work was supported by the Grant of the Korean Ministry of Education, Science and Technology (The Regional Core Research Program/Institute of Logistics Information Technology).

References

1. EPCglobal Inc., http://www.epcglobalinc.org/
2. EPCglobal Inc., The Application Level Events(ALE) Specification version 1.1 Ratified Standard, Part I: Core Specification (2008)
3. EPCglobal Inc., The Reader Protocol version 1.1 Ratified Standard (2006)
4. EPCglobal Inc., The EPCglobal Architecture Framework (2005)
5. Mohd Hashim, S.Z., Mardiyono, Anuar, N., Wan Kadir, W.M.N.: Comparative analysis on adaptive features for RFID middleware. In: International Conference on Computer and Communication Engineering, ICCCE, pp. 989–993 (2008)
6. Bornhoevd, C., Lin, T., Haller, S., Schaper, J.: Integrating Automatic Data Acquisition with Business Processes - Experiences with SAP's Auto-ID Infrastructure. In: VLDB, pp. 1182–1188 (2004)
7. Palazzi, C.E., Ceriali, A., Monte, M.D.: RFID Emulation in Rifidi Environment. Dipartimento di Matematica Purae Applicata Universita degli Studi di Padova, 4–13 (2009)
8. Frischbier, S., Sachs, K., Buchmann, A.: Evaluating RFID Infrastructures. In: Workshop RFID Intelligente Funketiketten - Chancen und Herausforderungen, Erlangen, Germany (July 2006)
9. Rifidi, http://www.rifidi.org/

Adaptive Optimal Global Resource Scheduling for a Cloud-Based Virtualized Resource Pool

Lingli Deng, Qing Yu, and Jin Peng

Department of Network Technology, China Mobile Research Institute
Unit 2, 28 Xuanwumenxi Ave, Xuanwu District, Beijing 100053, China
{denglingli,yuqing,pengjin}@chinamobile.com

Abstract. This paper proposes to employ linear programming algorithms for global resource scheduling to reduce the extra cost for power consumption and operation expenditures, for remote resource access in a cloud-based resource pool with concrete restraints of the networking environment. The scheduler adapts the problem modeling granularity and solution which corresponds to the differential demands of the various stages of a continual process for the initial construction and subsequent operation of a cloud-based resource pool. In particular, the proposed algorithms takes into account resource configuration, service deployment and real-time load, among other factors, to strike a tradeoff among the scheduling performance, response time and computation cost. Different environment modeling methods are provided according to the specific location of networking resource bottleneck. A simple greedy algorithm is provided for a small-scale pool with abundant networking resources.

Keywords: resource scheduling, operations research, cloud computing.

1   Introduction

The combination of virtualization technology and grid-computing platforms brings a brand-new way for resource consolidation and utilization [1]. The on-demand allocation and dynamic flow of virtualized resources among VMs on top of a single physical server are essential for its appealing features, such as promoted resource utility, ensured service quality and reduced user possession cost. With the continual development of virtualization technology, e.g. the emergence of non-stop VM migration [2] and other mechanisms [3], on-demand resource scheduling among VMs across physical severs become technically feasible.

However, traditional scheduling techniques for virtualized resources [4][5], bounded in a single physical server. Besides, they adopt static solutions, with no considerations for the consequences of environment evolution (e.g. resource configuration, service deployment and real-time load).

This paper proposes an adaptive optimal strategy, for the global resource scheduling VIMA, a cloud-based resource pooling architecture proposed by China Mobile for its Distributed Service Network (DSN) [6]. The proposal not only aims to promote resource utility through fine-grained global resource sharing mechanisms, but also makes use of an in-depth constraints-expenditure analysis for remote resource accesses

J.J. Park et al. (Eds.): STA 2011, CCIS 186, pp. 231–240, 2011.
© Springer-Verlag Berlin Heidelberg 2011

in its linear programming modeling to tradeoff the performance promotion with scheduling computation cost. It features with a complexity-adaptive problem analyzing methodology, which may be applied to scheduling scenarios besides VIMA.

Specifically, our contributions include: 1) a "minimal cost flow" model established for the problem analysis and resolution of the global resource scheduling strategy, with considerations for networking constraints and remote resource access expenditure; 2) an adaptive modeling scheme proposed for a resource pool, where the scheduler adapts its states to adjust the problem modeling granularity and resolution algorithms corresponding to the differential demands of various construction and operation stages; 3) a configurable set of parameter modeling methods provided to adjust to the specific location of resource bottleneck in an operating resource pool; and 4) a simple greedy algorithm for a small pool with abundant networking resources.

The rest of this paper is organized as follows: Section 2 briefly reviews related work on VM resource scheduling. Section 3 describes VIMA, the cloud-based resource pooling architecture, as our motivating scenario for cost-efficient global scheduling of virtualized resources. In section 4, we establish a minimal-flowing model and provide parameter modeling methods for the static global scheduling problem, which serves as a basis for our adaptive problem solving design of the flowing scheduler, presented in Section 5. We conclude our paper in section 6.

2   Related Work

Ever since the overwhelming success of Amazon EC2 (Elastic Compute Cloud) [1], "cloud-based resource pool" has been the buzz word throughout the IT industry, including private clouds for infrastructure resource integration within an organization and public clouds for infrastructure capacity leasing to outside customers.

In a cloud-based resource pool, resources of a server running virtualization software are divided into logically-independent virtual machines (VMs) as units to accommodate service systems, bringing forward the local scheduling problem to determine the optimal resource reassignment among VMs on a single server.

For instance, dynamic scheduling of the local CPU resource focuses on the optimal strategy designing, e.g. [4] establishes an economic model and a greedy quasi-optimal algorithm for the optimal scheduling among different services for the local server's CPU resource to maximize the profit in terms of the violation penalty of the Service Level Agreement (SLA), energy consumption expenditure and resource usage price.

On the other hand, dynamic scheduling of the local memory resource faces difficulties in order to schedule the local memory on a virtualized platform. Therefore, most of the previous work concentrates on the relevant mechanism design to conquer difficulties, e.g. memory usage acquisition and demand prediction, rather than the optimal scheduling strategy. Few works on the strategy field are too simple to be applied to the global setting. For instance, assuming each VM is assigned the equal service priority, [5] designs a recursive algorithm, iterating between each VM pair, to search for a local memory assignment scheme to reduce local page faults.

Although targeted at a different problem, the utility-cost analyzing methodology adopted by [4] in designing the local CPU resource scheduling for a server accommodating several service systems is most analogous to our optimal planning problem modeling method. However, our proposal differs from these static solutions in its dynamically adaptive modeling scheme, proposed for the differential demands of the various construction and operation stages of a resource pool, where the mathematical model as well as the relevant resolution algorithm can be adjusted to the environment manually by the system administrator. To tradeoff between the algorithm complexity and the scheduling performance, the scheme starts from a simple algorithm with acceptable modeling precision and least complexity to minimize the scheduling delay for computing an acceptable assignment, and refines its problem modeling/algorithm (with higher precision and complexity) as soon as the scheduling performance falls below the predefined threshold.

3 Motivating Scenario

On the contrary to the traditional core network architecture for telecommunication systems (e.g. IMS [7]) where dedicated customized devices for different applications are deployed in a physically separated way, China Mobile proposes a Virtualization-Based Merging Architecture (VIMA) for its Distributed Service Network (DSN) [6], aiming at providing internet services as well as traditional telecommunication services via common computing platforms (e.g. PC servers) instead of customized devices to reduce CAPEX (i.e. capital expenditure) [8]. Its major applications, VoIP and Streaming, both P2P based, manifest strong complementarities in resource consuming pattern to each other. Through the introduction of system virtualization technology [9], having a single group of physical servers serving as the basis for having various service entities running as virtual machines (or VMs for short) simultaneously within the resource pool, VIMA not only shields the heterogeneous resource platforms of physical servers beneath from the upper services, but also realizes flexible resource scheduling amongst different VMs. It is expected to deliver high-efficient resource-sharing among various P2P applications, while enforcing separation of them.

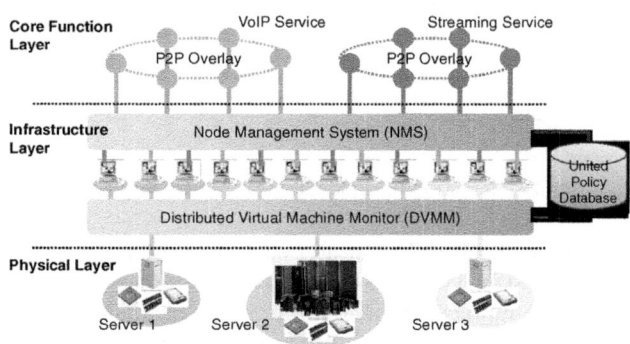

Fig. 1. The illustrative Architecture of VIMA in DSN

As shown in Fig. 1, VIMA is located at the infrastructure layer beneath the Core-function layer of the DSN network. More specifically, DSN is composed of:

1) *Core-function layer* realizes several abstract capabilities and relevant interfaces for telecommunication applications above. Each service subsystem performs service-specific request-handling operations using virtual resources provided by the Infrastructure layer beneath (in the form of VMs).

2) *Infrastructure layer* provides abstract network capabilities, such as computation, storage and session-control, to the service providing layer, through on-demand resource scheduling among various services.

   a) *Node management system* is responsible for handling the dynamics of DSN function nodes (i.e. peers in the above P2P service system), as well as load-balancing between different DSN nodes through user requests redirection techniques from the service's perspective.

   b) *United policy database* is responsible for the decision-making according to various demands of physical resource allocation and scheduling, e.g. deployment policies[10], migration policies[11], flowing policies[3], etc.

   c) *Distributed Virtual Machine Monitor* is responsible for enforcing the scheduling decisions of the policy database on the virtualized resource pool, where each physical server hosts a few virtual machines running as service-relevant software entities in the correspondent service subsystem.

3) *Physical layer*, consisted of a set of physical servers owned by the operator for the DSN core network, provides concrete physical capabilities (i.e. physical resources, such as CPU, memory and disk etc.) to fulfill the resource provision and scheduling decisions made in the Infrastructure layer.

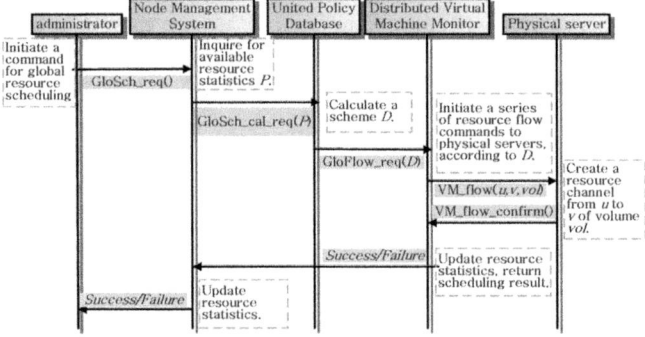

Fig. 2. Entity interaction for global resource balancing: the manual case

The proposed optimal scheduling strategy can be used as part of the united policy database in DSN VIMA when the virtualized resources are flowing on-demand among VMs on different physical servers. Fig. 2 shows an illustrative scenario, where the administrator manually triggers the process: the administrator sends a re-schedule request to the DSN NMS; the latter requests the policy database to compute a resource assignment scheme based on the distribution of available resources and hands it over to DSN DVMM, who divides the scheme into a series of resource flowing commands between server pairs; execution results are returned to DNS NMS to update resources records. The DSN NMS may be configured to monitor the global resource utility periodically, and automatically triggers the process accordingly.

4 The Basic Problem Modeling

Given a flow network $G(V,E)$, in which each edge $(i, j) \in E$ has capacity $c_{ij} \in R^+$ and unit transportation cost $b_{ij} \in R$, and each vertex i has a supply $s_i \in R$. If $s_i < 0$, i is called a sink. If $s_i > 0$, i is called a source. The Minimal Cost Flow (MCF) problem[12] consists in supplying the sinks from the sources by a flow in the cheapest way, i.e:

$$\min \Sigma^n_{i=1} \Sigma^n_{j=1} b_{ij} f_{ij}$$

$$\text{s.t.} \quad \Sigma^n_{j=1} f_{ij} - \Sigma^n_{k=1} f_{kj} = s_i \qquad i = 1 \ldots n$$

$$0 \leq f_{ij} \leq c_{ij} \qquad \text{for edge } (i, j)$$

In the following, a flow network as an instance of MCF [13], which can be solved by existing well-known algorithms [14][15]), is established for the global optimal scheduling problem among individual physical servers in terms of both networking bandwidth constraints and service resource consuming expenditure. Two methods are given respectively for server-bounded and network-bounded environments. [1]

4.1 Modeling Supply/Demand s_i

To start with, we map the global scheduling problem into a transportation problem from a set of resource supplying nodes (i.e. resource abundant servers) to a set of resource consuming nodes (i.e. resource insufficient servers).

Once the global re-scheduling is triggered, the DSN NMS subsystem can deduce the supply/demand s_i of each physical server i through its real-time monitory statistics, including the server's current available resource and the resource utility of each VM.

A resource abundant physical server i with $s_i > 0$ (i.e. its supply for resource) corresponds to a source in the flow network, while a resource insufficient server j with $s_j < 0$ (i.e. its demand for resource) corresponds to a sink. The supply/demand of the other network nodes (LAN networking equipment such as switches) equals to zero.

4.2 Modeling Edge Capacity c_{ij}

For the second step, we map the real-time networking bandwidth constraints between server pairs of a cloud-based resource pool to the correspondent edge capacity in the flow network model. Specifically, we present two methods for different resource-bounded environments with consideration of realistic networking architecture.

It is worth notice that in the MCF model, the capacity parameter puts a limit on the flow along the edge in question. However, in our specific scheduling problem, where the flow depicts the hardware resources (e.g. memory) shared across physical servers, the edge capacity is meant to model the networking bandwidth constraint, which cannot be measured directly through the same measurement units as the shared resource. Hence we adopt the following method to transform bandwidth constraints into variables measurable by the resource measurement unit as the flow capacity.

---

[1] To reduce the problem, we only consider a single type of concrete hardware resource that can be uniformly measured across server platforms, such as unit amount (e.g. 1MB) of memory.

Without loss of generosity, assume that constant m depicts the bandwidth consumption of accessing a unit amount of remote resource for a unit amount of time. For instance, in terms of remote memory access, given the service type and the amount of memory accessed, one can deduce the bandwidth consumption directly from the data traffic between the consumer and provider. The flow capacity between (physical server pair) i and j is defined as:[2]

$$c_{ij} = d_{ij}=m \tag{1}$$

4.2.1 Logic Pooling Method for Server-Bounded Environments

Since the networking bandwidth between servers is abundant, the only limit comes from the available NIC bandwidths of the servers. Hence, networking devices (e.g. switches) can be ignored for MCF modeling. Specifically, the servers constitute the flow network's node set; and the edge capacity between nodes i and j is defined as:[3]

$$d_{ij}=\min \{band(i); band(j)\} \tag{2}$$

In realistic settings, on may detect the end-to-end available bandwidth between i and j through networking devices as the direct input for d_{ij}.

4.2.2 Physical Pooling Method for Network-Bounded Environments

Since networking devices (e.g. switches and wiring) become bandwidth bottleneck, the specific networking topology becomes relevant in the edge capacity modeling. Specifically, local switches plus servers constitute the flow network's node set; and the edge capacity between nodes i and j is defined as:[4]

$$d_{ij}=\min \{band(i); band(j); band(w_{ij})\} \tag{3}$$

For realistic networking environments, the flow monitoring function of switching devices can be utilized to acquire real-time statistics for link bandwidth allocation d and its utility v, therefore one may use $d(1-v)$ directly as the input for d_{ij}.

4.3 Modeling Unit Transportation Cost b_{ij}

For the third step, we map the extra resource consumption expenditure for global scheduling between server pair i and j (e.g. the impact of bandwidth consumption on the service quality) to the transportation cost b_{ij} in the flow network.

4.3.1 Logic Pooling Method for Server-Bounded Environments

The server set constitutes the flow network's node set. And the remote access cost for a unit amount of i's local resource is defined as below[5], where operator $\otimes$ is employed to calculate the marginal cost for a unit amount of remote resource scheduling, whose practical meaning is determined by the administrator for realistic considerations (e.g. *max* for conservative settings, *min* for optimistic settings, or × for compromise):

---

[2] Where d_{ij} depicts real-time bandwidth constraint between i and j, defined below.
[3] Where function *band* returns a device's available bandwidth.
[4] In which w_{ij} depicts the wiring between devices i and j.
[5] Where function *profit* returns a node's service profit for acquiring a unit amount of local bandwidth, and *penalty* its service penalty for releasing a unit amount of local bandwidth.

$$p(i) = profit(i) \otimes penalty(i) \tag{4}$$

The unit transportation cost from node i to j is defined as below, where operator $\oplus$ combines two nodes' local costs, whose practical meaning may as well be specified for further considerations (e.g. *max* for conservative settings, *min* for optimistic settings or + for compromise):

$$b_{ij} = p(i) \oplus p(j) \tag{5}$$

4.3.2 Physical Pooling Method for Network-Bounded Environments

The local switches as well as servers constitute the flow network's node set. And the unit remote access cost for server node i's resource is defined as:

$$p(i) = profit(i) \otimes penalty(i) \tag{6}$$

The unit transportation cost between switch node i and its neighboring server node j is:

$$b_{ij} = p(j) \tag{7}$$

The unit transportation cost between switch node i (with m direct server neighbors) and its neighboring switch node j (with n direct server neighbors) is defined as the combination of both switch's neighboring servers' unit remote access costs:

$$b_{ij} = (\Sigma^m_{k=1} \, b_{ik}) \oplus (\Sigma^n_{l=1} b_{jl}) \tag{8}$$

The unit transportation cost between server pair i and j is defined as:

$$b_{ij} = p(i) \oplus p(j) \tag{9}$$

5   Adaptive Global Resource Balancing

In the above, we present alternatives for abstracting MCF parameters from realistic environments that differ in resource arrangement and network topology. Moreover, according to the concrete networking settings, as a result of the relaxing of some realistic restrictions, the MCF model itself can be reduced to simplified instances which can be solved by efficient heuristic algorithms. On the other hand, even if the networking settings remain the same, during the operation of a cloud-based resource pool, with the deployment of new services, the resource bottleneck may migrate.

Hence, we propose an adaptive scheme to locate a properly accurate flow model for a given pool at a given time point, in order to strike a tradeoff between scheduling efficiency (i.e. the global resource utility after re-scheduling) and algorithm complexity. The scheme starts from the algorithm with acceptable modeling precision and least complexity to minimize the scheduling delay for computing an acceptable assignment, and refines its problem modeling/algorithm (with higher precision and complexity) as soon as the scheduling performance falls below a predefined threshold.

5.1   Adaptive Modeling and Resolving

For a small-scale resource pool with abundant networking bandwidth, where the capacity constraints and transportation cost can both be ignored in problem modeling, the "Minimal Cost Flow" problem is reduced to "Simple Match" between the nodes' demand and supply, which can be solve efficiently by simple algorithms below.

```
Simple-match (G)
  begin
    sort the sources into a queue O in descending
supply;
    sort the sinks into a queue I in descending demand;
    repeat
      get the heads of I and O, server i and j;
      if |s_i|>|s_j|:
        add i→j:s_j into D;
        update s_i=s_i+s_j;
        insert server i into queue I;
      if |s_i|<|s_j|:
        add i→j:s_i into D;
        update s_j=s_i+s_j;
        insert server j into queue O;
    until I =null
    returen D; //the output global scheduling scheme
  end.
```

For a large-scale resource pool with complicated networking architecture, the transportation cost for remote resource scheduling is non-trivial:

On one hand, when the networking system is light-loaded, where the capacity constraints for remote resource accessing can be ignored, one may choose a method for the transportation cost modeling based on the expected scheduling performance:

1) He/she may adopt a cost modeling method, and the "simple match" problem is refined to "transportation problem"[12], another special instance of MCF.

2) Besides, he/she may as well choose other even simpler method according to the realistic settings. For example, the number of hops between server pairs can be utilized as a simplified version of the logic modeling method, resulting in the "Shortest Path Problem"[12], another special instance of MCF.

On the other hand, when the networking system's real-time load grows to a threshold, one may add the capacity modeling into the flow networking model, and the "transportation problem" model is thereby refined into the general MCF[12]:

1) If the resource bottleneck resides on the server side, the logic pooling method is preferred for modeling transportation cost.

2) Otherwise, if the resource bottleneck resides on the networking device's side, the physical pooling method is preferred for modeling both transportation cost and capacity constraints.

5.2 Adaptive Scheme Applied to DSN VIMA

Correspondent to the automatic triggering case stated in Section III, the adaptive scheduling process is illustrated by Fig. 4: To adopt the above stated adaptive scheme, the global resource scheduler for the DSN VIMA architecture needs to adapt its problem modeling according to the platform's real-time resource utility, and adjust its correspondent problem resolution algorithm to tradeoff the expected scheduling performance and computation delay.

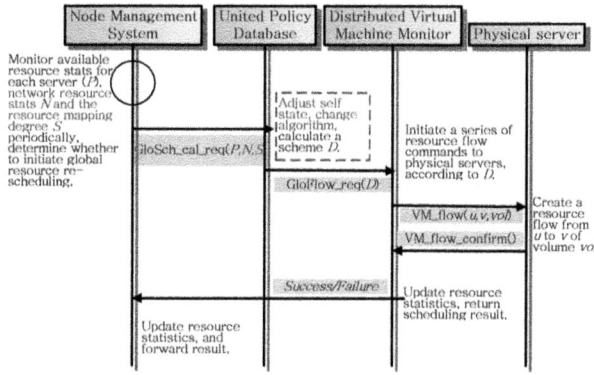

Fig. 3. Adaptive global resource balancing: the automatic case

5.3   Life-Time Evolution for Global Resource Scheduling

Moreover, the proposed adaptive methodology may be applied to the resource scheduling problem analysis and resolution for the continual process of the construction and operation of a cloud-base resource pool.

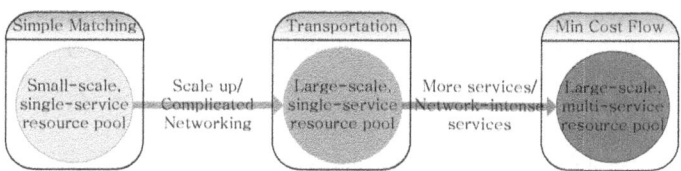

Fig. 4. Illustrative modeling adaptation for pool evolution

Fig. 5 shows an example of such life-time evolution for adaptive global scheduling:

An enterprise may start cloud construction for a given internal service system, resulting in a small-scale, single-service resource pool in the beginning, whose global scheduling problem can be efficiently solved by "Simple Matching" algorithm.

However, the pool's networking topology may become increasingly complicated as more and more servers are added into the cloud platform to meet the developing service's growing resource needs, the adaptive scheduler should shift to the "Transportation" problem modeling, as the scheduling performance may decrease as the simple modeling is too coarse-grained to reflect the increasing differential remote resource access expenditures between server pairs.

Following the success of single-service cloud, the enterprise may choose to incorporate other services on the pool, leading to a large-scale, multiservice platform. Since the internetworking is likely to be crowded by traffic of various services (some of them may itself be network-intense applications), the scheduler could shift to general "Minimal Cost Flow" model to take the bandwidth constraints into consideration in calculating the optimal global scheduling arrangements.

6 Conclusion

This paper proposes to employ linear programming algorithms for global resource scheduling to reduce the extra cost for remote resource access in a cloud-based resource pool. The scheduler adapts the problem modeling granularity and relevant resolution algorithms to the differential demands of various stages of the continual construction and operation of a cloud-based resource pool, corresponding to its resource configuration, service deployment and real-time load, to tradeoff among resultant scheduling performance, response time and computation cost.

References

[1] Ec2, http://www.amazon.com/ec2/
[2] Clark, C., Fraser, K., Hand, S., Hansen, J., Jul, E., Limpach, C., Pratt, I., Warfield, A.: Live migration of virtual machines. In: Proc. of the 2nd Conference on Symposium on Networked Systems Design & Implementation, vol. 2, p. 286. USENIX Association (2005)
[3] Song, Y., Wang, H., Li, Y., Feng, B., Sun, Y.: Multi-Tiered On-Demand Resource Scheduling for VM-Based Data Center. In: Proc. of the 2009 9th IEEE/ACM International Symposium on Cluster Computing and the Grid, pp. 148–155. IEEE Computer Society, Los Alamitos (2009)
[4] Chase, J., Anderson, D., Thakar, P., Vahdat, A., Doyle, R.: Managing energy and server resources in hosting centers. In: Proc. of the Eighteenth ACM Symposium on Operating Systems Principles, pp. 103–116. ACM, New York (2001)
[5] Zhao, W., Wang, Z., Luo, Y.: Dynamic memory balancing for virtual machines. ACM SIGOPS Operating Systems Review 43(3), 37–47 (2009)
[6] White Paper of DSN (Distributed Service Network) v2.0. Department of Network Technology, China Mobile Research Institute (2010)
[7] Camarillo, G., Garcia-Martin, M.: The 3G Multimedia Subsystems: Merging the Internet and the cellular worlds. John Wiley and Sons, Inc., Chichester (2004)
[8] White Paper of DSN (Distributed Service Netowrk) v1.0. Department of Network Technology, China Mobile Research Institute (2008)
[9] Barham, P., Dragovic, B., Fraser, K., Hand, S., Harris, T., Ho, A., Neugebauer, R., Pratt, I., Warfield, A.: Xen and the art of virtualization. In: Proc. of the 9th ACM Symposium on Operating Systems Principles, pp. 164–173 (2003)
[10] Sotomayor, B., Montero, R., Llorente, I., Foster, I.: Virtual infrastructure management in private and hybrid clouds. IEEE Internet Computing 13(5), 14–22 (2009)
[11] Wood, T., Shenoy, P., Venkataramani, A., Yousif, M.: Black-box and gray-box strategies for virtual machine migration. In: Proc. of the 4th USENIX Symposium on Networked Systems Design and Implementation, pp. 229–242 (2007)
[12] Hillier, F., Lieberman, G.: Introduction to Operations Research, 9th edn. McGraw Hill Education, New York (2009)
[13] Ahuja, R., Magnanti, T., Orlin, J.: Network flows: theory, algorithms, and applications (1993)
[14] Klein, M.: A primal method for minimal cost flows with applications to the assignment and transportation problems. Management Science 14(3), 205–220 (1967)
[15] Goldberg, A., Tarjan, R.: Finding minimum-cost circulations by successive approximation. Mathematics of Operations Research 15(3), 430–466 (1990)

Maximal Cliques Generating Algorithm for Spatial Co-location Pattern Mining

Seung Kwan Kim, Younghee Kim, and Ungmo Kim

Database Laboratory, School of Information and Commnication Engineering,
Sungkyunkwan University, 300 ChunChun-Dong, JangAn-Gu,
Suwon, Kyunggi-Do 440-746, Republic of Korea
libertas@korea.kr, younghees@gmail.com, umkim@ece.skku.ac.kr

Abstract. The spatial co-location pattern represents the relationships between spatial features that are frequently located close together, and is one of the most important concepts in spatial data mining. The spatial co-location pattern mining approach, which is based on association analysis and uses maximal cliques as input data, is general and useful. However, there are no algorithms that can generate all maximal cliques from large dense spatial data sets in polynomial execution time. We propose a polynomial algorithm called AGSMC to generate all maximal cliques from general spatial data sets; including an enhanced existing materializing method to extract neighborhood relationships between spatial objects, and a tree-type data structure to express maximal cliques. AGSMC constructs the tree-type data structures using the materializing method, and generates maximal cliques by scanning the constructed trees. AGSMC can support the spatial co-location pattern mining efficiently, and is also useful for listing maximal cliques of graph whose vertexes are a geometric object.

Keywords: Spatial Data Mining, GIS, Spatial Database, Spatial Statistics.

1 Introduction

Spatial co-location patterns are a subset of spatial features that frequently have neighbor relationships with each other [15]. For example, a set {hospital, pharmacy} may be an example of a spatial co-location pattern, because hospitals and pharmacies are frequently located near each other. The spatial co-location pattern is an important concept in spatial data mining, and can support decision-making in various domains (mobile services, ecology, earth science, biology, public health).

Several co-location pattern mining approaches have been proposed, and the approach based on association analysis is more useful than others [6]. This approach needs transaction-type data [16], as do the general association analysis methods [1]. The transaction-type data that are required for the spatial co-location pattern mining must include spatial co-location instances (instances of co-occurrent spatial features). However, general spatial data sets are a set or list of many spatial features with spatial positions; it does not include explicit spatial co-location instances. Thus, an efficient way to generate transaction-type data from general spatial data sets is needed.

J.J. Park et al. (Eds.): STA 2011, CCIS 186, pp. 241–250, 2011.
© Springer-Verlag Berlin Heidelberg 2011

A clique is a set whose elements comprise a vertex of an undirected graph and share edges with all other vertexes, and a maximal clique is one that is not included in other cliques. Maximal cliques can be used as transaction-type data by substituting spatial objects and neighborhood relationships for vertexes and edges, respectively [2,18]. General spatial data sets tend to be large in size (number of spatial objects), and density (the number of spatial objects located in a fixed area) is proportional to size. If the size of the spatial data set increases, the cardinality of maximal cliques increases at the same ratio; exponential amounts of time are required to generate all maximal cliques [4]. Thus, existing algorithms cannot efficiently generate all maximal cliques from such spatial data sets.

Spatial co-location pattern mining approaches, which are based on association analysis, may be classified into two groups. The first group internally exploits the association analysis algorithm, i.e., Aprori-like algorithm [1], but neither generates nor needs transaction-type data externally [6,7,13,17,20,22,23]. For this reason, the first group is restricted when using the association analysis methods; for example, these approaches are difficult to utilize relatively fast algorithms such FP-Growth [5], and to apply to special analysis such as quantitative association analysis [11,21], and fuzzy association analysis [19]. In addition, they require exponential amounts of time to check the spatial co-location instances internally. The second group exploits association analysis methods after explicitly generating transaction-type data. One of these approaches uses the maximal clique as transaction-type data, and requires exponential amounts of time to generate all maximal cliques [2,18]. The others use different transaction-type data with maximal clique, but they may miss some co-location instances [14,12].

Many studies have pursued the generation (listing) of maximal cliques. When the cardinality of maximal cliques is fixed, several algorithms can generate all maximal cliques in polynomial execution time [3,10]. However, when the cardinalities of maximal cliques increase linearly, they cannot generate all the maximal cliques in polynomial execution time.

In this paper we make the following contributions. First, we enhance the existing materializing method [23], which can extract all neighborhood relationships between spatial objects. Second, we propose a special tree-type data structure that has the ability to represent maximal cliques. Third, we propose a polynomial algorithm that can generate all maximal cliques from general spatial data sets. It constructs the tree-type data structures, and generates maximal cliques by scanning the completed trees. Trees are constructed as followings: for all nodes, only filtered candidates are generated as real nodes using the materializing method. Fifth, we verify that the proposed algorithm is polynomial, through experiments with synthetic and real spatial data sets.

The proposed algorithm has the following advantages. First, it generates maximal cliques from general spatial data sets efficiently than existing exponential algorithms, since they are mostly dense and large. Thus, it can efficiently support co-location pattern mining. Second, also in maximal clique problem of a geometric graph [8], whose vertexes have a spatial position (Euclidean coordinate), it is useful. Third, it can easily be carried out in parallel, and can therefore make full use of powerful computing resources.

The remainder of this paper is organized as follows. In Section 2 we enhance an existing materializing method, and propose a tree-type data structure to express maximal cliques. In Section 3 we exploit our revisions to propose a polynomial algorithm that generates all maximal cliques. In Section 4 we present an experimental evaluation of our proposed method, and in Section 5 we offer our conclusions.

2 Materializing Method and Data Structure

In this section we define a new term on maximal clique, enhance an existing materializing method, and propose tree-type data structure alongside way to construct the data structure. They are exploited to design a polynomial algorithm that generates transaction-type data from general spatial data sets in the next section.

2.1 Materializing Method

Spatial co-location instances and cliques have the same meaning, if the spatial objects and the neighbor relationships between them correspond to the vertexes and the edges of undirected graph respectively. So, we define maximal clique, which can be used as transaction-type data for spatial co-location pattern mining, with a new term, as follows.

Definition 1. (Spatial Maximal Clique, SMC): Given a spatial data set, a set consisting of spatial objects, $SD = \{O_1, \ldots, O_N\}$;

(1) Spatial clique is a set, whose all elements (spatial objects) have neighbor relationships with each other.
(2) Spatial maximal clique (short of SMC) is a spatial clique, which is not included in the others.

Then, we use the star neighborhoods instance, which was first introduced in the Join-less algorithm [23], as the materializing method. The star neighborhoods instance is a set of the center object and other objects in its neighborhood. In order to use it in designing the algorithm to generate SMCs efficiently, we enhance its definition as follows.

Definition 2. (Star Neighborhoods Instance, SNsI): In Definition 1;

(1) $\text{SNsI}(O_j) = \{O_i \mid \text{distance}(O_i, O_j) \le d$, where $1 \le i \le N$, $1 \le j \le N$, and d is a distance threshold$\}$ is the star neighborhoods instance of O_j, and O_j is the label of $\text{SNsI}(O_j)$. In other words, $\text{SNsI}(O_j)$ is the set consisting of O_j and the other spatial objects located within distance d from O_j, i.e., having neighbor relationships with O_j.
(2) $\text{NsP}(O_j) = \{O_i \mid O_i \in \text{SNsI}(O_j)$ and $i < j$, where $1 \le i \le N$, and $1 \le j \le N\}$ are the neighbors that precede O_j.
(3) $\text{NsF}(O_j) = \{O_i \mid O_i \in \text{SNsI}(O_j)$ and $i > j$, where $1 \le i \le N$, and $1 \le j \le N\}$ are the neighbors that follow O_j.

Let us assume that there is a spatial data set which consists of nine point-type spatial objects as shown in Fig. 1 (a), and the distance threshold of neighbor relationship is equal to a radius of circle in Fig. 1 (b) or (c), where the big circles of

Fig. 1 (b) and (c) are in same size. For example, SNsI(1) and SNsI(2) consist of the spatial objects located in circles of Fig. 1 (b) and (c), respectively. In the same way, the other SNsIs are generated. Finally, a set, which consists of spatial objects in each circle of Fig 1 (d), is an SMC, where each circle of Fig. 1 (d) is as half as that of Fig. 1 (b). Table 1 shows all SNsIs and SMCs in the case of Fig. 1.

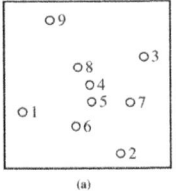 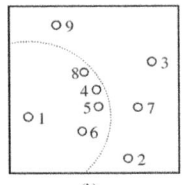 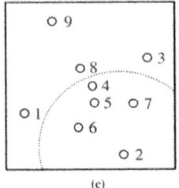 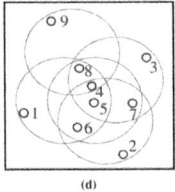

(a)   (b)   (c)   (d)

Fig. 1. Example Spatial Data Set (a) Raw Data Set (b) SNsI of 1 (c) SNsI of 2 (d) SMCs

Table 1. Example of SNsIs and SMCs

SNsIs	NsPs	Labels	NsFs	SMCs
SNsI(1)	{}	1	{4,5,6,8}	{1,4,5,6,8}
SNsI(2)	{}	2	{4,5,6,7}	{2,4,5,6,7}
SNsI(3)	{}	3	{4,5,7,8}	{3,4,5,7,8}
SNsI(4)	{1,2,3}	4	{5,6,7,8,9}	{4,5,6,7,8},{4,8,9}
SNsI(5)	{1,2,3,4}	5	{6,7,8}	-
SNsI(6)	{1,2,4,5}	6	{7,8}	-
SNsI(7)	{2,3,4,5,6}	7	{8}	-
SNsI(8)	{1,3,4,5,6,7}	8	{9}	-
SNsI(9)	{4,8}	9	{}	-

2.2 Tree Representing Spatial Maximal Cliques (TRSMC)

We can express more than one SMC with a tree-type data structure. Every element of an SMC has neighbor relationships with all the other spatial objects, and we can express such relationships by a node and its descendents of a tree. First, we define tree-type data structure, which can express and generate all SMCs from each materialized data set, i.e., each SNsI, as follows.

Definition 3. (Tree Representing SMCs, TRSMC): In Definition 2, for a spatial object O_i, the tree (which represents all SMCs to be generated from the SNsI(O_i) with the minimum number of nodes) is called TRSMC(O_i) or TRSMC of O_i, and its detailed definition is as follows.

(1) Each node is an element of $\{O_i\} \cup \text{NsF}(O_i)$.
(2) A set that consists of all nodes of each full path is an SMC.
(3) For a parent and its son nodes, if O_i is a parent node of O_j, then $i < j$.
(4) For an older brother and a younger brother nodes, if O_i is an older brother node of O_j (i.e., O_i locates at the left side of O_j), then $i < j$.
(5) For a node N, ANs(N) represents a set consisting of N's ancestors.

For example, all TRSMCs as shown in Fig. 2 (a) can express all SMCs of Table 1.

We must be able to generate TRSMCs from the given spatial data sets. We can generate each TRSMC, if we can generate all its nodes. In order to generate all nodes of a TRSMC, we use the way to generate candidate nodes and filter them. The proposed way to generate the candidate nodes is as follows.

Definition 4. (Candidate Children of a TRSMC's node, CCs): In Definition 3, given a node or candidate node N and $ANs(N) = \{AN_1, \ldots , AN_H\}$, $CCs(N) = [\bigcap_{k=1}^{H} NsF(AN_k)] \cap NsF(N)]$ are the Candidate Children of N, but O_i is a candidate root for itself.

For an illustration, we construct the 4th TRSMC like Fig. 3 (b). If 5 is C, then $ANs(5) = \{4\}$. Thus, $CCs(5) = NsF(4) \cap NsF(5) = \{6,7,8\}$.

Next, we contrive the way to check whether a candidate is a real node as follows.

Definition 5. (Condition for a Candidate to be a Node): In Definition 4, $(\forall l)(\exists m)$ $[(SS_l \neq \emptyset \wedge PS_m$ is a spatial clique$)] \rightarrow C$ is a node of TRSMC, but $NsPC(C) = \emptyset \rightarrow C$ is a node of TRSMC; where $NsPC(C) = [\bigcap_{k=1}^{H} NsP(AN_k) \cap NsP(C)] \cup$ $[NsF(AN_1) \cap \bigcap_{k=2}^{H} NsP(AN_k) \cap NsP(C)] \cup [CCs(AN_H) \cap NsP(C)] = \{NPC_1, \ldots , NPC_J\}$, $SSs(C)$ $= \{SS \mid SS = C \cup CCs(C) - NsF(NPC_l)\} = \{SS_1, \ldots , SS_J\}$, $PSs(C) = \{SS_1 \times SS_2 \times \ldots \times SS_J\}$ $= \{PS_1, \ldots , PS_K\}$, $1 \leq l \leq J$, and $1 \leq m \leq K$.

For example, when 5 of the 4th incomplete TRSMC in Fig. 3 (b) is a candidate C, $NsPC(5) = [NsP(4) \cap NsP(5)] \cup [NsF(4) \cap NsP(5)] \cup [CCs(4) \cap NsP(5)] = [\{1,2,3\} \cap \{1,2,3,4\}] \cup [\{5,6,7,8,9\} \cap \{1,2,3,4\}] \cup [\{5,6,7,8,9\} \cap \{1,2,3,4\}] = \{1,2,3\}$. $ss_1 = \{5\} \cup CCs(5) - NsF(1) = \{7\}$, $ss_2 = \{5\} \cup CC(5) - NsF(2) = \{8\}$, and $ss_3 = \{5\} \cup CCs(5) - NsF(3) = \{6\}$; so, $SSs(5)$ is $\{\{6\},\{7\},\{8\}\}$. $PSs(5) = \{6\} \times \{7\} \times \{8\} = \{6,7,8\}$, and one element of $PSs(5)$, $\{6,7,8\}$ is a spatial clique. Thus, 5 is a real node. For another example, when 3 of Fig. 3 (b) is a candidate root, $NsPC(3) = \emptyset$; thus, 3 is a real node.

Lastly, we introduce another problem and its solution. In Definition 5, if $SSs(C)$ includes many large elementary sets, then the product set $PSs(C)$ will include too many large elements. So, it may require too much time to assess whether more than one PS is a spatial clique. The solution is as follows.

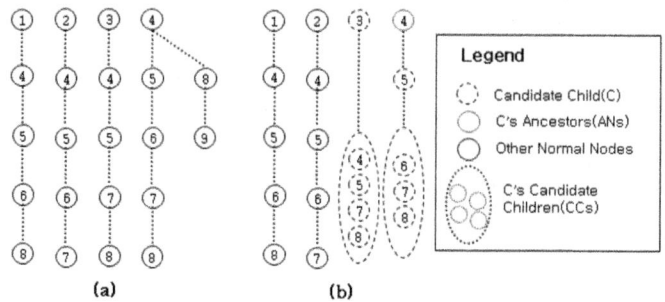

Fig. 2. TRSMCs (a) Completed TRSMCs (b) Not Completed TRSMCs

Definition 6. (Condition for more than one PS to be a Spatial Clique): In Definition 5, $(\forall l)\,(\forall n)\,(\exists o)\,[EO_{(n,o)}$ has neighbors in $SS_l] \rightarrow (\exists m)\,[PS_m$ is a spatial clique], where $EO_{(n,o)} \in SS_n$, $1 \le n \le J$, and $1 \le o \le |SS_n|$.

As an illustration, $EO_{(2,3)}$ is the third element of SS_2.

3   Algorithm Generating Spatial Maximal Cliques

In this section we design and describe an algorithm to generate SMCs based on the materializing method and the tree-type data structure mentioned in Section 2. We call it the Algorithm Generating Spatial Maximal Cliques (short for AGSMC).

The AGSMC is described in Fig. 3, and its detailed steps are as follows. First, it generates every SNsI by Definition 2 in Step (1). Next, it selects the label of each SNsI as a candidate root in Step (3), because all spatial objects are candidate roots. In Step (4), it then generate candidate children of candidate root by Definition 4, and

Algorithm AGMSC
Input:
  (1) *d*   /* diameter of SMC */
  (2) *SD*   /* Spatial Data Set, List of Spatial Objects */
Output:
  (1) *SMCs* /* Spatial Maximal Cliques, List of Lists of Spatial Objects */
Steps:
  (1) Generate *SNsIs* using *d* and all elements of *SD*
  (2) **For Each** *SNsI* **Do**
  (3)   Select Label of *SNsI* as Candidate Root, and Assign to *CR*
  (4)   Generate *CCs* as *CR*'s Candidate Children, and Compute *NsPC* of *CR*
  (5)   **If** (Check_Candidate using *CR*, *NsPC*, and *CCs*) **Then**
  (6)   Create Root, and Assign to *R*
  (7)   Call Construct_TRSMC with *R* and *CCs*
  (8)   **END If**
  (9) **End For**
  (10) **Return** *SMCs*

Procedure Construct_TRSMC
Input:
  (1) *PN*   /* Parent Node */
  (2) *CCs*   /* Candidate Children of Parent Node */
Steps:
  (1) **If** (Is_Reached_Leaf) **Then**
  (2)   Scan the Path from Leaf to Root, and Add Spatial Maximal clique **to** *SMCs*
  (3)   **Return**
  (4) **End If**
  (5) **For Each** *CC* **Do**
  (6)   Select *CC* as Candidate Node, and Assign **to** *CN*
  (7)   Generate *CCCs* as *CN*'s Candidate Children, and Compute *NsPC* of *CN*
  (8)   **If** (CheckCandidate using *CN*, *NsPC*, and *CCCs*) **Then**
  (9)   Create Node with *PN* and *CN*, and Assign to *N*
  (10)   Call Construct_TRSMC with *N and CCCs*
  (11)   **End If**
  (12) **End For**

Fig. 3. Algorithm Generating Spatial Maximal Cliques (AGSMC)

computes the variable NsPC of the candidate roots by Definition 5. Next, it evaluates whether the candidate root is a real root by Definitions 5 and 6 in Step (5). After that, the filtered candidate root is created as a real root and transferred to the Procedure Construct_TRSMC that is called in Step (7). Finally, all SMCs generated are returned in Step (10).

The Procedure Construct_TRSMC is also described in Fig. 3. First, it assesses whether it is reached to a leaf; if so, it scans the path from the leaf, generates an SMC, and is returned, in Steps (1) to (4); otherwise, it carries out the remainders of steps, and they are similar to the main steps of the AGSMC.

We see that the AGSMC can generate a TRSMC for each SNsI independently, and it can be carried out in parallel. So, parallel processing such as multi-processing or multi-threading may be applied easily to AGSMC.

4 Experimental Evaluation

We used synthetic and real spatial data sets as experimental data sets. We generated SMCs from these spatial data sets, and summarized the execution times. The experiments showed that the time complexities of the AGSMC are $O(n^2)$ and $O(n^5)$ respectively when the algorithm processes the general spatial data sets, the density of which is fixed and proportional to the number of the objects.

4.1 Experimental Spatial Data Sets

First, we generated variable random spatial data sets of several densities and sizes (as shown in the first row of Table 2) as synthetic spatial data sets for use in experiments. In order to generate data sets with fixed density, we distributed spatial objects randomly inside a 200 × 200 square meter study area, increasing the study area at a ratio proportional to the number of spatial objects. In order to generate data sets with density proportional to the number of spatial objects, we distributed spatial objects inside the same study area without increasing.

Table 2. Experimental Spatial Data Sets

Data Name	Data Size (Number of Spatial Objects)	Density
Synthetic Random Data Sets	10 K, 20 K, 30 K, 40 K, 50 K	Fixed or Proportional to Data Size
Topographical Map Data	40 K, 46 K, 52 K, 59 K, 65 K	
Land Units Map Data	20 K, 30 K, 40 K, 50 K, 60 K	

We then used a digital topographical map data with a building layer and a digital land unit map data with an urban planning layer, as real experimental data sets. We generated variable real spatial data sets with several densities and sizes as seen in the second and the third rows of Table 2 by filtering spatial objects randomly from the original spatial data sets. There are 65,000 spatial objects in the original topographical map data, and 60,000 in the original land unit map data. In order to generate data sets with fixed density, we filtered spatial objects by decreasing the original study area. On the other hand, in order to generate the data sets with density proportional to the number of spatial objects, we filtered spatial objects without decreasing the original study area.

4.2 Experimental Results

Fig. 4 shows the results of experiments. The labels of the vertical and horizontal axes of each graph indicate the execution time (seconds) and the number of spatial objects, respectively. The input of the Function $G(n)$, n denotes the number of spatial object of spatial data set to be processed by the AGSMC, and the output of the Function $G(n)$ denotes the execution time of the AGSMC. $C \times F(n)$ is the asymptotic upper bound function of $G(n)$, where every notation of $C \times F(n)$ is described in Table 3. Fig. 4 and Table 3 show that the degree of $F(n)$ corresponded to $G(n)$ on the spatial data sets with fixed density is two, and the other degree is five. Thus, the time complexity of the AGSMC on the general spatial data sets (which has a fixed density) is $O(n^2)$, and the complexity of the AGSMC on the general spatial data (which has a density proportional to the number of spatial objects) is $O(n^5)$.

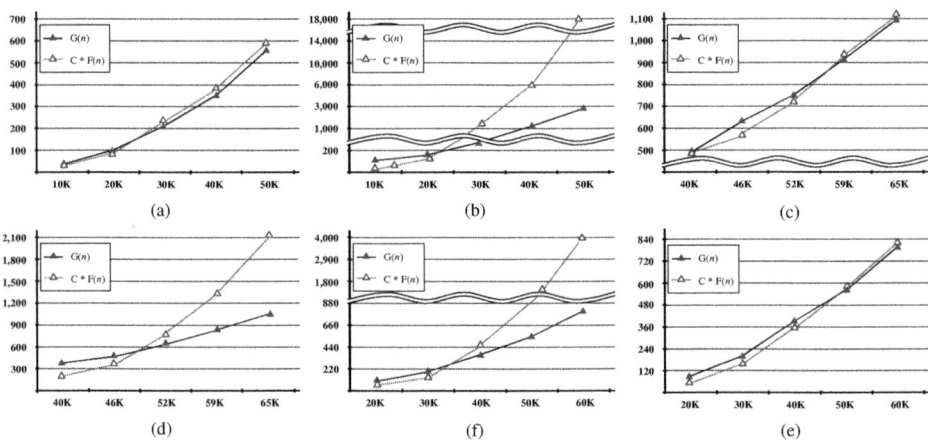

Fig. 4. Execution Time Required to Process (a) Synthetic Random Data Sets with Fixed Density and 50m Diameter of SMC (b) Synthetic Random Data Sets with Density Proportional to n and 50m Diameter of SMC (c) Topographical Map Data with Fixed Density and 200m Diameter of SMC (d) Topographical Map Data with Density Proportional to n and 200m Diameter of SMC (e) Land Unit Map Data with Fixed Density and 60m Diameter of SMC (f) Land Unit Map Data with Density Proportional to n and 60m Diameter of SMC

Table 3. Execution Time of Generating SMCs from Synthetic Even Spatial Data Sets

Data Name	Density	Upper bound Function	
		C	F(n)
Synthetic Random Data Sets	Fixed	$1/(2,070)^2$	n^2
	Proportional to n	$1/(7,000)^5$	n^5
Topographical Map Data	Fixed	$1/(1,941)^2$	n^2
	Proportional to n	$1/(14,000)^5$	n^5
Land Units Map Data	Fixed	$1/(2,100)^2$	n^2
	Proportional to n	$1/(11,500)^5$	n^5

When the data set to be processed is large enough, the polynomial algorithm is more efficient than exponential algorithms. So, we did not conduct comparative experiments of the proposed algorithm and the existing exponential algorithms.

5 Conclusion

Spatial co-location pattern mining is a useful method for decision making in space-related domains. The spatial maximal clique is a significant concept in the spatial co-location pattern mining approach, which relies on association analysis. The spatial maximal clique is used as transaction-type data, which is critical to the association analysis; however there are no existing algorithms that can generate all spatial maximal cliques from general spatial data sets in polynomial execution time. Spatial data sets are mostly dense and large; therefore, spatial maximal cliques may not be useful without efficient algorithms to generate them. By exploiting the follows, the materializing method enhanced, and the tree-type data structure proposed; we proposed a new algorithm that can generate all spatial maximal cliques in polynomial execution time. Our algorithm is useful for discovering spatial co-location patterns in the general spatial data sets, and can easily use parallel processing. Moreover, it is just as, if not more, useful for listing maximal cliques of a geometric graph.

References

1. Agarwal, R., Srikant, R.: Fast Algorithms for Mining Association Rules. In: Proceedings of 20th Conference on Very Large Databases (1994)
2. Al-Naymat, G.: Enumeration of maximal clique for mining spatial co-location patterns. In: Proceeding of IEEE/ACS International Conference on Computer Systems and Applications (2008)
3. Chiba, N., Nishizeki, T.: Arboricity and subgraph listing algorithms. SIAM Journal on Computing 14(1), 210–223 (1985)
4. Downey, R., Fellows, G., Fixed-parameter, M.R.: tractability and completeness II: On completeness for W [1]. Theoretical Computer Science 141(1-2), 109–131 (1995)
5. Han, J., Pei, J., Yin, Y.: Mining Frequent Patterns without Candidate Generation. In: Proceedings of ACM-SIGMOD International Conference on Management of Data (2000)
6. Huang, Y., Shekhar, S., Xiong, H.: Discovering Co-location Patterns from Spatial Datasets: A General Approach. IEEE Transactions on Knowledge and Data Engineering 16, 1472–1485 (2004)
7. Jiang, Y., Wang, L., Lu, Y., Chen, H.: Discovering both positive and negative co-location rules. In: Proceedings of the 2nd International Conference on Software Engineering and Data Mining, pp. 398–403 (2010)
8. János, P.: Towards a Theory of Geometric Graphs. In: Contemporary Mathematics. American Mathematical Society, Providence (2004)
9. Johnson, D.S., Yannakakis, M.: On generating all maximal independent sets. Information Processing Letters 27(3), 119–123 (1988)
10. Makino, K., Uno, T.: New Algorithms for Enumerating All Maximal Cliques. In: Hagerup, T., Katajainen, J. (eds.) SWAT 2004. LNCS, vol. 3111, pp. 260–272. Springer, Heidelberg (2004)

11. Martínez-Ballesteros, M., Troncoso, A., Martínez-Aĺvarez, F., Riquelme, J.C.: Mining quantitative association rules based on evolutionary computation and its application to atmospheric pollution. Integrated Computer-Aided Engineering 17(3), 227–242 (2010)

12. Morimoto, Y.: Mining Frequent Neighboring Class Sets in Spatial Databases. In: Proceedings of the 7th ACM SIGKDD International Conference on Knowledge Discovery and Data Mining, pp. 353–358 (2001)

13. Qian, F., Yin, L., He, Q., He, J.: Mining spatio-temporal co-location patterns with weighted sliding window. In: Proceeding of IEEE International Conference on Intelligent Computing and Intelligent Systems, vol. 3, pp. 181–185 (2009)

14. Rinzivillo, S., Turini, F.: Extracting spatial association rules from spatial transactions. In: Proceedings of the 13rd Annual ACM International Workshop on Geographic Information Systems, pp. 79–86 (2005)

15. Shekhar, S., Chawla, S.: Spatial Databases: A Tour. Prentice Hall, Englewood Cliffs (2003)

16. Tan, P.N., Steinbach, M., Kumar, V.: Introduction to Data Mining. Addison-Wesley, Reading (2006)

17. Valley, N., Lin, Z., Lim, S.: Fast Spatial Co-location Mining Without Cliqueness Checking. In: Proceedings of the 17th ACM Conference on Information and Knowledge (2008)

18. Verhein, F., Al-Naymat, G.: Fast Mining of Complex Spatial Co-location Patterns Using GLIMIT. In: Proceedings of the 7th IEEE International Conference on Data Mining Workshops, pp. 679–684 (2007)

19. Weng, C., Chen, Y.: Fuzzy association rules from uncertain data. Knowledge and Information Systems 23(2), 129–152 (2010)

20. Xiao, X., Xie, S., Luo, A., Ma, W.: Density Based Co-Location Pattern Discovery. In: Proceedings of the 16th ACM SIGSPATIAL International Conference on Advances in Geographic Information Systems (2008)

21. Yin, Y., Zhong, Z., Wang, Y.: Mining quantitative association rules by interval clustering. Journal of Computational Information Systems 4(2), 609–616 (2008)

22. Yoo, J., Shekhar, S.: A Partial Join Approach for Mining Colocation Patterns. In: Proceedings of ACM International Symposium Advances in Geographic Information Systems (2004)

23. Yoo, J., Shekhar, S.: A Join-less Approach for Mining Spatial Colocation Patterns. IEEE Transactions on Knowledge and Data Engineering 18, 1323–1337 (2006)

Author Index